£4.99

The Medieval British Literature Handbook

Literature and Culture Handbooks

General Editors: Philip Tew and Steven Barfield

Literature and Culture Handbooks are an innovative series of guides to major periods, topics and authors in British and American literature and culture. Designed to provide a comprehensive, one-stop resource for literature students, each handbook provides the essential information and guidance needed from the beginning of a course through to developing more advanced knowledge and skills.

The Medieval British Literature Handbook

Edited by
Daniel T. Kline

continuum

Continuum
The Tower Building   80 Maiden Lane
11 York Road   Suite 704
London SE1 7NX   New York, NY 10038

www.continuumbooks.com

British Library Cataloguing-in-Publication Data
A catalogue record for this book is available from the British Library.

ISBN: 978–0–8264–9408–5 (hardback)
       978–0–8264–9409–2 (paperback)

Library of Congress Cataloging-in-Publication Data
Kline, Daniel T.
   The medieval British literature handbook / Daniel T. Kline.
      p. cm.
   Includes bibliographical references.
   ISBN 978–0–8264–9408–5—ISBN 978–0–8264–9409–2 (pbk.) 1. English
literature—Middle English, 1100–1500—History and criticism—Handbooks,
manuals, etc. 2. Civilization, Medieval, in literature. I. Title.
   PR255.K56 2009
   820.9'001—dc22

                                                        2008028878

Typeset by RefineCatch Limited, Bungay, Suffolk
Printed and bound in Great Britain by CPI Antony Rowe,
Chippenham, Wiltshire

Contents

Contents

Detailed Table of Contents

(Available online at
www.continuumbooks.com/resources/9780826494092)

Introduction; Medieval and Middle English Literature in
US, UK and Canadian Classrooms; Medieval and Middle
English Literature in American Classrooms; Medieval

and Middle English Literature in UK Classrooms;
Medieval and Middle English Literature in Canadian
Classrooms; Factors Influencing Middle English
Offerings; The Problem of Language; Incorporating
Manuscripts; Linking Reading and Writing; Travel-Study;
Experiential Learning; Popular Culture and Film;
The Web; Traditional Pedagogy

Acknowledgements

The editor gratefully wishes to thank the following individuals and institutions for permission to cite from their texts:

- Baker Publishing House for Joan Ferrante and Robert Hanning's translation of Marie de France's *Lanval*.
- The British Library for the image of the death of Wat Tyler, from Jean Froissart's *Chroniques* (1460–80), MS Royal E.1 fol. 175r., © All Rights Reserved (The British Library Board, license number: UALASK01).
- The Council of the Early English Text Society (EETS) for *Morte Arthure*, E. Brock (ed.) EETS Original Series 8, London, 1865; *The Babees Book: Early English Meals and Manners*, F. J. Furnivall (ed.), EETS Original Series 32, London, 1868; *Cloud of Unknowing and The Book of Privy Counselling*. P. Hodgson (ed.), EETS Original Series 218, London, 1944; and *Mankind*, in *The Macro Plays*, Mark Eccles (ed.), EETS Original Series 262, London: Oxford University Press, 1969, 153–84; and 'Of Feigned Contemplative Life' from *The English Works of Wyclif Hitherto Unprinted*, F. D. Matthew (ed.), EETS Original Series 74, London, 1880.
- Julia Bolton Holloway has graciously made available additional material related to women mystics and the contents of chapter three at her website (http://www.umilta.net/Continuum.html).
- Heinle/Arts & Sciences, a part of Cengage Learning, Inc., for *The Riverside Chaucer*, Larry D. Benson, (gen. ed.) Boston: Houghton-Mifflin, 1987.
- Madeline Jeay and Kathleen Garay, editors of the McMaster University *Scriptorium* (www.mw.mcmaster.ca/scriptorium/), for their translation of Christine de Pizan's 'Letter to the God of Love'.
- The National Library of Scotland for *The King of Tars*.

The editor would also like to thank Stephen Barfield and Philip Tew for the chance to develop this project, to applaud the contributors for their stellar work, and to recognize the unfailing patience and constant helpfulness of Colleen Coalter and Anna Fleming at Continuum.

List of Illustrations

General Editors' Introduction

The Continuum *Literature and Culture Handbooks* series aims to support both students new to an area of study and those at a more advanced stage, offering guidance with regard to the major periods, topics and authors relevant to the study of various aspects of British and American literature and culture. The series is designed with an international audience in mind, based on research into today's students in a global educational setting. Each volume is concerned with either a particular historical phase or an even more specific context, such as a major author study. All of the chosen areas represent established subject matter for literary study in schools, colleges and universities, all are widely taught and are the subject of ongoing research and scholarship. Each handbook provides a comprehensive, one-stop resource for literature students, offering essential information and guidance needed at the beginning of a course through to more advanced knowledge and skills for the student more familiar with the particular topic. These volumes reflect current academic research and scholarship, teaching methods and strategies, and also provide an outline of essential historical contexts. Written in clear language by leading internationally-acknowledged academics, each book provides the following:

- introduction to authors, texts, historical and cultural contexts
- guides to key critics, concepts and topics
- introduction to critical approaches, changes in the canon and new conceptual and theoretical issues, such as gender and ethnicity
- case studies in reading literal, theoretical and critical texts
- annotated bibliography (including selected websites), timeline and a glossary of useful critical terms.

This student-friendly series as a whole has drawn its inspiration and structure largely from the latest principles of text book design employed in other disciplines and subjects, creating an unusual and distinctive approach for the undergraduate arts and humanities field. This structure is designed to be user-friendly and it is intended that the layout can be easily navigated, with various points of cross-reference. Such clarity and straightforward approach should help students understand the material and in so doing guide them through the increasing academic difficulty of complex, critical and theoretical approaches to Literary Studies. These handbooks serve as gateways to the particular field that is explored.

All volumes make use of a 'progressive learning strategy', rather than the traditional chronological approach to the subject under discussion so that they might relate more closely to the learning process of the student. This means that the particular volume offers material that will aid the student to approach the period or topic confidently in the classroom for the very first time (for example, glossaries, historical context, key topics and critics), as well as material that helps the student develop more advanced skills (learning how to respond actively to selected primary texts and analyse and engage with modern critical arguments in relation to such texts). Each volume includes a specially commissioned new critical essay by a leading authority in the field discussing current debates and contexts. The progression in the contents mirrors the progress of the undergraduate student from beginner to a more advanced level. Each volume is aimed primarily at undergraduate students, intending to offer itself as both a guide and a reference text that will reflect the advances in academic studies in its subject matter, useful to both students and staff (the latter may find the appendix on pedagogy particularly helpful).

We realize that students in the twenty-first century are faced with numerous challenges and demands; it is our intention that the Handbook series should empower its readers to become effective and efficient in their studies.

Philip Tew and Steven Barfield

Introduction

Daniel T. Kline, University of Alaska Anchorage

Chapter Overview

The Lure of the Medieval

Contemporary Western culture is fascinated with the Middle Ages, and this allure takes a myriad of forms, in both high and low culture, and appears in serious and not so serious manifestations. Some of the most popular recent books and movies, like the *Lord of the Rings* trilogy (whether J. R. R. Tolkein's books or Peter Jackson's movies) and J. K. Rowling's Harry Potter books, refract medieval concerns. *World of Warcraft*, the hugely popular MMORPG (Massively Multiplayer Online Roll Playing Game), just passed *ten million* players worldwide, and other many video, computer and console games derive their structures, conventions and characters from medieval genres and history thanks, at least in part, to the influence of *Dungeons and Dragons*. The Society for Creative Anachronism (SCA) holds festivals across North American and Europe. Medieval and Renaissance 'faires' are a staple in many communities, and LARPers (Live Action Role Players) live out their medieval fantasy lives in weekend communities. A decade or so ago, when Diana,

Princess of Wales, and Mother Theresa, the saintly nun of Calcutta, died within a few days of each other in September 1997, it seemed that the world stood still, if even for a moment, to remember their lives and to mourn their passing. What could be more *medieval* than a princess and a nun? Could it be that in some important ways the Middle Ages have never really ended?

At the same time, the medieval period has become a reference point for political controversy and cultural unease in the post-9/11 West. Our political leaders tell us that we are in the midst of war with an ideological enemy who wants to take the world back to the era before the Crusades, the signal political event of the medieval period. Shortly after 9/11, US President George W. Bush stated, 'This crusade, this war on terror, is going to take awhile' (Holsinger 2007, 6). In the wake of the US response to 9/11, Osama bin Laden stated that 'The crusader war against Islam has intensified . . . The world is split in two. Part of it is under the head of infidels [President] Bush, and the other half under the banner of Islam' (see 'Bin Laden' and 'Remarks'). The Crusades thus denote for both friend and foe a 'clash of cultures' that still affects contemporary society. In this Manichean perspective, each side rereads the medieval period differently, for their own purposes, and both sides appear bent on reviving these medieval conflicts but with far deadlier modern weaponry. In these usages, the medieval period is the 'Dark Ages', a backward period filled with indiscriminate, even casual, violence. Such a caricature merits Marcellus Wallace's pronouncement in *Pulp Fiction* that he was going to have his henchmen 'get medieval' on an enemy who brutalized him (see also Dinshaw 1999).

These examples demonstrate, I think, the allure of the medieval period: its ability to sustain so many contradictory yet productive reinterpretations. The medieval period remains recognizable enough to lull us into believing we understand it, but it also remains steadfastly alien enough to remind us that it is not our own time. This paradox – the pastness of the present and the presentness of the past – not only marks the popular and political uses of 'the medieval', it also impacts the academic study of medieval literature, history and culture. As opposed to earlier scholars, many of whom sought for the abiding 'truth' of the Middle Ages – a complete understanding of the period that transcended the vagaries of specific cultures, particular disciplines and variegated mentalities – contemporary literary scholars embrace the diversity of the past and employ a range of analytical tools to explicate the stunning variety of medieval culture. By giving up the quest for the universal 'truth' of the Middle Ages – as an era of uncomplicated faith, political uniformity or cultural regression, for example – critics have gained something much more important, a sense of the elusive, ongoing and mutually interdependent complexities of medieval civilization(s) in relation to our own time. Literature provides a privileged avenue into understanding the Middle Ages, and *The*

Continuum Handbook of Medieval British Literature introduces the variety of texts produced in England from the twelfth to sixteenth centuries and the analytical methods, theoretical approaches, critical perspectives and key critics of contemporary medieval study.

Dreaming the Middle Ages

In an important essay 'Dreaming the Middle Ages', novelist, semiotician and medievalist Umberto Eco notes the pervasive European and American interest with the Middle Ages, an interest that has only increased in the 30 years since Eco wrote his essay. In contrast to ancient Greece and Rome, which provided classical ideals that the West embraces but contemplates at some remove, Eco argues that we (as contemporary Westerners) still live within medieval structures and institutions – reviving them, rearranging them, patching them up and then dwelling in them again and again. He writes, 'We no longer dwell in the Parthenon, but we still walk or pray in the naves of the cathedral' (Eco, 'Dreaming', 68), much in the same way we use banks, wear glasses, study in universities, live in nation-states and struggle with the balance between church and state, all of which have their roots in the Middle Ages (64–8). In fact, Eco identifies ten different contemporary (re)configurations of the medieval period (68–72):

1. 'as a *pretext*' (68) for placing contemporary characters into an historical situation, as in historical novels and films.
2. 'as a site of an *ironical revisitation*' (69) in which contemporary fantasies are be worked out.
3. 'as a *barbaric age*, a land of elementary and outlaw feelings' (69), a dark age in which passion rules triumphant, heroes rule by brutal personal charisma, and culture hardly wards off nature's hostility.
4. 'of *Romanticism*, with their stormy castles and their ghosts' (68–9), a place of melancholy rumination and ruination.
5. 'of the *philosphia perennis*' (70), from whose wellsprings draw many contemporary theologians and philosophers.
6. 'of *national identities*' in which 'the medieval model was taken as a political utopia, a celebration of past grandeur' (70).
7. 'of *Decadentism*' (70), of the fin-de-siecle aesthetes whose fascination turned towards the extremes of human experience.
8. 'of *philological reconstruction*' (70), those academic investigations that 'help us, nevertheless, to criticize all the other Middle Ages that at one time or another arouse our enthusiasm (71).
9. 'of so-called *Tradition*, or of occult philosophy' (71) in which all thought is essentially a manifestation of a single hierophantic mystery.

    10. as 'the expectation of the *Millennium*' (72), whose warning is both ever present and always looking ahead.

Scholars have refined this shaggy, selective listing as the study of *medievalism* – a branch of reception theory studying how different cultures understand and reproduce medieval concerns – grows (see, for example, Bloch 1996; Biddick 1998; Trigg 2002; Marshall 2007; Fugelso 2007). Yet these different versions of the Middle Ages are not mutually exclusive, and we can see the residue of these ideas in books like *The DaVinci Code*, movies like *Braveheart*, and simulacra like The Excalibur casino in Las Vegas, as well as in some academic research. (See Chapter 7: Emerging Approaches).

Nonetheless, Eco's overall argument is well taken: The medieval period has never really left us, in a sense, though it is continually in the past. In a follow up written ten years later ('Living in the New Middle Ages'), Eco comments upon another salient feature of the Middle Ages that I believe characterizes our own period as well: 'The Middle Ages preserved in its way the heritage of the past but not through hibernation, rather through a constant retranslation and reuse; it was an immense work of *bricolage* [improvisation], balanced among nostalgia, hope and despair' (Eco, 'Living' 84). One of the geniuses of contemporary Western culture is exactly this ability to reconstitute the past for the purposes of the present, whether political or commercial, for entertainment or war, in scholarship or popular culture. Because we still live in the penumbra of medieval institutions, the Middle Ages seem in some ways familiar to us, yet strange enough for us to know that they are not really our historical moment. The simultaneous familiarity and alterity of the medieval period creates for us, I think, an endless source of fascination.

Approaching the Middle English Period

The *Continuum Handbook of Medieval British Literature* addresses the attraction we have to the cultures of the Middle Ages as expressed in the variety of textual production in England from 1200 to 1500 CE at the same time it articulates the range of contemporary academic approaches to that same literature. Eco concludes 'Dreaming the Middle Ages' with a call that the chapters in the *Continuum Handbook* each contend with and together throw into relief. Eco writes, 'before rejoicing or grieving over a return of the Middle Ages, we have the moral and cultural duty of spelling out what kind of Middle Ages we are talking about' (72). Indeed, with so many versions available, what kind of Middle Ages are we talking about? It is to these related questions that I now turn in the balance of this Introduction:

- What are the defining parameters of the Middle Ages?
- What scholarly concerns and questions mark the contemporary study of literature of England's medieval period?
- What ethical demands does this kind of study put upon readers of medieval literature?

This Introduction thus (1) addresses the medieval period as defined by contemporary literary critics of Middle English (ME) literature; (2) articulates the social, cultural, historical and discursive parameters that are the active concern of current scholarship in ME and (3) demonstrates that scholarship is neither disinterested nor objective (in the old-fashioned sense) but is actively involved with, and influenced by, issues of pressing contemporary concern. Medieval scholars are sensitized to the fact that scholarship is not simply an 'ivory tower' exercise, removed from all practical reality. Scholarship and teaching on both sides of the Atlantic occur in institutional contexts that are embedded within contemporary political realities, so the current critical preoccupation with issues like gender and identity, race and oppression, ethnicity and conflict, theology and violence, postcolonial thought and national identity both affect, and are affected by, these contemporary issues.

What I find so exciting about studying the Middle Ages is the way scholars question what we *thought* we knew in order to push to the scholarly conversation into provocative new areas and thereby to extend the knowledge about the past and ourselves we call the Middle Ages. The same process of questioning that so energizes scholarly investigation, however, often proves baffling or even frustrating to those who, for understandable reasons, want to know the *results* of that research more than to explore the *process* of getting there. So what this Introduction does is to contrast some 'common wisdom' concerning the Middle Ages with contemporary literary and historical analysis. As a result, we can examine the scholarly process as well as its results and assess the implications of this new understanding of ME literature. By questioning common presuppositions, scholars open up new avenues of investigation and the potential for new insight.

Redefining the Period

Traditionally speaking, 'the Middle Ages' denotes a roughly one thousand year period from the Fall of Rome in 476 CE to around 1500 CE (plus or minus a generation), and the *Middle* Ages sit between the ancient and modern periods in the conventional tripartite schematic division of Western history (ancient, medieval and modern history). On the one hand, the medieval period is conventionally separated from the *ancient* world at the moment when Odovacar (Odoacer), a Roman general but Germanic chieftain, compelled Romulus Augustulus to abdicate the throne in 476 CE, thereby ending the Western Roman Empire. (The realm persisted in the East as the Byzantine Empire, centred in Constantinople, until 1453). On the other hand, the medieval period is separated from the *modern* era by a number of social, political and cultural developments clustered around the year 1500 CE: in 1485 the Battle of Bosworth field in England ended the War of the Roses and saw the rise of the Tudor dynasty; in 1492 Columbus famously 'sailed the ocean blue' and contacted the North American continent; in 1517 Martin Luther nailed his 95 Theses to the door of the Elector's Chapel at the University of Wittenberg and initiated the Reformation. Many scholars point to other events as forerunners of modernity: c. 1450 Gutenberg's introduction of mechanical printing with moveable type, which William Caxton introduced to England in 1476; the 1453 fall of Constantinople to the Ottoman Empire and Ferdinand and Isabella's 1492 expulsion of Islam from Al-Andalus (Spain). Within this 1,000 medieval era, scholars often refer to the Early Middle Ages (c. 500–1000 CE), the High Middle Ages (c. 1000–1200 CE), and the Later Middle Ages (1200–1500 CE), though the boundaries between eras is flexible depending upon academic discipline and subject of study. It is important to think of these labels like the road signs on a map: In the same way the signs point towards a destination but are not themselves the road, so too the period *labels* indicate historical differences but are not themselves a reality. (See Chapter 2: Historical Timeline and Chapter 8: Rethinking the Boundaries and Fifteenth Century Literature.)

Along with clarifying the historical range under discussion, we need to put to rest another misconception. The medieval period is like the proverbial middle child who gets lost between siblings: It is not quite the place of origin and it is always on the way to something else. Thus, those who study the medieval period especially protest terminology too often still used to denote the era, that of 'the Dark Ages' followed by 'the Renaissance'. Of course, when Odovacar took the throne in 476, Rome did not cease to exist nor was the sun blotted out in the sky to initiate a dark, backward era of irrational belief and bad teeth. This generally pejorative term traces its origin to Petrarch's (d. 1374) famous letter to Agapito Colonna in which he states that he 'did not wish for the sake of so few famous names to guide my pen so far and through such *darkness*' (qtd. in Eisenstein 295; emph. mine). Using the Latin term *tenebrae* (darkness, shadow) most likely to indicate the difficulty of wading through medieval histories or the irregularities of medieval Latin (when compared to classical Latin), Petrarch's term became synonymous with the period prior to his own, particularly through the work of nineteenth-century historians like Jacob Burkhardt (*The Civilization of the Renaissance in Italy*, 1860). A term like the '*Renaissance*' (lit. *rebirth* in French) implies that the medieval period was so deficient that the ensuing period marked completely new form of culture, usually identified with 'Renaissance humanism'. Much in the same way Eco identified ten different 'Middle Ages', each serving a different end, so too the medieval period has served as the 'Other' against which historians elaborate the distinctiveness of their own, usually modern, periods of study. More recent historians note that these period markers are more artificial than actual and characterized by as much continuity as discontinuity. As a result, contemporary scholars have dropped the appellation 'Dark Ages' generally and use 'the Early Modern Period' to refer to what used to be called the Renaissance. When 'the Dark Ages' (or sometimes 'the Heroic Age') is used in European historiography, it is confined to the Early Middle Ages and indicates the dearth of materials limiting traditional historical investigation.

To add one more piece to the puzzle, not only does the schematization of time pose a problem for the study of medieval literature, so too does the question of geography, or more broadly, *place*. One geographical area within the medieval period might be embroiled in a completely different set of historical and cultural circumstances than a nearby region. (See Chapter 6: Location, Territorialization, Cartography.) Two examples illustrate the complex interaction of time and place and should serve to caution against applying simplistic labels too quickly. In the first, as David Wallace demonstrates in his superlative *Chaucerian Polity: Absolutist Lineages and Associational Forms in England and Italy*, when Chaucer visited Italy in the 1370s as a representative of the English crown, he did not pass through a gate that said on one side, in effect, 'You are leaving medieval England' and on the other, 'You are now entering Renaissance Italy' (1997, 9), though historians commonly classify fourteenth-century England as 'medieval' and the same period in Italy as the 'Renaissance'. It is quite unlikely that Chaucer saw himself and London as subservient to a superior Italian culture, and certainly Chaucer did not see himself as a 'medieval' person. In the second, we should be especially careful, for example, to take into account geographically specific concerns when examining medieval institutions and practices. This is especially true when considering, for example, 'the Church', one of the most easily misunderstood facets of medieval culture. We must always keep in mind that the Church in Western Europe means what we now term 'the Catholic Church', headed by the Pope, the Bishop of Rome. The Roman Catholic Church in the west split from the eastern Greek Orthodox Church, headquartered in Constantinople, in 1054. This 'East-West Schism' sent Rome and Constantinople on different historical trajectories that became vastly more complicated during the crusading era (1095 – c. 1300) as Western powers moved east into the Holy Land. Nonetheless, the Catholic Church encompassed a wide variety of theological views, political stresses and local practices. While it is tempting to consider 'the Church' to be an inviolable, monolithic entity that held dictatorial, even absolute, sway over all of culture, the fact is that despite the Church's best efforts, even after the educational and bureaucratic dictates of Lateran IV in 1215, local adherence to Rome's direct-ives was often uneven, and doctrinal purity was beset by heterodox beliefs like Catharism (in France) and Lollardy (in England) (See Chapter 2: Crisis in the Church at Home: Lollardy). The Church's situation is further complicated in the ME period by The Great Schism (1378–1417), when two and then three different popes were proclaimed and the papacy was seated in Avignon, France, rather than Rome (see Chapter 2: Crisis in the Church Abroad: The Great Schism). Labels like 'the Church' or 'the medieval' are useful, to a point, until they overpower our ability to see through them.

Although the literature, culture and history of the Middle Ages has laboured under these kind of misconceptions, some readily recognizable landmarks allow us to orient ourselves in late-medieval English culture, as Brian Gastle demonstrates in Chapter 2 (Historical Context). Key for England is the domestic struggle between church and state that led to the Magna Carta and the external controversy of the Great Schism. England was likewise beset by the natural calamities of famine and plague in the fourteenth century, and political unrest between the ruling and labouring classes, as well as the power struggles between competing noble families, affected literary production in later medieval England. In fact, the changes initiated by the Norman Conquest appear to have a greater influence on contemporary literary analysis than any distinction between medieval and modern, to judge by the recent *Cambridge History of Medieval English Literature* (Wallace 1999), for the *Cambridge History* begins its examination of medieval literature in 1066 and effectively excludes Old English (or Anglo-Saxon) literature prior to 1066, decisively separating Anglo-Saxon from ME literature. (See Chapter 2: When Did Middle English Literature Begin?) Recognizing that the literature of Anglo-Saxon England requires its own volume, *The Continuum Handbook of Medieval British Literature* focuses on literature produced after 1066, when William, Duke of Normandy became King of England, and concentrates particularly on the literature of the fourteenth and fifteenth centuries. The vernacular texts produced in England from 1066 to 1500, more commonly known as ME literature and widely taught in American and British higher education, provide the focus for this volume and the chapters that follow.

Extending the Medieval

As a result, the contributors to the *Continuum Handbook* follow the recent investigations of medieval scholars who see as permeable the boundary between the medieval and Early Modern period and who extend the range of what might be considered *medieval* texts and culture. As Nancy Bradley Warren notes in Chapter 8 (Changes in the Canon), medieval British literature's centre of gravity has shifted in the last 20 years from Chaucer's fourteenth century towards the fifteenth century of Lydgate and Hoccleve, Julian of Norwich and Margery Kempe and medieval drama and romance. We have also long known, for example, that 'medieval' drama persisted late into the sixteenth century, and 30 years ago, Lawrence M. Clopper noted that some manuscripts of the *medieval* Chester plays are in fact seventeenth-century artefacts (1978). Previously viewed as an era of 'dullness' and superficiality (see Lawton 1987), the fifteenth century is now seen as a period of cultural ferment and contestation, distinctive in itself and not simply a step in the transition to modernity, as poets and writers reacted to their changing cultural and political milieu. (See Chapter 8: Rethinking the Boundaries and Fifteenth Century Literature.)

At the same time scholars have questioned the temporal parameters of the medieval period, pushing the medieval ever further into modernity, they have also interrogated the spatial and geographical dimensions of the Middle Ages, as traditionally defined. In Chapter 6, Matthew Boyd Goldie's examination of 'Key Primary Literary Texts' provides an example of this trend in his analysis of Marie de France's *Lanval*. Although traditionally classified as a twelfth-century French writer, Marie likely lived in England (perhaps at the court of Henry II and Eleanor of Aquitaine), and while *Lanval* was originally written in Anglo-Norman French, it found wide circulation in ME translation (see Bloch 2003). Perhaps even more importantly, it is an Arthurian tale full of Celtic details and as such deals with the complexities of Britain's legendary court and king. Likewise, Diane Cady begins her discussion of 'Issues of Sexuality, Gender and Ethnicity' (Chapter 11) with Christine de Pizan, a fifteenth-century French writer, who engaged in an international literary dispute, the *Querrelle de la Rose*, over the misogynistic depiction of women in the *Roman de la Rose*, one of the most influential texts of the later Middle Ages. Extending the limits even farther, David Wallace's most recent work, *Premodern Places: Calais to Surinam, Chaucer to Aphra Behn* (2004), confidently elides the traditional boundaries between medieval and Early Modern and the Old World and the New. In other words, the old boundaries of medieval studies are under siege, and while they have served useful purposes in the past, contemporary scholarship challenges the very nature of 'the medieval'.

Part and parcel of this reassessment of the temporal and geographical boundaries of the Middle Ages is the recognition that medieval England itself was a multicultural, multilingual, cosmopolitan culture. Whereas previous study of medieval Britain concentrated upon the textual production of England's population centres and dominant dialects (London, East Anglia and the West Midlands, for example), current research is sensitized to the many simultaneously overlapping linguistic communities throughout medieval England (See Chapter 3: Literary and Cultural Contexts; Chapter 5: Patricia Clare Ingham and Michelle Warren, *Postcolonial Moves* [2003] and Jeffrey Jerome Cohen, *The Postcolonial Middle Ages* [2000]). Likewise, what the 1999 *Cambridge History of Medieval English Literature* sacrifices temporally, it increases linguistically by considering writing in Latin, Anglo-Norman and the varieties of ME as well as literature written in Wales, Ireland and Scotland. Chaucer's peer and friend, John Gower, exemplifies this multilingualism, for he composed major works in English, French and Latin (See Chapter 1: Crisis in the Church Abroad – The Great Schism), as Chaucer himself was undoubtedly trilingual. As Warren argues in Chapter 8, perhaps the best proof in the academic change of perspective towards the 'internationalization' of ME literature is the inclusion of Anglo-Norman literature and greater numbers of female authors in the eighth edition of the venerable *Norton Anthology of English Literature* (2006), one of the most widely used literary anthologies in college classrooms in North America and the United Kingdom. (See Chapter 8: The Impact of Feminism and the Expansion of the Canon.)

As detailed by Gail Ashton (Chapter 5: Ingham, Warren, Cohen), John Ganim (Chapter 7: Postcolonial Criticism) and Diane Cady (Chapter 9: Postcolonial Studies), postcolonial theory has likewise enriched traditional understandings of medieval literature and culture (See also Chapter 6: Location; Chapter 7: Postcolonial Criticism, Chapter 8: Multilingualism and Chapter 9: Postcolonial Studies). England's long history is one of multiple conquests and colonization, beginning at least with the Romans in 43 CE, continuing with the Vikings in the eighth to tenth centuries, and culminating with the French in 1066. Seen through the lens of postcolonial theory, originally developed to critique the British Empire's colonial legacy, medieval English literature and culture is now being examined, paradoxically, as a *premodern postcolonial* phenomenon. Drawing upon the work of Patricia Clare Ingham, Geraldine Heng and especially Jeffrey Jerome Cohen, medieval postcolonial theory 'refuse[s]', as Ashton writes, 'western modernity as a fact of history' and treats Englishness as a hybrid construction, drawing upon indigenous traditions (English, Irish, Welsh and Scottish) and extraterritorial and continental contacts (Irish, French, Dutch, Spanish and Italian). Postcolonial theory has especially disclosed additional dimensions in the representation of alterity and otherness, the Eastern and exotic, and the marvellous, monstrous and gigantic (Chapter 5: Jeffrey Jerome Cohen, *Of Giants* [1999] and Chapter 6: Alterity, Chapter 9: Issues of Sexuality, Gender, and Ethnicity).

Despite its seeming isolation at the edge of Europe, England has never been an island fortress, and the permeability of its shores means that its writers were constantly in contact with the Continent and pan-Mediterranean world and, later, with pan-Atlantic and even Pacific cultures. For example, in

Chapter 3, 'Literary and Historical Contexts', Julia Bolton Holloway traces the movements of a number of female mystics and documents their relationships to their English counterparts in pilgrimages across Europe and to Jerusalem (see Figure 3.1: Pilgrimages of Medieval Women). As a result of its geographical locale and highly mobile population even in the Middle Ages, medieval England also produced a fascinating body of travel and pilgrimage literature like Mandeville's *Travels* and *The Book of Margery Kempe*, whose increasing significance is reflected in its now canonical status. The principle impact of these approaches to medieval studies is simple: Our ideas in (and of) the present affect the way we understand the past.

Expanding the Canon

The academic reassessment of the geographical and temporal boundaries of 'the Middle Ages', as well as the increasingly interdisciplinary approaches of medieval scholars, is paralleled by concomitant changes in the *canon* of medieval literature. Once dominated exclusively by male authors, usually poets, often tied to prestigious institutions, patrons or movements, the medieval canon is increasingly devoted female authors, prose and dramatic works, encyclopaedic and mystical materials, and a great variety of cultural and historical 'texts' (rather than more traditionally defined 'literature'.) Changes in the canon, or what Warren calls 'the body of material written in Middle English deemed "authoritative" and hence worthy of scholarly attention' (See Chapter 10: 'Authoritative' Texts), have been driven by several forces, including feminism, New Historicism and postcolonial studies. First, feminism has driven the recovery of medieval texts by, for, and about women, bringing into focus large numbers of texts generally excluded from serious literary analysis by previous generations and expanding the canon to include hagiography (saints' lives); domestic, epistolary and courtesy literature; and mystical, visionary and theological texts. Because these materials (1) did not meet the narrow aesthetic definition of 'literature' in the past and (2) did not lend themselves to the tidy interpretive dictates of New Criticism, they received little attention by previous generations of literary scholars, and if they were mentioned at all, it was usually in the context of historical studies. Women were responsible for the creating a vast array of medieval texts, but because they generally were not, like Chaucer, *artists* but housewives and gentlewomen, nuns and mystics, they failed to gain critical recognition. Second, New Historicism's emphasis on cultural 'discourses' questions the separation between 'literary' and 'historical' texts and interrogates the disciplinary distinctions that artificially cleave texts into categories like fact vs. fiction, history vs. literature, secular vs. sacred or prose vs. poetry. Paul Strohm, for example, sets different types of texts in relation to one another to read them productively with, and against, each other as part of the same 'textual environment'. The confluence of feminist and New Historicist concerns finds expression in the increased attention to late medieval social movements like Lollardy or the 1381 Revolt. An intensely literate phenomenon, Lollardy was embroiled in controversies over the interpretation and dissemination of biblical texts and theological treatises, the place of gender in lay education, and the very status of the English language itself. (See Chapter 3: John Wycliff and Chapter 8: Changes in the Canon.)

Additionally, the redefinition of 'the medieval' as a more broadly construed temporal, geographical, multilingual and international period has led to a wider variety of texts to study. (See Chapter 8: Multilingualism, International Contexts, and Postcolonial Concerns.) As Warren demonstrates, the trad-itional canon of Chaucer, Langland, the *Pearl*-Poet, and the mystery plays has been supplemented by Margery Kempe, Julian of Norwich, and a bevy of female mystics; didactic texts the *Ancrene Wisse* and *Hali Meidhad*; historical texts like Froissart's *Chronicles* and Richard Maidstone's *Concordia*; hagiographical texts like *The South English Legendary* and *The Golden Legend*; theological treatises related to Lollardy and virginity; and fifteenth-century authors like John Lydgate, Thomas Hoccleve and Osbern Bokenham. How-ever, rather than being seen simply in the context of their cultures – where history provides the background and literature hovers in the foreground – these writers and texts are, in current medieval studies, firmly embedded in the warp and woof of medieval culture, simultaneously shaping, and being shaped by, the social and political forces of their historical moment. No longer focused solely upon so-called artistic or literary texts alone, medieval scholars today are as likely to read a legal document, court record, household letter or historical account as they are to read a Canterbury Tale. Even better, reading a court record with the Wife of Bath, as Paul Strohm does with his famous essay 'Treason in the Household' (1992) or examining the texts of the *Katherine Group* in relation to the *Second Nun's Tale* as Joyce Wogan-Brown does, mutually illuminates each text in surprising and productive ways. In Chapter 4, Matthew Boyd Goldie offers an example of this kind of historicist analysis as he reads the play *Mankind* over and against a Lollard text, *The Tretise of Miraclis Pleyinge*.

Perhaps counter-intuitively in light of the expansion of the medieval canon, the study of medieval literature has also deepened in its focus upon very specific local discursive cultures, narrowing and deepening the field of investigation, as in Ralph Hanna and Sheila Lindenbaum's analyses of London literary and institutional cultures. In addition to the examination of particular medieval institutions like religious orders, universities, trade guilds, civic festivities and ritual practices, contemporary scholars have also revealed the complex distinctiveness of specific locales, urban and rural. Long examined as England's major metropolitan area and as the home of traditionally studied writers like Langland, Gower and Chaucer, London has emerged in the last decade as a city of immense cultural complexity and textual density in which governmental regulations, historical records and literary productions exist side-by-side, often mutually reinforcing one another. Scholars like Sarah Beckwith have re-energized the study of the mystery plays, another staple of traditional literary interest, by moving beyond the simple play-text and considering the drama within the spiritual, social and symbolic economies of an entire city – in this case, York (*Signifying God*, 2001). Even an entire region can be 'read', as Gail Gibson did with East Anglia (*The Theater of Devotion*, 1989). Simply put, the expansion of the medieval canon has led to a parallel redefinition of medieval literature itself and a more sophisticated understanding the mutual inter-relationships of literature to history, culture and politics.

Theorizing the Texts

Previous generations of medievalists carried a rather arcane set of tools unlike many other literary scholars, all of which were necessary to deal with source material in different languages. A ME critic would likely be skilled in *historical linguistics* and *philology* (the study of the development of languages and etymological derivation of words), *paleography* (the historical study of handwriting styles), *codicology* (the study of manuscripts and manuscript production), as well as conversant in Latin, Anglo-Saxon, different dialects of ME, French and German. With a generously expanded sense of the *text* and *textuality* rather than just *literature* narrowly defined, much of the best literary scholarship now combines these traditional skills with inventively interdisciplinary approaches, combining literary, historical, cultural, theological, iconographic and architectural insights with increasingly sophisticated analytical methods drawn from the social sciences, including anthropology, sociology, psychology and economics. So, if recent literary analysis has redefined the temporal and geographical boundaries of the medieval period and if the canon of medieval literature has expanded to include previously unknown or ignored texts, scholars today add to that professional arsenal the theoretical innovations of the last 40 years both to revisit well-known texts with new eyes and to examine new documents for the first time. (See Chapter 7: Changes in Critical Responses and Approaches.)

Although it is perhaps an over-generalization, it is helpful to think about medieval studies as leaning towards either historicist (particularly New Historicist) or psychoanalytic approaches (particularly Lacan). On one hand, New Historicism analyses literary texts within the competing discourses of their historical moments, synchronically, as a kind of slice through time. In the Introduction to his influential anthology, *New Historicism*, H. Aram Veeser identifies five presuppositions informing New Historicist analysis: (1) 'every expressive act is embedded in a network of material practices', (2) 'every act of unmasking, critique and opposition uses the tools it condemns and risks falling prey to the practice is exposes', (3) 'literary and non-literary "texts" circulate inseparably', (4) 'no discourse, imaginative or archival, gives access to unchanging truths nor expresses inalterable human nature' and (5) 'a critical method and a language adequate to describe culture under capitalism participate in the economy they describe' (xi). Invigorated by Marxist concerns via Foucault's archaeological and genealogical work, New Historicism levels the distinction between literary and non-literary texts; denies the possibility of transcendent, transhistorical truths; focuses upon specific moments of production, reception, interpretation and consumption of texts and discourses; and ideally understands its complicity in the systems it unmasks. (See Chapter 5: Lee Patterson, *Chaucer and the Subject of History* [1991], Chapter 7: Marxism to New Historicism, and Chapter 8: New Historicism and Blurring the History / Literature Divide).

On the other hand, psychoanalytically inflected critics approach medieval culture diachronically across time, somewhat ahistorically, through a long history of ideas about subject formation, psychological processes and the relation of individuals to culture (See Chapter 5: Carolyn Dinshaw, *Chaucer's Sexual Poetics* [1989] and *Getting Medieval* [1999]). One of the great virtues of Lacanian thought, as it was with Freud's previously, is that both psychoanalytic thinkers created remarkably flexible systems whose formulations changed over the years. For example, Freud developed three different models for understanding the psyche: the structural model (ego, superego and id), the topographical model (conscious, preconscious and unconscious) and the economic model (drives vs. instincts) (Sadler et al. 1998). Each model and its associated mechanisms can be brought to bear upon literary texts and cultural concerns, each resulting in different conclusions. 'Returning to Freud' through structuralist linguistics and Kojeve's lectures on Hegel, Lacan's thought was likewise in constant revision, and the Lacan of 'the Mirror Stage' and 'the three registers' (the imaginary, symbolic and real) differs from the Lacan of 'the four discourses' and mathemes and ultimately from the knots and topological puzzles of the late-Lacan (see Rabaté 2003; Lacan, 'Mirror Stage' 1982, 2005).

Historicists sometimes polemically castigate psychoanalytic critics for their 'universalism' (for applying contemporary concepts to medieval subjects as if the psyche were a stable, universal entity), and psychoanalytic thinkers sometimes berate historicist critics as 'fetishists' (for investing inappropriately in the fragments of an unrecoverable past) (see Patterson 2001; Sebastian 2006).

However, much of the best medieval theory today is being developed by scholars – like Paul Strohm, Jeffrey Jerome Cohen, Louise Fradenberg and Geraldine Heng, to name just a few – who creatively bridge these gaps to create new theoretical spaces, remarkable formulations, and critical insights.

When thinking about the development of literary theory and its application to medieval texts, we should therefore think not so much in terms of a linear development, of one paradigm giving way tidily to the next, as much as we should imagine the interaction of ideas, and suggestive fragments of ideas, in constant and sometimes discordant colloquy. As new approaches develop, they do not simply leave earlier concepts behind as much as push ahead and loop back upon themselves anew, carrying the entire history of dialogue forward into new areas, different questions and related concerns in new disciplinary and institutional contexts. As Gail Ashton (Chapter 5), Bonnie Millar (Chapter 6), John Ganim (Chapter 7), Diane Cady (Chapter 9) and Sol Neely (Chapter 10) each detail in their own ways, medieval literary criticism has developed dynamically in conversation with, and often in critique of, the broader currents of literary and cultural theory. Borrowing a concept from physics, literary theory is thus a non-linear dynamical system, in which certain suggestions serve as attractors, drawing other ideas into their orbits and providing a conceptual structure, before morphing again into something new.

As the chapters in the *Continuum Handbook* make clear, not only have medieval scholars harnessed contemporary theory in the service of medieval texts, they have also been at the cutting edge of theoretical innovation. The influence of critics like David Aers, Jeffrey Jerome Cohen, Carolyn Dinshaw, Bruce Holsinger, Karma Lochrie, Lee Patterson, Miri Rubin and Paul Strohm reach beyond medieval studies, traditionally conceived (See Chapter 6: Critics.) In fact, as Bruce Holsinger demonstrates, the close relationship of medieval studies to the innovations of post-structuralist theory is far from accidental (*The Premodern Condition* 2005), for some of the most important thinkers in the theoretical pantheon sharpened their formulations either as medievalists or in the close analysis of medieval culture. Georges Bataille trained as a medievalist at the École Nationale des Chartes and worked at Bibliotheque Nationale as an archivist. Bataille's essay on the First World War destruction of the famous cathedral, 'Notre-Dame de Rheims', marks his entry into the world of loss, expenditure and excess, 'the general economy', and his life-long project, *La somme athéologique*, is a response to Aquinas's *Summa Theologiae* (26–52). Bataille influenced every French thinker from the 1930s onward, and Holsinger traces Foucault's concern for medieval culture back to Bataille as well, with Bataille's *The Trial of Gilles de Rais* serving as a model for Foucault's *I, Pierre Revière* (52–6). Lacan's important *Seminar VII: The Ethics of Psychoanalysis* finds its shifting, 'archaeophiliac' center in Lacan's engagement with 'courtly love as anamorphosis' (78). Critiquing Lacan, Julia Kristeva likewise returns to quintessentially medieval material in her 1983 *Tales of Love* (*Histoire d'amour*), especially in the fascinating essay on the Virgin Mary and Kristeva's own experience of pregnancy, 'Stabat Mater'. Pierre Bourdieu's influential concept of *habitus*, 'a "feel for the game" shared by all those living within a certain cultural moment or sphere and a collective disposition that in turn generates social practices, modes of human subjection and symbolic forms' (102), first emerged in his translation and introduction to Erwin Panofsky's influential *Gothic Architecture and Scholasticism* (94–113), in which both architectural and theological scholasticism worked by reconciling oppositions. Holsinger even finds in the second half of Derrida's epic *Of Grammatology* the dismantling of 'the theological scaffoldings of Enlightenment historiography and in particular the Rousseauist fantasy of a Dark Age of linguistic barbarism' (115). *Of Grammatology*'s apophatic or negative theology operates through Derrida's use of Emmanuel Levinas's 'liturgical temporality' that is itself ethical (See Chapter 10: The Ethical Turn: From Discipline to Responsibility.) Holsinger writes, 'Liturgy exists and is performed not in direct relation to God, but in the subject's relation of obligation to the neighbor who bears a trace of God and whose face the subject can recognize but never fully know' (131). Thus, in terms of Sol Neely's argument in Chapter 10, the 'ethical turn' in post-structuralism is less a recent reactionary development and more the outworking of deconstructive critique, historical criticism and resistant politics. Holsinger's final figure is Roland Barthes, whose readerly and writerly program in *S/Z* demonstrates an 'awed devotion to the hermeneutical proliferations embodied in the exegetical culture of the medieval West' (153). The five codes of Barthes' reading of Balzac in *S/Z* (the proairetic, semantic, cultural, hermeneutic and symbolic codes) are themselves an elaboration of the medieval (for Barthes', Ignatian) 'four senses of scripture' (the literal, allegorical, moral and anagogical dimensions of holy writ).

Mapping New Approaches

We begin to see, then, that the theoretical developments most important to contemporary literary analysis are themselves not necessarily external, modern impositions upon medieval literature but a (re)recognition of what appears already latent within medieval culture itself:

- The hybrid multicultural, multiethnic and colonial identities of the British Isles and the intercultural interaction of Muslim, Judaic, and Christian cultures (postcolonialism);
- The role of women as producers and consumers of texts (feminism); the

mutual interpenetration of literary and historical textualities (New Historicism);
- The genre-violating and conception-busting excessiveness of medieval textuality itself that effaces authors, disperses authority, displaces conceptual hierarchies and remains perpetually self-subverting (post-structuralism) and
- The ancient practice of midrash, which creates dialogue and extends the text without foreclosing it (ethical criticism).

The *Continuum Handbook* itself also explores new and emerging areas of scholarship in greater detail, with many chapters pushing into new territory. John Ganim (Chapter 7) discusses the 'Emerging Approaches' of ecocriticism, theology and theory and metamedievalism. Nancy Bradley Warren (Chapter 8) raises the prospect of 'Revising the New Orthodoxy'. Diane Cady (Chapter 9) looks at the intersections of race, gender and sexuality. Sol Neely's Chapter 10, 'Mapping the Current Critical Landscape', leads us to consider the necessity for an ethical criticism, one that is self-critical and anti-sacrificial no matter the theoretical approach.

To this list, I would add two areas of investigation that are gaining momentum in medieval studies, one driven by social and historical concerns and the other by formalistic and aesthetic issues. In the first case, historical research into medieval children, families and households is being matched by the concurrent analysis of these subject positions in medieval texts. Largely resulting from two generations of feminist investigation, families, households and individuals are being examined in their specific geographical and historical settings and particular lifespans. In other words, the problem of subjectivity – of the development of the individual and the individual's place in the wider society – has gained a diachronic as well as synchronic aspect: Human persons (and their representations in literature) emerge at a specific moment in time (synchronic) but are also figures in constant flux, movement and change through time (diachronic). What an earlier generation might have called 'human developmental psychology' is being supplanted by a more broadly based cultural understanding of 'the life course'. As a result, the medieval institutions associated with childhood and youth, particularly parenting and discipline, secular and spiritual education, apprenticeship, chivalric and monastic training, courtship and marriage rituals, are receiving greater attention (see, for example, Hanawalt 1986, 1993, 2002).

In the second case, the perception that literary theory has distanced readers from the literature itself, or otherwise obscured the rhetorical and literary features of the text, is giving rise to a new formalism and a renewed sense of aesthetic appreciation (Levinson 2007). 'New Formalism' appeared first among American poets in the 1970s and 1980s as a response to the excesses of free verse and confessional poetry (though some would look back as far Richard Wilbur's 1947 inaugural collection, *The Beautiful Changes*), and the New Formalists returned to metrically precise rhymed verse and traditional poetic forms (see Shapiro 1987; McPhillips 2005). The criticism of medieval literature has likewise awakened a renewed sense of aesthetics, returning to the formal structures and stylistic attributes of the text with theoretically informed eyes (Lerer 2003) or turning to appreciate the artistic complexity and linguistic subtlety of previously overlooked bodies of literature (Canon 2004, 2008).

Outline of the *Handbook*

The *Continuum Handbook* introduces both ME literature and key contemporary approaches to ME literature. The volume also includes specific historical, cultural and theoretical material designed to create a strong foundation for further study in medieval literature. Although it is not necessary to read the chapters in order, the volume moves from general historical backgrounds, into detailed readings of specific texts and particular critics and then finally to key theoretical considerations. Each chapter is also packed with cross references to associated topics in other chapters.

In particular, the *Continuum Handbook* is organized in sections, each composed of several chapters:

- Chapter 1:   Introduction
- Chapters 2–3:   Historical Context for the Study of ME Literature
- Chapters 4–5:   Case Studies in ME Texts and Critics
- Chapters 6–9:   Extended Analysis of Specific Critical Issues in ME Literature
- Chapter 10:   Where is the Study of ME Literature Moving?

Specific chapter details are as follows. Chapter 1, the 'Introduction' by Daniel T. Kline (University of Alaska Anchorage) provides an orientation to the medieval period as recently redefined and the impact of that redefinition on the study of ME literature. Chapter 2, 'Historical Context' by Brian Gastle (Western Carolina University), deftly outlines the key historical events of the ME period (c. 1200–1500), both domestic and international, that shaped English culture and affected ME literature. Chapter 3, 'Literary and Cultural Contexts' by Julia Bolton Hollow (Florence, Italy) with Daniel T. Kline, supplies brief descriptions of specific persons, texts, genres, topics and issues foundational to a strong understanding of ME literature. In Chapter 4, 'Case Studies in Reading I', Matthew Boyd Goldie (Rider University) offers four case studies highlighting contemporary approaches to ME literature as he examines (1) Marie de France's *Lanval*, (2) representations of the 1381 Revolt, (3) *The Book of Margery Kempe* and (4) the play *Mankind* in relation to *The Tretise of Miraclis Pleyinge*. Following Goldie in Chapter 5, Gail Ashton (Independent Scholar) looks at key contemporary ME critics (Lee Patterson, Carolyn Dinshaw, Karma Lochrie, Jeffrey Jerome Cohen and Patricia Clare Ingham and Michelle Warren) and details their distinctive contributions to ME criticism. In Chapter 6, Bonnie Millar (Castle College), paralleling Holloway's 'Literary and Cultural Contexts' in Chapter 3, assesses 'Key Critics, Concepts, and Topics' in the contemporary study of ME literature and provides helpful, compact descriptions of key issues and thinkers. John Ganim (University of California Riverside) follows in Chapter 7 with an incisive history of 'Changes in Critical Responses and Approaches' that outlines the development of ME criticism over the last 30 years, concluding with an examination of the newest theoretical approaches. Nancy Bradley Warren (Florida State University) in Chapter 8 deals specifically with 'Changes in the Canon' to identify the cultural forces and to evaluate the literary movements that have expanded the range of material studied by current ME scholars. Key among these is feminism, New Historicism and postcolonialism. In Chapter 9, 'Issues of Sexuality, Gender and Ethnicity', Diane Cady (Mills College) takes on a cluster of issues absolutely central to contemporary literary study and details the critics and topics that make sexuality, gender, ethnicity, and race central to many current analyses. Finally, Sol Neely (Purdue University) in Chapter 10, 'Mapping the Current Critical Landscape', assesses the last 40 years of ME criticism and challenges ME critics to move towards 'ethical exegesis'. As a result, there is a certain amount of helpful overlap in many of the chapters to demonstrate how a particular issue – say, gender – is treated in different texts, by different critics, according to different approaches.

No single volume could adequately do justice to the great wealth, variety and complexity of ME literature and culture. The *Continuum Handbook* has not attempted to do so, nor does it offer a seamless account of ME literature and criticism. Instead, the different emphases in the volume, many indicated by internal cross references, and the scholarly friction between the respective authors' approaches, encourage creative exploration of the ME texts themselves and critical interrogation of the critical theories as well. The *Continuum Handbook* is less concerned with providing tidy answers as it is with spurring continued thought and discussion. The Study Questions at the end of each chapter are an initial push into class discussion and personal investigation, including a series of 'Web Quests' designed to propel further research. The volume concludes with ancillary material that supports the central chapters of the *Handbook*. The Reference section serves several functions: (1) it provides full bibliographical citations for the parenthetical references incorporated into the text of each chapter, (2) it offers brief annotations of each cited source and (3) it suggests additional readings for further study. Finally, Susan Oldrieve (Baldwin Wallace College) has prepared an appendix on 'Teaching, Curriculum, and Learning' that briefly surveys ME and medieval literature courses in the US and UK and highlights 'best practices' that should be helpful both to in the study and teaching of ME literature. This chapter is available on the Continuum website.

It is appropriate to conclude the *Continuum Handbook* with a chapter on pedagogy because each contributor is an experienced classroom teacher, and the anthology itself is designed for classroom use. So, I would like to end with an anecdote that summarizes, in a way, what I have attempted to illustrate in this Introduction. During a class discussion concerning affective piety and religious devotion in the Middle Ages, I asked if anyone knew what an 'icon' was. Of course, I had in mind a religious image used as an aid to prayer or worship. There was one of those rather long silences, until a student raised her hand tentatively and said, 'It's one of those little pictures on the computer screen that you click to make something happen'. Initially chagrined, I was then struck by the pertinence of the analogy between the religious and technological definitions of 'icon', and as a class we began to chart out the correspondences: both are visual links to an invisible realm; both require a kind of activation to be effective; both require specialized knowledge to understand and properly implement; both pack an entire history into a rather simple image; both enable, to the uninitiated, a kind of power, or even magic. (If you have forgotten that feeling, just sit down in front of a computer screen with someone unfamiliar with complex software and watch their reactions.) In class we found many other connections together, for the cultural information compressed into any software program's visual field provides a living, contemporary analogue to any program of medieval stained glass, statuary or iconography. Both sets of icons require a commensurate effort to understand, to employ, and to decode. As Eco argued, as the reactions to Princess Diana's and Mother Theresa's death reminded us, and as the anecdote of the icon demonstrates, perhaps the Middle Ages have never really ended at all, just changing forms and remaining forever familiar yet unalterably alien.

Study Questions

1. Define the following terms in your own words:
   - MMORPG
   - Medievalism
   - The Middle Ages
   - The Middle English Period
   - The Dark Ages

- The Church
- The Canon
- Palaeography
- Codicology
- Synchronic/Diachronic

2. The Introduction references a number of contemporary medieval phenomena. What others can you identify? What in those other examples seems more medieval vs. more modern? Another way to approach this question is to examine each of Eco's ten medieval 'dreams' and brainstorm examples for each.
3. What is the relationship between 'medieval studies' (strictly defined as the study of the medieval period) and the study of 'medievalism'? How, if at all, do the two areas overlap?
4. Many commentators point to the development of the printing press as a defining feature of the modern period. What cultural effects did the introduction of the printing press and moveable type have throughout Europe, and why would this initiate a new historical moment? In comparison, the late twentieth century saw the development of new communication technologies, particularly digital communication and the internet. What are the cultural effects of these new digital technologies? Is it possible that we are now undergoing similar cultural changes? Why or why not?
5. What kinds of ethical issues are involved in studying another time, another place and another culture? Do writers and researchers have any kind of moral obligation in how they conduct their work or argue their points of view? What are some of the issues involved, if any, and why should it even matter?
6. *Web Quest*: Unfortunately, the Middle Ages are often associated with cultural backwardness, ignorance, fanaticism, and violence. Do a quick search for the term 'medieval' or 'Middle Ages' to see how many usages are negative vs. how many are neutral or even appreciative. In what contexts, venues or publications do these different connotations of the terms appear? Why do you think this is the case?
7. *Web Quest*: Search the web for uses of the terms 'crusade(s)' or 'crusader(s)' in regard to post-9/11 political events and identify (1) who uses the terms, (2) in what contexts and (3) to what purposes? Are the references made with any historical grounding? That is, is there any relationship between the contemporary reference and medieval events, or are the references lacking a clear relation to the medieval crusading phenomena?
8. *Web Quest*: Look up the term 'medievalism' and record the range of activities, approaches and materials that fall under that rubric. Of those aspects of medievalism that you research, which are the most intriguing? Why?
9. *Web Quest*: The question of 'periodization' is currently of great interest in medieval studies. Search the web for different approaches, definitions and criticisms of the traditional tripartite structure of Western historiography (ancient, medieval, modern). What are the advantages and disadvantages of such an approach? What insights do such an organizational structure foster, and what kind of problems does that same structure introduce?

10. *Web Quest*: Taking the common chronological boundaries traditionally given for the medieval period in the West (roughly 500–1500 CE), investigate several non-Western cultures to ascertain the typical chronological boundaries or eras that characterize those cultures, like:

    - The Far East: China, Japan and Korea
    - South and Southeast Asia: India, Thailand and Cambodia
    - Sub-Saharan Africa: Kenya, Nigeria, Ghana, Lesotho and South Africa
    - Central and South America: Mexico, Guatemala, Ecuador and Peru

What comparisons can you see between not only (1) the historical events that were happening at approximately the same time in different places across the globe, but also (2) the kinds of literature that was being produced in those areas and (3) the kinds of labels historians have applied to those disparate cultures and different eras. Creating a basic timeline might be a helpful way to visualize these connections.

2 Historical Context for Middle English Literature

Brian Gastle, Western Carolina University

Overview

Middle English (ME) literature stretches from roughly 1100 through the fifteenth century. The historical events that shaped English literature during this period were equally monumental. From the Battle of Hastings in England to the Battle of Agincourt in France, from the Crusades in the Holy Land to the Peasant's Revolt and the march on London, from the Black Death to the deposition of Richard II, the events of the later Middle Ages provided a rich backdrop that both affected and was affected by the literature of the period. While no common thread ties all of these events together, the period does reflect an interesting kind of parallelism, for both the beginning and the end of ME literature are marked by significant events that would redefine English national identity. This chapter explores a number of these events, not to force direct parallels between the events and specific ME works, but rather to highlight the rich relationship between two. First, beginning with the Norman Conquest, it investigates the significant changes in language that occurred during the period and some of the continental events affecting England during the time, such as the Crusades. Second, it discusses some of the social, religious and political events in England that parallel events abroad (such as the Schism in the Church on the Continent and the heretical Lollard movement in England). Finally, it addresses three major political struggles that served to redefine the country and the literature at the end of the Middle Ages: the Hundred Years' War, the Deposition of Richard II and the War of the Roses. (See Chapter 1: Extending the Medieval.)

When Did Middle English Literature Begin?

Medieval English literature in general is usually divided into two main categories: Old English (OE) literature (also known as Anglo-Saxon literature) and ME literature. Since language changes gradually over time, it is often difficult as well as inappropriate to assign specific dates for dividing such periods. Fortunately, however, for students and scholars the origins of ME literature can be traced to a single, specific historical event: the Battle of Hastings, on 14 October 1066, during which William I definitively ended English self-rule and installed a French-speaking aristocracy and attendant bureaucracy, forever changing English language and literature.

Historical and Political Change after 1066

From the late fourth through the sixth centuries, the Angles, Saxons, Frisians and Jutes had invaded England from northern Europe, conquering and displacing the indigenous Celts, but Vikings also subsequently harassed these invaders all the way into the eleventh century, when Danish kings replaced Saxon kings of England. In 1042, Edward the Confessor took the throne of England from the Danes and held it for two decades against both Danish incursions and opposition from other English nobility. (See Chapter 3: Geoffrey of Monmouth, *History of the Kings of Britain*.)

Edward named William, Duke of Normandy, his successor, in part because the Normans aided Edward in his acquisition of the crown. When Edward died in January of 1066, Harold I (Harold Godwinson), a Saxon lord and opponent of Norman rule, claimed the crown. A second Harold, Harold Hardraada, a Norwegian warrior and descendant of the Danish kings of England (and no friend of the Normans), invaded northern England and captured land as far south as York. The Saxon forces, under Harold I, defeated the Norwegians on 26 September 1066 (marking the last major Scandinavian invasion of England until 1974 and ABBA's hit song 'Waterloo'). The very next day, 27 September 1066, William landed in Hastings, England, to defend his claim to the throne. The Battle of Hastings occurred on 14 October 1066, and the Normans defeated the Saxons after two days of fierce fighting. By the end of the year, William had swept through the country and subdued the English nobility, and he was crowned King of England in London on Christmas day, 1066. (See Chapter 3: The Bayeux Tapestry.)

Artistic and Linguistic Change after 1066

William's conquest opened a new chapter in English literary history. Most notably, French became the official language of the state and of the aristocracy, and would remain so until the fourteenth century. For over 200 years after the Conquest, artistic literary production in England focused upon French forms, styles, genres and subjects. In fact, ME literature – from its genesis in the eleventh century, to its heyday in the fourteenth, and to its eventual transmutation into Early Modern (formerly called Renaissance) literature – could be characterized as an attempt to create and define English national identity. The play between French and English traditions is even further complicated by the fact that many medieval English texts were written in Latin, the international language of medieval Europe. England was truly a multilingual nation, and that multilingualism reflected the political turmoil of the times. (See Chapter 8: Multilingualism, International Contexts, and Postcolonial Concerns.)

In addition to these political changes, one of the most important effects of the Norman Conquest upon English literature was linguistic change. The English language changed dramatically after the Norman Conquest. It gradually lost its inflections (word suffixes that controlled meaning) and relied more on word order for meaning. French words became a more significant part of English vocabulary, and often the French form of a word became the more socially prestigious usage. For example, the following words originally meant the same thing, but have now come to carry much different connotations:

- 'stench' (OE *stenc/stincan*) and 'aroma' (OF *aromat*): the French have an *aroma* and the English *stink*
- 'ask' (OE *ascian*) and 'demand' (OF *desmande*): the English, as subordinates, *ask* and the French, as superiors, *demand*.
- 'cow' (OE *cu*) and 'beef' (OF *boef*)

That last example typifies the political and social effects of this language shift. When the animal was prepared and placed on the table in front of the aristocracy, the French word was used. When the Anglo Saxon peasant was in the field working, that peasant had to beware of Anglo Saxon 'cu'-pies.

We especially see this influx of French vocabulary in legal, military, social, ecclesiastical and governmental terms. Because the Norman conquerors controlled political life, they brought to English the words *exchequer, administer, nobility, garter, brooch, siege, captain, jury, judgment* and many others. Later authors took full advantage of such French etymologies and cognates to develop their own characters and events. For example, when Chaucer wants to highlight the inappropriate gentility of his Prioress, not only does he say she can only speak French that she learned at school, but her portrait in the *General Prologue* is replete with French cognates (*divine, simple, morsel, plesaunt, charitable, tretys* etc.), many of which appear to have entered the language not long after the Norman Conquest. Such subtle diction exemplifies how historical events help to shape ME literature, and the Prioress's portrait also demonstrates how those changes affected both political and religious discourse (I. 118–62).

The Crusades and the Expansion of Church Power

Being a Christian in medieval western Europe meant being what is now termed Roman Catholic; the authority of Holy Church, the authority of the Pope, and the power bestowed upon clergy (as the only path to salvation) were well established. Catholic doctrine so permeates ME literature that it is nearly impossible to extricate such beliefs from that literature. During England's violent transformation in the eleventh century, the Church expanded its reach into the Holy Land through the Crusades. While French and German aristocracy fielded most of the Christian forces during the Crusades, England participated comparatively little; only Richard I – the Lionheart – went on crusade during his reign. Nonetheless, the cultural effects of the Crusades resonated for over two hundred years.

For ME literature, the Crusades provided rich matter both as an explicit subject and as background or metaphorical material. No ME literature embraced the Crusades as fully as continental literature, such as the Old

French *Song of Roland*, but several ME Romances allude to the Crusades. However, the proliferation of continental romances, which idealized the courtly crusading warrior and crusader culture, influenced romance production in England. Arthurian literature, such as the *Alliterative Morte Arthure* and Malory's subsequent *Le Morte d'Arthur*, depict King Arthur as a Crusader to further establish his Christian legitimacy to the crown. While Boccaccio's great Italian work, the *Decameron*, sets several tales during the Crusades, the English poet John Gower would later draw upon the Crusades more circuitously in his Tale of Constance in the *Confessio Amantis*, as would Chaucer in his version of the Constance story, the *Man of Law's Tale*. Chaucer complicated his Knight's portrait in the *General Prologue* by referring to crusading battles in which the Knight had fought, but not all of which were successful for the Christians. The Crusades also led to a flourishing of travel and trade between the East and the West, which gave rise to the rich travel and pilgrimage literature of the later Middle Ages. (See Chapter 3: Arthurian Literature and the 'Matter of Britain': *Chanson de Roland* and the 'Matter of France'; and Fall of Troy and the 'Matter of Troy'.)

The Power of the Church at Home: From Thomas Becket to the *Magna Carta*

In spite of England's relative distance from the Crusades, the Church's power in England grew, thanks in part to two historical events – the murder of Thomas Becket and the adoption of the *Magna Carta* – that reverberated through the literature of the period. In the twelfth century, Henry II named Thomas Becket, his long-time friend and Chancellor, to the post of Archbishop of Canterbury, the most senior ecclesiastical position in England. In contrast to his earlier role as the King's chief ally, Beckett consolidated Church lands and protected them from secular control and taxation, battling Henry for years in the courts and waging a political war for the autonomy of the Church in England. In 1170, four knights, possibly incited by the King, violated the sanctity of the church as a refuge from violence, entered Canterbury Cathedral and murdered Beckett on the stairs leading up to the choir. One contemporary account of the murder is quite gruesome, stating that the knights cut the top of Beckett's head off and 'scattered the brains with the blood across the floor' (Grim). Both the Church and the people of England were outraged at the murder, which led to greater sympathy for the Church throughout the land, and Beckett became one of the most significant saints of England, with a shrine established at the very place he was murdered. Chaucer later sets this shrine as the destination for the pilgrimage in his *Canterbury Tales*: 'The hooly blissful martir for to seke' (I.17). (See Chapter 3: Pilgrim and Travel Literature.)

The conflict between secular authority and Church rule continued into the early twelfth century when, in 1215, the first version of the *Magna Carta* was issued. While the *Magna Carta* is best known for its influence on constitutional law and democracy, it also strengthened the Church's authority in England. The *Magna Carta* was issued several times from 1216 (King John) to 1297 (Edward I). It granted specific rights both to the Church in England and to English nobles, and it freed the Church almost completely from secular authority in England. This freedom allowed the Church to weather internal conflicts during this period, such as heretical movements and the Great Schism.

Crisis in the Church Abroad: The Great Schism

From the eleventh century, a number of forces variously consolidated and fractured the power of the Church throughout Europe. For example, the Knights Templar, a military and religious order, had risen to power with the blessings of the Church in the early twelfth century, in part through crusading, but by the early fourteenth century, their power had so threatened the Church that they were persecuted as heretics. During that time, the Church enacted its own sweeping reforms during the fourth Lateran Council of 1215. A number of that council's edicts shaped the organization of the Church and its relationship to parishioners for centuries. Lateran IV adopted the word 'transubstantiation' for the literal transformation of Eucharistic wine and bread into the blood and flesh of Christ, began the process to establish Fraternal orders (Friars), outlined basic prayers and defined the Seven Sacraments – baptism, confirmation, Eucharist, confession, matrimony, holy orders and extreme unction – as aspects of the ideal Christian life. (See Chapter 3: Monastic Orders.) Even though Lateran IV attempted to set basic parameters of Christian faith, ME texts developed a range of responses to Catholic doctrine and practices, from explicative works such as the morality play *Everyman* and Chaucer's *Parson's Tale*, to critiques of abuse such as *Piers Plowman*, to gendered investigations such as the *Book of Margery Kempe* and Julian of Norwich's *Showings*. Additionally, in the twelfth century, the rise of the universities in Paris and Oxford coincided with increased education of parishioners, greater interrogation of ecclesiastical rules and growing dissatisfaction with the system itself. (See Chapter 3: Schools and Literacy and Universities.) While much of the Church's turmoil occurred too far away to affect England directly, in the later Middle Ages ME literature drew upon both far reaching Church politics and local ecclesiastical problems, some of which paralleled England's tumultuous relationship with France.

The years 1378 to 1417 – a time known as the Great Schism or Avignon Papacy – marked a troubled period in Church history, one that medieval

English writers acknowledged. From 1309–77, seven popes (all of whom were French) had held the papacy in Avignon rather than in Rome. The initial move to Avignon in 1309 was defended as a security measure to protect the Pope from armed militias in Rome. But the political ramifications of the move intensified as subsequent popes remained in the familiar, more modern and far more luxurious papal seat in Avignon. The political effects of the move were unavoidable, and the great Italian poet Francesco Petrarch referred to Avignon as the 'Babylon of the West'. In 1378, Pope Gregory XI moved the papacy back to Rome, but upon his death opposing factions established two different popes, one in Rome (Urban VI) and one in Avignon (Clement VII); thus began the period generally referred to as the Great Schism. At times there would be two or even three popes until the Council of Constance ended the Schism in 1415. While the papacy had been under attack before, never had its own members created such division, forcing all of Europe take sides. Needless to say, during this period of fragmented and weakening papal power, the English did not support the French pope, but they were interested in a resolution. John Gower attacked Clement both in his long Latin poem *Vox Clamantis* and in his ME poem *Confessio Amantis*, but in his short Latin poem 'De Lucis Srutinio' ('An Examination of Light') he urged reunification. Additionally, like many of his contemporaries, Gower saw the Schism as a catalyst for other, more local, problems, namely the heretical movement known in England as Lollardy. (See Chapter 4: The 1381 Revolt.)

Crisis in the Church at Home: Lollardy

Lollardy was a religious movement of the late fourteenth through the fifteenth century in England that the Church deemed heretical, but it possessed a wide following and often benefited from powerful supporters and protectors, such as John of Gaunt, uncle to Richard II and father of the subsequent Henry IV. Lollardy developed out of the teachings of the Oxford theologian John Wyclif (c.1320–84), and therefore its adherents are sometimes also called Wycliffites. However, Wyclif was not the leader of the movement, and Lollardy did not follow a single common text or doctrine. Rather, Lollards held various beliefs that they judged central to reforming the corruption they saw in the church. They believed that the Bible and preaching should be more accessible to the laity, so they enacted the first translation of the entire Bible into ME (centuries before the King James or Authorized Version) and preached not in Latin but in the vernacular. They believed that laymen, not just the ordained clergy, should have the power to perform sacraments. They opposed many of the doctrines of the Church, including transubstantiation. Their religious teachings also led to questioning of the social and political status quo in England. For example, John Ball, a leader of the 1381 Peasants' Revolt who appears in many ME poems, was a Lollard preacher. Upon the death of John of Gaunt, and especially after John of Gaunt's son Henry IV took the throne, Lollards were persecuted relentlessly in England, and in 1427 Wyclif was burned as a heretic and his ashes cast into a river; it is unlikely that this had much effect on him, since he had been already dead for some 43 years. Yet even with such dedicated persecution, Lollards appear to have remained in England well into the Early Modern period, and many of the Protestant tenants of the Reformation echo Lollard doctrines. (See Chapter 3: Lollardy and John Wyclif.)

Just as Lollardy had both its proponents and persecutors among the sacred and secular authorities, so too did it have both among authors of the period. Literature criticizing abuses of the Church proliferated in late medieval England, and sometimes it is difficult to determine whether a work is specifically Lollard in sentiment or if it is merely participating in a long tradition of anti-clerical or anti-fraternal literature. Such works might criticize friars (*anti-fraternal*) or merely general corruption among members of the church (*anti-clerical*). William Langland's long dream vision *Piers Plowman* is often read as a Lollard poem, given its focus upon the humble plowman, Piers, and its emphasis upon personal piety leading to salvation. Some medieval contemporaries associated the character of Piers himself with the revolt, as if he had been a real person participating in the event. Other authors, like John Gower, criticized Wyclif and the Lollards as heretical and dangerous to the social order of England. In the Epilogue to the *Man of Law's Tale*, the Host accuses the Parson of being a Lollard (II.1173), and the Shipman then interrupts, saying that he will hear no preaching from someone who would 'springen cokkel in our clene corn' (II.1183). It is difficult to know whether medieval audiences saw the Parson justly criticized as a Lollard who sows dissent, or if they believed him to be pious and the Shipman as too coarse to benefit from such a sermon. Either way, Chaucer's critique of simony and abuses in the Church emerged as part of the growing vernacular secular literary traditions, but such criticisms of the Church also appeared in more explicitly religious literary texts. (See Chapter 3: Geoffrey Chaucer.) In the early fifteenth century *Book of Margery Kempe*, Margery is often considered a heretic because she travels the countryside speaking of her discussions with God and Jesus, but she carefully defends herself against these claims since being considered a Lollard might have led to her imprisonment or death. (See Chapter 4: Margery Kempe, *The Book of Margery Kempe*.)

The Book of Margery Kempe is also part of a larger literary tradition in the later Middle Ages known as mysticism. Medieval mystics, such as Margery Kempe, Julian of Norwich and Richard Rolle, were particularly interested in their individual spiritual relationship with God, the 'mystical' rapport between the temporal self and the divine almighty. While the authors of a number of mystical and devotional texts (such as *The Cloud of Unknowing*) are unknown, many were composed by women who were either lay people (like Margery Kempe) or members of religious communities (like Julian of Norwich). This textual form of feminine spirituality often upset secular and sacred authorities alike. Julian, for example, refers to God as both a Mother and as a Father figure, while Margery Kempe calls upon her visions to help resolve personal and political disputes she encounters during her travels. The profoundly personal spirituality of medieval mystics undermined traditional roles of the clergy, and just as the nature of spirituality and religion was transformed from within, so too was the secular feudal order thrown into chaos from disruptive external pressure. (See Chapter 3: Birgitta of Sweden, Catherine of Siena, Christina of Markyate, *Cloud of Unknowing*, Walter Hilton, Julian of Norwich, Margery Kempe, Nicholas Love, Marguerite Porete, and Richard Rolle and Chapter 3: Contemplative Literature.)

Famine and Plague

England in the fourteenth century experienced a number of events that greatly diminished its population and strained its socio-economic resources. The first of several famines, probably caused by climate changes, struck in 1315 and lasted for at least two years, killing some 10–20% of England's population of 5–7 million. More debilitating and better known is the Black Death (Bubonic Plague) that swept across Europe and reached England in 1348. The Black Death was spread in part by the bite of fleas, which transmitted the disease across Europe on the backs of the ubiquitous black rat (*Rattus rattus*). Mortality rates are unclear; estimates range from one-third to two-thirds of the population of Europe, but the death rate was probably somewhat less in England because the colder Northern climate restricted its spread. As people died, survivors looked for ways to deal with the loss.

A veritable cult of death emerged. Visual representations of the Dance of Death arose in frescoes and art. In Italy, Giovanni Boccaccio set his celebrated *Decameron* against the backdrop of the plague. In England, chroniclers like Henry Knighton describe its effects on the country, referring to the plague as a worldwide catastrophe. Surprisingly perhaps, the plague tends not to figure prominently in ME literature, but rather it serves as a dark backdrop to its themes and issues. For example, even though Chaucer's *Canterbury Tales* is modelled on Boccaccio's *Decameron*, it does not rely upon the plague as a narrative force in the way the *Decameron* does. The Old Man in the *Pardoner's Tale* is 'forwrapped' (VI.718) like a corpse prepared for burial, and Chaucer sets his version of the story during the Plague, unlike his sources and analogues, but the images do not contain the stark morbidity found in Boccaccio's descriptions of plague-ridden Florence. (See Chapter 3: Giovanni Boccaccio and *Wynnere and Wastoure*.)

Labour Unrest and the Peasants' Revolt

One of the most immediate effects of the plague of 1348 was a substantial decrease in the labour force. As farmers and field hands died, fewer and fewer crops were harvested, which contributed to greater mortality due to famine. As the size of the labour force declined, workers recognized one of the basic laws of economics: Labour shortages lead to higher wages. For the first time, English workers began demanding better pay for their work.

In the 1349 Ordinance of Labourers, King Edward III dictated that workers should work for their pre-plague wages. This edict did not go over well with the workers (although the landowners appreciated it), and it served as the first in a number of attempts at fixing prices, stabilizing wages, and controlling the workforce. The Statute of Labourers (1351) attempted to reinforce the Ordinance of Labourers by setting a 'maximum wage' – as opposed to modern minimum wage laws – and stiffer penalties for charging excessive wages or demanding exorbitant prices for goods. These heavy-handed controls on peasant labour, in conjunction with a substantial tax in 1377, fueled a great uprising, known formerly as the Peasants' Revolt, or more currently, the 1381 Revolt, for recent research has demonstrated that far more than just commoners and peasants were involved.

A group of rioters from Kent and Essex marched on London in June 1381, led by Walther 'Wat' Tyler, Jack Straw, and the aforementioned Lollard priest John Ball who, according to biased chroniclers like Thomas Walsingham, used Langland's *Piers Plowman* as a rallying cry. The crowd attacked London, selectively burning the palace of John of Gaunt (uncle to Richard II and father to the future Henry IV), destroying official charters and administrative files, and executing the Archbishop of Canterbury and other notable members of the London elite. They demanded the abolition of serfdom and the dismissal the King Richard II's counsellors, whom they viewed as corrupting the King. (See Chapter 3: William Langland, *Piers Plowman*.) The crowd was not opposed to the monarchy; rather it decried oppression of the commons by a corrupt and abusive aristocracy under the King. The 14-year-old Richard II took advantage of their patriotism and, during a meeting with the rebels outside of London, promised to consider their demands. Meanwhile the Mayor of London struck down Wat Tyler. (See Figure 4.2 – The Death of Wat Tyler.) After Tyler's death, Richard managed to disperse the crowd; subsequently all the leaders and many of the participants were found and imprisoned, tortured, or executed. (See Chapter 4: The 1381 Revolt.) This attack against the social basis of English culture, threatening to undermine an already shaky feudal hierarchy, profoundly affected the literary imagination of the time, although not all authors seemed to side with the rebels. In Chaucer's *Nun's Priest's Tale*, for example, the cacophony of the barnyard is likened to the noise of 'Jakke Straw and his meynee' (VII.3394). In his *Vox Clamantis*, Gower, a fierce supporter of Richard II (until he became a fierce supporter of Henry IV), uses the events of 1381 to show the increased corruption of society, and in his *Vox*, Gower likens supporters of the revolt to supporters of the Antichrist. Chaucer and Gower both seem to decry such strife because it can lead to anarchy, and England could not afford such internal turmoil given the threats from abroad it was facing during that time.

The Hundred Years' War

As if the ravages of famine and plague in the fourteenth century were not enough, the long wars with France further burdened England's populace. The Hundred Years' War began as a dispute over the English monarch's rights to territories on the continent, especially Gascony (in southwestern France). When Charles IV, King of France, died in 1328, the French crowned Philip, Charles' cousin, as king. However, King Edward III of England also claimed the right to the throne of France, at least according to the English interpretation of feudal law and primogeniture (the right of the first born son to inherit the crown), since Edward's mother was Charles's sister. England had also long held lands in the north of France that stemmed from ancestral ties associated with William the Conqueror's titles.

In 1337, Philip tried to take advantage of Edward's preoccupation with the Scots (who were fighting England for independence) by claiming Gascony, harassing the coast of England, and supporting the Scottish rebels; the first open hostilities of the Hundred Years' War between England and France had begun. England often managed to defeat the French through the early fifteenth century, notably at the famous battles of Crécy, Poitiers, and Agincourt, but the tide turned in 1429 at the battle of Orléans where, led by the famous French martyr and saint Joan of Arc, the French defeated the English. By the early 1450s the English had been driven out of all of the French territories except Calais, and the Hundred Years' war was all but over.

While few ME writings deal directly with the war, the changing backdrop of English society colored much of the writing from the period. Perhaps nowhere is this more evident than in Arthurian literature. Arthuriana can be traced back far earlier than the ME period, yet it is during the later Middle Ages that a number of notable and influential Arthurian works appeared on the literary landscape, from Chrétien de Troyes in twelfth-century France, the

Gawain-poet in fourteenth century and Malory in fifteenth-century England. Chrétien's romances represent the flowering of the French Arthurian tradition and focus on French knights such as Lancelot. British knights, such as Gawain, might be portrayed as honourable in the French romances but were often criticized, condemned, or derided for their inability to rise up to chivalric standards. The thirteenth-century French prose *Tristan*, for example, depicted Gawain as an evil murderer. (See Chapter 3: Geoffrey of Monmouth, *History of the Kings of Britain*, Arthurian Literature and the 'Matter of Britain', and The *Pearl*-Poet).

But Arthur is, after all, king of the Britons, and during the Hundred Years' Wars England reclaimed Arthurian myths to define its own political and religious character. The late fourteenth century *Sir Gawain and the Green Knight*, as well as the contemporary *Wedding of Sir Gawain and Dame Ragnelle*, focuses not upon a French knight but upon Gawain, whose literary lineage was traced back to pre-conquest England (his name may be Welsh in origin) and who appears in early English works such as William of Malmesbury's *Gesta Regum Anglorum* (*The Deeds of the Kings of England*) and Geoffrey of Monmouth's *Historia Regum Britanniae* (*The History of the Kings of England*). The reclamation of Arthuriana for England did not stop with appropriating just character or plot, however. Many of these later ME romances were written in alliterative verse – which repeats the sounds at the beginnings of the words, as in the opening line of *Sir Gawain and the Green Knight*, 'Sithen the sege and the assaut was sesed at Troye' – rather than the end-rhymed verse of their French predecessors, which was based on similar inflectional endings long dropped from ME. Scholars debate the extent to which alliterative verse survived as a vernacular tradition from earlier OE alliterative verse (an alliterative *tradition*), or whether it was resurrected in the fourteenth century as a way to establish a separate English literary tradition that simply hearkened back to earlier OE forms (an alliterative *revival*), but whatever the case, much of the ME Arthurian literature does not follow the French tradition in either content or form. As for Gawain's character in particular, about 20 years after the end of the Hundred Years' Wars – at the height of the internal conflict that would become known as the Wars of the Roses – the great British knight Gawain would again be represented as problematically as the earlier French tradition, this time in Malory's *Morte d'Arthur*. (See Chapter 3: Arthurian Literature and the 'Matter of Britain'.)

English Monarchy and the Deposition of Richard II

Ongoing conflicts with France, the ravages of the plague, and religious discontent were not the only factors wreaking havoc on late fourteenth-century English society. Post-Conquest England had repeatedly seen its share of upheaval in the monarchy, but the perceived failings of Richard II and his eventual deposition in 1399 by Henry IV influenced ME literature in ways more directly than virtually any prior monarchical event. Richard II was the son of Edward the Black Prince and grandson to the reigning Edward III when, in 1376, his father, next in line for the throne, died. When Edward III died the following year, Richard became King of England at the age of 10. During Richard's minority a number of advisors (most notably his uncle, John of Gaunt) in effect ruled the country in his name, but as Richard's actions during the 1381 Revolt suggest, he was already thinking of himself as the anointed monarch of the realm.

Richard II eventually removed a number of long-standing and high-ranking nobles and replaced them with a trusted inner circle of friends. He fostered a sense of aesthetic refinement at court that, for many of his fellow countrymen, smacked somewhat of French gentility. He pursued peace more than any of his Plantagenet forefathers, seeking resolution with the Irish (after successful campaigns there in 1395–6), signing a truce with France (after marrying princess Isabella of France), and refusing to pursue a campaign against the Scots. At home, he continued to levy increasing taxes on his subjects, thus alienating many of the powerful members of the merchant classes. In 1398 Richard banished his cousin, Henry Bolingbroke, son of John of Gaunt, for ten years. When John of Gaunt died, Richard seized all Bolingbroke's possessions, inciting Henry to return to England with force to reclaim his lands and goods. In 1399, while Richard was on a campaign in Ireland, Henry swept through Southern England, gathered powerful allies and entered London. Some leaders, especially the aristocracy who felt snubbed by Richard, and the merchants who felt over-taxed, welcomed his return with open arms and urged Henry to take the crown himself. Upon Richard's return, Bolingbroke forced him to abdicate the throne, and Henry was crowned as the first Lancastrian (a different branch of the House of Plantagenet, the royal house of English Kings, from which Richard II descended) King of England. Richard was subsequently imprisoned in the Tower of London, where he died (or some say, was murdered) in 1400. With the reign of Henry IV came renewed hostilities with France, increased conservatism at court, and rising persecution of social and religious liberties enjoyed during Richard's reign.

The literature of Richard II's reign (Ricardian Literature) was often interested in proper rule, a common theme throughout the Middle Ages. Ricardian political allegory and social commentary ran the gamut from the overt to the oblique. For instance, the Prologue to the B Text of *Piers Plowman* includes the famous scene where a bell is placed around a cat's neck (the 'belling of the cat'), which is commonly read as an allegory for John of Gaunt's role as advisor to and guardian of the young Richard II, and this image reappeared elsewhere, such as in the short political allegory, 'On the Times'. Poems such as *Richard the Redeless* and 'There is a busche that is forgrowe' further criticized Richard's protected counsellors. In the late 1380s, John Gower dedicated the first version of his *Confessio Amantis* to Richard II, but his subsequent revisions in the 1390s shifted that dedication to Henry IV.

This militant change of monarchs, rather than the approved succession defined by primogeniture, called into question the authority and validity of the monarchy itself, a concern that Henry IV addressed throughout his reign by making every attempt to legitimize his rule, usually by pursuing both war with France for ancestral lands and by supporting his new Archbishop, Arundel, in Arundel's crackdown on religious dissent at home. Lancastrian political literature is markedly more restrained in its criticism of the Crown than was Ricardian literature. Whereas a political poem such as *Richard the Redeless* referred to specific people and criticized particular policies during Richard II's reign, Lancastrian political poems such as *Mum and the Sothsegger* were much more circumspect in their criticisms. Lancastrian poets like Thomas Hoccleve and John Lydgate enjoyed almost laureate status in part due to their overt Lancastrian sympathies. Henry IV and Henry V both supported Lydgate's poetry, as well as Lydgate's promotion of Chaucer, to further create an English literary and linguistic identity. Lydgate's works reflect this patronage. For example, Lydgate's *Siege of Thebes* echoes language from the Treaty of Troyes, the agreement that named Henry V successor to the crown of France after the English victory at the Battle of Agincourt. Well into the Early Modern period, authors such as Shakespeare (in his history plays devoted to Richard II, Henry IV and Henry V) helped legitimize the Lancastrian dynasty, even as that dynasty was threatened from within by baronial conflicts. (See Chapter 3: John Lydgate.)

The Wars of the Roses and the Transition to the Early Modern Period

After the closing battles of the Hundred Years' War in the 1450s, English nobles began amassing local armies to protect their lands from civil unrest. The Wars of the Roses, as later history would refer to it, represented a battle over the throne between the House of York and the House of Lancaster, both of whom traced their lineage to Edward III and therefore claimed right to the throne. The Wars of the Roses lasted from 1455 to 1487 and all but ended with the accession of Henry VII to the throne in 1485. With the rule of Henry VII and his son Henry VIII in 1491, there came about a consolidation of power in the monarchy and in the merchant classes. This consolidation of power eventually allowed England's imperial ventures subsequent to Columbus' 'discovery' of America in 1492. (See Chapter 1:

Redefining the Period and Extending the Medieval, and Chapter 3: War of the Roses.)

Apart from the political and social upheaval caused by the war, the end of the fifteenth century saw a major shift in the English language. William Caxton's introduction of the printing press to England in 1476 brought with it, among other things, greater regularization of the language, since the press was able to disseminate large numbers of like texts. It also ushered in an era wherein more people of all classes would have access to literary production in the vernacular. (See Chapter 3: William Caxton.) Even prior to Caxton, vernacular texts spread throughout the countryside, due in part to increased manuscript production. At the same time, vernacular drama carted across the countryside, or was performed by the brethren of guilds, in towns and cities like Chester and York. The proliferation of medieval drama in the fifteenth century helped secure the vernacular as a literary commonplace, just as Caxton imprinted the vernacular on a new book culture. Throughout the fourteenth and fifteenth centuries, English underwent subtle but ongoing shifts in pronunciation, so much so that the language of fourteenth- and early fifteenth-century literature is dramatically different with respect to pronunciation from literature of the sixteenth and seventeenth centuries due to a phenomenon known as 'the Great Vowel Shift'. The British Isles contained (and will probably always contain) a rich variety of regional dialects, but Chaucer's London dialect eventually became the English standard from the Early Modern Period onwards.

Conclusion

The same features that mark its beginnings mark the end of ME literature's historical era: a war that helped define English national identity and the ongoing transition of a language. Even so, the literature of the later Middle Ages is not exclusively about war, or politics, or religion, or strife. On the contrary, as you shall see throughout this volume, ME literature is rich and varied, and it is interested in the same things in which many of us today are interested, like humour, loss, desire, anger, frustration, adventure, fear, and, of course, the many forms of love. But those historical events particular to the Middle Ages, the historical context which this chapter only briefly touches upon, shaped the way medieval authors wrote about those issues and help make ME literature both recognizable in its passions and yet fascinating in its eccentricity.

Study Questions

1. Briefly summarize the important characteristics of the following historical events and social movements, including their dates:

   - The Conquest/Invasion of England
   - The Martyrdom of Thomas Becket
   - The *Magna Carta*
   - Lateran IV
   - The Ordinance of Labourers and The Statute of Labourers
   - The Great Schism/Avignon Papacy
   - Lollardy
   - The Plague
   - The Peasants' Revolt
   - The Deposition of Richard II

2. For a work of ME literature that you are reading or have read, list the adjectives used to describe specific characters. Using an etymological dictionary, identify whether those words derive from French or English/Germanic origins or from some other language.

3. Given the events of 1066, why do you think there is relatively little literature that remains in ME from the twelfth to thirteenth century?

4. Today, Christianity is divided into a number of denominations (Catholic, Episcopalian, Lutheran, Baptist and many others). How do you think the late medieval period differed from the contemporary period by having a unified and centralized Church?

5. King Arthur is one of the most recognizable figures from the Middle Ages. What effect would it have to associate him with the Crusades?

6. Compare two different accounts of the Crusades and discuss their relative approach to 'the enemy' and to the Crusades themselves, for example, in:

   - An Arab account: Al-Makrisi's Account of the Crusade of St. Louis in the *Medieval Sourcebook* (http://www.fordham.edu/halsall/source/makrisi.html).
   - A Christian Account: Guy, A Knight: Letter from the Sixth Crusade in 1249 in the *Medieval Sourcebook* (http://www.fordham.edu/halsall/source/1249sixthcde-let.html).

7. Make a list of the changes that Lollards wanted to make to the Church. For each one, discuss the ramifications of that change and how it would affect the power and role of the Church in England. See, for example, the following online sources that discuss Lollard beliefs and propositions, including:

   - The Harvard Chaucer Page (http://www.courses.fas.harvard.edu/~chaucer/special/varia/lollards/lollards.html).
   - The *Catholic Encyclopedia* entry on Lollardy: (http://www.newadvent.org/cathen/09333a.htm).
   - The Lollard Society, an academic organization devoted to the study of Lollardy: (http://lollardsociety.org).

8. The next time you are in a classroom, or any room with a number of people (especially friends and family), note how many there are and imagine half of them being dead within the year (roughly the European mortality rate of the plague of 1348). How do you think that would that affect your world? Imagine how you might deal with such loss and compare that to how you see death handled in ME literature versus contemporary accounts.

9. Compare and contrast the Deposition of Richard II with changes of power in contemporary societies in the First, Second and Third Worlds. What accounts for the similarities and differences?

10. *Web Quest*: Do a web search for the term 'crusade(s)' or 'plague(s)' and identify the different uses to which the terms are put. How many are used with a contemporary political or social slant? How many are used as a historical reference to the medieval period? What kinds of websites use the terms and in what ways? What are the strengths and weaknesses of using such historically inflected terms for contemporary situations?

Middle English Timeline, 1066–1492

Date	Historical and Cultural Events	Ruler	Literary and Cultural Texts
Eleventh Century			
1066	• Edward the Confessor Dies • Harold II (Harold Godwinsson) crowned • Harold Hardraada of Norway invades England – defeated at Stamford Bridge by Harold II • William Duke of Normandy invades • Battle of Hastings – William defeats Harold II • William I (the Conqueror) crowned first Norman King of England	Edward the Confessor, Harold II (Godwinsson), William I	
1067	• Work begins on Tower of London	William I	
1072	• William I invades Scotland	William I	
1086		William I	• *Domesday Book* completed
1087	• William I dies • William II crowned	William II	
1095	• Pope Urban preaches the First Crusade • Eight crusades take place between 1096 and 1270	William II	
1099	• Crusaders capture Jerusalem	William II	
Twelfth Century			• *Mabinogion* (Welsh Epic) • Geoffrey of Monmouth (Welsh), *Prophecies of Merlin* (1135) and *Historia Regum Britanniae* (1137) • *The Owl and the Nightengale* (late twelfth century)
1100	• William II assassinated • Henry I ascends to the throne	Henry I	
1129	• Empress Matilda (daughter of Henry I and widow of Emperor Henry V) marries Geoffrey the Handsome (Count of Anjou; Plantagenet)	Stephen	

Date	Historical and Cultural Events	Ruler	Literary and Cultural Texts
1141	• Matilda deposes Stephen • Matilda then driven out by an uprising and Stephen is restored to the throne	Stephen Matilda Stephen	
1143		Stephen	• William of Malmesbury (d. 1143), *Gesta Regum Anglorum* and *Historia Novella* narrates English history from 1066, includes references to Arthur as an historical person.
1152	• Henry (later Henry II) marries Eleanor of Aquitaine (formerly married to King of France)	Stephen	
1153	• Henry of Anjou (son of Matilda) invades England and forces Stephen to name him heir to the throne	Stephen	
1154	• Henry II crowned	Henry II	
1155	• Henry II appoints Thomas a Becket as Chancellor	Henry II	
1160–80		Henry II	• Wace, *Roman de Brut* • Chretien de Troyes (at French court) • Marie de France (at English court), *Lias* and *Fables*
1162	• Henry II appoints Thomas Becket Archbishop of Canterbury	Henry II	
1170	• Becket murdered	Henry II	
1189	• Richard I (Coeur de Lion, the Lion Hearted, son of Henry II and Eleanor of Aquitaine) crowned	Richard I	
1190	• Richard I leads the Second Crusade	Richard I	
1191–4	• Richard conquers Cyprus and Jaffa; makes peace with Saladin; captured by Duke Leopold of Austria; turned over to Emperor Henry VI; ransomed and returned to England	Richard I	

Date	Historical and Cultural Events	Ruler	Literary and Cultural Texts
1193	• First English merchant guild established	Richard I	
1199	• John Lackland, youngest son of Henry II, crowned	John	
Thirteenth Century			• *Nibelungenlied* (German epic) • Gottfried von Strassburg, *Tristan and Isolde* (c. 1210) • *Roman de la Rose* – Guillaume de Lorris (c. 1235) and Jeun de Meuns's continuation (c. 1275) • Thomas Aquinas (d. 1274), *Summa Theologica*
1200–25		John	• Layamon's *Brut* • *Ancrene Riwle* (aka *Ancrene Wisse* – manual for anchoresses) • The 'Katherine Group'
1207–13	• John and Pope Innocent III altercations over Archbishop of Canterbury appointment	John	
1209	• Cambridge University founded	John	
1213	• John agrees to be subject to the Pope	John	
1215	• *Magna Carta* establishes feudal rights of barony, provides rights in England to the Church, protects property from the crown • Fourth Lateran Council	John	
1216	• Henry III crowned (at age 9)	Henry III	
1221	• Dominicans establish order at Oxford	Henry III	
1224	• Franciscans at Oxford and Cambridge	Henry III	
c.1240	• 'Great Council' now referred to as 'Parliament'	Henry III	

Date	Historical and Cultural Events	Ruler	Literary and Cultural Texts
1250–99		Henry III	• *King Horn, Floris and Blauncheflur, Havelok, Arthour and Merlin, Sir Tristrem* (metrical romances) • Roger Bacon, *Opus Majus*
1269	• Rebuilding of Westminster Abbey	Henry III	
1272	• Edward I ('Longshanks') crowned	Edward I	
1274	• Dominicans at Cambridge	Edward I	
1290	• Edward I expels all Jews from England	Edward I	
1295	• Representative Parliament – First Parliament to include broad representation	Edward I	
1296	• Edward I deposes John Balliol from throne of Scotland	Edward I	
1297	• William Wallace of Scotland defeats English army	Edward I	
1298	• Edward I defeats William Wallace and re-takes Scotland	Edward I	
Fourteenth Century			• Dante's *Divine Comedy* (1307–21) • Petrarch • Giovanni Boccaccio: *Filostrato* (1335), *Filocolo* (1338), *Decameron* (1351) • *Gesta Romanorum* (c. 1350) • *Mandeville's Travels* (c. 1357)
1300–50		Edward I	• *Ywain and Gawain* • *Bevis of Hampton* and *Guy of Warwick* (romances) • Robert Mannyng *Handlyng Synne* • *Land of Cokaygne*
1305	• Capture and execution of William Wallace	Edward I	

Date	Historical and Cultural Events	Ruler	Literary and Cultural Texts
1306	• Robert the Bruce leads Scottish rebellion and is crowned King of Scotland	Edward I	
1307	• Edward I dies (en route to battle Robert the Bruce) • Edward II crowned	Edward II	
1314	• Robert the Bruce defeats Edward II at the Battle of Bannockburn achieving Scottish independence	Edward II	
1315	• Great Famine in England		
1327	• Edward II deposed, murdered • Son Edward III crowned king	Edward III	
1333	• Edward III defeats Scots	Edward III	
1337–40	• French invade Aquitaine • Edward III declares himself King of France • Hundred Years War begins (ends 1453)	Edward III	
1346	• Battle of Crécy – Edward III invades France and defeats larger French force	Edward III	
1348	• Order of the Garter established • Black Death (bubonic plague) reaches England (30–50% of English population dies)	Edward III	
1349	• Ordinance of Labourers	Edward III	
1350–99		Edward III	• *Pearl* manuscript (c. 1400), includes four texts: *Pearl, Patience, Cleanness* (*Purity*), *Sir Gawain and the Green Knight* • *Alliterative Morte Arthur* • *Winner and Waster* (Alliterative)
1351	• Statute of Labourers	Edward III	
1356	• Battle of Poitiers – Edward the Black Prince (eldest son of Edward III) captures King John II of France	Edward III	

Date	Historical and Cultural Events	Ruler	Literary and Cultural Texts
1360–70		Edward III	• Chaucer, *Romance of the Rose* (trans.) • William Langland, *Piers Plowman* (A-text)
1361	• Plague in England	Edward III	
1362	• English language required in court pleas	Edward III	
1368	• Duchess Blanche – wife of John of Gaunt, Duke of Lancaster (son of Edward III) – dies	Edward III	Chaucer, *Book of the Duchess* (after Blanche's death)
1370–80		Edward III	• John Gower, *Cinkante Balades* and *Mirour de l'Omme* • York Corpus Christi plays (first references)
1373	• John of Gaunt leads invasion of France	Edward III	
1374	• John of Gaunt returns to England and assumes control of government (during old age of Edward II and illness of the Black Prince)	Edward III	
1376	• The 'Good Parliament' • Death of Edward the Black Prince • John Wyclif calls for reforms	Edward III	
1377	• Edward III dies • Richard II (aged 11, son of the Black Prince and grandson of Edward II) crowned • John of Gaunt controls government during Richard's minority • 'Bad Parliament' reverses decisions of the 'Good Parliament' of 1376	Richard II	• William Langland, *Piers Plowman* (B-text)
1378	• Great Schism (aka Western Schism or Papal Schism) begins – Papal courts and rival Popes in Rome and Avignon	Richard II	

Date	Historical and Cultural Events	Ruler	Literary and Cultural Texts
1380–90		Richard II	• Wycliffite English Bibles • *Cloud of Unknowing* • Chaucer, *House of Fame, Parliament of Fools, Troilus and Criseyde,* Boethius' *Consolation of Philosophy* (trans.); *Canterbury Tales* begun • John Gower, *Vox Clamantis, Confessio Amantis*
1381	• Peasants' Revolt • Wyclif denies transubstantiation	Richard II	
1388	• 'Merciless Parliament' condemns advisors of Richard II	Richard II	• Julian of Norwich, *Showings*
1389	• Richard II (aged 22) assumes power	Richard II	
1390–99		Richard II	• *Parliament of Three Ages* and *St. Erkenwald* • William Langland, *Piers Plowman* (C-text) • *Pierce the Ploughman's Crede* • Chaucer, *Canterbury Tales* (in process) and *Treatise of the Astrolabe* • Henry Knighton, *Chronicle*
1399	• Death of John of Gaunt • Gaunt's son, Henry of Bolingbroke, deposes Richard and is crowned Henry IV • Richard II murdered	Henry IV	
Fifteenth Century			• Christine de Pisan (d. 1431) • Gutenberg Bible (1450)

Date	Historical and Cultural Events	Ruler	Literary and Cultural Texts
1400–50			• Stanzaic *Morte Arthur* • Hoccleve, *La Male Regle* (c. 1406) and *Regiment of Princes* (c. 1412) • *Dives and Pauper* • Lydgate: *The Troy Book* (c. 1420), *Siege of Thebes* (c. 1422), *Pilgrimage of the Life of Man* (1428), *Fall of Princes* (c. 1438) • Early Paston Family Letters • *Book of Margery Kempe*
1400	• Owen Glendower of Wales rebels against England	Henry IV	Chaucer dies
1401	• Persecution of the Lollards	Henry IV	
1406	• Henry, Prince of Wales, defeats Welsh	Henry IV	
1413	• Henry IV dies • Henry, Prince of Wales, becomes Henry V	Henry V	
1414	• Lollard Revolt – Sir John Oldcastle executed	Henry V	
1415	• Battle of Agincourt – Henry V invades and defeats France	Henry V	
1414–7	• Council of Constance ends Great Schism	Henry V	
1422	• Henry V of England and Charles VI of France die • Henry VI (9 months old) King of England (Humphrey, Duke of Gloucester is Regent)	Henry VI	
1429	• Joan of Arc rescues Orleans English siege	Henry VI	
1430	• Joan of Arc captured	Henry VI	
1431	• Joan of Arc burned as a witch • Henry VI of England crowned King of France in Paris	Henry VI	
1436	• Henry VI assumes power at age of majority	Henry VI	

Date	Historical and Cultural Events	Ruler	Literary and Cultural Texts
1450–99			• Cycle Plays: The *Towneley Cycle* and the *N-Town Plays* • *Mankind* • John Capgrave, *Chronicle of England* • Sir Thomas Malory (d. 1471), *Le Morte d'Arthur*
1453	• Hundred Years' War ends	Henry VI	
1454	• Richard, Duke of York, Regent during Henry VI's insanity	Henry VI	• Gutenberg press
1455	• Henry VI (Lancaster) removes Richard (York) • War of the Roses (Civil War) begins between houses of York and Lancaster (1455–87)	Henry VI	
1485		Henry VII	
1492	• Columbus contacts West Indies	Henry VII	

3 Literary and Cultural Contexts: Major Figures, Institutions, Topics, Events, Movements

*Julia Bolton Holloway, Florence, Italy
with Daniel T. Kline*

Chapter Overview

Setting the Context

Late medieval England was pan-European and influenced by Continental and Mediterranean culture through the continuing use of Latin. It was also shaped by oral story telling in the vernacular, the Romance languages deriving from Latin in southern Europe, and the Germanic languages in northern Europe. In the British Isles, the earlier layers of Celtic and Pictish culture that had become Christian and maintained a knowledge of Roman and Greek civilization were later overrun by the Jutes and Anglo-Saxons. The Anglo-Saxon *scop* (shaper, poet) treasured a 'word-hoard' of vocabulary, history and identity through memory. These invaders in turn became Christian and also, with the aid of Irish scholars, studied Biblical and Latin literature, as did Bede in Northumbria. English culture then forever changed in 1066 by the French-speaking Normans ('Northmen'), who went as far as Ireland and the border of Wales. The powerful Norman culture extended also to Sicily and to the Jerusalem Kingdom, which the Normans seized in 1099, while Iceland, with its saga literature, preserved Anglo-Saxon for centuries.

The Languages of Britain

Although 'Old English' (OE) describes the English language before 1066, post-1066 language and culture, with its admixture of French, is called Middle English (ME). The British Celtic language (Brittonic) is still spoken and written in Wales and in Brittany; a related Celtic language (Goidelic) is spoken and written in Ireland and Scotland. Chaucer's London dialect, situated at the economic and political centre of late-medieval England, emerged as the de-facto standard, displacing other dialects and earlier languages to the margins of the British Isles and Continent.

Like the spoken tongues of the British Isles, the written languages of medieval England present a fascinating multicultural history. Celts used Ogham, a phonetic alphabet of straight and slanted lines, while runes and our phonetic alphabet extended from the Mediterranean to Iceland and Greenland. Like Ogham, runes were typically inscribed on tombstones, swords, and on stone, metal and wood. The spread of literacy was closely linked with the Bible as a book written first on papyrus scrolls and then in parchment *codexes* (or bound books). Irish monks collated the Latin Bible with Greek and Hebrew texts, as in the *Codex Amiatinus* and created lavish and beautiful illuminated manuscripts like the *Book of Kells*. Monasteries copied and preserved secular books (like Terence's *Comedies* and Roman histories) as well as religious texts. The institutions associated with wealthy manors, towns and the Crown kept financial records and inventories both in Latin and in the vernacular. (See Chapter 8: Multilingualism, International Contexts and Postcolonial Concerns.)

Textual Communities and the Medieval Book

Scribal (or written) literature was produced in 'textual communities'. Monasteries, whose scribes generally copied manuscripts in Latin, formed the most persistent and longest-lived textual communities in England, from the time of Celtic Christianity to Henry VIII's dissolution of the monasteries. Books were written out by hand, each copy being different, until the introduction of the printing press into England. The front (*recto*) and backs (*verso*) of pages are numbered as 'folios' or leaves. Monasteries generally consisted of a church, against which was built the cloister, with a square garden and well at its centre, representing Paradise. Around the cloister would be a scriptorium for writing out books, a library for keeping them in, a dormitory for the monks to sleep in, and a refectory for their meals, as well as storerooms for grain and other produce. Monasteries produced Bibles and liturgical texts in Latin as well as biblical and theological commentaries and universal histories. Oblates (boys given by their parents to monasteries) were trained in Latin and Gregorian chant; hagiographical texts (saints' lives) were often read during meals in the refectory. These writings about saints, like the Voragine's *Golden Legend*, include stories from many cultures and often depicted valorous Christians overcoming violent persecution. Because the canon of saints was cosmopolitan so also are these stories intensely multicultural. An example is Chaucer's *Man of Law's Tale*, whose Christian heroine, Constance, first marries an African Muslim ruler and then a pagan Northumbrian king.

The universities, offshoots of cathedral schools, belong likewise to the clerical world and shared in its literature, but specialized in rigorous training in Aristotelian logic. University curriculum was compartmentalized into the *trivium* (grammar, rhetoric, dialectic), the *quadrivium* (arithmetic, geometry, astronomy, music), and the 'Queen of Sciences', theology, mirroring the guild structure of apprentice, journeyman, master. After completing cathedral or grammar school, students qualified as master and then doctor, reflected still in our Bachelor, Master and Doctoral degrees. The upbringing of the nobility was sometimes traumatic, for young boys were often sent to a different noble family to be trained as a page, then a squire, and finally a knight. Young girls were often sent to other families as well to be trained as servants or ladies-in-waiting.

The monasteries spoke of the three divisions or 'estates' of society: those who prayed (monks), those who fought (knights) and those who laboured (ploughmen). The culture of those who prayed revolved around biblical, religious and theological texts. The culture of those who fought produced their own distinctive literature, preferring 'Romances', initially denoting what was translated from the Romance languages, such as French, and later applying to the literature of knights on quests for a lady's love, and pseudo-genealogies about the Matter of Troy, the Matter of Britain (Arthur), the Matter of France (Charlemagne). Workers in the countryside and in the towns knew of the monastic and courtly writings largely through oral means. Peasants during the 1381 Revolt sang out lines from *Piers Plowman*. Left out of the ideal paradigm are the merchants and townspeople, who came to emulate the nobility while, at the same time, seeking piety. Courtesy and conduct books, training manuals describing the proper training of young people, emerged in towns and manors, and their literature drew from multiple sources and produced such a rich kaleidoscope of literature. Margery Kempe had Birgitta's *Revelationes* and other works of contemplative direction read to her by priests. Wealthy and politically important patrons commissioned the copying of both secular and sacred manuscripts, while other families compiled anthologies of texts across several generations. Many manuscripts were copied in monastic scriptoria, but the later Middle Ages saw the emergence of secular commercial copy houses where scores of manuscripts were prepared, copied, illuminated and sold.

Persons and Texts, Movements and Events

Adam Easton
A Benedictine monk of Norwich who taught Hebrew at Oxford, Easton translated the whole Bible from that language and was deeply versed in Pseudo-Dionysius and the Victorines. He wrote in defence of Pope Urban VI the *Liber Defensorium Potestatis Ecclesiasticorum*, for which he was made Cardinal of England though he was later imprisoned and tortured. He affected Birgitta of Sweden's canonization in 1391, and he worked closely with the editor of her text, Hermit Bishop Alfonso of Jaén. He was present in Norwich with the manuscript of Birgitta's *Revelationes* at the time Julian was composing the Long Text of her *Showing* in which the *Revelationes* is quoted.

Alliterative Morte Arthure
Using Geoffrey of Monmouth and Layamon's *Brut*, and used in turn as a source by Sir Thomas Malory, this poet writes about the Arthurian past and creates a quasi-epic work. The English won the Battle of Agincourt because of their use of the long bow made from yew, these trees being protected in the realm for this purpose and planted in graveyards. The following is found in the fifteenth-century Robert Thornton manuscript:

Thane bowmene of Bretayne brothely ther-aftyre Bekerde with bregaundez of ferre in tha laundez, With flonez fleterede thay flitt fulle frescly ther frekez, ffichens with fetheris thurghe the fyne maylez; Siche flyttynge es foule that so the flesche derys, That flowe o ferrome in flawnkkes of stedez. (ll. 2095–2100)	Then the British archers fiercely fought with foreign brigands in that land, with fletched arrows they shot the men, piercing with feathers through their fine mail; such shooting is foul that hurts the flesh so much, that flies far into the flanks of steeds.

Amherst Manuscript, British Library Additional 37,790

A compilation written for a woman contemplative, which includes works by Richard Rolle, Marguerite Porete, Julian of Norwich, Jan van Ruusbroec, Henry Suso and others, written out by the same scribe who copied Guillaume de Deguileville (St. John's College, Cambridge, G.21) and Mechtild of Hackeborn's *Book of Ghostly Grace* (British Library, Egerton 2006), all in ME. Julian's Short Text is dated 1413.

Anchoress

A large section of medieval Latin and English literature consisting of writings giving advice to anchoresses, women who lived in solitude, often in a single room, usually beside a church in its graveyard. Among these are Aelred of Rievaulx's *De Institutione Inclusarum*, the *Ancrene Wisse*, Walter Hilton's *Ladder of Perfection*, the *Cloud of Unknowing*, while Julian of Norwich's *Showing of Love* is a work written by an anchoress. Male recluses of this type were called anchorites.

Ancrene Wisse (*Ancrene Riwle*) and the *Katherine Group*

A series of manuscripts were written after 1214 in early ME and Latin to give spiritual direction for a group of anchoresses and to present women saints, such as Sts. Margaret and Katherine, as models for female readers.

Arthurian Literature and the 'Matter of Britain'

The Celtic King of Britain, largely legendary but a figure of great use in political literature, was known throughout Europe and in the Crusaders' Jerusalem Kingdom, though the Anglo-Saxons, apart from La3amon in his *Brut*, ignored it. It is likely that Breton minstrels singing the legend to Norman lords in England, Sicily and Jerusalem popularized the cycle. Includes texts like *Mabinogion*, Geoffrey of Monmouth, *History of the Kings of Britain*,

Alliterative *Morte Arthure, Sir Gawain and the Green Knight,* and Malory. (See Chapter 5: Ingham and Warren, and Cohen.)

Archbishop Thomas Arundel (1353–1414)
Archbishop, also Chancellor, Arundel was the leader in suppressing the Lollard movement about John Wyclif, whose supporters had included Queen Anne of Bohemia and Richard II's uncle, John of Gaunt, Duke of Lancaster. Exiled by Richard II, he returned to England with the support of Henry IV (when Duke of Lancaster) and was reinstituted in 1399. In 1408, Arundel's *Constitutions* forbade the translating of the Bible into English, forbade laypeople, especially women, to teach theology, and called for Wycliffe's writing to be examined for heresy. The *Constitutions* are enumerated as follows:

    I. That no one can preach without a licence.

   II. On the punishment for those preaching without a licence.

  III. That the preacher must conform or be punished.

  IV. Of the penalties for preaching on the sacraments of the altar and other sacraments against the Church's teaching.

   V. That no teacher with only an MA or BA instruct children about the sacraments.

  VI. That no book or treatise of John Wyclif may be read, before it is examined.

 VII. That no text of Holy Scripture may be translated into English.

VIII. That no one join those opposed to these conclusions, propositions and good customs.

  IX. That no one may question the Articles Holy Church determines.

   X. That no chaplain may celebrate in the Canterbury Archdiocese without testimonial letters.

  XI. That at the University of Oxford an inquisition should be held each month concerning these principles.

 XII. Of the penalties for countering these.

XIII. Of the procedures to be followed in such cases.

Auchinleck Manuscript
National Library of Scotland, Advocates Manuscript 19.2.1, is a compilation of many early ME texts written out in an Anglo-Norman convent. It contains saints' legends, together with *St. Patrick's Purgatory,* and romances of *Guy of Warwick, Sir Degare, Amis and Amiloun, Floris and Blancheflur, Sir Bevis of Hamtoun, Arthur and Merlin, Lay le Freine, King Alisaunder, Sir Tristram, Sir Orfeo, King Richard the Lion Heart,* and *Horn Child,* together with Lives of the Virgin and other texts that date this manuscript to c. 1330–40. Some of the

texts are a mixture of ME and Norman French (a *macaronic* text includes multiple languages).

The Bayeux Tapestry

The Bayeux Tapestry recounts, in embroidery on linen carried out by women with images and Latin text, the historical event of the Battle of Hastings at the Norman Conquest of England. (See Chapter 2: Historical and Political Change after 1066.)

The Bible

Chaucer's *Man of Law's Tale* mentions an ancient Bible (II. 666). Such Bibles were produced in Ireland and England (*Book of Kells, Lindisfarne Gospels* and others), using splendid Celtic interlaced 'Carpet Pages', from Islamic influence. Adam Easton later sought to translate the Bible from the original Hebrew into Latin, while John Wyclif and his followers translated it from the Latin Vulgate into ME. The Bible used in the medieval period is the Vulgate, originally translated by St. Jerome, and his supporters, the mother and daughter Sts. Paula and Eustochium. The modern version closest to the Vulgate is the Douay-Rheims version.

Birgitta of Sweden (d. 1373)

A Swedish noblewoman, Birgitta was governess to King Magnus and the mother of eight children. Initially, Bishop Hemming of Abo was her ambassador to the Kings of France and England and Magister Mathias, who had studied Hebrew under Nicholas of Lyra in Paris and who translated the Bible from that language into Swedish for her, was her spiritual director. On her husband's death at Alvastra, following their pilgrimages together to and from Compostela, Birgitta established a monastery in the King's Castle of Vadstena, then journeyed to Rome during the year of the Black Death. She worked with ecclesiasts in Sweden and in Italy, producing the many-volumed *Revelationes*, which she sent to the Kings of England and France and to other heads of state pleading for peace in Europe. She died in 1373 following her return from Jerusalem and Bethlehem. Birgitta's *Revelationes* were widely influential. Richard Lavenham, Richard II's confessor, lectured on them at Oxford, and copies exist in Latin and ME. Julian of Norwich's *Showing of Love* quotes Birgitta of Sweden's *Revelations*. Margery Kempe had Birgitta's *Revelations* read to her, and she later imitated Birgitta's pilgrimages and literary activities.

Giovanni Boccaccio

Giovanni Boccaccio's *Filostrato* in Italian was the source for Chaucer' *Troilus and Criseyde*, and Boccaccio's *Decameron* influenced Chaucer's *Canterbury Tales*.

Boethius, *Consolation of Philosophy*
Written in Latin, with the full knowledge of Aristotle and Plato, by a learned
late Roman statesman, imprisoned and awaiting execution, this text, one of
the most influential of the medieval period, was translated into OE by King
Alfred, into ME by Chaucer, and into early modern English by Queen Elizabeth I. Combining both poetry and prose, the *Consolatio* is in the form of a
dream vision in which Lady Philosophy consoles Boethius as he awaits his
death. It was used as an argument against depression, the 'wanting of will' as
Julian of Norwich calls it, or 'wanhope', which is despair, the antidote being a
responsible, reasonable freedom of will. (See Chapter 10: Literature and
Commentary.)

Catherine of Siena (1347–80), *The Orcherd of Syon*
Catherine of Siena dictated the *Dialogo* in Italian to her secretaries. A manuscript translating it was found at Brigittine Syon Abbey and printed as *The
Orcherd of Syon*. It opens with a preface describing the orchard at Syon Abbey
in Richmond within which the Brigittine nuns walked and contemplated. The
text is organized as a metaphorical garden, an image of Eden, with seven
parts of five chapters each, each indicating a contemplative path. We can
picture them in their Clarissan (Franciscan) grey habits, black veils and white
crown and cross on them intersected with five red roundels for Christ's
wounds that Birgitta, in a vision, had designed for them as they read about
the Dominican tertiary Catherine of Siena, herself garbed in white and black.
A related Syon Abbey publication is *The Myrroure of Oure Lady*.

Cattle Raid of Cooley/Tain bo Cualgne (c. 1150)
From the Ulster Cycle, Ireland's great epic, in which King Aillil acquires the
White Bull of Connaught, for which his Queen, Mebd, strives to acquire his
equal, the Brown Bull of Cooley, acquiring him from Daire, and of the great
warrior Cuchulain.

William Caxton (c. 1422–92)
The first English printer, Caxton learned his trade in Bruges where, with
Colard Mansion, he translated and printed the first English text in 1473,
Recuyell of the Historyes of Troye. He then established a printing press at
Westminster in 1476, where his first text was probably an edition of Chaucer's
Canterbury Tales. His early printed texts also include *Dictes or Sayengis of the
Philosophres* (1477), his translation from the Latin of the *Golden Legend* (1484),
his translation from the French of *The Book of the Knight of the Tower* (1484), and
Malory's *Le Morte d'Arthur* (1485). Wynkyn de Worde, who moved the press
to London, succeeded Caxton.

Chanson de Roland and the 'Matter of France'

The *Song of Roland* was sung by Taillefer at the Battle of Hastings in 1066, and its Anglo-Norman manuscript is not in France but in Oxford's Bodleian Library, having earlier being owned by the Oseney Abbey Chaucer mentions in his *Reeve's Tale*. Its propaganda against Saracen culture is not warranted by historical facts. Charlemagne journeyed to Spain as an ally of the Muslims, Haroun al Raschid sent him the gift of an elephant (whose tusks were turned into the Olifant and chess pieces), and the rear guard with 'Hrolandus' was attacked not by Saracens but by European Gascons. Its hero 'Hrolandus', then 'Roland', and later 'Orlando', is from Brittany and thus 'British', in a Norman poem. The 'Matter of France', as Wace called it, reverberated throughout Europe and especially in Norman regions such as Sicily and the Crusaders' Jerusalem Kingdom, though it was less popular in England. Affected by the crusading ethos against Islam, the poem categorically states: 'Pagans are wrong, Christians are right!' (*Paien unt tort e Chrestien unt dreit*, l. 1015). (See Chapter 9: Race Studies and Postcolonial Theory.)

Geoffrey Chaucer (c. 1340–1400)

Chaucer's context is courtly and diplomatic. He served as a page in noble households and had access to French and later Italian literature. He translated Boethius and the *Roman de la Rose*. His earlier works are *The Book of the Duchess, The Legend of Good Women, Troilus and Criseyde*, a scientific *Treatise on the Astrolabe*, written for his little son Louis. His *magnum opus* is the unfinished *Canterbury Tales*, which combines fabliaux, saints' legends, beast fables, romances, moral tales told by male and female pilgrims, and it ends with a penitential treatise, shaped as a sermon told by a (possibly) Wycliffite Parson. (See Chapter 5: Lee Patterson, *Chaucer and the Subject of History* and Carolyn Dinshaw, *Chaucer's Sexual Poetics*.)

Children and Childhood

If the broader culture 'knows' anything about children in the Middle Ages, it is that medieval culture didn't know anything about children and childhood. They were considered 'little adults' with whom medieval parents had little if any emotional connection, and children (especially girls) were driven as quickly as possible out of the home and into adult roles, particularly marriage. However, medieval historians have tried to put firmly to rest Philippe Ariès' fundamental though flawed analysis of medieval children and childhood that is the source of these misconceptions (1962). The research of Barbara Hanawalt, Ronald Finucane, Nicholas Orme, Shulamith Shahar and others has emphasized the existence of parental care, community investment, legal consideration, theological reflection and literary investigation of medieval children and childhood from a wide range of source material and in a number of European regions. These investigations into the children, families and households of the predominantly Christian west are being matched by exciting new work in medieval Judaic (Ivan Marcus, Elisheva Baumgarten) and Islamic (Avner Giladi) culture as well.

Medieval authorities did indeed recognize distinct phases of childhood from birth through adolescence, and although the demarcations differ, the early life course was often understood in seven-year increments (from birth to age 7 as *infancia*, ages 7 to 14 as *pueritia*, and ages 14 to 21 as *adholenscia*), and throughout the medieval period a wide variety of texts were created specifically for children (Kline 2003). Medieval English law also recognized important age distinctions. In general, both boys and girls could be contracted to marry at age 7, and boys could be married at 14 and girls at 12, though (ideally) neither could be compelled and either could break the marriage contract by paying a fee. Wardship practices also complicated the understanding and place of young boys and girls. For example, a child became an orphan when the *father* died, not both parents as in contemporary practice. Feudal wardship separated guardianship of lands and chattels from guardianship of the body, and as a result, feudal wards might have a complex network of guardians and overseers who were not their parents. (See Chapter 3: Courtesy and Conduct Literature; Didactic Literature; Guillaume de Deguileville, *The Pilgrimage of the Life of Man*; Paston Letters; Saints' Legends [Hagiography].) [DTK]

Christina of Markyate (c. 1100–55)
Christina became an anchoress, then founder of the nuns of St. Albans. The St. Albans Psalter is associated with her, likewise an unfinished *vita* in Latin that includes snatches of vernacular English. Christ says to her in Latin: ' "Rejoice with me", and in English, "My Sunday daughter" ' (*letare mecum. ait anglico sermone. myn sunendaege dohter*).

Christine de Pizan (1363–c. 1434)
Daughter of an Italian astrologer at the French court, this brilliant writer had the run of the King's library when a child and wrote books counseling kings, nobles, queens and ordinary women how to conduct their lives. Her *Book of the City of Ladies* references St. Augustine's *The City of God*. *Le Chemin de Longs Estude* is a feminist version of Dante's *Commedia* and Virgil's *Aeneid* where Christine is guided by the Sybil into the knowledge of all things. Christine recasts Greco-Roman mythology from a female standpoint in the *Epistle of Othea*. She oversaw the production of her most beautifully illuminated manuscripts with images showing herself as writing them. Though France and England were at war against each other, her son was page to the Earl of Salisbury and her books were treasured and translated into English. She also

championed feminine virtue against the misogyny of the *Romance of the Rose* in the international *Querelle de la Rose*. (See Chapter 9: Christine de Pizan and the *Querelle de la Rose*.)

Cloud of Unknowing

Deeply influenced by Pseudo-Dionysius and the Victorines, this author likely wrote treatises of spiritual direction, including *Deonise Hid Diunite*, which have been assumed to be addressed to a young Carthusian laybrother of 24 years of age lacking Latin. However, from the constant use of gender-sensitive language throughout and from the use of scriptural examples centred on women, these texts could equally as well have been written for a young woman solitary of 24. The text advocates an apophatic (imageless) spirituality. Contemplation rather than knowledge is seen as the showing or revelation of divinity, as in the following prayer:

þis is Seinte Deonise Preier
    þou vnbigonne & euerlastyng
Wysdome, þe whiche in þiself arte
þe souereyn-substancyal Firstheed,
þe souereyn Goddesse, & þe
souereyn Good, þe inliche beholder
of þe godliche maad wisdome of
Cristen men: I beseche þee for to
drawe us up in an acordyng abilnes
to þe souereyn-vnknowen and þe
souereyn-schinyng hei3t of þi derke
inspirid spekynges, where alle þe
pryue thinges of deuinytee ben
kouerid and hid vnder þe souereyn-
schinyng derknes of wisest silence,
makyng þe souereyn-clerest
souereynly for to schine priuely in
þe derkyst; and þe whiche is – in a
maner þat is alweys inuisible &
vngropable – souereynli fulfillyng
wiþ ful fayre cleertees alle þoo
soules þat ben not hauyng i3en of
mynde. (ll. 14–24)
	This is St Denis' Prayer
	    O eternal and everlasting
	Wisdom, who are in yourself the
	highest substantial Prime, the
	highest Goddess and the highest
	Good, the inward beholder of the
	spiritual wisdom of Christian men,
	I beg you to draw us up in like
	capacity to the highest unknown
	and greatest shining height of the
	dark inspired speakings, where all
	the secret things of divinity are
	covered and hid under the greatest
	shining darkness of wisest silence,
	making the highest clearness
	greatly to shine secretly in the
	darkest, and which is in a way
	always invisible and unfelt, highly
	fulfilling with most beautiful
	clearness all those souls who lack
	the eyes of the mind.

Confessional Manuals
The adoption of Aristotelian taxonomies in universities encouraged priests trained there to categorize and discuss the Seven Deadly Sins: Lust (Lechery), Gluttony, Greed (Avarice), Pride, Envy, Anger (Wrath) and Sloth (*acedie* or depression) required confession before a good death. These lists inform other literary texts, such as *Piers Plowman*, Chaucer's *Pardoner's Tale*, and the morality play *Mankind*.

Contemplative Literature
A category of literature whose aim is to assist in the contemplation of spiritual matters, including Aelred of Rievaulx; *Ancrene Wisse*; Walter Hilton, *Ladder of Perfection*; *Cloud of Unknowing*; Julian of Norwich, *Showing of Love* and Nicholas Love, *Mirror of the Blessed Life of Jesus Christ*. (See Chapter 8: The Impact of Feminism and the Expansion of the Canon and Rethinking the Boundaries and Fifteenth Century Literature.)

Corpus Christi Plays
Generally refers to the great cycle plays of York, Chester, Towneley and N-Town. In the later Middle Ages, it became customary at York, Chester and other places for the trade guilds to perform biblically based plays in ME, particularly during the season of the Eucharistic feast of Corpus Christi. Of these manuscripts, the Towneley manuscript contains the finest plays, some of which are attributed to a brilliant and distinctive writer called the Wakefield Master. The N-Town plays are preserved in a single manuscript that incorporates a variety of materials, including a series of plays based on the life of the Virgin Mary. The Chester Plays were revised into a consistent stanza form late in their history, and the York Plays were controlled by the city council, which fined poor acting and shoddy production. During the Reformation, the play books were called in for censorship and the play cycles, for want of their texts, died out. In one of the most famous medieval plays, the Wakefield Master's *Secunda Pastorum* or 'Second Shepherds' Play from the Towneley Plays, the shepherds complain about current issues like landowners, taxes, and women while simultaneously witnessing the birth of Jesus. (See Chapter 4: *Mankind* and *The Tretise of Miraclis Pleyinge*; Chapter 6: Spectacle and Authority; Chapter 7: Interdisciplinarity and Synthesis.)

Courtesy and Conduct Literature
Written and compiled primarily to assist rising middle-class and aristocratic families in raising their children (or training servants), courtesy books (which could be in prose or verse) offered advice in proper manners, deportment, language, and the personal accoutrements necessary for a successful life or for finding a spouse. Related to the earlier *facetus* literature, examples include

'How a Good Wife Taught Her Daughter', 'How a Good Man Taught His Son', *Stans puer ad mensam*, and John Russell's *Book of Nurture*. (See Chapter 1: Mapping New Approaches.) Concerned with proper table manners in polite company, *The Babees Book* (c. 1475) poetically advises its young charges:

> A, Bele Babees, herkne now to my lore!
> Whenne yee entre into your lordis place,
> Say first, 'god spede;' And alle that ben byfore
> Yow in this stede, salue withe humble Face;
> Stert [jump up] nat Rudely; komme Inne an esy pace;
> Holde vp youre heede, and knele but on oone kne
> To youre sovereyne or lorde, whedir he be.
>
> And yf they speke withe you at youre komynge,
> Withe stable Eye loke vpone theym Rihte,
> To theyre tales and yeve yee goode herynge
> Whils they haue seyde; loke eke withe your myhte
> Yee Iangle nouhte, also caste nouhte your syhte
> Aboute the hovs, but take to theym entent
> Withe blythe vysage, and spiryt diligent. (ll. 57–70) [DTK]

Courtly Love
Emerging among the troubadours, trobaritz, and noble courts of twelfth-century France, courtly love or *amour courtois* names the sacrificial love of a knight for his beloved lady, and as proof of his love the knight often goes on a quest against insurmountable odds or superhuman foes to prove his devotion. This sacrifice, rather than the erotic fulfilment of their love, ennobles him and transforms his devotion into spiritual fulfilment. The twelfth-century *Art of Courtly Love* by Andreas Capellanus details the 'rules' of courtly love. However, given its name by Gaston Paris in an 1883 essay and popularized in C.S. Lewis's *Allegory of Love* in 1936, 'courtly love' is now widely believed to be more of a literary convention than historical practice. (See Chapter 4: Marie de France, *Lanval*.)

Dante Alighieri
Geoffrey Chaucer, Adam Easton and perhaps Julian of Norwich all display knowledge of the Italian and/or Latin writings of Dante Alighieri, author of *The Divine Comedy*.

Didactic Literature
Refers to any literature whose purpose is to teach, whether children or adults. Gower's *Confessio Amantis*, addressed first to Richard II and then to Henry IV,

could be considered a didactic text. The medieval period also saw a wide variety of texts devoted to the teaching of children and youth, ranging from *abecedaria* (ABC poems like 'The ABC of Aristotle'); instruction in the rudimentary prayers and precepts of Christianity, including the Pater Noster, Ave Maria and Apostle's Creed ('primers' like Plimpton MS 258 or *The Lay Folks Prayer Book*); exemplary tales that doubled as Latin instruction (Cato's *Distichs*, Aesop's *Fables*, *The Fables of Avianus*); the training of novice monks (Aelfric's *Colloquy*), courtesy and conduct literature (*The Babee's Book*, 'How the Good Wife Taught Her Daughter'); and Latin primers, whose lessons the 'litel clergeon' of Chaucer's *Prioress's Tale* ignores in favour of learning the *Alma Redemptoris*. (See Chapter 1: Mapping New Approaches and Chapter 8: The Impact of Feminism and the Expansion of the Canon and New Historicism and Blurring the History/Literature Divide.) [DTK]

Double Monastery
Anglo-Saxon seventh-century Whitby, Northumbria; Brigittine fifteenth-century Syon, London. These monasteries had fine libraries and produced a rich literature, conversant with classic and contemplative learning, with both men and women under an Abbess.

Dream Vision
Dream vision narratives, in which the narrator or main character is transported in a dream into a heightened state of spiritual and contemplative awareness, are given in Bede, *St. Patrick's Purgatory*, Christina of Markyate, Dante, Birgitta, Chaucer, Christine de Pizan, *Wynnere and Wastoure*, *Piers Plowman*, Julian of Norwich, *Pearl*, Usk's *Testament of Love*, James I's *The Kingis Quair*, Margery Kempe and John Lydgate.

Ellesmere Manuscript
This magnificent illuminated manuscript (abbr. El) of Chaucer's *Canterbury Tales*, now at the Huntington Museum, San Marino, California, is one of the two earliest versions of Chaucer's *Canterbury Tales*, the other being the Hengwrt Chaucer (abbr. Hg) in the National Library of Wales. Both manuscripts appear to have been copied by the same scribe c. 1400–05, though Hg is regarded as slightly earlier and more faithful to Chaucer's text. Prepared for a significant patron, El seems to have been 'cleaned up' by the copyist (for example, many lines lacking strict iambic pentameter or featuring rougher end-rhymes seem to have been improved), and includes the *Canon's Yeoman's Tale*, which is lacking in Hg. [DTK]

Fall of Troy and 'Matter of Troy'
A common preoccupation of many late-medieval writers, Chaucer (*Troilus and*

Criseyde), *Sir Gawain and the Green Knight*, Henryson (*Testament of Criseyd*) and Lydgate (The *Troy Book*) – often drawing upon on Boccaccio and Guido da Colonna – the history of Troy was particularly important as London was sometimes called New Troy, *Trinovantium*. In this way, Trojan stories were seen as a 'distant mirroring' of their own moment in time.

Geoffrey of Monmouth, *History of the Kings of Britain*
Written in Latin by a Welshman giving the Celtic history of Britain, Geoffrey's *Historia*, which influenced many ME works, tells the story of Arthur. (See Chapter 3: Arthurian Literature and the 'Matter of Britain'.)

John Gower (c. 1330–1408)
A contemporary of Chaucer's, John Gower wrote in Latin (*Vox Clamantis* or 'the voice of one crying' recounting the Peasant's Revolt), in French (*Mirroir L'Omme* or *The Mirror of Humanity*) and in English (*Confessio Amantis* or *The Lover's Confession*.) Chaucer dedicated *Troilus and Criseyde* to 'moral Gower' and 'philosophical Strode' (V. 1856–57), and Gower praised Chaucer at the end of the *Confessio*. (See Chapter 4: The 1381 Revolt.)

Guillaume de Deguileville (b. c. 1294), *The Pilgrimage of the Life of Man*
Influenced by the *Roman de la Rose*, the Cistercian monk creates a lengthy three-part vision poem of the *Pilgrimage of Man, of the Soul, and of Jesus Christ*. Translated into ME and later printed by Caxton, it is written out by the same scribe who copied the Amherst Manuscript containing Julian of Norwich and Marguerite Porete's works, as well as another manuscript containing Mechtild of Hackeborn's *Book of Ghostly Grace*.

Henry IV (1367–1413)
Henry Bolingbroke, son of John of Gaunt, Duke of Lancaster, took England from Richard II, and was crowned Henry IV. He vowed a Crusade to recapture Jerusalem but died instead from leprosy, contracted on his pilgrimages, in Westminster Abbey's Jerusalem Chamber. He is interred in Canterbury Cathedral. Unlike his father, he opposed Lollardy, seeing it as a threat to the State as well as to the Church. He had Lollards executed as both traitors and heretics. (See Chapter 2: English Monarchy and the Deposition of Richard II.)

Henry V (1387–1422)
Born in Wales, Henry V reigned from 1413 to 1422 and nearly united the crowns of England and France with his famous victory at Agincourt and his relationship to Catherine of Valois, daughter of Charles VI of France. The Treaty of Troyes stated that Henry V would inherit the throne of France when

Charles VI died. However, Henry V died before Charles, leaving the infant Henry VI as putative ruler of both countries and leading to renewed conflict in the Hundred Years' War. A successful military leader throughout his career, Henry V instituted English as the language of state. (See Chapter 2: English Monarchy and the Deposition of Richard II.) [DTK]

Henry VI (1421–71)

The only son of Henry V, Henry VI ruled under a regency (including Humphrey, Duke of Gloucester; Henry Beaufort, Bishop of Winchester; and John, Duke of Bedford) until age sixteen when he assumed personal rule. Generally regarded as a weak-willed though deeply spiritual ruler, Henry VI married Margaret of Anjou but eventually lost control of France and of his faculties. The ensuing power vacuum led to the War of the Roses. Considered a saint, Henry VI was imprisoned and executed in the Tower of London in 1471. (See Chapter 2: The Wars of the Roses and the Transition to the Early Modern Period.) [DTK]

Walter Hilton (d. 1396), *The Ladder of Perfection*

Head of the Augustinian Canons at Thurgarton Priory, Hilton is best known for the spiritual treatise, *The Ladder of Perfection*, a description of the soul's internal pilgrimage to spiritual Jerusalem. Written in two parts, the *The Ladder of Perfection* begins with spiritual advice to an Anchoress. It repeatedly uses the Pilgrim's Prayer, 'I have nought, I am nought, I seek nought but sweet Jesus in Jerusalem'.

Histories

The chronological accounts of institutions, royalty, countries and even the world, often blending fact, fiction and partisan politics. Gildas, Bede's *Ecclesiastical History of the English People*, Wace, Layamon, Geoffrey of Monmouth, Higdon's *Polychronicon*, Froissart's *Chroniques*, Walsingham's *Historia Anglicana* and Capgrave's *De Illustribus Henrici* are examples.

Thomas Hoccleve (c. 1368–1426), *The Regiment of Princes*

Known as a Lancastrian poet, Hoccleve was also Chaucer's friend and bureaucratic colleague. Hoccleve wrote *The Regiment of Princes* for Henry V, then still Prince Hal. He was a clerk in the office of the Privy Seal and wrote what is now termed 'Hoccleve's Series' (*Complaint, Dialogue* and *Learn to Die*). He also translated Christine de Pizan's *L'Epistre au Dieu d'Amours*. Once relegated to the 'dullness' of the fifteenth century, along with his more prolific contemporary John Lydgate, Hoccleve, as well as Lydgate, are now recognized as important artists in their own right and not simply as Chaucer's followers, both for the quality of their work and their cultural importance in the Lancastrian era. (See Chapter 8: Rethinking the Boundaries and Fifteenth Century Literature.) [DTK]

James I of Scotland (1394–1437), *The Kingis Quair*
A prisoner of the English in the Tower of London, King James I of Scotland composed an allegory in seven line Chaucerian stanzas, known from its use by this king as 'rhyme royal'. The semi-autobiographical dream vision is based on Boethius, and Chaucer's *Knight's Tale* is written in Middle Scots (Anglian) dialect and is titled *The Kingis Quair* ('The King's Book').

Julian of Norwich (c. 1342–1416), *Showing of Love*
An anchoress of St. Julian's Church in Norwich, she wrote different versions of the *Showing of Love*, which survive in various manuscripts now at Westminster Abbey, Paris' Bibliothèque Nationale, and the British Library. The Short Text in the Amherst Manuscript, which dates itself 1413, is thought to be earlier, composed soon after 1373, though its self-censorship is typical of texts written during the period of Lollard persecution by Archbishop Chancellor Arundel. The Long Text in the Paris and Sloane Manuscripts is divided into chapters, the Sloane providing comments in the style of the Birgittine *Revelationes*, written by Julian's editor. She translates directly from the Hebrew Bible into ME, before the King James Bible, and it is possible that Adam Easton, who effected Birgitta of Sweden's canonization as a saint and who had taught Hebrew at Oxford, may have been her editor for the Long Text. All versions present the contemplation of the Virgin and the vision of the hazelnut in the palm of Julian's hand: 'And so in this sight I saw that he is everything that is good as to my understanding. And in this he showed me a little thing the quantity of a hazel nut, lying in the palm of my hand as it seemed, and it was as round as any ball. I looked on it with the eye of my understanding, and I thought, "What may this be?" And it was answered generally thus, "It is all that is made" ' (Reynolds and Holloway 2001). (See Chapter 3: Contemplative Literature.)

Margery Kempe (d. after 1438), *The Book of Margery Kempe*
The daughter of John Brunham, Mayor of Lynn, Margery married and, like Birgitta of Sweden, bore many children and went on far-flung pilgrimages. Chaucer has his Wife of Bath make the same pilgrimages as does Margery Kempe, but without her piety. Margery dictated her *Book* to various authorities, though the first version was likely written down by her daughter-in-law from Gdansk, familiar with Birgitta's similar book. At one point Margery is accused of being Sir John Oldcastle's daughter and is nearly burned at the stake. She describes visiting Julian of Norwich, and her account of their conversation rings true. Castigated by early critics as a 'hysteric', Margery's

achievement is now recognized as one of the most important in ME. (See Chapter 4: Margery Kempe, *The Book of Margery Kempe*.)

William Langland, *Piers Plowman*
The alliterative dream vision *Piers Plowman* is said to be written by William Langland and is set in Malvern, Westminster and London. It exists in three versions (the A, B and C versions). However, Jill Mann has argued the order should be altered: the C and A versions being Langland's later response to Archbishop Arundel's censorship of Lollard teachings, and the B version, chanted at the 1381 Revolt, reflecting Wycliffite sympathies, being the original. In its allegory Will, as sinning Everyman, has a vision of Christ as Piers the Plowman, who begins as a Moses figure giving the Law, then becomes a Christ as Samaritan, and finally as a failing Piers or Peter, the Church at the Schism betraying Christ. Much of what we know about Langland is extrapolated from Passus 5, an autobiographical passage, in the C version. Piers Plowman initiated a series of plowman tales, dedicated to social and anti-clerical critique, that include *Pierce the Ploughman's Crede* and *The Plowman's Tale*. John Bowers recently has argued that Chaucer's Plowman, brother to the Parson in the *General Prologue*, remains without a tale largely in reaction to Langland's great achievement. (See Chapter 4: The 1381 Revolt; William Langland, *Piers Plowman*; *Mankind* and *The Tretise of Miraclis Pleyinge*.)

Lollardy
From the Latin *lollius* (weeds) or Dutch *lollaer* (mumbler), Lollardy initially described the theology derived from Oxford theologian John Wyclif's (d. 1384) teachings. Wyclif criticized what he saw as theological inconsistencies (transubstantiation, indulgences) and ecclesiastical abuses (clerical wealth, power and immorality) in the medieval church. The Wycliffite Bible is the first translation into ME, and the Lollards advocated lay education in the scriptures. Their sermons, treatises and the Wycliffite Bible are in fine manuscripts, lacking images or ornamentation, accurately transcribed and collated with each other. Lollardy soon became associated with heresy in general (William Sawtry) and found a sympathetic audience among the gentry, some of whom, like Sir John Oldcastle and his 1414 rebellion, extended their theological positions into political revolt. (See Chapter 2: Crisis in the Church at Home: Lollardy.)

Nicholas Love (c. 1410), *Mirror of the Blessed Life of Jesus Christ*
The Carthusian Prior at Mount Grace Charterhouse in Yorkshire translated the Franciscan *Meditationes Vitae Christi*, encouraging lay people's pious devotion through the affective contemplation of episodes in the Virgin Mary's life. Widely circulated in manuscript and early print editions, Love's *Mirror of*

the Blessed Life of Jesus Christ was authorized by Archbishop Thomas Arundel as a means of countering the Lollard movement among the laity.

Luttrell Psalter (c. 1335)
The British Library's Luttrell Psalter is richly illuminated with scenes of East Anglian agriculture and culture. The grotesque faces of the peasants may well derive from the actors' masks in Terence manuscripts. Used with the *Promptorium Parvulorum* (the earliest Latin-English dictionary, written for schoolchildren in Lynn and including their games) it offers a revealing context for reading Chaucer, Langland, Julian, Margery and the Corpus Christi Plays.

John Lydgate (c. 1370–1451)
A Benedictine monk at St. Albans Abbey and later Prior, Lydgate was perhaps the most prolific writer of the later English Middle Ages, composing more than 145,000 lines and writing in nearly every genre (including ceremonial pieces, mummings, saints' legends, dream visions and classical stories about Troy and Thebes). One of Chaucer's early followers, his *Siege of Thebes*, a prequel to the action of the *Knight's Tale*, is a continuation of the *Canterbury Tales*. (See Chapter 8: Rethinking the Boundaries and Fifteenth-Century Literature.)

Lyric Verse
Rhyme had been a characteristic of the Celts, the Irish, the Welsh, the Breton, but not of the Anglo-Saxons. Irish monks had scribbled rhyming lyrics on the edges of their Latin manuscripts, including one about Pangur Ban, a monk's white cat chasing mice while his master chases scholarly references. Friars inherited from their founder, St. Francis of Assisi, the idea of creating spiritual lyrics in the vernacular rhyme, composed to the same tunes as were secular love songs. Generally these are anonymous but often are exceedingly fine. Not a few ME lyrics play with the tension of sexuality in the Spring and Lent's simultaneous mandatory abstinence from sexuality, for example: 'Lenten is comen with love to toun'. One of the most famous, 'Sing, Cuckoo' is a motet sung in ME and Latin simultaneously celebrating Nature and Christ, for which we have the music as well as the words written out by a monk at Reading Abbey.

Mabinogion
The Welsh cycle of the *Mabinogion* gives Celtic tradition that is also present in the Arthurian cycles. It divides itself into four 'Branches', each named after a character in its opening tales, 'Pwyll', 'Branwen', 'Manawydan' and 'Math'. The earliest surviving manuscript, writing down these oral tales, is called the 'White Book of Rhydderch', and the complete version is in the 'Red Book

of Hergerst'. The title appears to refer to a boy's education, which may be the theme of the Pryderi son of Pwyll cycle in the four Branches. The early manuscripts date from the fourteenth century, but the material is likely much older (twelfth century).

Sir Thomas Malory (c. 1405–71), *Le Morte d'Arthur*

Most scholars accept that the author of the *Morte d'Arthur* is the Warwickshire knight, Sir Thomas Malory of Newbold Revel. While in prison for unknightly deeds during the violence and social breakdown of the Wars of the Roses, Malory passed the time by writing in Tudor English the matter of Arthur inherited from the Celts and French, creating from these stories a chain of romances leading up to the final tragedy of Arthur. (See Chapter 3: Arthurian Literature and the 'Matter of Britain' and Geoffrey of Monmouth, *History of the Kings of Britain*.)

Sir John de Mandeville, *Travels*

Sir John de Mandeville, likely an Anglo-Norman knight from St. Albans (though some scholars doubt his existence), wrote a travelogue into which he put all other travel books to which he had access. In the *Travels*, Mandeville claims to have ventured to the Far East, sojourned in the Holy Land, and trekked to all the great cities of Europe, Asia Minor and as far as China. He recounts 'anthropophagi [cannibals] and men whose heads do grow beneath their shoulder' that he says he has not seen, while describing monkeys, bamboo and bananas. He wrote in Anglo-Norman and his account was quickly translated into ME. (See chapter 3: Pilgrim and Travel Literature.)

Marie de France, *Lais*

Although little is certain about Marie's life (she likely was at the court of Henry II and Eleanor of Aquitaine), she is regarded as the author of three (and possibly four) texts: the *Lais* (tales of courtly love), a version of Aesop's *Fables*, *St. Patrick's Purgatory*, and perhaps a Life of St. Audrey. Dante speaks of *lais* in connection with the lovers Paolo and Francesca in *Inferno* V, and Chaucer calls his *Franklin's Tale* a Breton lay. (See Chapter 4: Marie de France, *Lanval*)

Mirk's *Festial*

A compilation of ME sermons written by John Mirk to be preached on the Saints' Days, which often incorporate historical legends, biblical accounts, moral exempla, and contemporary stories, including those of pilgrims.

Monastic Orders

Founded by Benedict of Nursia (529), the Benedictines or Black Monks are the major order in Western Christendom. The Black Monks of the English

Congregation were powerful and wealthy, crowning England's kings at their Westminster Abbey. The Cistercians or 'White Monks' (1098), emerged out of the reforms launched at Citeux Abbey in France and in England mainly built their abbeys in Yorkshire. The Carthusians, founded by St Bruno (1084), live in houses about a cloister in silence as if hermits in the desert. The Franciscans or Grey Friars (1209) follow the Rule of St Francis, the Italian saint devoted to poverty and preaching. The Dominicans (Black Friars), founded by Spanish St Dominic (1215), emphasize education and preaching, originally against the Albigensians (Cathars) in France, The Carmelites (White Friars) claim descent from Elijah on Mount Carmel. The Augustinians lived as canons or as hermits. Benedictines, Cistercians and Carthusians are cenobitic monks (that is, they live in cells about a cloister in a monastery). Franciscans, Dominicans, Augustinians and Carmelites are medicant friars (that is, they beg for their upkeep). Individuals, like Richard Rolle and Julian of Norwich, could be hermits and anchoresses. Monks and friars were often the target of satirical and reformist literature.

Mystery, Morality and Miracle Plays
A traditional way of categorizing medieval English drama, *mystery* plays (from the French *mystere* or 'guild') describes the biblically based cycle plays of medieval England (York, Chester, Towneley [erroneously called the Wakefield Plays in the past] and N-Town [sometimes called *Ludus Coventriae* or the 'Coventry Plays' in the past], as well as other plays preserved in single or fragmentary manuscripts). *Morality* plays denote dramas based upon personification allegory in which characters represent virtues and vices (as in *Everyman* and *Mankind*). *Miracle* plays commonly indicated a catch-all category that include saints' plays (like the Digby *Mary Magdalene*) and other drama (like the *Croxton Play of the Sacrament*). The mystery plays were performed on pageant wagons (processional staging) or upon fixed stages throughout town, while the morality and miracle plays often suited a travelling company with fewer players and less need for dramatic machinery. In Celtic-speaking Cornwall, there is evidence of an outdoors Roman-type theatre in the round being used for a vast production of biblical dramas, while a touring company used similar outdoor theatres in the round or other spaces for the *Castle of Perseverance*, *Wisdom*, *Mankind* and other plays in the Macro Manuscript. (See Chapter 3: Corpus Christ Plays; Chapter 4: *Mankind* and *The Tretise of Miraclis Pleyinge*; Chapter 7: Interdisciplinarity and Synthesis.)

Paston Letters
Letters written by members of a large and powerful merchant family in East Anglia, roughly spanning the fifteenth century (1422–1509) demonstrate the socio-economic roles men and women played in late medieval English

society. In addition to the Paston Letters, two other sets of late-medieval correspondence family survive: the Lisle and Stonor letters.

The *Pearl*-Poet

Likely the author of the four texts of Cotton Nero A.x. (*Pearl, Cleanness, Patience* and *Sir Gawain and the Green Knight*), the *Pearl*-Poet (also known as the *Gawain*-Poet) is widely recognized as one of the most sophisticated and technically accomplished writers of late-medieval England, on a par with Chaucer. The dream-vision *Pearl* recounts a Dreamer's extended dialogue with the courtly *Pearl*-child. *Cleanness* (sometimes called *Purity*) is an extended homily upon the theme of spiritual purity and sinfulness. *Patience* retells in verse the biblical tale of Jonah. *Sir Gawain and the Green Knight*, a poetic tour-de-force combining alliterative verse and end-rhyme, is perhaps the finest Arthurian romance in English. The author appears to be lay but deeply versed in theology, blending this playfully with the disparate world of court and castle. The equally brilliant though less studied *St. Erkenwald*, recounting the life of London's patron saint, is often attributed to this anonymous author because of similarity of style, language and approach.

Francesco Petrarch

Italian writer, whose tale of Griselda is used by Boccaccio in the *Decameron* and by Chaucer in the *Clerk's Tale* of the *Canterbury Tales*. His sonnets are also echoed in Chaucer's *Troilus and Criseyde*.

Pilgrim and Travel Literature

Examples include Adamnam, *Arculf's Voyage*, Orosius, 'Elena', 'Andreas', Guthrithyr, Icelandic Sagas, Old English lyrics, 'The Wanderer', 'The Seafarer', the Irish *Voyage of Bran, Voyage of St. Brendan, St. Patrick's Purgatory*, Margaret of Jerusalem, Mandeville's *Travels*, Birgitta of Sweden's *Revelationes*, Margery Kempe's *Book*. Using ships and horses or on foot, medieval people could travel extensively, participating in different cultures. Langland's *Piers Plowman* and Chaucer's *Canterbury Tales* satirize pilgrimage. See also Figure 3.1: Pilgrimages of Medieval Women, outlining women's pilgrimages, in which medieval women, like Birgitta and Margery Kempe, imitate earlier women like Saints Helen and Paula.

—————————	Helena of York, Rome, Sinai, Jerusalem, Bethlehem, Constantinople
····················	Egeria of Spain, Sinai, Jerusalem, Bethlehem, Constantinople
- - - - - - - - -	Paula and Eustochium of Rome, Jerusalem and Bethlehem
— — — — —	Guthrithyr of Iceland, Vinland and Rome
—··—··—··—··	Bridget of Ireland and Sasso
—···—···—···	Margaret of Jerusalem, Beverly, Froidmont
— — — — —	Birgitta of Sweden, Compostela, Rome, Jerusalem, Bethlehem
—··—··—··	Margery Kempe of Lynne, Compostela, Rome, Jerusalem, Bethlehem

Figure 3.1: Pilgrimages of Medieval Women

Marguerite Porete (d. 1310), *The Mirror of Simple Souls*
Marguerite Porete, associated with the Beguines, first had her book burned at Valenciennes, and then she herself was burned at the stake in Paris in 1310 for it. Nevertheless, this book of contemplative Pseudo-Dionysan theology, originally written in Old French, was preserved in ME translations in three manuscripts, one of which, the Amherst Manuscript in the British Library, also contains the Short Text of Julian's *Showing*, Jan van Ruusbroec's *Sparkling Stone*, an extract from Henry Suso's *Horologium Sapientiae*, and writings by Richard Rolle.

Promptorium Parvulorum
The first Latin-English Dictionary, its title meaning a 'store room for children', written by a recluse in Margery Kempe's town of Lynn, this work is given in Julian's and Margery's dialect and includes much information on the games medieval schoolboys played and on their intimate household details. (See Chapter 3: Children and Childhood.)

Richard II (1367–1400)
He became king as a boy when his grandfather Edward II died after his own father, the Black Prince, had been buried in a magnificent tomb beside St. Thomas Becket's shrine. As a youngster Richard II showed great courage during the Peasants' Revolt and then became unpopular. He was married first to Anne of Bohemia, daughter of the Holy Roman Emperor, in a magnificent double coronation ceremony in Westminster Abbey designed by Cardinal Adam Easton at the Pope's bidding. Anne, deeply beloved by the people, died of the Black Death at Sheen. Richard's second wife was the child bride Isabelle, Princess of France. No children were born to either marriage. Richard's male favourites were accused of corrupted the realm, resulting in conspiracies against him, and Richard had his uncle the Duke of Gloucester murdered for participating in them. Eventually Richard II was forced to abdicate, dying in prison, with Henry Bolingbroke, John of Gaunt's son, succeeding to the throne as Henry IV. (See Chapter 2: Labour Unrest and the Peasants' Revolt and English Monarchy and the Deposition of Richard II, and Chapter 4: The 1381 Revolt.)

Richard Rolle (c. 1300–49)
Rolle chose as a young man to quit Oxford University and become a hermit, and as a contemplative he composed many texts, both in ME and in Latin, often writing these to Margaret Kirkeby, a Cistercian contemplative nun who later inherited his hermitage as anchoress. His most important works are *The Fire of Love* and *The Prick of Conscience*, and he is similar to Henry Suso and John of the Cross, leaping into song from the midst of prose.

He died at Hampole in 1349 and his women followers sought his canonization. In the Amherst Manuscript, some of Rolle's Latin writings are translated by Richard Misyn, Carmelite Prior of Lincoln, into ME for Margaret Heslyngton.

Roman de la Rose, Guillaume de Lorris and Jean de Meun
The first part of the *Roman de la Rose* is a courtly allegory (authored by de Lorris); its continuation by de Meun is considerably more coarse and realistic. Written in the Loire region in French, it is a dream vision of a Lover and his Rosebud and it is filled with debates by its various characters. One of the most widely circulated texts of the late-Middle Ages, many of the *Roman's* manuscripts are superbly illuminated. Chaucer translated it, adapted it to his own purposes and drew from it for many of his own works. Christine de Pizan later was involved in an international controversy over the *Roman's* misogyny, *Querelle de la Rose*. (See Chapter 9: Christine de Pizan and the *Querelle de la Rose*.)

Romance
The word 'Romance' comes from what is told or written in the Romance languages derived from Latin. Romances were stories generally about love and adventure among the upper classes, particularly chivalric (or knightly) romances. Developing into a pan-European phenomena, they came to be composed in Irish, in Icelandic and in other vernacular languages not derived from Latin. Common examples include *Sir Orfeo, King Horn, Beves of Hampton, Sir Gowther*, Chaucer's *The Knight's Tale, Sir Gawain and the Green Knight*, Malory's *Le Morte d'Arthur* and Henryson's *Testament of Cresseid*. (See Chapter 3: The Matter of Britain, The Matter of France, The Matter of Troy). (See also Chapter 5: Jeffrey Jerome Cohen, *Of Giants*; Chapter 5: Patricia Clare Ingham and Michelle Warren, *Postcolonial Moves* and Jeffrey Jerome Cohen, *The Postcolonial Middle Ages*; Chapter 7: Postcolonial Criticism; Chapter 8: Multilingualism, International Contexts, and Postcolonial Concerns; Chapter 9: Race Studies and Postcolonial Theory).

Saints' Legends (Hagiography)
One of the most popular medieval genres of the Middle Ages, these are *hagiographical* texts (lit. *holy writing*) or lives of the saints, as in the Vercelli Manuscript (St. Helen, St. Andrew), the *Katherine Group* (St. Katherine, St. Margaret), Laud Misc. 108 (early *South English Legendary*), the *Golden Legend* (all the saints), Chaucer's Second Nun's Tale (St. Cecilia), *St. Erkenwald* (Bede's St. Earconwald). (See Chapter 8: The Impact of Feminism and the Expansion of the Canon.)

Schools and Literacy

Although noble and aristocratic families often could afford private tutors for their children or send them to monastic institutions to be educated, elementary schools in England were primarily of two types: grammar schools (which concentrated upon education in Latin) and song schools (which focused upon teaching the antiphon and elements of the Mass). When thinking about medieval literacy, it is important to make two distinctions: first, the difference between reading and writing and, second, the distinction between reading and writing in the vernacular and in Latin. In general, more people could read than write, and more people could read or write in English than in Latin, but it would be incorrect to say that, in general, medieval people were 'illiterate'. (See Chapter 1: Mapping New Approaches and Chapter 3: Children and Childhood, Didactic Literature.) [DTK]

The Scottish Chaucerians

King James I of Scotland, who had been imprisoned by the English and educated by them, was the initiator of the school, using 'rhyme royal' in his *Kingis Quair*. Other Scottish Chaucerians include Robert Henryson, author of the Boethian and Chaucerian *Testament of Creseid*, and William Dunbar, author of the *Golden Targe* and other works. They are Lowland Scots from the area around Edinburgh, who were Anglian settlers, not Celtic Highlanders and Islanders. Robert Henryson describes preparing to write his *Testament of Cresseid*, during a cold Scottish Lent:

I mend the fyre and beikit me about,	I mend the fire and warm myself
Than tuik ane drink my spreitis to comfort	Then take a drink to comfort my spirits
And armit me weill fra the cauld thairout.	And arm me well from the cold about.
To cut the winter nicht and mak it schort	To cut the winter night and make it short
I tuik ane Quair and left all uther sport,	I take a Book and left all other sport,
Writtin be worthie Chaucer glorious	Written by worthy Chaucer glorious
Of fair Cresseid, and worthie Troylus.	Of fair Cresseid and worthy Troilus.
(ll. 1–7)	

Sermon Literature

Sermons that could be preached are given in the Vercelli Manuscript, *Mirk's Festial*, *Jacob's Well*, the *Gesta Romanorum*, the Franciscan preaching manual *The Fasciculus Morum*, William Langland's *Piers Plowman*, Julian of Norwich, Margery Kempe and Lollard literature. (See Chapter 3: Mirk's Festial).

Three Estates

A traditional way to classify medieval society: those who pray (Monk), those who fight (Knight), and those who work (Plowman), resulted also in their specific literatures: Literature for the Cloister, Monks, Nuns, Hermits, Anchoresses (Monk); Literature for Court and Castle (Knight); Literature for Town and Village (Plowman).

Universities

Oxford and Cambridge came into being in the twelfth century. Oxford holds pride of place, with teaching recorded from 1096, the title Chancellor from 1214, and the college masters recognized as a *universitas* or corporation from 1231. Cambridge was founded in 1209 when students fled hostile towns-people in Oxford, and a Chancellor is attested to in 1226. They adopted the Greco-Arabic model, which excluded women and emphasized Aristotelian taxonomies, while living with stress between 'town and gown'. Oxford's University College, Balliol, and Merton were founded in the thirteenth century. After finishing their grammar school education, teenaged boys entered university, primarily to study theology, medicine or law. Chaucer's Clerk is a student at Oxford, and the *Reeve's Tale* features rowdy Cambridge students.

Thomas Usk (d. 1388), *The Testament of Love*

While in Newgate Prison awaiting his 1388 execution by hanging, drawing and quartering, Usk wrote the *Testament of Love*, a prose allegory, modeling it on Boethius' *Consolation of Philosophy*, similarly written while awaiting execution. The work, addressed in an acrostic, which includes the author's name, to a 'Margaret' or pearl, borrows from Chaucer's *Troilus and Criseyde* and *Knight's Tale*. As a Controller of Customs at the same time as Chaucer was Comptroller of Customs for the port of London, it is likely that Chaucer and Usk were acquainted. It is also a paradigm for King James I of Scotland's *The Kingis Quair*.

Virginity

As complex an issue as there is in medieval culture, virginity derives from the example set by Mary, Jesus' mother and the Apostle Paul's injunctions to remain sexually pure (1 Corinthians 7). Doctrines advocating virginity were elaborated throughout the Early Middle Ages in the writings of Patristic Fathers like Jerome's *Adversus Jovinianum* ('Against Jovinian') and in hagio-graphical tales of virgin martyrs (the *Katherine Group's* tales of Sts. Juliene, Margarete and Katherine, for example). Virginity became closely identified with feminine spirituality generally, and even married couples could enter into a 'chaste marriage' (Margery Kempe). *Hali Meidhad* ('Holy Maidenhood') is an excellent example of a ME text that compiles previous Latin writings on virginity into a didactic treatise addressed *ad status* or 'to the estate' or social group. Paralleling the 'three estates' of nobility (those who fight), clergy (those who pray), and peasantry (those who work), the three 'feminine estates' – those social positions appropriate for women – were virgin, wife, and widow. Thus, the study of virginity touches upon nearly every aspect of medieval culture – family and marriage, feminism and patriarchy, lay and clerical spirituality, political alliance and male privilege and so on. (See Chapter 3: Anchoress, *Ancrene Wisse* [*Ancrene Riwle*] and the *Katherine Group*, Saints' Legends [Hagiography]). [DTK]

Voyage of Bran and *Voyage of St. Brendan*

A mystical Irish text, closely related to figures in 'Branwen Daughter of Llyr' in the *Mabinogion*, of a voyage to the Otherworld, told in verse and prose, part pagan, part Christian. Verse and prose mixed together tell the story of Bran being encouraged by a woman, bringing a branch of apple blossom to his palace, to set sail over the seas. The Irish also freely translated into their language classical Greek texts, such as the *Odyssey* (*Meirud Ulisse Mac Laertes*), unknown in this period in England. Perhaps a Christianizing of the *Voyage of Bran*, the *Voyage of St. Brendan* (c. 1150), who journeys from island to island in the Atlantic performing miracles, was popular throughout Europe. (See Chapter 3: Pilgrim and Travel Literature.)

Wars of the Roses (1455–89)

In the fifteenth century, England was torn apart by the struggle for the crown between the Lancastrian and York dynasties, not to be reconciled until the marriage between them wrought by the Tudors. (See Chapter 2: The Wars of the Roses and the Transition to the Early Modern Period and Chapter 4: Margery Kempe and *The Book of Margery Kempe*.)

Nigel Wireker (d. c. 1200), *Speculum Stultorum* ('*Mirror of Fools*')

A beast fable written in Latin verse, whose hero is a donkey, satirizing education, by a contemporary of Thomas Becket. Also known as Nigel de Longchamps, his work is quoted in Chaucer's *Nuns' Priest's Tale*. (See Chapter 3: The 1381 Revolt.)

John Wyclif (d. 1384)

An Oxford University Professor of Theology, his desire for worker priests, proficient in Biblical scholarship and able to communicate with the people the spirit of the Gospel, translated into ME, helped to spark a revolution in England, the 1381 Revolt. Wyclif was supported by John, Duke of Gaunt, the king's uncle, and perhaps by Richard II's Queen, Anne of Bohemia (though her support may have been enhanced after her death for Lollard purposes). Often considered a forerunner of the Reformation through his influence on Jan Hus, Wyclif attacked ecclesiastical abuses (excessive wealth, moral laxity), criticized the relationship between civil and church authorities, critiqued the doctrine of transubstantiation, advocated lay education and translated the Bible into English. Equally adept as a philosopher, Wyclif was attacked by the Benedictine Adam Easton of Norwich and 24 of Wyclif's teachings were condemned at the Earthquake Council at Blackfriars, London (1382). He died at Lutterworth Parsonage in 1384. The relationship between Wyclif and Lollardy is complex, and Wyclif's followers were sometimes condemned as Lollards and heretics, many being burned to death at the stake. Margery Kempe is at risk of such a condemnation and execution as she travels about England during the unrest associated with Sir John Oldcastle. Chaucer's ideal Parson is possibly a Wycliffite figure. Wyclif was declared a heretic at the Council of Constance (1415), his remains were exhumed, burned, and the ashes scattered in the River Swift at Lutterworth. (See Chapter 3: Archbishop Thomas Arundel and Chapter 4: Margery Kempe and *The Book of Margery Kempe*.) The tract, 'Of Feigned Contemplative Life' bears the hallmarks of Wycliffe's thought and advocates active preaching rather than reclusive contemplation, using Christ as the example:

> First whanne trewe men techen bi goddis lawe wit & reson þat eche prest owiþ to do his my3t, his wit & his wille to preche cristis gospel, þe fend. blyndiþ ypocritis to excuse hem by feyned contemplatif lif, & to seie þat siþ it is þe beste & þei may not do bo þe to-gidre, þei ben nedid for charite of god to leue þe prechynge of þe gospel & lyuen in contempla cion. See nowe þe ypocrisie of þis false seiynge; crist tau3t & dide þe beste lif for prestis, as oure feiþ techiþ , siþ he was god & my3te not erre; but crist preched þe gospel & charged alle his apostlis & discipl is to goo & preche þe gospel to alle men: þan it is þe beste lif for prestis in þis world to preche & teche. (p. 187)

Wynnere and Wastoure

A splendid though unfinished alliterative vision poem in which 'Wynnere', the folk who toil to produce, and 'Wastoure', the consuming class, debate with each other. It is a political allegory set in the time of Edward II and his son, the Black Prince, and makes use of the 'Honi soit qui mal y pense', 'Shame to him who evil thinks', of the Order of the Garter, used also at the ending of *Sir Gawain and the Green Knight*. (See William Langland, *Piers Plowman*.)

Study Questions

1. Briefly summarize the characteristics of the following social movements, cultural practices and literary figures, genres or texts:

- Anchoress/Anchorite
- Christine de Pizan
- Conduct and Courtesy Literature
- Contemplative Literature
- Didactic Literature
- Lollardy
- John Lydgate
- The Matter of Britain
- Monastic Orders
- *Piers Plowman*
- Pilgrim and Travel Literature
- Romance
- Saints' Lives/Hagiography
- The Scottish Chaucerians
- Virginity

2. Identify the author of the following texts (if known) and their dates, and using the traditional 'three estates' distinction (those who fight, those who pray, those who work) categorize the texts according to their institutional context and 'textual communities' as Literature for Court and Castle (Knight); Literature for Nuns, Hermits, Anchoresses (Monk); or Literature for Town and Village (Plowman). What factors influence your decision?

   - 'ABC of Aristotle'
   - *Alliterative Morte Arthure*
   - *Ancrene Wisse*
   - *Book of the City of Ladies*
   - *The Book of Margery Kempe*
   - *Canterbury Tales*
   - *The Ladder of Perfection*
   - *Mankind*
   - *Morte d'Arthur*
   - *The Orcherd of Syon*
   - Paston Letters
   - *Piers Plowman*
   - *Roman de la Rose*
   - *Showing of Love*
   - *Vox Clamantis*

   Using the above list as a starting point, discuss the strengths and weaknesses of categorizing literary texts according to their generic features or institutional contexts.

3. Consolidating material from a variety of entries, describe the kinds of educational opportunities available in the ME period. What kinds of education would be available to which children? Who would lead the education and where would the children receive it?

4. How would reading a manuscript differ from reading a printed text? An electronic text? Compare and contrast the implications of manuscript culture upon things contemporary people take for granted, like the access to and

distribution of texts, durability and ease of transport, costs to purchase or to reproduce, communal or shared reading and so on.

5. Based upon the entries in this chapter, identify texts and writers in languages other than ME or Latin. What does this variety indicate about the 'Englishness' of ME literature and culture?

6. *Web Quest*: Using Figure 3.1: Pilgrimages of Medieval Women, trace the routes that medieval women followed to different pilgrimage sites. What were the common destinations, crossroads, and ports of call? Using the web, follow one of the women closely in her pilgrimage and identify the likely sites along her route.

7. *Web Quest*: Investigate scribal practices to identify the stages necessary to copy a manuscript, from preparing the skin, 'pricking' the surface, and copying the text.

8. *Web Quest*: One of the things that distinguishes the study of ME from more recent literatures is its foundation in medieval material culture (the production, distribution, and reading of manuscripts). Make a web search for medieval manuscripts related to the texts and figures in this chapter and record their official names and current physical locations, note their physical characteristics, and ascertain their contents. For example, one of the things you should look for is the manuscript's 'shelf mark'.

9. *Web Quest*: Investigate the life and library of Sir Robert Cotton, an important seventeenth-century antiquarian. What kinds of texts did he collect? What are some of the most famous from his library? Who had access to his library, and what ultimately became of it?

10. *Web Quest*: The study of Lollardy has become central to ME studies because it combines literary, theological, political, and social concerns. As a starting point, do a web search on 'Arundel's Constitutions' to get the full text of this important document. Identify contemporary situations that parallel each of the Constitution's thirteen points, and if so, how are these contemporary situations similar to and different from this medieval precedent?

4 Case Studies in Reading I: Key Primary Literary Texts

Mathew Boyd Goldie, Rider University

Chapter Overview

The following study examines the ways that Middle English (ME) writers work in productive tension with a variety of contemporary concerns: First, Marie de France's *Lanval*, originally written in Norman French but also translated into ME, explores the antagonisms between gender and genre, and society and sexuality, in court culture. Second, representations of the 1381 Revolt describe the principal players, especially the labourers, in ways that shape the reader's interpretation of the rebels' motivations, actions and outcomes. Third, Margery Kempe's *Book*, a story of the worldly and spiritual life of a fifteenth-century woman and the first autobiography in English, shows how her very public mystical experiences reiterate and reveal normative societal codes of gender and Latinity. Finally, the morality play, *Mankind*, whose bawdiness nevertheless teaches religious truths and moral concepts, is set in contrast to *The Tretise of Miraclis Pleyinge*, a contemporary document that objected to plays to illuminate the risks involved in pedagogical methods that have the potential both to reinforce and to disrupt societal norms. Each of these texts, therefore, explores medieval writers' difficult and telling engagements with the world around them.

Marie de France, *Lanval*

Marie de France wrote beast fables, a vision of purgatory, and *lais* (or *lays*) or short romances intended to be sung. Along with her contemporary Chrétien de Troyes, Marie wrote and worked in England during the reign of Henry II (1154–89). Marie's *Lanval* is a *lai*, and its setting, characters and actions exhibit many characteristics that are typical of this genre. The action occurs in two spaces: the civilization of King Arthur's court and the countryside of a magical queen. In a romance, the knight typically leaves civilization and goes out into nature. He often meets a lady and falls in love, and he subjects himself to the woman, which ennobles him. The lady is mysterious and often distant, and the knight undergoes a test, sometimes a quest, for a love that is true and freely given. This romance plot is often seen as a form of 'courtly love', a commonly used term that has recently come under question. A basic feminist analysis of the text might focus on the representation of women in *Lanval*, that is, whether the women in the text conform to or deviate from stereotypes. However, *Lanval* is more complicated and opens itself up to a more sophisticated gender analysis. From the start Marie introduces problems that complicate the romance so that the *lai* becomes an exploration of the tensions between genre and gender, and between society and sexuality. (See Chapter 6: Gender; Chapter 7: Feminism and Gender Studies and Chapter 9: Feminism).

The Court Setting

The majority of the poem's action takes place in Arthur and Guinevere's court. From the start the Arthurian court is not an idealized space (ll. 5–38). The lords and ladies at Cardoel have been forced to retreat from Scottish and Pictish attacks. Arthur 'distributes', in the sense of negotiates the settlement of, 'wives and lands' as an authoritative king should. However, he 'forgets' Lanval, and 'none of [Arthur's] men favored him either'. Lanval has the ideal qualities of a knight in a romance – 'valour', 'generosity', 'beauty' and 'bravery' – but these qualities make the other knights envy him. The narrator suggests a particularly nasty implication of their jealousy: 'if something unpleasant happened to him', they 'would not have been at all disturbed'. Lanval's problem is that he is 'far from his heritage' and has 'spent all his wealth'. He is consequently 'depressed and very worried', and in a direct address to the audience of 'lords', the narrator says that we should not be 'surprised' that Lanval is 'sad' because he is a nobleman from another land (l. 429).

Lanval rides out of Arthur's conflictual court and into the country (ll. 39–133). In romance, nature is not an innocent or sympathetic force. It is a place of 'fairie', of wondrous and sometimes threatening occurrences. Sure enough, when Lanval lies down on the banks of a stream near a field, two beautiful and exquisitely dressed women lead him to their lady, who is wealthier than Octavian or Semiramis, the legendary ruler of Assyrian armies. Somewhat atypical is Marie's explicitly erotic description of the lady. She is 'dressed only in her shift', and 'her whole side was uncovered, / her face, her neck and her bosom'. She immediately and, characteristically for a romance, declares her love for him, and Lanval similarly falls in love with her straight away. As he should, he also submits himself, giving his will over to her, and she gives herself, both body and goods, to him. Notice a little later (ll. 185–90) the innuendo of the 'entremet' that particularly pleases Lanval. So far Marie has diverged from some of the more expected characteristics of a romantic *lai*, including realism that upsets the idealistic harmony of such a place as Arthur's court. Arthur is remiss, the knights are vindictive, and Lanval has run out of money. More typical is the fact that the country outside the court is a place for miraculous happenings and magic. The lady gives Lanval anything he wants. Her gifts redress what Arthur neglected to give Lanval – wife and lands. Accordingly, each location may be contrasted as follows (see Figure 4.1: Comparing the Courts of Arthur and the lady).

Arthur and Guinevere's Court	The Lady's Court
Cardoel	in countryside
place of gift giving	servants of great beauty
gift giving unequal	place of immense wealth
Lanval poor and alone	place of erotic women
knights wish ill of Lanval	love bonds
Lanval far from home	magical promise

Figure 4.1: Comparing the Courts of Arthur and the Lady.

The conditions of the lady's gift are clear (ll. 143–70): Lanval will get whatever he wants, including her body, *only if* he does not reveal her existence or what she has given him. Lanval returns to the Arthurian court, immediately proves his generosity by dispensing gifts to all, and secretly sees his lady (ll. 201–18). The knights, led by Gawain, no longer neglect Lanval. (See Chapter 5: Karma Lochrie, *Covert Operations* and *Heterosyncracies*).

The Ladies' Approach

This happy equilibrium is short-lived, however, because Guinevere notices Lanval's sudden largesse. Guinevere approaches Lanval in an orchard and brazenly offers her love to the knight if he will 'just tell me your desire' (l. 266), but a *lai* is a short romance, and the narrative moves quickly. It is more important to note that her request quite clearly goes to the heart of the tale, for what is his 'desire'? At this precise moment Lanval's desire is to be with his love, so he can't tell Guinevere the truth without breaking his pledge to his lady. One lady, one realm and one desire is being opposed to the other. Lanval refuses Guinevere (ll. 273–74) in part because it would betray Arthur, and Guinevere's response is quite extraordinary (ll. 275–86). She viciously accuses him of faults that have little place in a romantic *lai*: he is a queer, a coward, a cripple and a kind of heretic. Lanval responds just as rashly by breaking his promise – he tells Guinevere about his love. Though Guinevere appears to react in a stereotypical manner as a sexually rapacious and frustrated woman, a more nuanced gender analysis encourages attention to all the implications of her and Lanval's responses. What does Lanval say that is so upsetting to Guinevere? What else might be upsetting to her?

In the next section of the tale (ll. 303–471), from Guinevere's tirade to the approach of the lady's court, the Arthurian court's response to Lanval reveals the *lai*'s complexity through three different characters and groups: Guinevere, the knights in the legal proceeding, and Arthur. In terms of the knights, the process of trying Lanval is similar to actual legal procedures used in the twelfth century, a realistic description unusual in a *lai*. Lanval has to defend himself in court or be 'burned or hanged' (punishments suitable to a common criminal rather than a courtly knight of noble heritage), and the barons (his peers) are to try him. Lanval is summoned to court, Arthur consults with his council on what to do, Gawain has to pledge that Lanval will appear when required and the Duke of Cornwall announces the accusation. Lanval's fellow knights are concerned that he will commit suicide. We see in these actions a complicated realism again take over the genre of romance. Arthur tries to influence the trial, but the most interesting part is his accusation of Lanval (ll. 367–70): He has made a foolish boast and his love is 'too noble' if his lover is indeed more 'beautiful' and 'worthy' than Guinevere. Lanval's relationship to his lady is a threat not only to Guinevere but to Arthur as well.

The opposition between Arthur's court in the city and the lady's extra-ordinarily rich and magically powerful court in the country continues when the lady's maids and the lady herself reappear (ll. 471–628). The approach of these women has a ritualistic quality that echoes the first time Lanval was approached on the banks of the stream: first two girls, then two more and finally the lady. Once they see her, the Arthurian court agrees that the lady and her female courtiers are indeed more beautiful, more rich and more well-mannered in court etiquette than anyone has seen before. Thus Lanval's words to the queen are proven true. His love exists; she is more beautiful and wealthy than Guinevere; and everyone witnesses this truth. Also, if Guinevere and the lady are in some ways stereotypical representations of women throughout literary history, the ending of the *lai* is not. In the closing lines (ll. 629–46), the lady rides out from Arthur's court and, as she departs, Lanval uses a 'great stone' to mount on the horse behind her. The lady has the bridle while he is her passenger, and they ride off to the island of Avalon, the mythical place where Morgan le Fay will transport Arthur upon his death.

The Critique of the Arthurian Court

One way of analysing *Lanval* is to think about class in relation to gender. What is important here is that Lanval's 'love is much too noble', that is, the quality of his own love and not only his love object. One of the conventions of romance, after all, is that the knight's love ennobles his character. Is there something about love itself, or a kind of fictional desire, that is potentially disturbing to the social order? In *Lanval* a combination of the mysterious feminine realm and Lanval's desire is a challenge to Arthurian (or more broadly courtly) society and its inherent contradictions. For example, Arthur initially overlooks Lanval, so the Arthurian court is beset from the beginning by inequality. Lanval becomes integrated into society only because he gets the love and wealth that had been unfairly denied him, and these from a royal and foreign woman. Lanval is no longer overlooked so much that his fellow knights wished him dead. When pressured, the knight has to prove his love against extraordinary accusations of same-sex desire, being a cripple and inducing ungodliness. Courtly society must set in motion extensive legal machinery to prove his guilt, a process that can be manipulated and influenced by those in power. *Lanval* thereby reveals the factors that are hidden but necessary for a society such as Arthur's to function. That is why Lanval and his lady must leave at the end. Their love cannot exist within such a space because it upsets hierarchies and threatens to expose what is kept hidden: that Arthur's patriarchal court is a corrupt, unjust and repressive place. (See Chapter 10: The Ethical Turn: From Discipline to Responsibility.)

The 1381 Revolt

The broader changes in society brought about by famine, plague and anti-fraternal and Lollard dissatisfaction with Church institutions came to a head in the summer of 1381 when villagers and rural workers in Essex, Kent and other areas refused to pay poll taxes (a kind of flat or head tax). (See Chapter 2: Crisis in the Church at Home: Lollardy and Famine and Plague.) They then resisted arrest, killed a number of minor officials and attacked the property of local land and businesses owners. They amassed in London, capturing and killing the Archbishop of Canterbury and the Treasurer. King Richard II, only 14 years old, confronted the rebels and negotiated with them through Wat Tyler, a rebel leader, to bring about peace. Richard II promised the rebels amnesty for their crimes, but when they agreed to leave London, he sent out officials to execute, imprison and fine those involved. This event is known as the Revolt or Uprising of 1381. (See Chapter 2: Labor Unrest and the Peasants' Revolt.) Contemporary writers acknowledged the Revolt, and this section analyses Jean Froissart's *Chroniques*, John Gower's *Vox clamantis*, Geoffrey Chaucer's *Nun's Priest's Tale*, William Langland's *Piers Plowman* and *The Anonimalle Chronicle*.

Froissart, *Chroniques*

Representations of the 1381 Revolt include artworks, poems and chronicle histories. Whether they are poetic responses or more seemingly objective chronicle accounts, these interpretations are written after the fact. Consider, for example, Jean Froissart's *Chroniques*, a history probably written within seven years of the Revolt. Several illuminated copies of Froissart's French chronicle survive, and each usually shows scenes from the Revolt. The image shows two incidents. On the right and facing right, King Richard II addresses the commoners. On the left are London and the forces of Richard

Figure 4.2: The Death of Wat Tyler
[MS Royal 18 E.1 fol. 175r., Jean Froissart's *Chroniques* (1460–80)
(c) All Rights Reserved. The British Library Board. Licence Number: UALASK01]

and the Mayor of London, William Walworth. Walworth is about to mortally injure Wat Tyler. (See Figure 4.2: The Death of Wat Tyler.)

Gower, *Vox clamantis* and Chaucer, the *Nun's Priest's Tale*

John Gower, a contemporary of Geoffrey Chaucer and William Langland, wrote a Latin poem called *Vox clamantis* (or *Voice of One Crying*) that includes descriptions of the Revolt. Gower's *Vox clamantis* is a book-length dream-vision allegory in which a series of dreams contain figures and actions that signify on more than one level. Gower wrote much of the poem in 1378 and returned to it after 1381 to add the first book in which he casts Wat Tyler as a 'Jackdaw', a jay or crow. Gower's allegory depicts the peasant 'mob' as monsters, 'wild beasts', the devil and other evil Biblical figures. He distinguishes among the kinds of beasts – asses, oxen, swine, dogs, cats, foxes and birds – and he describes each in terms of its physical behaviour (See Figure 4.3: Gower's Allegorical Beasts).

The significance of the rebel behaviour is revealed when they act in ways that overturn or usurp their usual natural activities. For example, instead of being harnessed and domesticated, the asses 'jumped through open fields' and were 'wild and untamed'. The animals also want different and more luxurious things than they usually have. Thus, the asses desire 'greater delicacies' rather than the regular 'field grasses'. They also have the effect of 'driving' others out of their homes and try to take the place of the horses.

Geoffrey Chaucer was in England and possibly in London during the Revolt. His only extended (and oblique) representation of this calamitous event is in the *Nun's Priest's Tale* in the *Canterbury Tales*. A beast fable about a rooster called Chaunticleer, one of his wives called Pertelote and a fox named Russel, the *Nun's Priest's Tale* depicts Chaunticleer having a dream about a red beast attacking him, and he and Pertelote disagree about the interpretation of the dream. Ultimately, the fox enters the farmyard and tricks Chaunticleer into singing with his neck outstretched and his eyes closed. Russel grabs him by the neck and runs out into the countryside, and the Nun's Priest describes the farm's widow, daughters, other people, dogs, cattle and hogs all running out after the fox and Chaunticleer (VII. 3375–401). Chaucer draws an analogy between the animals' noise and that made by 'Jakke Straw and his meynee' – a supposed leader of the Revolt and his companions.

William Langland, *Piers Plowman*

The date of 1381 is also important for William Langland's *Piers Plowman*. Like Gower's *Vox clamantis*, *Piers Plowman* is a complex dream-vision poem in which the narrator, Will, has a series of dreams about societal and spiritual matters. It includes animals such as rats, but its focus often lies elsewhere. It is an extended allegory in a series of *'passus'* or steps that are peopled by allegorical figures and institutions: Holy Church, Lady Meed, False, Saint Truth and the unlearned Piers Plowman, among many others. Unlike a simpler allegory, however, *Piers Plowman* explores the meanings of the figures in terms of their strengths, weaknesses and contradictions as they interact with each other. For example, Lady Meed signifies a range of meanings from reward, to repayment, and even to bribery and corruption.

	Asses	*Oxen*	*Swine*	*Dogs*
Behaviours	• unchecked by bridles • jump through all fields • bray and terrify citizens • 'violently wild and untamed' • useless and refuse to carry	• refuse the plowman • do not allow themselves to be led • 'raging' • refuse their duty • 'threatening' foreheads and raised u-horns • emit 'sulpherous flames' • damage city and countryside • leave their labour • lay waste to the farms	• band together • damage the soil • set cities on fire • trampled crops • ruined grain	• only lowly acts • barked at men's heels • bare their teeth • grouped together • lay in 'soft beds'
Desires	• 'vainglory' • 'greater delicacies' than grass • others' homes • to take horses' places • 'jeweled saddles' and combed manes • lions' skins • 'to enjoy lofty things'	• 'to bear their necks upright' • better grain • no work	• fine wines • a real bed • noble buildings in the city	• to devour 'anything and everything fat' • had 'insatiate hunger' • satanic savagery • great 'wrath'

Figure 4.3: Gower's Allegorical Beasts.

The composition history of Langland's poem is also complicated. It is believed that Langland revised the poem several times to produce three major versions called the A, B and C versions. A is a shorter poem of 2,567 lines written about 1377 and primarily deals with community reform. B is a reworking of A some time between 1377 and 1381 with nine added *passus* that almost trebles its length to 7,242 lines. Version C is a reworking of B some time after 1381. The poem survives in about 50 manuscripts in the various versions, so it was relatively popular and widely distributed. Many of these texts also mention the name of a priest associated with the Revolt called John Ball. In one historical chronicle, John Ball is accused of sending a letter to the commoners of Essex that urged them to follow the example of 'Peres Ploughman' and to rebel against the lords (Dobson 1983, 380–81). Langland's central character, it seems, had become a rallying cry for the rebels. This seems to be the motivation behind Langland's revision of the B version of his poem because in the C version he removed much of what may be considered its revolutionary content. (See Chapter 3: William Langland, *Piers Plowman*.)

Piers Plowman is the hero of Langland's poem in that he leads the people to St. Truth. However, in many cases it is difficult to perceive how the rebels could have found him to be an inspiration for their cause. For example, Langland specifically alludes to the Statute of Labourers, a piece of legislation passed in 1351 that extended an earlier Ordinance of Labourers (1349), both of which sought to limit the demands of labourers (ll. 312–20). Because plagues had reduced the population, some labourers were able to demand higher wages and choose where they might work. The Ordinance and Statute set wages at pre-plague levels and prevented labourers from relocating for better, and better paid, work. (See Chapter 2: Famine and Plague.) Langland writes that common labourers cursed the king and his council because their laws punished common men and made them subject to Hunger. In the rest of this *passus*, Langland's allegory explores the nature of work, the role of the estates in labour and what can be done with peasants who refuse to work. The farmers begin to work, but then they slack off and start to drink and sing. A character called Waster appears and curses Piers and his plough. A Knight threatens Waster and the other labourers, but this seems to have little effect. Piers therefore calls upon Hunger, who reduces the workers' demands and restores the former order. However, Hunger refuses to leave and, when Piers complains of hunger himself, Hunger's advice is unrealistic: Don't eat. Finally, Hunger goes to sleep, then the labourers ply him with ale, and the result is societal chaos at the end of the *passus*. (See Chapter 3: *Wynnere and Wastoure*.)

The Anonimalle Chronicle

Several chroniclers recorded their impressions of the 1381 Revolt. One is *The Anonimalle Chronicle*, so called because the author of this French text is unknown. The author's impressions of the Revolt are immediate and vivid, and they are also less overtly opinionated. At the beginning of the excerpt dealing with the uprising (177–79), the author examines the causes of the Revolt and describes the unfair taxes and unjust ways of collecting them that were one of the causes of the rebellion's outbreak. He also describes the roles that Wat Tyler and John Ball played (180), and he shows them to be leaders with clear and not unreasonable ideas. King Richard also is close to the model of a good leader (181–86): He summons his council and listens to their advice, he tries to help his lords escape from the tower, he is 'thoughtful and sad' when he observes London burning, and he attempts to negotiation with the commoners. The peasants in these passages are violent, but they also seem to know clearly what they want. They articulate their demands, and they reject any that they consider unreasonable.

The scene on the grass at Smithfield (186–89), the same scene the Froissart illuminator depicted (see Figure 4.2), is in many ways the climax of *The Anonimalle Chronicle's* narrative of the Revolt. Much of the interest lies in trying to interpret the behaviours of Wat Tyler, the king and the mayor. It also lies in trying to perceive what the anonymous author of the chronicle thought of these three players and their actions. Is Wat Tyler depicted as proud or merely coarse? Given the king's use of Tyler's head and his subsequent punishment of the rebels, is Richard disingenuous when he agrees to the rebel demands? Is Tyler's reaction to the valet justified? Is the mayor's reaction to Tyler's action justified? *The Anonimalle Chronicle* is complex and subtle in its representation of the events.

Comparing Accounts of 1381

We can compare and contrast the authors' representations of the causes of the Revolt, of the leaders of the king's party and the rebels' party and of the rebels. Consider, for instance, how much each author explores the reasons behind the outbreaks of violence. How much attention does each text devote to the causes? How justified or irrational do the causes seem? How appropriate are the violent outbreaks? How is the royal party and the king depicted? What attention does the text pay to the king's motivations and actions? In terms of the rebel leaders, what do the authors describe as their motivations? How rational and thoughtful are they? What are their faults? We can also begin to compare and contrast each author's depictions of the rebel

Representations of Rebels	Organized	Individuated	Rational	Beastly
Jean Froissart, *Chroniques*	X	X	X	
John Gower, *Vox clamantis*	X	X		X
Geoffrey Chaucer, *Nun's Priest's Tale*				X
William Langland, *Piers Plowman*	X	X		X
The Anonimalle Chronicle	X	X	X	

Figure 4.4: Comparing Representations of the 1381 Rebels.

group or groups as follows (See Figure 4.4: Comparing Representations of the 1381 Rebels).

If we look at the chart and re-examine the artworks, poems and chronicle representations of the rebels, we can see that the Froissart illuminator presents the peasants as organized, somewhat individuated and, from the image of their ordered force, rational. Gower also presents the rebels as organized though for the wrong reasons. In *Vox clamantis* they band together, but their reasons for doing so are opaque. Their aspirations to 'greater delicacies', 'riches', freedom from servitude and certain kinds of labour and better food are the products of irrational desires. They are misled by the organizers and are like devilish madmen. Chaucer shares with Gower and Langland the comparison of the rebels to beasts though his tone is less accusatory and malicious. Langland is close to Gower in depicting the rebels as organized, individuated and beastly. Like Gower, he represents them as stepping out of their proper roles in a society held together by the reiteration of people's expected functions within the three estates. *The Anonimalle Chronicle* is one of the most complex. Like the illuminator of the Froissart chronicle, he does not depict the peasants as beasts. Instead, they have demands, they voice them clearly, they reject what they deem unacceptable, and, though certain leaders such as Wat Tyler might be uncouth, they are well-meaning towards the king. However, they are vengeful towards those directly responsible for the taxes and other things they find oppressive. These narrative complexities make the accounts of 1381 Revolt a fascinating and productive study.

Margery Kempe, *The Book of Margery Kempe*

A similar diversity of responses may be found among the people who encountered Margery Kempe in the fifteenth century and among present-day readers of her *Book*. Contemporary readers of *The Book of Margery Kempe* continue to be troubled by the spiritual and social life of a middle class woman in the early fifteenth century because Kempe makes her spiritual experiences so public and so demonstrative. It is not enough for Kempe to have private, 'homely' visions and bodily events, as she calls them; she also publicizes them widely. She cries and roars in crowded areas, she wants to convert her husband and others to her way of life, she appears to preach, she publicly debates with clerics and she makes a great effort to have her story written down. Some readers respond to her exertions reactively and wish she would be quiet or at least private – until, perhaps, they notice that the men of her book share those same sentiments. These clerical and municipal authorities also want Kempe to conform to stereotypical women's roles and spiritual behaviours.

Margery and the Performative

The concept of the *performative* can help us to think through the issues related to Kempe's spirituality. The performative, as articulated by theorists such as Judith Butler, Eve Sedgwick and others, suggests that words and gestures are not simply expressions of an individual's inner emotions and thoughts. Instead, they make things happen. The most common example is of the wedding vows where the moment of saying 'I do' actually changes the social and relational status of the speakers. These words are not original to the speakers, and they don't merely have an effect. The moment of saying them is the moment of effect when the speakers themselves as well as their relationship to each other become different; their words, in effect, change reality. In addition, a society's dominant norms, which we can term *hegemony* and are more implicit than explicit, are maintained by constant reiteration. So in saying 'I do', couples not only change their legal and social status to being married partners, but they also implicitly maintain the legal and social system of marriage itself: property rights, legal privileges, rights over a partner's body, public recognition of commitment, heteronormativity and so on. (See Chapter 6: The Body.)

The concept of the performative does more, however, than provide another way of describing society because it suggests that people's words and gestures are never wholly individual, are not based on anything natural, nor are founded upon a universal indisputable truth. Instead, words and actions conform to society's hegemonic rules and norms, which are themselves sustained by repeated reiteration, constant citation and continued performance. The question then becomes not so much where these rules all started but how society's norms continue so powerfully to shape our lives, even when we are not aware of them or their repetition. The concept of the performative suggests, however, that social hegemony is not an impregnable or unified whole but can contain contradictions. Moreover, individuals can, again unintentionally as much as intentionally, deviate from hegemony. These performative actions might even reveal the structures (and reiterations) that sustain these norms and thus enable a critique of medieval hegemonic practices. (See Chapter 6: Identity Formation and Performance and Spectacle.)

Hegemony: Gender and Latinity

What might we consider hegemonic in the ME period? Two powerful societal and literary forces come to bear on Margery Kempe: *gender* and *Latinity*. They sometimes work together, and sometimes they clash. First, by *gender* we can think of the expectations that confronted a middle-class medieval woman in England. She was expected not only to marry, manage a household with children and often look out for her husband's business affairs but also to generate income independently of him. Second, as Chaucer's *Wife of Bath's Prologue* illustrates, according to *Latinity*, women exist in a social and spiritual hierarchy with virgins at the top, widows below them, married women next and unmarried sexually active women at the bottom. (See Chapter 9: The Place of Chaucer's Wife of Bath.) A woman should be subject to her husband and men in general. Latinity designates the institutional Church and religious discourses that attempted to structure fully not only religious but also secular life. Latinity thus also includes a linguistic hierarchy in which Latin is the sign of literacy and authority, whereas vernacular English is not as authoritative and comes to be suspect due to Wycliffitism. A religious woman was often the object of Latinity's formulations, yet, excepting women saints, a women could not really contribute to a discussion about religion, gender or a woman's place in society. If she did, she likely would be cast as potentially heretical in England because she would most likely compose and read in the vernacular (and frequently orally) rather than in Latin or in writing. If she were to lead a religious life, she would be expected to be decorous, quiet and preferably enclosed or isolated from human community (an anchoress). If a woman wanted to contribute her life story to the Latin discourse of the Church, her narrative would need to conform to the generic conventions describing saintly women. According to literary norms of Latinity, the religious woman must demonstrate that (1) she has always had religious visions or other revelations, (2) she discloses them in confidence to a male and supportive confessor (a religious authority and her spiritual superior) and (3) her own life and story are only important in that they reveal the truth of God to a potential audience so that it may also follow a righteous path. (See Chapter 6: Transmission and Authority.)

Kempe's actions and words are performative in the sense that they reiterate but also expose hegemonic norms of gender and Latinity. In what follows, we will examine the interactions of gender and Latinity because a private life was considered more suitable for a religious woman working within the vernacular whereas Kempe leads a public, mixed life of religious and secular vocations within a context where Latin religious authorities were largely male. First, Kempe's performed words and actions complicate but also enable her to establish an independent status as both a married and religious woman. Second, when she carries this identity outside the home to public spaces, she runs into further complications that she must overcome. Third, when she encounters powerful religious male authorities who work within institutions based on Latinate authority, Kempe has to adapt her performance to a new set of secular and religious approaches to gender and Latinity in order to transform the world around her. This she achieves with varying degrees of success.

Kempe's Personal Crisis

Kempe is a combination of wife and middle-class business woman who comes from a fairly powerful and wealthy family in King's Lynn in East Anglia. In the first chapter of *The Book of Margery Kempe* (Staley 2001, 6–8), we learn that she 'went out of her mind' following the birth of a child (Kempe had 14 children) and an incomplete confession interrupted by an insensitive priest. She had visions of devils and 'slandered' all her family and friends until Jesus appeared to her and restored her wits. After she regained her faculties, her husband gave her back the keys to the household 'buttery', despite the servants' protests, when it became clear that she would not simply give away all of the household's goods. A 'buttery' such as this was a large, possibly room-sized, pantry, a storage area for all the household goods. In effect, Kempe is being restored to managing the whole household, a position that was rightfully hers as overseer of the most important family economic site.

Kempe continues to live in a manner fitting for a middle-class woman but that we come to see as prideful (Chapters 8–10). That is, her taste for secular fashion clashes with religious codes of behaviour. At this point, Kempe is still tied to her high social position as the mayor of Lynn's daughter. She also tries to practice brewing, a traditional business for women, and then she attempts milling, but both businesses fail. Kempe finally realizes that she is meant for a spiritual life, but becoming a nun, the traditional role for religious women, is not an option. Instead, she has to perform spiritual actions and religious work while still maintaining a secular life.

Such a feat requires Kempe to negotiate constantly between the norms of a middle-class wife and female religious. She has given up money-making, but she is still married and has children, both of which tie her to her body and to the world in this life. In her pursuit of spiritual purity, Kempe renounces sexual pleasure, which takes some time, as does her husband's trans-formation. She initially gives up 'desire to commonly flesh with her husband' but not the 'debt of matrimony' itself (10–11). That is, she is legally bound to have sex with her husband according to medieval custom, but doing so detracts from her spirituality and he initially refuses to abstain. Her con-versations with Jesus, God and Mary also are performative in the sense that they help to resolve these problems. In Chapter 11 (18–20), the demands of marriage and spirituality clash once again, but Jesus' words to Kempe, which she repeats to her husband, move them to find a solution. Her husband wants to sleep with her, but she says she would rather 'be slain than we should turn again to our uncleanness'. In concession, he ultimately states three demands: He wants her to sleep in the same bed with him, eat on Fridays (she has forsaken food and drink on that day) and to pay off his debts, and he will then allow her to go on a pilgrimage to Jerusalem. Kempe prays, and Jesus tells her that her fasting has in fact worked. She can now concede to her husband that she will eat on Friday, and she will pay off his debts so long as he promises not to ask her to fulfil the marriage debt again. Her husband agrees, but murmurs, 'Thou art no good wife'.

Kempe also struggles with the fact that she has had children. In terms of her spiritual life, Kempe sees her children as a sign of her having sex, and they therefore tie her to affairs of the earth rather than a contemplative life. Although she is ashamed to talk with Jesus because she is still 'paying the debt' to her husband and having children, Jesus assures, 'believe right well that I love wives also, and specially those wives who would live chaste, if they might have their will'. Again, her mystical conversations perform a role of reconciliation, for Jesus tells her she should not have any more children (29). He outlines the religious hierarchy of virgins at the top, but he comforts her with the idea that he also loves her. His mother, the Virgin, also appears to model for her – perform for her – the role of religious woman who is also a mother. (See Chapter 3: Virginity.)

Kempe's Public Spirituality

Kempe's spiritual life is also performative in the sense that it helps her to change the structure of society around her. Although she is still a married woman, the essential nature of the marriage has changed. Kempe might be seen to be carving out a space within marriage for a middle-class woman who wants to remain married but also wants to give up the marriage debt, recon-cile her role as mother and practice her religious life. However, as we can see, the recognition of this new space is limited to her bedroom and household with her husband, a constricted, narrow, private sphere. Encouraged in her spiritual conversations, Kempe soon expands that sphere of influence.

In Chapter 15 (24–7), Jesus tells her that she should wear white, which would be a very visible, public sign of virginity. Kempe rightly considers that if she dresses like a chaste woman, 'I dread that the people will slander me. They will say I am a hypocrite and wonder upon me'. Note at this stage that the reader's appreciation of Kempe's situation is different from her audiences within her *Book*. We know that she has an agreement with her husband and is living a chaste life, but people of her own time will not understand how a married woman with children could be chaste or, further, a virgin. However, the medieval spiritual hierarchy for women was not a set, inflexible series of levels. A woman could move up and down it according to her status. Unlike today when we think of virginity as something one 'loses' forever, medieval notions of sexuality were more alive to a person's inner state. Kempe has already ascended from a married woman having sex to a married woman living a chaste life. It is an orderly step then to become a chaste woman on a par with being a virgin. Indeed, by wearing white, she is attempting to perform virginity. Nevertheless, Kempe's narrative highlights the fact that an internal change is not enough. It would in fact be hypocritical for her to be chaste in her private life and not in her public appearance. Appearances, something for which she was previously criticized, are still important, but here they have become important because they affirm and declare her new spirituality. Jesus advises Kempe at about the same time to visit the Bishop of Lincoln so he can perform the religious rites usually associated with widows entering a nunnery. In doing so, Kempe not only wants the ceremony in order to transform her status, but such a ceremony also alters the rite itself. Advised by clerks who had earlier asked Kempe 'many hard questions', the bishop is hesitant about performing such a different rite, this time for a married woman. Kempe's efforts to have her new status publicly acknowledged are frustrated, and she has to accept spiritual acknowledgment of future virginal status (39). She turns her efforts to perform her spirituality publicly in other directions. Each time her inner, 'homely' visions reiterate hegemonic norms and, by making them fully transparent, threaten to disclose underlying contradictions in gendered expectations and Latinity.

In terms of Latinity and its paradigms, Kempe's performance of the mystical life crosses the border between her middle-class gendered status and the religious life, extends the parameters of acceptable religious action and reveals the contradictions within Latinity's power. First, her mystical life is very intimate, physical and often painfully violent. As Caroline Walker Bynum has pointed out in *Holy Feast and Holy Fast*, this was an acceptable path for holy women in the later Middle Ages. However, as *The Book of Margery Kempe* reveals, Kempe gradually and insistently turns her inner life outward. Her spirituality performs again in the sense of transforming the spaces and society around her. Second, several of Kempe's revelations make clear that her mystical experiences are not disembodied. At one point, Jesus observes to her that 'you have so great compassion for my flesh that I must need have compassion for your flesh' (134). Most significantly, Kempe's spiritual performances include 'plenteous tears and many violent sobbings' (11). When she makes the long and arduous pilgrimage to Jerusalem, she comes to Mount Calvary, the place of crucifixion. There 'she fell down and cried with loud voice, wonderfully turning and twisting her body on every side, spreading her arms abroad as if she should have died, and could not keep herself from crying or from these bodily movings' (51–2). Kempe is troubled by her reactions, but she also comes to understand them as 'free gifts of God' that she should in turn impart to others (24). Kempe's intense spirituality is performative in the sense that it not only changes herself, it is also very public and transforms the spaces around her. Sometimes the onlookers are sympathetic, as with Julian of Norwich and Kempe's confessors. Sometimes, however, the public is antagonistic, and the effect of Kempe's witnessed spirituality is to demonstrate a further difficulty of Kempe's experiences for herself and to expose the small-mindedness and understandable but ultimately mistaken awareness of others. The publicity of her spirituality reveals others' shortcomings.

Kempe's Confrontations with Authority

Kempe's public spirituality is most revealing when she encounters the clerks and other members of the Church because she confronts expectations about how a woman should experience and demonstrate a spiritual life. Often her behaviours expose a nexus of religious and gender preconceptions and ingrained norms. At Canterbury 'she was greatly despised and reproved because she wept so hard, both by the monks and the priests and by secular men', and 'her husband went away from her as if he had not known her and left her alone among them' (21–3). A powerful monk says he wishes she 'were enclosed in a house of stone so no man could speak with [her]'. Soon, the whole town is threatening to burn her as a heretic. Fortunately, two men rescue her and take her back to an inn. Her failure to transform public spaces seems also to play out in another situation, in Leicester (81–8), when the mayor puts her in jail because of her crying and outbursts. The steward of the Earl of Leicester threatens 'to oppress her and lie with her', and her travelling companions are also imprisoned. Eventually, Kempe has to appeal her case to abbots, who test her on her Articles of Faith to prove that she is not a Wycliffite. (See Chapter 3: Lollardy.)

Kempe's encounters with the clergy in York (chapters 50–52) are also performative in that her words demonstrate her orthodox spirituality and the hypocrisy of those around her, furthering her efforts to have others recognize her spirituality and to change their own sense of Latinity and its religious precepts. When she is then brought before the Archbishop of York (90–95), one of the most powerful church leaders in England, Kempe demonstrates her ability at not only getting out of very dangerous situations but also at strategically defeating her opponents. Again, she uses their Latinity, their religious discourse, against them. First, the Archbishop's 'household' scorns her, swearing at her and accusing her of Lollardy. She admonishes them for swearing, and they leave 'as if they were ashamed'. Second, Kempe is then brought before a full court of the Archbishop, the doctor and clerk who examined her before, and many other clerics. She is tested again on the Articles of Faith to see if she is a Wycliffite, but she knows them very well and fully agrees with them. Finally, in exasperation, the clerks say, 'We know well that she knows the Articles of our Faith, but we will not suffer her to dwell among us, for the people have great faith in her dalliance, and perhaps she might pervert some of them'. Finally, the Archbishop tries to get her to leave his diocese and, when she refuses, he tries to get her to swear that she will not 'teach nor challenge the people in my diocese'. Again she refuses, citing Biblical authority for her 'to speak of God'. A clerk steps in and counters that the Bible also says that a woman 'shouldn't preach'. Kempe responds again, 'I preach not, sir; I go in no pulpit. I use but communication and good words'. Another interjects that she tells bad tales about priests. When the Archbishop orders her to disprove this, she instead retells a tale about a priest who does not live up to priestly ideals. Thus, each time religious authority figures try to trap her, she out-manoeuvres them. Her words to them are performative in the sense that she uses their charges against her spirituality against them. At the same time, she publicly and effectively turns people away from their attacks and changes their minds about her. Her responses also gradually pare away her oppositions' stratagems until the naked power that lies behind their efforts is exposed. The Archbishop finally just wants to get rid of her from his area and pays someone to do it. (See Chapter 3: Archbishop Thomas Arundel.)

Writing *The Book of Margery Kempe*

By way of conclusion, we might note the complicated nature of *The Book of Margery Kempe* itself, and the internal narrative of Kempe's attempts at having her story written down can also be read in terms of the performative. It has been called the first autobiography in English, yet it is written in the third person; Kempe is referred to throughout the book as 'this creature'. Kempe struggled to have the book written down more than once. These efforts are closely parallel to the performative aspects of spirituality elsewhere in her *Book*.

The priest-scribe recounts the complicated story of how he came to write the *Book* in his prefatory materials (3–6). After an Englishman, married and living in the Low Countries or what is now Germany, wrote a near illegible version of Kempe's *Book* and died soon thereafter, her second scribe, the priest, offered to read and rewrite the illegible manuscript. At that time, however, 'there was so much evil spoken of this creature and of her weeping' that the slander affects the priest-scribe so that he becomes too frightened to continue. In the end, only divine grace restores his resolve and his eyesight and enables him spiritually and physically to read the text. He goes on not only to rewrite the earlier text but also to write the second book. That is, Kempe's spirituality not only affects her but transforms her scribe and, in a sense, transforms the very text of her narrative so that it becomes legible to her scribe and communicable to her audience. (See Chapter 3: Margery Kempe, *The Book of Margery Kempe*.)

Overall, Kempe's words and actions are performative in the sense that they alter the spaces and peoples around her as well as her own subjectivity, yet these words and actions are often not of Kempe's own volition. They are Jesus' words or God's commands. Sometimes they make her able still to be a 'good wife' and a religious woman, but in each case the context around her has to change in order to accommodate a slightly different set of gender norms and religious practices. In many cases Kempe's words perform in the sense that they might be seen to reiterate and re-enforce social hegemony. When she encounters Latinity in religious authority figures, her words often paradoxically have the effect of calling clerics to a seemingly more moral and truer religious understanding. In several instances, however, her words perform in the sense that they expose the self-serving and corrupt aspects of medieval gender and Latinity.

Mankind and *The Tretise of Miraclis Pleyinge*

Various kinds of play – performance spectacles – were important in the ME period, from occasional jesters and acrobats at fairs to the large-scale productions of morality and mystery or cycle plays. The anonymous fifteenth-century play *Mankind* is thought to be associated with the cathedral of Bury St. Edmunds, a large and important religious abbey in Suffolk in the East of England. Most plays were important events that drew people from all parts of society and bolstered the monetary and spiritual economy of the town or area that staged them. However, a few people objected to these forms of entertainment precisely because they were popular. In what follows, we will examine what *Mankind* teaches audiences and how it teaches them in the light of a contemporary critique of plays, *The Tretise of Miraclis Pleyinge*. (See

Chapter 3: Mystery, Morality, and Miracle Plays and Chapter 6: Performance and Spectacle.)

Mankind is typical of morality plays in that it dramatizes a perpetual struggle between good and evil for possession of the individual soul. This battle, which involves burlesque and bawdy humour in *Mankind*, is heightened by the threatened imminence of death after the brevity of life. The characters in morality plays are personified figures of human virtues, vices and institutions. On one side in *Mankind* is Mercy, the embodiment of the last possible hope for humankind. On the other side are the mischievous and devilish characters, Mischief and his 'helpers' New Guise, Nowadays and Nought. The play later introduces another character to assist these forces in the figure of Titivillus. In the middle, pulled between the two sides, is Mankind, a simple farmer who represents all humanity. *Mankind* can be divided into three main parts: lines 1–412 in which the characters are introduced and Mercy warns Mankind about temptation, lines 413–733 in which the devilish characters successfully cause Mankind's downfall and lines 734–913 in which Mercy redeems him. Thus, the narrative structure goes from forewarning, to fall, to redemption.

The *Tretise* and Wycliffite Concerns

The Tretise of Miraclis Pleyinge is a Wycliffite text and is unique in that it addresses medieval drama at length and in detail. It is structured in the fashion of an academic discourse. After an introduction, it presents an opposing argument point by point and then, taking each point in turn, attempts to demonstrate the falsity of those arguments. That is, it presents orthodox defences of plays and then tries to demolish those contentions. Even though the *Tretise* author is arguing against miracle, that is cycle, plays and not morality plays such as *Mankind*, it is interesting to examine *Mankind* in the light of the *Tretise*. By trying an experiment to defend the play against the *Tretise*'s charges, we can gain insights into potential faults in the Wycliffite objections to plays. More important, defending the play against the charges the *Tretise* brings against miracle plays foregrounds the topic of pedagogy, a key concern for the Lollards. Ultimately, it will help answer the following questions: What does the morality play *Mankind* teach? Are the methods it uses to suggest those lessons effective, or do they detract from the message? Can a convincing argument against the *Tretise* author be presented? (See Chapter 3: Lollardy and John Wyclif.)

First, let us understand the *Tretise* author's objections to plays. The introductory section lists the following (264–66):

- The miracles that Christ and the saints performed were effective for belief, so to use those miracles in 'bourde [jest] and pleye' is against that belief and is using the Lord's name in vain.
- Christ meant his miracles in earnest; to make play and plays out of them will take away the fear of sin.
- Our life on earth in imitation of Christ should be full of penance because Christ gave his body for us, so to play in ways that 'reversen penaunce' is to reverse Christ's works.
- The plays reverse the discipline, respect and the meekness we should have for Christ and Biblical teachings.
- Plays are 'lustis of the felyssh and mirthe of the body', not spiritual devotion; no one can serve both 'masters'.
- The plays have the effect on audiences of making them lecherous and of encouraging debate among themselves rather than simply being patient and fearing God.
- Laughter at the plays is taking the Word of God as a joke.

In the listing of presumably orthodox defences of miracle plays and the attempt to overturn these defences (267–72), more of the *Tretise* author's objections come clear:

- A defence of the plays is offered that they are for the 'worship of God'. The *Tretise* author objects that they are not for this purpose but give more pleasure in this world rather than looking forward to the next, and they are like idolatry in that they are worship of a false representation or else they are either empty signs or lies.
- Another defence is that people viewing the plays will recognize how corrupting and persuasive the devil characters are and will therefore avoid their own vices such as pride. The *Tretise* author sees the opposite effect: Not only are individuals but whole communities are 'perverted' by plays and turned towards earthly 'vanitiees'.
- Another defence is that the plays lead people to devotion as shown by their weeping. The *Tretise* author objects that audiences are only weeping at the plays themselves and not out of contrition for their own sins.
- A further defence is offered that plays are better than other forms of play; they are effective in reaching people who are attracted to games and are more effective than other religious representations such as paintings because they are live. The *Tretise* author objects that plays are in fact worse than other forms of play because people will be led to confuse holy ideas with sinful ones. In fact, some paintings are better because they do not lead people to bodily 'shrewidnesse' (wickedness) because they are less lively and life-like.

Mankind's Characters

The character Mankind's problem in *Mankind* is clear; he is of mixed estate. In his opening speech (ll. 186–204), he introduces himself: 'My name is Mankinde. I have my composicion / Of a body and of a soull, of condicion contrarye. / Betwix them tweyn is a grett division'. He knows he should 'renunce' 'voluntarye dysires', and it grieves him 'To se the flesch prosperouse and the soull trodyn under fote'. He therefore appeals to Mercy to help him, and she counsels (ll. 226–44): 'The temptacion of the flesch ye must resist like a man'. Before she leaves him, she adds (ll. 293–96), 'Be ware of New Gyse, Nowadays and Nought. / Nise [foolish] in ther aray, in language they be large; / To perverte yowr condicions all the menys shall be sowte'. She also points out in particular to look out of Titivillus (ll. 301–304), who is 'worst of them all'.

In the second part of the play, these devilish characters tempt and taunt Mankind. Mankind initially repels New Guise, Nowadays and Nought with his spade and resolves to keep them away with God's help (ll. 376–412). However, Mischief calls in Titivillus, the fiend, to help. Titivillus, stalking Mankind invisibly, puts a wooden board under the ground so Mankind cannot dig with his spade, steals his seeds and eventually takes away the spade so that Mankind becomes frustrated (ll. 525–550). When Mankind prays for help, Titivillus interrupts his piety. Discouraged in all respects and exhausted, Mankind bursts out that 'Of labure and preyer, I am nere irke of both; / I will no more of it, thow Mercy be wroth'. He chooses instead to sleep (ll. 551–88). These actions are all hints of Mankind's imminent fall. The play suggests he verges on anger, one of the seven deadly sins, in his defence against New Guise, Nowadays and Nought; hubris in thinking he can do this without God's help; and sloth in that he decides to sleep instead of praying and going to church. Tellingly, it is the needs of the body, with Titivillus' help, that make him interrupt his prayers. Titivillus, still invisible, whispers in the sleeping Mankind's ear that Mercy is discreditable and dead because he stole a horse, ran away from his master and was hanged for the offence. He advises Mankind to renounce Mercy and, ironically, 'Arise and aske mercy of New Gyse, Nowadays, and Nought' (ll. 589–606). Mankind awakes and, fed up and believing Titivillus, goes looking for the three rascals. They are happy to get their revenge on Mankind when he asks 'mercy' (l. 658). They humiliate him, convict him in a mock trial and Mischief makes Mankind swear to commit adultery, rob, steal and kill (ll. 661–725).

Mercy's reappearance the turning point in the play and begins Mankind's path to redemption. Upon finding him again, Mercy laments Mankind's condition (ll. 734–71), complaining that 'Mankinde is so flexibull'. In a thematically significant play on words, which is typical of some of the clever writing in this play, Mercy says he is 'Man onkinde'. When Mankind appears again before Mercy (ll. 811–900), he falls to his knees and prays for forgiveness. Although he does not consider himself worthy, Mercy grants him pardon. In the final scene (ll. 901–15), Mercy, alone on stage, addresses the audience and advises the people gathered there to consider their own sins, to remember that all the world is vanity and to seek the everlasting life after death. Thus, Mankind's temptation, fall and redemption functions as an *exemplum* – a warning and a model – for all humanity.

Structure and Subversion

The overall structure of the play in itself seems to be a defence against several of the charges that the *Tretise of Miraclis Pleyinge* brings against dramatic performances. It uses the allegorical figures to teach contrition, penance and the right path to Mercy. It suggests, in orthodox fashion, that Mercy can redeem all, even the most sinful and despairing. However, the ribald characters complicate such an easy defence. After all, they seduce Mankind and might appeal to audience members. They are funny, clever, witty and cunningly subversive. The most outstanding feature of *Mankind* is its sophisticated and obscene word play, much of which includes the audience. Indications in the play suggest it was staged in an enclosed space such as a hall, so the audience might have been sitting all around the play area and thus close to, if not in the midst of, the action. For example, the ribald characters parody Mercy right in the play's opening. Immediately after Mercy's eloquent and Latinate speech at the opening, Mischief pokes fun at it precisely for being so aureate (ll. 45–72). Slightly later (l. 124), New Guise says disgustedly of Mercy's speech that it is too 'full of Englisch Laten'. Nowadays asks Mercy to translate into scholarly language some very scatological words and eventually tells him '*Osculare fundamentum!*' or 'kiss my ass!' (ll. 128–42). Later, these characters invite the audience to join them in an obscene 'Cristemese songe' (ll. 331–43). Before Titivillus enters, New Guise, Nowadays and Nought also take up a collection from the audience, thus implicating the people watching the play in paying to bring on the most diabolical character, the one who leads to Mankind's downfall (ll. 459–70). Other audience interactions are incidental, yet they continue to entangle the viewers in the devilish machinations. For example, when Mankind is finally overwhelmed with frustration and lies down to sleep, Titivillus warns the audience to be quiet or else he will fine them, and besides, they will see a clever 'game' before they leave (ll. 589–93). Presumably the audience keeps quiet while he corrupts the sleeping Mankind.

Is it possible that the *Tretise* author is correct in condemning plays because they appeal to an audience's 'lustis of the fleyssh and mirthe of the body'?

Surely the audience finds funny at least some of these instances of wordplay and of parody. The *Tretise* author also wants to ban plays because they teach disrespect for the word of God, and it is in places precisely these kinds of words from Mercy's mouth at which the other characters poke fun. There is too much pleasure gained from sympathizing with the nefarious characters. What might be worse, the *Tretise* author continues, is that plays, in including so much live bodily (and bawdy) humour in front of large audiences, are worse than any other form of art because they are more effective in corrupting large groups of people than other art forms. Moreover, perhaps the play is only teaching that, as New Guise says, quoting Psalms, '*Cum sancto sanctus eris et cum perverso perverteris*' ('With the holy, you will be holy, and with the perverse you will be perverted', l.324).

One way of resolving the problem and defending the play against the *Tretise*'s objections is to try to discern how much and at what points in the play the audience sympathizes with Mischief, New Guise, Nowadays, Nought and Titivillus. This is a difficult consideration. Some of the answer may have to do with when these characters cross a line, not so much in terms of propriety but more in terms of morality. First, for instance, even if the audience shares in some of the fun of corrupting Mankind, surely they do not like and will not follow Mischief when he encourages him to steal and murder. Part of the fun lies in the gleeful obviousness of Mischief's machinations. Second, we might also mount a fairly strong defence of the play if we consider that audiences can enjoy, for example, the wordplay that parodies Mercy's devout and authoritative speeches while, at the same time, having a critical distance on the mockery. It seems that the *Tretise* author underestimates the audience's emotions and intelligence in this respect. Finally, some critical distance on the play may be reinforced by how it is staged. Unfortunately, we have no idea from the surviving manuscript as to how evil the bad characters looked nor how exaggerated their actions might have been. Nevertheless, it is interesting to consider how the play might be staged, costumed, and performed to encourage some critical distance from the action, a measure of distance that might allow both recognition and repulsion.

Playing and Pedagogy

What, in the end, does the morality play *Mankind* teach? Is its humour and ribald action more or less effective in conveying its messages? These are important questions to consider. *The Tretise of Miraclis Pleyinge* objects that people are misled and enjoy the action of plays rather than turning to themselves, examining their own faults, and being contrite. We might conclude that this at least overlooks the fact that the character Mankind, our representative, models the very human propensity towards corruption, yet he returns back to a better path. It also seems to underestimate the ability of audiences to see and sympathize with derision and temptation yet not imitate the actions that follow. The ultimate question in siding with the *Tretise* or not is whether it is bad enough just to have sinful ideas in mind. The case of *The Tretise of Miraclis Pleyinge* suggests the perils of undervaluing audience intelligence and the ability of play watchers and readers more generally to comprehend complex and even contradictory texts. *Mankind* and the *Tretise* might serve as a warning to present-day audiences of medieval literature not to delimit the richness of themes, characters, and styles in what we read. Instead, we can pay attention to the complexities of how the texts react to contemporary concerns about gender, sexuality, revolution and pedagogy – concerns that we share today but that are also subtly different at this moment in the Middle Ages. By doing so, we can avoid stereotypes about medieval literature and medieval societies at the same time that we understand more clearly another time and our own.

Study Questions

1. Define the following terms in your own words:

   - Wheel of Fortune
   - Romance
   - *Lai*
   - The Three Estates
   - Dream-Vision
   - Lady Meed
   - Hegemony
   - Performative
   - Latinity

2. Marie de France's *Lanval* is an unconventional romance in many ways. As you reread, consider:

   - What is atypical about *Lanval* in terms of the settings?
   - What is atypical about *Lanval* in terms of the characters?
   - What is society (the court, social organization and social processes) like in the *lai*?
   - What is sexuality like in the *lai*?

3. Gather all the moments in *Lanval* when the narrator comments on the action. Analyse them. At what moments in the story does the narrator choose to comment? What does the narrator say? How individual and distinct is the omniscient narrator? Does he or she have a character? Can you identify the narrator with the author, Marie de France, or is the narrator impersonal?

4. Given the traditional expectations of a romance *lai*, how does *Lanval* both meet and also violate those expectations?

5. Consider the illustration of Richard II with the 1381 rebels in London:

   - Describe the rebels' forces in the scene on the right. Do they appear threatening? Organized? Individuated? What expressions can you see on the faces?
   - Describe King Richard II in the scene on the right. What appears to be his attitude towards the rebels?
   - Describe King Richard II and the men accompanying him in the scene on the left. What appears to be his attitude towards the action occurring in front of him? Compare and contrast Richard in the left scene with Richard in the right scene.
   - Describe the action between Mayor Walworth and Wat Tyler. What is Wat Tyler doing while the Mayor wields his sword?

6. The accounts of the 1381 Revolt show how the authors' points of view affect the interpretation of the events. Take a recent political event in the news and compare different written accounts of that event. In what ways do these recent news stories parallel the different accounts of the 1381 Revolt?

7. Consider the representation of peasants in the same and other dream-visions, fables and other poems. You might look at other *Canterbury Tales*, Marie de France's fables or other *lais*, *Sir Gawain and the Green Knight*, cycle plays, Sir Thomas Malory's *Morte d'Arthur*, or other texts. Are peasants commonly associated with beasts or beast-like attributes? Are other characters such as knights or ladies associated with these attributes?

8. Describe at least three ways Margery Kempe disturbed the gender expectations of her time. How did members of Kempe's society react to her actions? Similarly, describe three ways that Kempe dealt with the social and religious obstacles she encountered.

9. What are the primary arguments *The Tretis of Miraclis Pleyinge* makes against 'playing' of different types? What assumptions motivate those arguments? How does Mankind address those criticisms, either implicitly or explicitly?

10. Web Quest: Taking *The Tretis of Miraclis Pleyinge* as a critique of a form of medieval popular culture (drama), compare and contrast the *Tretis* with (for example) the controversy surrounding violence in contemporary video games and their effects on young people. Use the web to find (and document) accounts pro, neutral, and con about the effect of video and console games on contemporary game players. Do any of the contemporary accounts summon arguments similar or complementary to those marshalled in the *Tretise* against plays and play-going? How do contemporary arguments compare to those made in the *Tretise*, and upon what basis do contemporary critics make their cases against gaming?

Case Studies in Reading II: Key Literary and Theoretical Texts

Gail Ashton, Independent Scholar

Perhaps the greatest difficulty in writing on the impact of key thinkers or seminal works in any field is making the selections. Undoubtedly, readers will be able to track my own inclinations and preferred methods of research between the lines of my explorations in this chapter while the claims of those who are, by necessity, omitted (Paul Strohm and Louise. O. Aranye Fradenburg to name but two) are pressing. However partial the selection, my aim is to examine crucial and persistent concerns in medieval studies: that is, notions of history and historicist enquiry, the competing claims of the present on the past (and vice versa), and the impact of contemporary theory on 'past' texts. I recognize that any summary of complex argument is potentially reductive and the broadly chronological sweep of my chosen theorists is equally hazardous, especially given my assertion of discontinuities rather than progression. Nevertheless, I begin with Lee Patterson in order to establish some fundamental and influential ideas before opening out to Carolyn Dinshaw, Karma Lochrie, Jeffrey Jerome Cohen and postcolonial theory.

Lee Patterson, *Chaucer and the Subject of History* (1991)

The influence of Lee Patterson's *Chaucer and the Subject of History* (1991) on medieval studies is inestimable. Patterson's argument in this key work rests upon an understanding of Chaucer as uniquely placed to critique the complex and competing interrelationship between 'the individual and the social' in late medieval England (425). Chaucer, he says, offers us the traditional 'universals' of literature. At exactly the same time, Chaucer's writing is 'socially contingent' (423), concerned with 'attitudes' and the particularities of his historical context rather than moral truths (168), even though he rarely explicitly references events specific to his own world (24). This middle ground vantage point comes from the ambivalence of Chaucer's own social position. Patterson infers from the life records that Chaucer participated in a variety of groups (merchants, courtly or aristocratic, and civil servants), yet remained marginal to them all as a 'slightly distanced insider' (198). In this way, he was able to negotiate the universal and the particular that so interests Patterson. To support this view, Patterson argues throughout for a literary development that sees Chaucer start as a 'makere' of courtly poems that are deeply invested in the ideologies of chivalry and nobility, before moving out from under this constraint to find a mode of writing 'at once oppositional and non-political' in the *Canterbury Tales* (49, see also 53–59). (See Chapter 7: Marxism to New Historicism.)

History and Subjectivity: The Place of Texts

I begin with these ideas to flag a potential fault-line – one that tracks its way throughout this chapter and its other seminal thinkers – in Patterson's otherwise invigorating and far reaching thesis about the nature of medieval history and subjectivity. The question of whether Chaucer is a radical or an orthodox writer continues to exercise present-day medieval studies and is probably irresolvable. However, the extent to which so many theorists seem to allow 'Chaucer' to stand as a key to late medieval literature is especially problematic. There are, too, implications for Patterson's idea of a history that presents as invariably local. His readings of Chaucer's texts depend on a swirl of other writings and specific fourteenth-century occurrences. Within this 'web', Patterson makes connections that depend, in part, upon inference and imagination. He claims that though there is no direct evidence in, say, the *Miller's Tale*, that links it to the Uprising of 1381, this is, nonetheless, the event influencing Chaucer as he wrote it.

Despite this, the impact of Patterson's methodology on contemporary medieval studies is huge. He combines close textual reading with careful analysis of other discourses (legal depositions, confessional writings, classical mythology, records of events) to place 'literature' within a discursive web where each component part interacts with and against its other contingent units. Equally, 'history' is understood not as a matter of archived fact or written record but as *textual*, as another discourse replete with vested interests and potential distortions. It is perhaps better recognized as what we would now term New Historicism, the impact of which is readily gauged by a glance at the current web pages of the New Chaucer Society. (See Chapter 7: Marxism to New Historicism and Chapter 8: New Historicism and Blurring the History/Literature Divide.)

The predominant thread of Patterson's argument is that Chaucer offers us ways of 'thinking socially': about him as a poet, about his poems, about issues crucial to his time (424). Chaucer's concern is with the 'social meaning' of the ways in which poetry interacts with its audiences, with class values and ideologies and/or with its particular context (47). Patterson suggests that our modern insistence that self or 'subjectivity' springs from the Renaissance obscures concepts like the 'social' (as a collective identity or set of values) and 'history' which (and here Patterson gestures towards later postcolonial work) we insist has an originary point from which all else proceeds in progressive and linear fashion. Patterson points to a wealth of late medieval writings of all kinds that work out a dialectic between inner and outer, private and public, or, in other words, subjectivity and history (8). So, in the socially-oriented *Tales*, we see a dialectic between the 'estates' of the *General Prologue*, for example, or character types that signal identity through social function, as well as (Chaucer's innovation) the more individual voices that cross-cut to offer instances of subjects 'caught in the very processes of self-construction' (30). (See Chapter 10: Materialist Criticism.)

What does Patterson mean when he speaks of the 'subject of history', though? Moreover, how exactly do we begin to think socially about Chaucer? Patterson contends that a late medieval understanding of history differed entirely from our notion of a forward moving trajectory. Medieval 'history' was, in fact, a transhistorical or philosophical ideal divorced from 'material reality' (86). Instead, it was conceived in Christian or spiritual terms as a state of exile or loss, an always harking back to antiquity or an imagined point of origin but doomed never fully to know it. As such, it was of value only for the way it affected our inner, spiritual self and not for what it might reveal of that self or our collective identities. The events of *this* history seemed irrational or random, subject to an ultimately indecipherable cosmic order or divine plan, and, so, could only be grasped by working out its allegorical meaning (see 84–96). In this sense, too, it was a problematic, imperfect time that always took us back to an originary moment (of perfection) that we could never fully see or reproduce (18).

History and Historicity: The Problem of Origins

Patterson exemplifies this notion by tracing the classical story of Thebes which, he suggests, presents history as a collision between the powerful forces of love and war in a labyrinthine tragedy that constantly replicates itself by re-enacting and re-telling the patterns of its own story (77, see also 65–83). He notes that Chaucer returns to this 'foundational' story (and to Trojan history as a point of origin for Western civilization) to revisit the implications of its constricting circularity and the painful 'failures' it invokes. The *Knight's Tale*, for instance, is set in a past in which Thebes and Athens represent different understandings of destiny and order. Other tales like the *Franklin's* or the *Wife's* begin 'Whilom' or long ago, while the *Troilus* is a 'poem of origins' (84) whose inconclusiveness – like other problematic 'endings' in Chaucer – shows how history, and any understanding of it, will always fail (163). Above all, Chaucer, he argues, both fully grasps this particular medieval concept of history *and* resists it in the way he simultaneously proposes and undoes the 'dream of origins' we can never realize (20).

In practical terms, this insistent referral back to a point of absoluteness or perfection is witnessed in the citing of authorities or sources that are then exposed as insufficient (think of the invented Lollius of *Troilus and Criseyde*

[I.394, V.1653]). Chaucer gives us examples of, or references to, antiquity but uses them to establish a critical distance from which to discard a philosophical, static ideal in favour of the 'specific and surprisingly antagonistic practices' of his historical present (243). This crucial re-conceptualization of history is the force through which Patterson's 'social thinking' works (168). The pilgrimage of the *Tales* never reaches the 'New Jerusalem' but is shaped as a parabola in which the *Parson's Tale* offers not 'resolution but . . . cancellation' (20). Its voices are oppositional and drift into a 'socially undetermined subjectivity' exposing rifts and empowering the present, rather than pointing backwards to an unattainable ideal (322). For Patterson, then, Chaucer's world is energized but also dissonant and ambivalent. It works with and against paradoxical 'histories': as past perfection, a pre-ordained reality already accomplished *and* as prospective, full of random, clashing events or discourses. (See his comments, for example, on the *Knight's Tale*, 222–30). As already noted, Patterson's innovative methodology similarly stirs up of antagonisms that produce rich and provocative interpretations of medieval literature, and even contemporary texts. Reading the *Knight's Tale* alongside the specifics of the 1390 Scrope-Grovesnor dispute over the right (or not) to bear a particular coat of arms shunts local, politicized 'history' into an allegory about the unravelling of chivalric ideology and the class solidarity it intersects (see 165–230). An analysis of antifeminist writings and the structures of medieval rhetoric inform the Wife of Bath's 'dilated discourse' (307) and resistant 'act of deliberate self-fashioning' (289). The confrontation of subjectivity and history is similarly delineated in Patterson's commentary on the *Miller's Tale* (244–79) and the *Pardoner's Prologue and Tale* (367–421).

The Miller and The Pardoner

For Patterson, the *Miller's Tale* is the 'false start' of the *Canterbury Tales* in every respect. To read it against the *Knight's Tale* is to witness its (ultimately failed) resistance to a problematic aristocratic public (i.e. social) identity and a 'social authority' repeated in Fragments II and III via the game of 'quiting' (281). The Miller consciously interprets 'to quite' as a retaliation rather than a match or a reward to give us a 'linguistic subversion' followed through in vocabulary that parodies the Knight's chivalric ideology. This is the means by which the tale asserts its own 'peasants' revolt' and turns back upon the governing class the very language it uses to regulate the lower orders. Patterson examines the documentary evidence of the event he contends is contingent to this tale, that is the 1381 Revolt. (See Chapter 2: Labor Unrest and the Peasants' Revolt and Chapter 4: The 1381 Revolt.) He argues that both clerical and chronicle accounts of the rebels and their actions censure a peasant consciousness invoked in the language of these documents as animal, sinful, or naturally 'fallen', even mad. The Miller picks up on and 'rewrites' these pejorative connotations. So, he celebrates the vitality of the natural world that, despite the seemingly random turns of the plot, is carefully ordered. Each character works through a particular aspect of this stigmatizing discourse in classic *fabliau* 'arse-about-face' style: society laughs at 'mad' John, Nicholas represents the heretic Ham of the Noah story, Absolon misappropriates the biblical Song of Songs to 'rectify' an authoritarian process of *exegesis*, Alison is the festive 'animal' nature that finally proves no more articulate than her 'Tehee' and so on (286). Patterson's reading bears cross-reference with Karma Lochrie's version of 'thinking socially' about this tale discussed later in this chapter. In the same way, his complex analysis of the Pardoner needs to be read alongside Dinshaw's intervention in the critical debate.

Carolyn Dinshaw, *Chaucer's Sexual Poetics* (1989) and *Getting Medieval* (1999)

At first sight, Carolyn Dinshaw's work appears poles apart from that of Patterson. Yet, as with other key thinkers in this chapter, the two share a fundamental concern with history and the nature of its representations in all kinds of narratives. *Chaucer's Sexual Poetics* (1989) was the first full-length work to bring questions inspired by a feminist enterprise to bear on a canonical medieval author. In it, Dinshaw draws together a range of sources from medieval patristic writings and Lacanian psychoanalytical works to modern anthropology and notions about incest. Her ideas centre upon two analogous activities: the ways in which medieval thinkers read (interpreted) and wrote texts, and the processes through which we construct gender in both contemporary and medieval worlds.

Gendered Hermeneutics

Medieval writers like St. Jerome have much to say on the practices of reading/interpretation and writing, or what is known as hermeneutics. Medieval hermeneutics described a written text as a captive, and usually pagan, woman, a body ready to be inscribed by a phallic stylus and/or 'glozed' by a man to bring out its hidden Christian doctrine or message. This (textual) body is a carnal and seductive one, clothed in letters designed to attract the reader's eye. For example, think of the way many modern readers are drawn to the Wife of Bath's startling portrait. This body must be stripped of that clothing or letters veiling the 'truth' accessible only to the practised, usually male, eye. The reader strips the textual body bare to re-clothe and domesticate it, cast it as a fecund 'wife', something possible only when its inner message is discovered. In this sense, medieval literary theory bears resemblance to the activities of a patriarchal world in which women are appropriated, exchanged and regulated by men, hence the feminist strand of Dinshaw's work. (See Chapter 7: Feminism and Gender Studies.)

Dinshaw pushes these ideas further, arguing that these different ways of reading – the literal one that reads only the letters or surface text *and* the allegorical unveiling of the text's meaning – are gendered feminine and masculine respectively. Yet, she contends, they are not sexed. In other words, anyone may take up either of these positions regardless of their biological sex. This innovation means that, throughout, she speaks of 'reading like (not *as*) a man' to seek truth or closure and of 'reading like a woman', perhaps superficially but also in ways more open to ambiguity. In turn, her advocacy of a specifically Chaucerian 'sexual poetics' offers Chaucer's short poem to his scribe, Adam Scriveyn, as a framework for her subsequent analysis of Chaucer's narrative art. Adam corrupts or 'rapes' Chaucer's manuscript as he copies it out. As such, its 'letters' deviate from an intention or 'truth' Dinshaw goes on to explore in a range of Chaucer's other poems. Adam's rape of the text subtends the idea of writing as a masculine act performed on feminine textual bodies, the gendered hermeneutics I have just described. Again, though, Dinshaw goes further and traces the medieval etymology of 'rape'. It indicates sexual violation, as we would understand it today but also abduction or seizure of property. Thus, Adam both appropriates Chaucer's words and intentions (the property of his text) to twist an apparent truth, and, also, invokes a sexual charge as he rapes – both signs and violates – Chaucer's poem (9). (See Chapter 10: Literature and Commentary.)

According to Dinshaw, then, if this (gendered) model of literary activity can slip between, and out of, reading like a man and reading like a woman, other categories, such as gender itself, equally become unmoored. Becoming the victim of scribal rape feminizes Chaucer. From this position, Dinshaw suggests, he is then able to get out from under some of the prevailing ideologies of his time to explore other, less closed perspectives (10). So, his 'poetics' is gendered in a way that unsettles a traditional medieval hermeneutics *and* produces works that are both of, and yet not, a late medieval context. There is nothing especially new in the suggestion that Chaucer occupies such a singular place in medieval literary history, but few ground it as carefully as Dinshaw does. She suggests that in Chaucer all literary activity or representation must be viewed as bodily, including the way that it 'enters into social interactions, as it functions in social organization, as it is assigned gender value in the transactions that constitute social structure' (15). Dinshaw is able to link medieval reading and writing practices and a feminist inquiry because in both the body of 'woman' signifies as a blank to be worked on and brought into line as a 'proper' body: that is, one which is clean and whole and bears a truth or moral message that is subject to patriarchal law.

Dinshaw's Pardoner

This timely intervention in medieval studies is ultimately perhaps not supple enough for twenty-first century theorizing. Certainly, Dinshaw's later work moves feminism into the realm of queer and gender theory even as she re-thinks, as well, concepts of history. Perhaps the best example of this theoretical shift is Dinshaw's writing on Chaucer's Pardoner in the *Canterbury Tales*. The hermeneutics Dinshaw depicts impacts upon both women *and* texts in what, she insists, is a specifically 'patriarchal' (in the sense of being controlled by men) and heterosexual dynamic (156). What, in 1989, she finds celebratory about Chaucer's Pardoner is that he problematizes this patriarchal model to offer a performance that is a key to the *Tales*. She argues that the Pardoner exposes the faulty mechanisms of a masculine-dominated world constructed through binary opposition precisely because he evades both extremes (156–84). We might see this at its simplest in the Pardoner's literal and figurative refusal to be stripped of his fashionable clothes or his alternation between heterosexual (his 'wenches', his proposed marriage) and homosexual display (his 'compeer' the Summoner). In textual terms, his clothed body is a 'refusal to know' prompted, for the most part, by the suggestion that beneath the clothes/the 'letter' of the text is an absence (for he has no balls) of meaning (159).

This is why Dinshaw describes the Pardoner as a figurative eunuch exemplifying what she calls a 'eunuch hermeneutics'. She elucidates this complex argument by linking ideas about actual eunuchry and spiritual understanding in classical and theological writings – as well as close reading Chaucer's text – to point up an association between the body and its constituent parts, and Lacanian psychoanalysis. She is particularly concerned with Lacan's notion of 'lack'. Here, the subject experiences an incompleteness borne of the necessary splitting from the maternal body and mother-child unity when entering the symbolic or social world and language. Dinshaw contends that the Pardoner's fake relics indicate this missing completeness, as do his probably 'missing' testicles. As a figuration of lack or absence, his performance shows up the instabilities of the binaries through which Western culture constructs the world. The Pardoner confuses those who attempt to interpret him, leaving his 'readers' unable to move from one opposition to the other and, so, mediate language. In short, he *is* neither one thing nor the other. At the same time, in what is perhaps a large jump in her argument, she suggest the Pardoner invites us to look beyond absence to the 'absolute Presence' of God at the end of the *Tales* (160, see also 183).

Later incursions into how the Pardoner means are far less resolute than this early manoeuvre (Dinshaw 1999, 113–42). There, Dinshaw brings to bear upon Chaucer's poem other historical and discursive encounters: the 1394 account of the activities of a male transvestite prostitute, John/Eleanor Rykener; Foucault's writings on sexuality and the Middle Ages; Kittredge's inflected, heterosexist and highly influential critical reading of the Pardoner; and Lollard and anti-Lollard medieval polemic. In this way, she seeks to highlight a nexus of indeterminacies, cross-cuttings and potential contagion. She argues that the Pardoner's 'illegible' and anomalous body (117), his 'queer' role playing and self-confessed hypocrisy, plus his position on the margins of the pilgrimage community, combine to send a 'natural' hetero-sexual norm into 'a queer skid' (113). The Pardoner's very queerness exposes the workings of this norm (126) and deconstructs what the rest of the *Tales* tries to assert as natural or essential. Though order is apparently restored by the final 'kiss of peace', the Pardoner casts a long, 'sodomitical shadow' over the pilgrimage as he continues to ride with the others on the way to Canterbury (121 and 136).

Queering the Medieval

Getting Medieval (1999), Dinshaw's later major work, meditates on 'queerness, community, and history' (144). In so doing, it re-imagines all three of these categories, largely through an analysis of sex. Dinshaw remains interested in the ways in which we constitute identities – individual and, above all, com-munal – based on sex, and what, in the process, we expel or *abject* to 'secure' them. She defines sex as 'heterogeneous, multiple, and fundamentally indeterminate', a series of acts, desires, identities or categories that are, by condition, slippery and difficult. Her project is not to pin these down but rather to 'embrace' their complexity (1). Like Lochrie, she is less concerned with what sodomy is, for example, and more interested in how and why it becomes a medieval 'unspeakable', with what is at stake in categorizing it as such (5). Specifically, she focuses on the interlinked and 'mutually constitutive' discourses of late medieval heresy and sexual deviancy (6). Dinshaw contends that what is presented as disorderly or threatening indi-cates how a community forms itself and subsequently polices what it chooses to keep 'inside' and normative.

Dinshaw builds, too, upon the intersection of past and present that lurks at the edges of her earlier work by exploring a range of literary and non-literary texts from both medieval and contemporary times, as I described in my discussion of the Pardoner. This provocative methodology seeks to extend our understanding of history (as we will see other theorists do), and takes 'sex' into a queer theoretical field. There 'queer' – which may be employed as noun, verb and/or adjective – seeks to dismantle 'natural', taken-for-granted binaries, like masculine/feminine or hetero/homosexual, and dislodge heterosexuality as a 'compulsory' norm. Rather, queerness challenges and historicizes a contemporary sex-gender-sexuality dynamic to show that it is neither natural nor progressive but, instead, vibrates across times and texts. Thus Dinshaw draws together what at first sight might appear eclectic or arbitrary, something that bears similarity with Karma Lochrie's work, discussed later. Dinshaw concentrates on a small number of English medieval texts written in London and East Anglia during the mid 1390s and mid 1430s: some of Chaucer's *Tales*, *The Book of Margery Kempe*, Lollard and anti-Lollard propaganda, John Mirk's manual for priests and a 1394 account of a transvestite prostitute working in London. These she places alongside consideration of contemporary thinkers and historians – Michel Foucault, Homi Bhabha, John Boswell, Roland Barthes – and analysis of works like Quentin Tarantino's film *Pulp Fiction* or Robert Glück's postmodern novel, *Margery Kempe*. (See Chapter 8: The Impact of Feminism and the Expansion of the Canon.)

The Touch of the Queer

The enterprise of *Getting Medieval* extends beyond instances of 'perversion' to consider a broader web in which events and attitudes are 'affective' not causal; that is, meanings shift according to context and location to brush up against each other, often in ambiguous or contradictory ways. This, Dinshaw argues, undoes any notion of a monolithic past. Instead, people, discourses, cultural phenomena, places, signs and signifiers are all charged, sometimes erotically (39), and reworked by 'touching' or intersecting other texts and contexts. Conventional distinctions, including the idea of history as progressive, dislodge. Meanings we take for granted, as natural or given, rupture or expose their gaps to leave us with indeterminacy (see 11–12). Dinshaw advocates, then, that we read specifically, attentive to particular discourses produced in a given context, *and* through contiguity – by making contact with, or going off in a tangent from, the web of effects in which all texts are placed (39). This is what she calls 'the touch of the queer', a notion she describes more fully in a 1995 essay called 'Chaucer's Queer Touches / A Queer Touches Chaucer'. This 'touch' may be literal or figurative but is, above all, a making contact with other texts, discourses, characters, places or histories. It is, too, a 'touch across time' that gives us 'discontinuous' histories (21) that track from the present to the past and back. However partial its connection, its result is to make us look again at what seems unthinkable, an endeavour she terms 'getting medieval'. She takes her title from Marcellus Wallace's threat to 'get medieval' on the ass of his male rapist in *Pulp Fiction*. Dinshaw argues that this retribution totalizes both a 'medieval' time and a heterosexual norm worked out by demonizing a homosexual 'threat'. In contrast, Dinshaw's use of the verb is more nuanced. For her, it means opening up the kind of queer, historical project I have just summarized to de-familiarize our 'natural' assumptions and expose what these norms have 'left out' (1). (See Chapter 7: Gender, Identity and Queer Studies.)

Karma Lochrie, *Covert Operations* (1999) and *Heterosyncrasies* (2005)

Karma Lochrie's writing is made key through her contribution to gender and queer theory, and thanks to her methodologies, both areas of overlap with Dinshaw. She employs a range of theoretical and historical sources – medieval and contemporary – to ground ideas that she subsequently illustrates via medieval literary and non-literary texts. What is particular about the two books I shall focus on, though, is the ways in which she draws together, yet keeps pliable, such a diversity of material to mine a 'middle ground' that compensates for her self-confessed eclectic approach (1999, 6).

Sodomy and Secrecy

There are two inter-connecting strands to Lochrie's thinking in *Covert Operations* (1999). The first re-conceptualizes medieval sodomy as a gender perversion that manifests as specifically feminine and not, simply, as an 'unnatural', homosexual opposite of heterosexuality. I return to this idea shortly. The other is an exploration of medieval technologies of secrecy. Lochrie's interest in secrecy and the 'secrets it keeps' arises from the ways in which it maps and secures knowledge (1). In turn, this structures the dynamics of power within specific cultural contexts and discourses to give rise to a practice of 'concealment' in which what is *not* said or made visible operates alongside and within what is spoken or seen (2). Even though this dynamic is oppositional, secrecy works *within* it, according to Lochrie, to expose its frayed edges, rather than directly to offer a mode of resistance (2). The 'covert' of her title is not the *actual* secrets of medieval culture but the practices or 'operations' that cover them. Some take particular form and it is these to which she attends: discourses of confession, the language and practice of medieval law and prevalent attitudes or 'forbidden practices' 'textualized' in books of secrets, or writings on gossip and sodomy. This approach generates fresh readings of medieval texts such as Pseudo-Albert the Great's *The Secrets of Women*, Gower's *Confessio Amantis, Sir Gawain and the Green Knight*, Chaucer's *House of Fame, Miller's Tale* and *Wife of Bath's Prologue and Tale*. Each concentrates on different aspects of the operations of secrecy to pull out a range of ideas that work in a kind of 'queer complementarity' (6). (See Chapter 4: Marie de France, *Lanval*.)

One instance is her revision of a medieval discourse of confession. Here she uncovers a double bind hinted at in the prevalence of theological manuals on how to elicit revelation of sin. The confessor must discover the secret (often sexual) sins of a penitent who both comes to confess yet may resist full disclosure. Once in possession of any secrets, the priest is bound to stay silent. For both participants in this one-sided intimacy there may be shame *and* pleasure in the exchange (see 14–32). This confusion of elements finds its way into literary texts and the gender ideologies they so often reveal, according to Lochrie (24). So, Albert the Great's *The Secrets of Women* or books like *Secrets of Secrets*, as well as a host of medical or scientific works, embed an understanding of the bodies and sexualities of women as dangerous secrets owned and exchanged by (usually religious) men. These kinds of secrets, she suggests, are predicated on a fear of the feminine and ensure that women are represented only as *being* the secret, not as having it (8–9). Yet, even within this notion, there exists a marginal, secret discourse of gossip that mimics and, so, undermines the structures of medieval confession to become a secret of its own threatening patriarchal discourse: think Wife of Bath (8).

Lochrie's textual analysis is especially helpful in negotiating the complex and conflicted spaces of the 'covert operations' she exposes. She argues, for instance, that secrecy 'haunts' *Sir Gawain and the Green Knight* through a model of confession suggestive of the structures of power that work through and within its depiction of chivalry (see 42–55). The poem dismantles these structures at exactly the same time as it produces them (7). Her delineation of its impulses of listen/tell, conceal/reveal, public/private, shame/laughter bear reading alongside Dinshaw's consideration of the same text in her article 'Getting Medieval' (1997) or Cohen's in *Of Giants* (1999). Lochrie asserts Gawain *as* the secret in this poem, and so 'reads' him from the position of the feminine. Yet hers is not a conventional gendered perspective primarily concerned with identity. Instead, she is interested in how and why he reveals himself at the end of the poem, in 'confession' rather than gender. The text's 'confessional structure' centres on 'pleasurable talk' – exchanged with both the Lady (in secret) and Bertilak (in public, yet also as a secret pact, the Exchange of Winnings) – *and* the 'confessional imperative' that impels Gawain's outpouring of shame over the gift of the green girdle (43). The erotic, and shameful, pleasure of these secrets is integral to a 'verbosity', or obsession with disclosure, that problematizes the ways in which we produce truth (54).

Secrecy and Gender

Discussing the *Miller's Tale* (read against Patterson's interpretation) is the means by which Lochrie follows through her ideas on the technologies of secrecy in relation to gender. Taking as her cue a French legal notion of 'coverture' (in which a wife is sexually and legally appropriated by the husband *and* protected by him), she delineates a medieval system of 'coversion'. Here, women are denied access to speech or their own bodies, which sets up a masculine mode of exchange (9). A wife becomes an 'open' secret within a culture that effectively erases her while the feminine is associated with a conflated privacy and secrecy that the masculine uncovers *to take for itself*. Through the genre of *fabliau*, with its compulsive and comic cuckolding, we might see some of this at work, as well as the anxieties such *coversion* provokes. Lochrie highlights her ideas with a play across meanings of 'privee' or 'pryvetee' (from God's secrets to Alison's 'private parts') and a range of secrets structuring the narrative.

It is not until the closing sections of *Covert Operations* that Lochrie begins to gather up the second strand of her work on sodomy upon which the later *Heterosyncrasies* (2005) hinges. She describes sodomy as perhaps the greatest medieval secret, a category confusion so menacing that it must not be spoken or disclosed. Her argument begins with a by-now usual appellation of medieval sodomy as a series of unnatural or disordered sex acts. Her innovation is to review that notion in a manoeuvre that has implications for gender and heterosexuality as 'a normative principle' that 'simply did not exist' for the Middle Ages; rather, sodomy is heteronormativity's 'best kept secret' (225). Instead of asserting sodomy simply as the unnatural – and often homosexual – pole of 'natural' heterosexual behaviour, she rereads medieval theological writings to position it as a (secret) 'gender pathology' hidden within an apparently heterosexual 'norm' (181). How, then, does she arrive at this conclusion?

Perversion and the Unnatural

Medieval sexuality was predicated on gender roles in sex, an active-passive opposition that designates an entire range of acts as unnatural, or sodomitic. These include many heterosexual activities; woman-on-top usurps 'proper' gender by making the male passive, and so on. At the same time, homosexual acts are frequently characterized as a 'feminine' disorder, because they were thought to be unchecked by masculine reason and produced soft or effeminate figures. All fall into the category of 'perverse'. Each is, says Lochrie, a *feminine* 'disorder' that defies proper gender roles. As such, sodomy becomes a gender perversion that also works *as though* it is feminine (10). Following this line of thinking, it too becomes a natural rather than an unnatural category as previously believed; one of the essential attributes of 'woman' in medieval thought is her association with nature and the flesh, with an appetite that is 'perverse, straying, unbridled' (203). So, what is natural – sodomy – is also perversely feminine and breaks the rules of gender. In which case, heterosexuality is dismantled by the secret of sodomy that sits at its heart. Once sodomy undoes these conventional binaries, 'queer' can no longer always be recuperated back into heteronormativity as its constitutive order. In other words, it cannot be expelled in order to 'guarantee' a heterosexual norm that remains haunted by that abjection and to which it remains integral. Neither can it operate as a force of resistance against it – by virtue of being its polar opposite – when that same 'heteronormative' remains 'illegible' in the medieval world (199).

Heternormativity and Heterosyncrasy

Instead, Lochrie's delineation of 'queer' – worked out more fully in her possibly more accessible study, *Heterosyncrasies* – is far more slippery than that of any of the theorists discussed this far. She coins the term 'heterosyncracies' to meld the 'hetero' of sexual desire and its particular, even odd, manifestations of 'idiosyncratic' (xix). This then becomes a lens through which to view medieval culture and assert her conviction that 'heterosexual' and 'heteronormative' demand further scrutiny. She returns to the idea that sodomy is more than a homosexual 'resistance' that invokes 'queer' (xiv). Homosexuality is but one aspect of sodomy, she suggests; we can equally find sodomy in a range of disorderly acts. Lochrie is especially concerned here to make visible a so far hidden feminine desire 'written out' of sodomy in many contemporary practices and in medieval theological writings on the subject. If sodomy is not a discrete opposition to heterosexuality, so, too, heterosexuality both opposes *and is complicit with* a number of other ideologies she redefines as 'queer', such as medieval virginity, medieval marriage and conjugal rights, or medieval notions of gender (xv). (See Chapter 7: Gender, Identity and Queer Studies.)

Her impetus is to 'rescue' medieval and contemporary times 'from the terrible presumption of transhistorical heteronormativity' (xxviii). In order to do this, Lochrie distinguishes 'heterosexual' from 'heteronormative'. She argues that the conflation of the two terms has consequences for now, for our 'readings of the past' *and* for a queer theoretical field (xii). She defines 'heterosexuality' as a specific desire for sex with the opposite sex, something that may also have moral or social consequences. 'Heteronormativity' simultaneously describes heterosexuality and embeds it as an assumption ('natural' choice) that shapes our world. In short, heteronormativity presents itself as a cultural 'average' that takes in ideas about sexualities, marriage and parenting, and passes as a given 'fact', quantifiable through surveys and data-gathering. Its inception, she insists, is entirely modern, an outcome of nineteenth- and twentieth-century statistical analysis. Ignoring this history, as we do, allows us to assume heterosexuality as a normative or governing principle for all times, and, therefore, as transhistorical. It is 'hardwired' into attitudes, behaviours, even scholarship (xiv). Equally, by establishing it in this way as standard, a host of other possibilities fall out of range, or, alternatively, present themselves only as deviant (xiv). Thus heteronormal 'slips a modern category into the premodern past in disguise' to disregard not only the 'historicity' of 'norms' but how such 'averages' actually 'produce' the very categories they seemingly describe (2).

Once again, Lochrie's sources are wide-ranging. She begins by mapping the processes of normativity in the present before moving out to rethink a pre-normative (medieval) sodomy that writes out female desires. Therefore, she rethinks the writings of Heloise to undo chastity as an ideal. Instead, Lochrie suggests, virginity is offered as a 'queer' space (46) that permits the indulgence of female same-sex desire (45). This refusal of marriage is set against a revisioning of an attack on celibacy in the Twelve Commandments posted on the doors of parliament by Lollards in 1365. Lollard disapprobation of chastity in favour of marriage and 'family values' is, Lochrie suggests, a 'larger cultural heteronormative reflex' rooted in anxieties about the disproportionate number of single women in late medieval England (50). Other chapters analyse medical texts to uncover medieval thinking on female anatomy and capacity for sexual pleasure. From this, she asserts a 'female masculinity' that takes various literary forms (xxvii) and is concluded in those 'queer virgins' (138), the figuration of the Amazon warrior-woman in literature, travel writings and medieval *mappaemundi*. These sections continue to unlace heteronormativity even as they also gesture towards a historicist enterprise of the kind Patterson proposed in 1991 and, hence, towards postcolonial medieval studies by linking readings about Amazons, Trojan historiographies and narratives of nation.

Above all, Lochrie's innovations find expression in the exploration of Chaucer's *Canterbury Tales* that runs throughout *Heterosyncracies*. She offers the *Tales* as a site where 'gender, sexuality, identity, and even literary genre might become unmoored' (136), a reading that demands consideration alongside those of all of the key thinkers in this chapter. Instead of a 'Marriage Group', she offers a 'queer' 'Virginity Group' (the *Knight's*, *Clerk's*, *Physician's*, *Prioress's* and *Second Nun's Tales*). So, too, she re-imagines the *Knight's* and the *Man of Law's* through the 'not normal' of Amazons and 'feyned', masculine mothers-in-law, and asserts a *'lingua queynte'* – literally, cunt-language – (97) central to what she argues is the Wife of Bath's refusal of heterosexual, married sex and a 'performance of female masculinity' (91).

Jeffrey Jerome Cohen, *Of Giants* (1999)

Cohen's innovation is, like Lochrie's, to read medieval texts through the lens of psychoanalysis. In particular, he explores notions of identity, both gendered and national, by focusing upon bodies, many of them monstrous, and upon moments in texts that relate to ideas about masculinity. I shall return to Cohen's contribution to postcolonial medieval studies later, but for now, I wish to take up the main strand of his seminal *Of Giants* (1999) to intersect gender and queer theory. (See Chapter 7: Gender, Identity, and Queer Studies and Chapter 7: Psychoanalytic Theory.)

The Body and the Giant

Cohen begins by tracing the figure of the giant as it appears in literature from the Hebrew Bible, to Welsh legend and Arthurian romance, and up into the present day in order to extrapolate its attributes. He suggests that the giant embodies a range of paradoxes. Both superhumanly masculine and excessive in form, it is also associated with a materiality that is often gendered feminine, through, for example, images associated with consumption or orality. Its gigantic form is grasped only in 'pieces' – a hand, a footprint that fills to become a lake, or a body so enormous it cannot be seen in totality. The giant inhabits wildernesses, banished from civilization, yet returns to haunt us, to smash cities or stand at the threshold of a hall. Above all, we fear and desire it, take horrific pleasure in looking at it, a moment Cohen terms a 'sticky gaze' (see 64 and 196). Often this looking is attached to familiar tropes in romance: dismemberment, beheading or decapitation. In particular, the traditional battle between the hero and the monster – *gigantomachia* – functions as a rite of passage to sexual and social maturity. Corporeal wholeness is set over and against a body in pieces. Typically, the giant's severed head bears messages about the limits of the body whilst the actual beheading becomes a 'violent moment of gender assertion' that brings into line 'fleshly excess' (the feminine) and pushes aside (abjects) unacceptable (homosexual) desire to secure heterosexuality (see 66–9). (See Chapter 6: The Marvelous/Monstrous.)

The giant embodies sexual aggression (towards both the hero and 'heroine' of medieval romance) and monstrous appetite or desire – witness, for instance, the Freudian overtones of its club or axe, its threat of rape or castration. Cohen argues that, as such, it is the chivalric hero's unacceptable double, everything that masculinity is not, a 'cultural body on which the codes that produce a safely gendered identity have failed to adhere' (102). Consequently, its defeat marks the limits of what that identity *should* be. Not surprisingly, then, it appears most often in literature when the boundaries of the body are in dispute (xiii).

Cohen's contribution to the field is, however, more than a description of the workings of *gigantomachia*. He grounds his ideas in Lacanian theory to posit monstrosity as a transhistorical phenomenon as applicable to medieval romance poems as to contemporary 'slasher' films or DVD games. His choice of methodology arises from an understanding of psychoanalysis as a force that shies away from an imposition of order or an insistence that 'persuasive ideologies work ... because they squelch contradiction and subversive *jouissance*' and instead unleashes 'their productive, disharmonious power' (70). As such, his interest and his innovation lie in suspending rather than resolving ambiguities. This is similar to Dinshaw's insistence in 'indeterminacies' and the refusal of easy resolution witnessed in the work of Patterson and Lochrie.

Monstrosity and *Extimité*

In this sense, the paradoxical nature of the giant is seen to embody what Lacanian psychoanalysis calls *extimité* and what Cohen terms 'the intimate stranger' or 'intimate alterity'. Here the monstrous is simultaneously other, beyond or outside the limits of human bodies and the human world, yet also familiar and foundational to that world and its identities. It too is a site of prohibition (against bodily pleasures) and desire or enjoyment, subject in effect to our 'sticky gaze'. This dual position ensures that it continually disturbs and evades our sight and understanding – hence the movement in literary depictions between super-size embodiment and little pieces. Cohen's key terms – 'subjectivity' and 'embodiment' – are used not as conventional binaries (person/body), but as interlinked processes: Subjectivity happens in and through bodies whose impulses are both inside and outside and constantly cross-connecting (xvii). It is this disturbing of categories that pushes Cohen's thinking into a queer theory that owes much to Dinshaw's delineation of how 'queer' is a general unhinging rather than purely a homoerotic moment.

For Cohen these cross-connections are inevitable because 'To be fully human is to disavow the strange space that the inhuman, the monstrous, occupies within every speaking subject' (4). We can absorb monstrosity but never fully assimilate it, not least because the monster has helped to create everything it subsequently menaces. Cohen likens this to the process of identity formation, imagined through the Lacanian 'mirror' that allows us to enter into the symbolic (social) world as fully formed, speaking subjects. On the one hand, we experience ourselves as a 'body-in-pieces'. On the other, we see ourselves as a coherent body or unified being, an image we (mis)take as conforming to what is inside and which Cohen calls a 'fabricated thing' (11). Both states, he asserts, whether in pieces or unified, are monstrous. The giant enters the equation as a point of origin, before we change from 'pieces' to 'embodiment' (22). At the same time, that embodiment is a fragile state, forever reaching back to what it thinks it has lost (an imaginary oneness with the maternal body). The giant is, then, both origin and loss (25), a piece of what Lacanian thinking calls the 'real'. The real, which is, in fact merely another effect or illusion, is the piece left over when we enter the symbolic or social world. It contains everything that the symbolic must exclude or suppress in order to permit culture to come together; that is, all that disturbs it, terrifies and thrills. Again, Cohen suggests the monster is a piece of the 'real', so that even when the hero conquers it a small piece of it settles inside his own body (94) where it remains, unassimilated, not coherent, but a queer site of unrest (see 93–5).

These ideas are seen in his discussion of *Sir Gawain and the Green Knight*. Cohen's exploration overlaps with Dinshaw's in 'Getting Medieval' (1997), in the sense that he, too, is interested in the complex working out of what it might mean to be a masculine, chivalric and heterosexual subject. Like Dinshaw, he scrutinizes Gawain's always-about-to-be-lost bodily control, citing, as she does, examples from the poem of near or actual dismemberment. Their main point of difference has important implications for queer theorists working in medieval studies. Cohen moves firmly away from Dinshaw's conviction that the poem, however queer, ultimately affirms heterosexuality. He suggests, instead, that both states prove impossible and leave us with category confusion. The cost of Gawain's apparently straight identity is, he argues, enormous. It is predicated on a series of dangerous games instigated through the agency of a woman (Morgan) and played out with a monster (Bertilak) who doubles as urbane host. At the end, Gawain stands outside the court, having refused Bertilak's invitation to join in the New Year revelry and laughed at by his Arthurian fellows who fail to grasp the import of his adventures. Equally, the *gigantomachia* motif unexpectedly permits no resolution of its conflicts. The giant – in this case the Green Knight – is not an abjected other opposed to chivalric identity, or a force to be overcome, for their battle is deflected (150–3). Instead, the Green Knight/Bertilak sits right at the heart of that identity and remains central to a circular motion that sees the poem move out from a 'history' of the fall of Troy and back again. In this sense, too, *Sir Gawain and the Green Knight* problematizes the idyllic Arthurian past that helps to construct so many narratives of nationhood for a medieval 'England' that is itself produced, at least in part, by modernity, a matter that is the subject of my concluding section.

Patricia Clare Ingham and Michelle Warren, *Postcolonial Moves* (2003) and Jeffrey Jerome Cohen, *The Postcolonial Middle Ages* (2000)

The emerging field of postcolonial medieval studies demands, yet again, re-conceptualization of a historicist enterprise. Postcolonialism has usually focused on the nineteenth and twentieth centuries, on modernity, a time often opposed to the pre-modern or medieval that functions as its defining other.

Western culture is constructed by and through the colonization of other times, bodies and places. In short, a binary is established whereby a Eurocentric space and time modernizes those other nations construed, by definition, as archaic or primitive, and, hence, in need of colonization. If we accept this view, then 'medieval' is defined exclusively through its premodern, 'dark' alterity; the ubiquitous 'scare quotes' highlight its irreconcilable sense of *difference*. Many medieval and postcolonial theorists have begun to challenge a limiting perspective that has special significance for the ways in which the medieval field situates itself. This section will examine, in particular, the writings of Cohen and Patricia Clare Ingham in order to explore notions of time, place and history. (See Chapter 7: Postcolonial Criticism; Chapter 8: Multilingualism, International Contexts, and Postcolonial Concerns; Chapter 9: Race Studies and Postcolonial Theory; See Chapter 9: Postcolonial Studies.)

Medieval Colonialism and the Modern West

In *Postcolonial Moves* (2003), Ingham and Michelle Warren refuse Western modernity as a fact of history. They suggest that it is, instead, an ideology that 'blocks certain routes to the past and thus maintains certain nationalist and historicist exclusions' (2). To question conventional periodization in this way is to 'enter into new kinds of historical dialogue' whereby history is reread: not homogeneous, or as a linear or progressive trajectory (teleogical), but as composed of continuities *and* ruptures (2). The effects of medieval colonialism – Christianization and Islamic conquest, the corresponding clashes and exchanges (commercial, martial, intellectual and cultural) between East and West – and a contemporary quest for our hidden origins (what Cohen calls 'originary fantasies') thus intermingle.

Such a project is not without difficulties for medievalists, and this is where I would like to begin. A strictly postcolonial emphasis derived from modernity becomes anachronistic when applied to the Middle Ages. However, collapsing historical periodization extends the limits of postcolonial theories. This broader sweep may be in danger of denying some of the specificities of medieval contexts. At the same time, according to Patricia Ingham, post-colonial medieval studies places histories, ethnicities and religions within the same central universals as matters of race, class and gender (9). As such, she argues, the methodologies of postcolonialism stress three interrelated strands, seeking to interrogate paradigms of place (geography), time (temporality) and related and/or hidden disciplines and fields (academic analysis). Post-colonial theory intersects, for example, historicist enquiry, gender and queer theory, matters that have been at the heart of this chapter. Each time, the search is for repressions, paradoxes and ruptures, for associations and re-appropriations: of 'colonial' or 'master' texts and authors, for instance, or transhistorical phenomena and tropes like monsters.

Cohen's impact on the theorization of medieval studies comes via post-colonialism as well as queer studies. Two works of particular note are *Of Giants*, discussed earlier, and his edited collection of essays, *The Postcolonial Middle Ages* (2000). In both, he, like Ingham, explores concepts of temporality, nationhood and history, largely through medieval romance texts such as *Sir Gawain and the Green Knight*, its numerous analogues and other versions, plus *Sir Gowther*, but also through historiography like Geoffrey of Monmouth's *History of the Kings of Britain* (*Historia Regum Brittaniae*). Perhaps the most crucial strand of Cohen's analysis is his call to reposition the Middle Ages in terms of narratives of history. Like Ingham, Cohen seeks to dismantle a modern/premodern divide and disrupt notions of medieval as a primitive waiting-to-be (colonized) space and time, a stepping-off point from the 'Dark Ages' into the Renaissance and Enlightenment. He commends recent attempts to begin this process, witnessed when 'post-colonial' loses its hyphen as a mark of synthesis and contiguity, an attempt to lose a colonial and its 'after' (or before). For Cohen, however, this dismantling does not go far enough.

Medieval Intertemporality

Cohen proposes that the field be opened up to an awareness of 'medieval' as a mid-point or in-between. Using the Lacanian notion of *extimité* or 'intimate alterity' outlined in my earlier consideration of *Of Giants*, in which everything is familiar yet also strange, Cohen mingles past/present, outside/inside, difference/same. Thus he doesn't entirely reject any sense of medieval as an 'undifferentiated alterity' or a far-away, in the past, point of origin that constructs the modern. Instead, he shifts emphasis to bring it in from outside (denied or excluded) and more towards a recognition that it is an 'always-already existed *alongside*' (3, emph. mine). In this respect, the 'Middle Ages' is both in and out of constitutions of modernity, moving backwards and forwards in time. To insist upon it as *past* is to keep it as a point of origin, separate from our contemporary world. To make it visible in that world is to recognize it as a 'traumatic effect', full of violence, pain and difficult suppressions (3–6). Medieval (*without* scare quotes) then becomes a difficult point of friction, rather than a border between pre and modern (6), a meridian or middle (3) that takes us away from a founding myth (which is nevertheless important) and into an in-between position to blur the difference between 'origin' and 'end' (colonial) (6). (See Chapter 6: 'History' and the Past.)

In this sense, Cohen rethinks notions of time. He suggests we can dismantle clear-cut, progressive and, ultimately, inadequate narratives of history by emphasizing what he terms the 'untimely' and *problematizing* notions of temporality. He urges us to explore cultural 'moments' through the lens not only of difference but of similarity. In this way, we might get out from under fantasies of former wholeness through which we embed dominant ideas about ethnicity, nationalism or gender (Ingham's 'universals'). Instead, we ought to view these 'moments' not as unified but as multiple sites of overlap, replete with internal conflicts and ambiguities. In such a manoeuvre – one remarkably similar to Patterson's tension between 'subject' and 'history' – what is marginal (Wales, Muslim, pagan, Jewish communities) might be repositioned as a centre in its own right.

Cohen's personal contribution to this enterprise explores questions about nationhood and collective identities through the figure of the monster (*Of Giants*). 'Monster' is the 'familiar stranger' embodying the fantasies we construct about the past (10–12). It is, too, foundational, an idea he explores through romance texts. Here Cohen addresses a typical Western myth that imagines a former time and place inhabited by a monstrous or savage race. This race is defeated by a hero who appropriates or colonizes its space to establish a new, 'civilized' and 'modern' nation. So, a number of medieval stories have giants creating or forming the landscape to project a 'history' upon its features. Or else, in a series of chapters on medieval 'foundational' romances, Cohen's 'mid-point' is witnessed in hybridity or miscegenation – giants spawned by the Albina princesses copulating with devils or angels in a mythic 'England', or the half-man, half-dog *cynecephalus*, the embodiment of a dangerous cultural other that might yet be brought to heel. Often, too, such monsters are translated as Muslim or Saracen (131–7). Equally, he interrogates the originary nature and alterity of 'medieval' via readings of the roles of Arthur and Brutus as points of identification for an 'English' nation which was itself a colonized space in the medieval period (143–52).

Though Ingham does not work out her arguments through Lacanian psychoanalysis as Cohen does, many of their thoughts intersect. Both view the Middle Ages as, in Cohen's words, an 'unbounded "middle space" ' (2000, 6) and call for similar manoeuvres within a medieval postcolonial field. Cohen lists several imperatives for those working at this interface, asking that we reconsider not only notions of time and space (East, West, Europe and England) but a series of identities or terms that we take for granted as 'truth': colonial, history, race, sexuality, pagan, Christian, Muslim etc. Patricia Ingham shares Cohen's concerns about the ways in which we narrate our pasts and its subsequent impact upon medieval studies. Her critique of postcolonial theory similarly extends its scope and forces it to reconsider convenient polarities. Both Ingham and Cohen suggest that though difference is important (East versus West, let us say), similarities cannot be ignored. Within what appears to be a unified group, there may also be small but significant differences. Ingham cites the Christians of Chaucer's *Man of Law's Tale*, some of whom are Roman and some Syrian. In this way, categories cut loose and make us think again about their apparent homogeneity. So, too, says Ingham we risk a 'double bind' by always accepting conventional oppositions and ignoring those 'traumatic' moments and places of conquest. She suggests that though much about 'medieval' is different, even dead, its particularity is not as clear-cut as we might assume. Rather, Ingham calls for an examination of the *problematics* of power across time. Acts of power (the ways in which different cultures and times colonize or suppress other bodies) are specific to context and time, but the tensions and difficulties they produce (its trauma) are, she argues, broadly similar (2003, 49–53). (See Chapter 10: Violence and Religion: Toward Anti-Sacrificial Readings.)

Contrapuntal Histories

Where Cohen confronts some of these issues through psychoanalytic theory, Ingham proposes a methodology organized around her innovative notion of 'contrapuntal histories'. The term is taken from music. There 'contrapuntal' is a notation composed of pricks or points running counter to the main melody or score. Transposed to postcolonial theory, Ingham's counter or contra-point is, then, those 'additional histories' running over or under dominant accepted ones (55 and 48). Such a move re-inscribes the alterity or difference of 'medieval' with its specificities and time-lag as *distinction* (48). It permits, too, exploration both of overlap between histories and territories of colonial rule *and* comparative analysis of time and place (temporalities and geographies). So, Ingham pushes forward Patterson's thinking about 'local' and contingent histories to advocate looking at the 'here' and 'there', at 'then' and 'now', at instabilities and oppositions (48), rather than securing 'accepted' grand narratives of history or allowing the sedimentation of categories and places – pagan, Saracen, Europe and the East (55).

In common with many postcolonialists in medieval studies, Ingham views Chaucer's *Man of Law's Tale* as a canonical text. Her critique pairs it with Conrad's similarly crucial (for modernity) *Heart of Darkness*. Both, she says, image colonialism through the intervention of ancient Rome. The unreliable narrators of each also engage the problematics of relating stories and histories as part of a colonial endeavour (55). Ingham's 'history' of academic criticism of the *Man of Law's Tale* points up some of the difficulties inherent in standard postcolonial readings, as I remarked earlier. Most of these readings highlight similarities between Islam-Christianity / Britain and Syria – often seen as exemplifying Chaucer's tolerance of religious and cultural 'others'. Instead, according to Ingham, they assert cultural *differences*, and so foreground a series of slippages that destabilize 'categories of difference' (61). Legal process and references to law punctuate the tale, revelatory not of the securing of 'us' and 'them', 'masculine' and 'feminine' (66) but of ambiguity and the ways such ideas are 'liable to shifts across time and space' (64–6). She suggests that Chaucer's tale shows how easily binary categories slip and cultural markers alter: Roman *and* Syrian Christians, pagans *and* Christians each with different status in Northumbria; Syria and Britain *both* colonized by Rome (60–1). (See Chapter 9: Intersections: Race, Gender, and Sexuality.)

In one way, then, medievalist postcolonial thinking both moves medieval studies forward and yet, in a discontinuous manoeuvre, returns us to the local and particular, to the contradictions and disjunctures with which I opened this chapter. So, too, individual theorists contribute uniquely to the field even as each remains contingent upon and responsive to the other. All of the thinkers explored in this section advocate indeterminacy while seeking to propose their own enterprise as key. It is, though, these ambiguities and contradictions that energize our own readings and keep the field alive.

Study Questions

1. Define the following terms in your own words:
   - Monstrosity
   - Nationhood
   - Sodomy
   - Queer
   - Heteronormative
   - Gender
   - Subjectivity
   - Postcolonial

   What, in your opinion, are their implications for medieval studies? Are these theoretical concepts anachronistic when applied to the Middle Ages? How much attention ought we to pay to medieval alterity?
2. List three to four key strengths and weaknesses of a key theorist you have read about in this chapter.
3. Think of three texts you've read that might be read from the theoretical perspective of historicism, psychoanalysis, postcolonialism, queer, gender or feminist approaches. Choose one text and one approach and make notes on how you might use its ideas in textual analysis.
4. Compare and contrast a range of views on Chaucer's Pardoner. Which do you find most convincing and why? Which seems the least convincing and why?
5. Describe the monstrous body, as outlined by Cohen, and its associative qualities. Why must this body always be made a spectacle? How do these ideas impact upon other texts with spectacular bodies, such as the torture

scenes of saints' lives, armouring scenes in chivalric and Arthurian romances, or the cultural icon of Christ's body for medieval persons?

6. What do you think Lochrie means when she writes of 'feminine perversion'? How is this integral to medieval discourses on sodomy (think about the 'woman who mounts', how the feminine is already perverse, and how it is made pathological and excluded)?

7. Having read the views of several theorists in this chapter, what do you understand by the term 'history' as applied to medieval studies?

8. Cohen remarks the apparent absence or reversal of *gigantomachia* in some important medieval romances – Breton *lais* like *Sir Launfal, Sir Orfeo, Floris and Blauncheflour*. How might we refine his ideas to open up these texts? Think about the doubled battle scenes in *Sir Launfal* (Launfal and his opponent/ Guinevere and Tryamour) or the monstrosity of the fairy world.

9. For Dinshaw and Patterson, the Pardoner-Wife is the crucial axis for the *Canterbury Tales*. Do you agree? Can you think of any other interpretive models for its study? Crucial to both Patterson's and Dinshaw's discussion of Chaucer's work is their insistence that he stands, in part, outside the ideological structures of his own time. In your view, is Chaucer, then, a more radical or more conservative writer?

10. *Web Quest*: Using your university or community library and/or internet search engine, find and record the bibliographical information (1) for other works by two or three ME critics discussed in this chapter and (2) for other literary or historical studies that reference ME critics discussed in this chapter. How has the work of these writers developed and how have other scholars put their writings to work?

6 Key Critics, Concepts and Topics

Bonnie Millar, Castle College

This chapter on key critics, concepts and topics provides an overview of the field of inquiry, in order to contextualize the topics addressed in detail in the subsequent chapters. It is divided into three main sections. The first section discusses of the origins, development and legacy of early critical work on medieval British literature together with its revision as more rigorous methodologies are used to scrutinize the literature. The second section, dealing with key concepts and topics, is divided into sub-sections that indicate the multiple interdisciplinary approaches used to address them. Finally, the third section surveys major critics, explaining their contributions to shaping this changing field of study.

A History of Early Criticism

Medieval British literature began to be studied and edited in the eighteenth century with Thomas Percy publishing his *Reliques of Ancient English Poetry* in 1765. This set a trend for small scale, private text publishing, with the Roxburghe Club producing limited runs of editions for members in the early years of the nineteenth century. By the middle of the nineteenth century, interest in medieval literature and culture grew with the historical novels of Walter Scott and the activities of Frederick Furnivall. Furnivall founded the Chaucer Society, dedicated to publishing early Chaucer manuscripts, and in the 1860s he began the Early English Text Society (EETS) to produce editions of Old and Middle English (ME) literary and cultural texts. Developments in comparative philology generated greater understanding of medieval works, and they were no longer viewed as barbaric but rather as part of a great national heritage. Henry Bradshaw, Frederick Furnivall, Walter Skeat and Israel Gollancz were the key figures at this stage, and their endeavours resulted in a canon of texts, works by authors like Chaucer who were associated with the medieval court and displayed a long tradition of Britain's literary riches (Matthews 1999). This was far from a new concept, for in the early fifteenth-century writers such as Hoccleve and Lydgate venerated Chaucer as the central literary figure of medieval England, a position that was solidified by Caxton's printing activities and formed the basis of the nationalistic Tudor agenda, vestiges of which still linger (Kerr 1957; Lewis 1954).

Hence the initial impetus in critical appraisals of ME literature consisted of philological, biographical and textual–codicological approaches. Scholars like Furnivall concentrated on establishing medieval texts and their sources, genres and authors. They endeavoured to uncover the authors of both individual works, attempted to group apparently similar stylistic texts, and tried to ascribe to them specific names and biographical details from historical records. In addition, these early scholars tried to establish the evolution and attributes of different genres and to categorize pieces of literature accordingly, with varying success (Loomis 1924; Trounce 1932–4). The problem with this approach is that no system of classification accounts for all texts, and a consensus as to the elements of each type has proved impossible to compile. The cause of the critical disparity is that the medieval authors created individual works, albeit in a specific mode, from traditional materials and freely used subject matter and generic features from different narrative modes and poetic forms. In addition, early analyses of ME literature exhibit the influence of late eighteenth-, nineteenth- and twentieth-century ideals, for instance confusing the terms 'romantic' and 'romance' (Kerr 1957). This scholarly desire to locate, define and categorize medieval texts fuelled the drive to establish the sources and analogues of medieval narratives and the endeavour to trace story elements to their ultimate origins. For instance, critics documented the mythic and Celtic origins of Arthurian figures. Others compared ME redactions with early French works, in order to ascertain precedence or to propose a hypothetical lost French original. Complementing these studies, critiques of style explored the use of motifs, imagery or sound. This work served to separate a canon of the literary texts deemed worthy of close analysis from those like fifteenth-century ME works, which were seen to be of little worth (Lewis 1954).

Subsequently, scholars tried to understand the diversity of texts by using more rigorous methodologies based upon the social sciences, such as Morton W. Bloomfield's historicist close textual analysis based on episodic structure (1970), Susan Wittig's structural approach focusing on narrative units (the motifeme, type-scene and type-episode) (1978) and Eugene Vance's application of theories of logic and narrativity to medieval works (1987). Northrop Frye (1957, 186–206), in his classic account using elements of psychoanalytic theory, focuses on the similarity of the medieval romance to the 'wish-fulfillment dream', with its 'childlike quality', its 'nostalgia' and the importance of adventure. A romance is a three-stage quest: *agon* (the conflict), *pathos* (the death-struggle) and *aganorisis* (the discovery and recognition of the hero). Frye's is basically a dialectical account of the archetypal conflict between the hero and his enemy. If we use the terminology of dreams, the critical approach can be summarized as the search for the libido that will relieve the subject of its anxieties concerning reality. Alternatively, we can express it through an analogy with ritual as the victory of fertility over the wasteland.

135

Thus, both critical and creative narratives are the products of a particular time and specific society, serving a cultural purpose while being read or written. They are instances of play, articulated social interaction through which the identities of the author/compiler and audience are joined. Literature functions as a catalyst for dialogue and debate, provoking the reader/listener into interacting with the text, and guiding the receiver into an awareness of the issues involved. By working through the past, we discover its strangeness, and this leads to the realization of our own inherent strangeness in the present.

The Relationship between History and Literature

Early historicist critics struggled to define the relationship between history and literature. Frederic Jameson (1981) discusses how 'all literature, no matter how weakly, must be informed by what we have called a political unconscious, that all literature must be read as a symbolic mediation on the destiny of community' (70) and that history is 'the experience of Necessity (a form of events)' (102). What Jameson means is that all ideas are constructed from cultural codes transmitted by the multiple elements that constitute a community whose elements continually interact and transect discursive boundaries. Narratives reflect these cultural negotiations in a variety of ways. Hayden White (1973, 7) notes that writers of history must mediate between the 'historical field' (the raw data, earlier histories) and an audience. He identifies five levels of conceptualization: chronicle, story, plot, argument and ideology. Thus the 'facts' (or events) have structures imposed upon them to make them meaningful (1978, 99, 110). Historical discourse is the form of story in which 'facts' or 'events' are organized, and the genre or conceptual paradigm is what makes history comprehensible. History is an attempt to explain the world, while literature is an endeavour to illuminate it. As Joseph J. Duggan (1981, 288) says of the epic, so too with medieval literary genres: historical matter is tailored to the 'synchronic system of relationships', the standard character types, usual settings, traditional scenes and conventional language. Therefore, meaning is the product of plot construction, narrative stance, social function, style, appeals to authority, characterization, genre, tradition, reception and author's purpose. It is not possible to appeal to any hard and fast rules; each text has to be examined on its own merits. Daniel Poirion (1978–9) similarly argues that there is a two-way relationship between literature and history, in that each bestows meaning on the other. Hence, each text has to be understood as an instance of the intersection of the writer's imagination with the society's ideological values. Although the study of medieval British literature is moving in new directions and utilizing new critical tools, many of the questions that engage scholars remain the same as those which have occupied critics since its inception. The differences lie in the way they conceptualize these issues and the texts they choose to interrogate. Current critical approaches are informed by the more complex ways in which we view our own subjectivities and societies, as well as our recognition of the limitations of previous critical methods and the impact of the long tradition of scholarly endeavour. (See Chapter 7: Marxism to New Historicism and Chapter 8: New Historicism and Blurring the History/Literature Divide.)

Key Concepts and Topics in Contemporary Medieval Literary Criticism

Agency

Bakhtin argues that knowledge and belief and intrinsically linked to support an authoritative discourse that is not open to dispute. Applicable to medieval Christian society, this model limits human agency in the production of knowledge, as it is deemed the provenance of the Divine. Human acquiescence to this hegemonic model ensures the maintenance of the power relations, the promotion of the common good, the sustainability of monarchy and the ultimate authority of God. In *The Parliament of Fowls*, Chaucer investigates the connections between knowledge, agency and power, where the authoritative figures of Affrycan and Nature explain the need to eliminate dissidence to those with limited agency (the narrator and the royal birds). Affrycan instills a reliance on book learning and the official discourse that subsumes worldly experience. Here, human agency is restricted, with the emphasis placed on divinely originated knowledge. Nature represents God, a monarchical figure who justifies the social structure and the birds' compliance. Humans are merely God's tools who enact the divine will, the only true form of knowledge and source of agency. In contrast, the dreams in *Troilus and Criseyde* are seen as authoritative texts, discourses that contour Troilus's and Criseyde's actions, but Pandarus's subversive interpretation suggests that resistance is possible.

Although Roland Barthes declared the Author to be dead almost four decades ago, authorial agency in medieval texts is constructed through self-dramatization, claims of following an established tradition (Marie de France alleges Breton *lais* as her sources), and taking one's lead from various sources. Alternatively authors can be self-effacing, downplaying their skill as when Chaucer's Franklin states he is 'a burel man' (III.716), a rhetorical trope called the *modesty topos*. Ultimately, agency is dependent on the nexus of social and cultural constructs, which are deemed sanctioned by a divine being who orchestrates knowledge and events, with possibilities for transgression present in the in-between spaces. As a theoretical term, agency thus denotes the subject or character's ability to negotiate structures of authority and systems of power.

Alterity and Racial/Ethnic Difference

The representation of *alterity* or *otherness* poses aesthetic and literary problems when the exigencies of the plot require foreign persons and cultures to be presented as in the cases when, for instance, Saracen princesses marry Christian knights. The figure of the Saracen 'other' forms a literary space where poetics, aesthetics and societal values are confronted and questioned (Speed 1990). Scholars taking their lead from Bakhtin's discussion of Rabelaisian carnival, the anthropological models of Mary Douglas and rhetorical reasoning promulgated by Paul de Man and Eugene Vance, who explore the discontinuities produced by alterity and antecedent textual representations. Alterity can be expressed through non-verbal behaviour (bowing, swooning), physical features, clothing and other cultural practices (Dinshaw 2001, Pearsall 1997). The recent finding of common ground between medieval and postcolonial studies has offered new perspectives from which to investigate encounters with the foreign and the shock of the different (Cohen 2003; Kabir and Williams 2005). (See Chapter 7: Postcolonial Criticism and (See Chapter 8: Multilingualism, International Contexts, and Postcolonial Concerns.)

The Body

Selves are encased in material bodies upon which are inscribed constitutive social discourses, like gender or religious belief, and medieval literature examines the encounters between fluid subjectivity and the alterity with which it is encompassed and penetrated. The body represents the site of housed subjectivity, where cultural, political, scientific and ideological discourses intersect. It can be analysed as a physical entity, a structure of parts or collection of genomes, and yet it can transcend these elements to become a site where knowledge can be created or where discourses can be inscribed. Claire Sponsler (1997) investigates the effects of the technologies of power, commodification and theatricality on constructions of medieval subjectivities. She uses a cultural historical approach that draws on Foucault's model of power, Judith Butler's conceptualizations of subjectivity and embodiment, Michel de Certeau and Terry Eagleton's theories of consumerism and Pierre Bourdieu's concept of 'habitus'. The 'habitus', which is composed of social agents who have internalized social values via the body, is an overarching structure that shapes human behaviour. Sponsler analyses the official pronouncements and prescriptions of conduct and attire that articulate a dominant social order. These discourses seek to achieve their objectives by appealing to subordinant groupings deemed in need of control. Paradoxically, due to their internal contradictions, they also facilitate the dissidence. Bodies evade complete control, and thus form a subversive space, capable of re-presentation in drag and sexually, socially or violently deviant forms which contest officially sanctioned modes of meaning and signification. As Clare R. Kinney (1994) argues, bodies are not only constructed; they are also deconstructed and even re-invented, as in Glenn Burger's 1997 reading of The *Miller's Tale*. Thus, bodies are not simply physical selves but complex cultural constructions that vary according to time and place.

Gender

Social theorists make the distinction between sex, a biological construct, and gender, a cultural construct (Rubin 1975). Gender likewise describes a movement, an act of becoming, and a part of the continuum where subject and object interact, and identity, space and time continually converge. Women's power was excluded from traditional patriarchal narratives, and women's agency likewise posed a threat to concepts of masculinity. Scholars increasingly devote attention to the multiplicities and complexities of medieval masculinities as well as femininities, and these gendered identities are forged through negotiations of embodiment, symbolism, power, social status and desire. Anthropology, psychoanalysis, cultural studies and performative theoretical models of gender underpin many of these critiques. In a widely influential study, Judith Butler (1990, 32–3) conceptualizes gendered beings as the products that result from the cultural 'regulation of attributes'. In the light of her theories, scholars consider the operation of acts and the articulation of spaces and how these operate within the 'compulsory' framework that governs gender construction in late medieval Britain. Rather than static entities, bodies are envisaged as fluid constructs where gender can be enacted or performed, and this performance confers meaning. The slippage of medieval gender ideology and its physiological basis is therefore a fruitful area of inquiry, as addressed by Vern L. Bullough and Gwen Whitehead (1999). (See Chapter 9: Feminism; Chapter 9: Gender Studies.)

For example, Mary Magdalene is a pivotal figure in gender debates, through whom issues pertaining to female social, political and religious status converge and reveal the interplay between spirituality and sexuality. These concerns are at the heart of the Digby *Mary Magdalene*, a complex miracle (or saint) play in which a whole host of late medieval religious (and specifically East Anglian) ideologies are contested. Theresa Coletti (2004, 5–6) provides a cultural reading of this saint's play, utilizing the body of scholarship on medieval female spirituality and setting the text in dialogue with East Anglian cultural artefacts that interpret religious phenomena through the frame of gender and mainstream literary works like Walter Hilton's *Scale of Perfection*. Coletti unravels the ideological negotiations in the Digby play's presentation of the Marseilles episode in which Mary converts the king and queen of Marseilles. The childless couple turns to God when they discover, after Mary's intervention, that they are to be blessed with a child. No sooner is all this accomplished than the queen dies and the king has to seek out the succour of St Peter and Mary Magdalene. On the one hand, the Digby play appears to endorse familial values and marriage while, on the other, it undercuts traditional values with other concepts of gender roles. Coletti investigates the play's invocation of Mary Magdalene as a sexual woman, 'a reconstituted virgin' (12), and her association with the Virgin Mary translates the differences between sinful secular world of gendered activity and the sacred ideal. (See Chapter 7: Feminism and Gender Studies; Chapter 7: Gender, Identity, and Queer Studies; Chapter 10: Feminism and Gender Theory.)

Identity Formation

Every *subject* – a literary-critical term for the individual person – is composed of disparate elements that cohere through identification with, and divergence from, transmitted cultural norms. Subjects are likewise interpellated, constituted through their naming and identifying with dominant societal codes and the creation of subjectivity fashions a space within which there is the potential for reworking these forms. Subjects are not so much a representation of these social codes, but result from continual negotiations between desire and language, and as subjects evolve, they adapt to, and shift between, discourses and power relations. Through writing and repetition, what Judith Butler calls *performativity*, we translate and adapt to the constantly changing cultural situations with which we are faced. The relationship between identity, subjectivity and power is fluid as human identity is confronted by issues of class, race, age and other social and political exigencies. In contrast, disguise is a means of examining the interplay between the individual and society, and it is employed in medieval romances to hide the identity – status, origin and lineage – of the hero while simultaneously engendering him (Crane 1997, 2002). (See Chapter 4: Margery Kempe, *The Book of Margery Kempe*.)

Medieval Britain was also subject to forces of immense change with religious reform movements, economic and environmental crises and the rise of civic and secular institutions, all of which affected individual identity formation. (See Chapter 2: Famine and Plague.) Because of the complexities of subject formation, critics have become increasingly preoccupied with the formation and evolution of English nationhood and the cultural anxieties concerning the state of the country. Derek Pearsall (2001) argues that despite two brief periods where it is possible to distinguish English national feeling (1290–1340 and 1410–20), the major impetus in formulating an English national identity coincided with the establishment of English as the national language (Turville-Petre 1996). (See Chapter 5: Jeffrey Jerome Cohen, *The Post-colonial Middle Ages* [2000]; Chapter 7: Postcolonial Criticism; See Chapter 8: Multilingualism, International Contexts, and Postcolonial Concerns; Chapter 9: Postcolonial Studies.)

Language and Literature

Critics increasingly realize that the compartmentalization of academic studies needs to be overcome. In order to analyse medieval British literature, we must be sensitive to the fundamentals of more than one language. Therefore, we need to determine the function of a text's language and its relationship to contemporaneous languages. In his introduction to *Multilingualism in Later Medieval Britain*, a volume of essays dealing with the history, practice and consequences of language interplay (2000, 3), D. A. Trotter discusses how the 'challenge of multilingualism' has inspired historical sociolinguistics and critical approaches to literature based on the textual analysis of 'code-switching', linguistic appropriation and language-mixing. Studies of modern bilingualism (Romaine 1995) inform the exploration of the ME and Medieval British (socio) linguistic situations, which in turn are illuminated by the historical data patterns. (See Chapter 8: Multilingualism, International Contexts, and Postcolonial Concerns.)

Location, Territorialization, Cartography

Through the textualization of territories and the treatment of texts as territories, lands and texts can be analysed, contained and interpreted. The use of 'discourses of embodiment' facilitates the expression of the inter-connectedness of space and time and the merging of disparate groups into a single discursive unity (Tomasch and Gilles 1996, 5–7). Naming and locating dangerous elements, particularly associating them with traditional figures and places, is a means of presenting the alien and exotic in a safe space, a position that allows them to be conquered and controlled. Jeffrey Jerome Cohen (1999, 5) argues that 'projecting a history upon the land is the mirror image of the process of identity formation' detailed by Lacan, who argues that an individual 'receives its selfhood' by 'seeing itself mimicked in the actions of another' or 'by gazing into a mirror'. The map thus becomes a mirror of national or corporate identity. Jennifer R. Goodman (1988) undertakes a comparative reading of chivalric literature and texts concerned with exploration. She endeavours to rediscover a body of literature, much of which is little known, such as fifteenth- and sixteenth-century prose romances that were held to be inferior prose translations or adaptations of earlier ME verse romances and French texts. Literary journeys to differing locales, real and imagined, wild and civilized are a means of exploring chivalric and corporate identity (Saunders 1993). (See Chapter 3: Pilgrim and Travel Literature.)

Marginal Voices

As the study of ME literature became an academic discipline, certain genres, authors and texts became canonized and received a great deal of attention, while others were excluded, particularly late medieval texts and those deemed 'popular'. Material focusing on the Robin Hood legend is a case in point. New texts and appraisals of the works related to Robin Hood, themselves the product of different periods and locales, are now becoming available. Renewed critical interest in these formerly marginalized texts have allowed literary critics to deal with their political implications, offer sociocultural readings and rehabilitate these formerly marginal texts and voices. Scholarly interest in reception theories has led to explorations of the possible meanings such narratives may have had for different receivers (listeners/readers), their potential reactions and the re-articulations of culture contained in popular forms like poems, plays and ballads. For instance, Barbara A. Hanawalt (1999) and Evelyn Mullally and John Thompson (1997) have published critical anthologies containing a number of papers on the liminality of the court and outsiders. Drawing on Mikhail Bahktin's cultural materialism and Raymond William's sociolinguistic theories readings of the production and consumption of culture, Peter Stallybrass (1999), Peter R. Coss (1999) and Richard Tardiff (1999) have read the Robin Hood tradition with its use of the mythology of the forest and courtly outsiders as an expression of cultural anxiety. Reappraisals of the fifteenth-century literature, particularly its political and aesthetic content, have led scholars to read this previously ignored literature as a self-conscious literary oeuvre invested with anxiety yet addressing political turmoil and intellectual fervour (Cooney 2001). (See Chapter 9: Feminism.)

The Marvellous/Monstrous

Marvels and magic are employed in medieval texts to generate complex situations that permit the exploration of human motivation, morals and self-hood and invite multiple responses and reactions. The use of magical objects, tests and encounters create an imaginative space where complex social, theological and moral issues can be safely explored, as in *Ywain and Gawain* where Ywain's receipt and loss of a magical ring at the hands of his beloved are used to discuss the limitations of his fidelity and performance as both knight and husband. Michelle Sweeney (2000), using a comparative approach that takes into account the intertextual nature of romances, examines the 'interactive' reception encouraged of the audience through magic's function as a literary tool linked to religion, history, science, philosophy and society. By invoking monsters, it is possible to examine the forms of humanity that fail to cohere to accepted cultural norms. These monstrous figures occupy a space where subversive, disruptive and dangerous forces can be examined in order to establish the positive and negative sides of the 'human' and its 'boundaries'. The *monstrous body* fails to be bound by dominant cultural codes and is not subject to social control. In overcoming the monstrous, as Jeffrey Jerome Cohen argues (1997, 226), the hero discovers how to direct the 'drives that traverse the body' and thereby becomes a unified human being. The monstrous is thus a useful medium for exploring the problems of identity-formation, the differences that are embedded in the individual. Initially, each subject is fragmented and struggles to achieve unity through internalizing culturally proscribed images, a la Lacan's 'mirror stage'. The monstrous body that fails to complete this process becomes a being represents an origin of human identity, the point from which humanity springs. Geoffrey of Monmouth's use of the Albina myth, in Cohen's 1999 reading, supplies an instance in which Brutus' triumph over the female giants in the founding of Britain subsumes the monstrous feminine and establishes it as an originary myth in which the maternal linked with the natural is erased in order that a masculine linguistic order can be established. Through opposing monsters and monstrous places to humans and civilization, it is possible to naturalize cultural articulations of power, gender and nation. (See Chapter 4: Marie de France, *Lanval* and Chapter 5: Jeffrey Jerome Cohen, *Of Giants* [1999].)

Orality and Textuality

As Derek Brewer (1997) argues, written and oral communication entails a prior knowledge of language and 'complete originality would be incomprehensible', for in 'traditional literature' (9) this situation is intensified because most narratives constitute 're-tellings' rather than original compositions (16). From the late eighteenth century, when the drive for originality and objective truth became priorities, repetition and retelling became denigrated as inferior, but Brewer persuasively argues that all narrative is in a sense an act of 'remembering', where the past is translated, appropriated and re-iterated, with repetition essential to this activity (18).

Literacy is influenced by orality and vice versa, with written texts displaying oral techniques and oral works incorporating book learning. Retelling conveys continuity, re-invents the past in accord with the needs of the present and generates new relevance from a traditional tale. Chaucer's use of traditional tales is analysed by Carl Lindahl (1987), and the features of traditional tales, with their cross-cultural and international qualities, are classified and documented by Stith Tompson (1955–8) and Antti Aarne (1971) using a historic–geographic methodology. In the Middle Ages, both the literate and illiterate relied on and trained their memories, for both literature and learning were communicated orally and tended to be encountered by listening as texts were read or performed aloud. Poetry in such a culture is improvised to some extent during performance, using various mnemonic techniques (Carruthers 1996; Doane and Pasternack 1991). Milmann Parry and Alfred Lord's studies of the Yugoslavian *guslars* (bards), together with more recent analyses by W. A. Quinn and A. S. Hall (1982) and Walter Ong (1982), illustrate how to interpret the traits of orally improvised works, how to comprehend literature intended to be read aloud and how to understand the differences between primary oral and literate cultures. Scholars and students alike need to query the very linguistic foundations of texts and unravel the various layers of embodied voices, both consciously and unconsciously interwoven into the texts we read today. Julia Kristeva's (1980) model of intertextuality furnishes a fruitful way to conceptualize 're-telling', dealing as it does with the multifarious voices in a text and the participation of both author and listener/reader in the production and consumption of meaning (although see Leicester's alternative view [1987]).

'History' and the Past

What exactly is 'history'? When we read historical texts, the important questions to ask are, What do we mean by 'history' and 'the past'? What did history, the past, mean for medieval society? Not only is the past re-invented in accordance with the needs of the present, it is essential to recognize that accounts of the past are imaginatively constructed narratives. Hence, contemporary medieval studies recognize the need for comparative analyses of literatures and histories, for two main reasons: first, to avoid cultural solipsism (believing that one type of discourse or development is normative, usually the one we prefer, and all others are deviant), and second, to test our readings and verify our hypotheses. In other words, 'history' is never simply about the past but likewise concerns the present. (See Chapter 8: New Historicism and Blurring the History/Literature Divide.)

The appearance of new editions of most of the dramatic texts and extensive research into early records has led to a re-evaluation of early twentieth-century theories concerning the origins of the drama, particularly the realization that E. K. Chambers' *The Mediaeval Stage* (1903) and other similar studies were heavily influenced by nineteenth- and early twentieth-century evolutionary models, a view refuted by O. B. Hardison (1965). The *Records of Early English Drama* project (*REED*) is an endeavour to uncover and edit all extant evidence of dramatic activity in each British county up to 1642 and has influenced subsequent studies of medieval English drama, providing a vast amount of previously inaccessible data concerning the contexts in which it occurred. What we have learned is that 'drama' is more than just a performance but is part of a larger network of dramatic texts and performances as well as the patronage, logistics and technology required to produce them. Theresa Coletti reviews the limitations of the historicist approach of using documentary evidence of dramatic origins and performance history as the basis of literary analysis (1990). Thus, drama recounts, generates and forms part of the past and history. (See Chapter 1: Extending the Medieval.)

One of the best examples of how contemporary medieval scholarship interrogates different constructions of history is found in the study of drama, particularly the ME civic or 'cycle' plays (the York, Chester, Towneley and N-Town plays). Late medieval drama translates biblical texts and theological commentaries into vernacular spectacles. Information provided by the extant manuscripts and the religious, civic and private records detailing the drama's history, revision and performance reveals a complex interplay with theological, political and literary texts generates meaning (Nisse 2005). In the current reappraisal of medieval English drama, Lawrence M. Clopper (2001) has questioned the accepted history of medieval drama as a renewal of classical tradition based on an amplification of the liturgy, arguing that liturgical development differs markedly from drama in intention and execution and that a vernacular lay performative tradition evolved independently from church-based drama. (See Chapter 1: Redefining the Period.)

Performance and Spectacle

One of the key components in the literature of late medieval Britain is its performative nature, which is grounded in the theatricality and the 'spectacular' nature of culture, as manifested in a variety of public celebrations; civic, religious and courtly festivities; and the ME mystery and morality plays. Paul Strohm (1992), Seth Lerer (1995), Laura Kendrick (1988) and John Ganim (1990) provide detailed readings of the independence of literary works and popular / public ceremony. The historicist approach favoured by Paul Strohm in exploring social constructions has been adapted by other scholars, who have combined it with anthropological conceptualizations of ritual, theatre and performativity – a model of the ability of discourse to produce that which it expresses and controls. *The Performance of Middle English Culture: Essays on Chaucer and the Drama* (Paxson, Clopper and Tomasch 1998) contains 11 essays which reflect the current drive for greater awareness of institutional and theoretical implications in the production of meaning, approaching the works of Chaucer and medieval drama from an inter-disciplinary standpoint grounded in close textual analysis and historically situating iconographical, anthropological and sociological mechanisms.

Even the idea of 'performance' is being reassessed. For example, the medieval terms for 'theatre' or 'drama' do not necessarily have modern implications when used in medieval contexts, and terms like 'play' or 'ludus' referred to disparate and not necessarily dramatic activities. Thus Lawrence M. Clopper's (2001) reappraisal of medieval performative spectacles and ME drama begins with a philological enquiry upon which he bases his larger project of providing a cultural history of the field. Clopper's analysis of the medieval terminology removes the spectre of classical comparisons and presents the material in its medieval context of political negotiation between clerical and secular institutions. Hence, Clopper concludes that dramaturgical performances were the material manifestations of pastoral care, power and prestige. Dramatic texts, like those at York and Chester, were subject to re-interpretation, re-presentation and revision in accordance with changing cultural needs and different theo-political controversies, and their production continued well into the seventeenth century. Lynn Forest-Hill (2000) com-pares the interaction between transgressive language, with its indebtedness to its social context, and words, action and audience in the fifteenth- and sixteenth-century biblical, moral and political drama. By considering these texts in relation to the moral prescriptions of sermons and laws concerning such discourse, she uncovers a liminal, subversive space between the society portrayed in the drama and the society in which it was produced and performed, a space where social critique and religious education prevail.

Transmission and Authority

The relationship between the physicality of texts and political/literary authority is complex, as it is through the material form the reader encounters the works. Textual authority can be re-enforced and self-constructed through the addition of illustrations, commentary or glosses and the selection of com-plementary accompanying works. In order to analyse its dynamics, many critics have incorporated a greater theoretical perspective, turning to models such as Foucault's power matrix to illuminate how manuscripts are 'the material outcomes' at the intersections of power's 'net-like organization' and to understand how texts are 'the meeting point of all the social interactions' in the 'circulation of power' (Riddy 2000, 5). For example, Riddy focuses on the relationship of prestige, authority and power in twelfth to sixteenth-century manuscripts, so when we turn to a medieval work, we need to establish how it was transmitted (in medieval manuscripts and modern editions) and that medieval and modern transmission affects the mode of circulation and the layers of scribal, editorial and critical activity (Symes 2007). (See Chapter 4: Margery Kempe, *The Book of Margery Kempe*.)

Critics

Any selection of contemporary critics will be partial at best and as a result incomplete, but the scholars listed below offer a range of critical perspectives, theoretical orientations and areas of study important to current trends in medieval studies.

David Aers

David Aers works on medieval theology, ecclesiology, literature and culture in England, publishing a range of works on Chaucer, Langland and the inter-sections of history, language, literature, religion, culture and ideology. In 'A Whisper in the Ear of Early Modernity: or Reflections on Literary Critics writing the "History of the Subject" ' (1992), Aers writes revealingly of the paradox whereby New Historicists and other recent 'radical' critics have con-structed the same understanding of an 'idealist' Middle Ages as earlier critics. They do not challenge the values at the base of the centre/margin distinction. His work has led to re-evaluations in the way we view medieval society to place spirituality, which he views as intrinsically connected to social and aesthetic concerns, to the centre of medieval studies.

Sarah Beckwith

Sarah Beckwith's work on medieval spirituality, embodiment, ritual and its literary expression, especially in drama, is of great significance to current understandings of these issues. In *Christ's Body: Identity, Religion and Society in Medieval English Writing* (1993), she argues that the human body is the bond between the self and society and that Christ's body symbolizes this relation-ship. His body, moreover, can be seen as a battleground in which personal identity and society, agency and structure, vie for position. Following this, she postulates in 'Ritual, Church and Theatre: Medieval Dramas of the Sac-ramental Body' (1992) that ritual does not necessarily consolide of social order. In *Signifying God: Social Relation and Symbolic Act in the York Corpus Christi Plays* (2001), she further develops this analysis, where she reads the mystery plays as a form of sacramental theatre, seeing a relationship between social actions and symbolism, in which the Corpus Christi plays are a mechanism of labour control (Beckwith 1994). Her reading highlights the ways in which theatre and theology – especially the sacraments – operate together through the body of Christ, the material presence of divine agency.

147

Louise O. Aranye Fradenburg

Louise O. Aranye Fradenburg in *City, Marriage, Tournament: Arts of Rule in Late Medieval Scotland* (1991), a study that continues to influence medieval criticism, conceptualizes the city not as an origin of change but as a locale in which change and human constructs are more visible. Personal identity is under constant threat from external perception, and individuals need to self-dramatize in order to align their self-perception with public modes of assessing worth as knight do in tournaments. Fradenberg's work offers rigorous new approaches to dealing with issues of sexuality, rethinking the ways in which history and theory – in particular queer theory – intersect and how these challenge expressions and perceptions of sexuality (Fradenburg and Freccero 1996). (See Chapter 7: Psychoanalytic Theory.)

Bruce W. Holsinger

Holsinger employs a historicist approach to compare disparate vernacular and Latin texts, dealing with a range of topics and their intersections. In *Music, Body and Desire in Medieval Culture: Hildegard of Bingen to Chaucer* (2001), he challenges traditional assumptions concerning the role of music, and through his insights into musicality he discovers further interconnections between literature, religion, sexuality, gender and culture, revealing them in a new light. Holsinger does not merely engage with medieval literature, philosophy, art, history and ideology; he also challenges the uses of medieval history, culture and literature at the hands of modern philosophical, sociological and literary-critical theorists (*The Premodern Condition*, 2005). (See Chapter 1: Theorizing the Texts.)

Stephen Knight

Stephen Knight publishes widely on medieval cultural studies, particularly on Arthurian literature, Robin Hood and Chaucer. His work on Robin Hood seeks to redress the lack of critical attention received by this figure, particularly to advance scholarship and to move beyond historical–biographical studies. He finds that social historians, interested in the 'real' Robin Hood, created an empiricist, individualist myth of their own. His work reveals a number of 'Robin Hoods', from the social bandit who represents local organic values pitted against the distant oppression of civic and religious authorities, to the gentrified Robin Hood of the sixteenth century who fights for the true hierarchy. He finds that Robin Hood legends change more considerably over time than does Arthurian matter, as there is little compulsory narrative, with tales of each in ascendancy according to the cultural and political climate of the period. Robin Hood material tends to be more prevalent in politically conservative eras where it provides a means of resistance.

Steven F. Kruger

Kruger approaches medieval texts with a meticulous eye for detail, deploying historical specificity and contextual information, before paring away the layers of meaning with a shrewd use of critical tools. In *The Spectral Jew: Conversion and Embodiment in Medieval Europe* (2006), he draws on Derrida's concept of spectres – ambiguous, paradoxical beings who appear to combine disparate and contradictory elements, and are both real and unreal. He argues that the past cannot be sealed off and laid to rest and that it inevitably affects and continuously influences the present. For Kruger, the lingering presence of Judaism is an instance of the queer. He notes how Jewish difference is inscribed on and through Jewish bodies. He carefully teases out the different elements that entwine to form human identity such as ethnicity and gender in a historically grounded study. (See Chapter 7: Gender, Identity, and Queer Studies and See Chapter 9: Queer Theory.)

Miri Rubin

Miri Rubin's *Corpus Christi: The Eucharist in Late Medieval Culture* (1991) opened up new avenues of reading medieval religiosity and embodiment that have become central to discussions of theology, the sacraments, gender debates and their cultural and literary manifestations. The Eucharist reveals the power of God orchestrating the forces of nature, just as any miracle does, but transubstantiation proves the reliability of the divine. The 'sacramental power' (1991, 50–1) of these regular events makes priests 'ritual performers of sacramental acts', connecting Christian society to God. She argues that processions offer multiple, contradictory and unstable meanings (1991, 49) rather than a single unified message. Basically, public processions are the scene of conflict through which people tried to work out their relationship to the community as a whole and their position in it, as one of those saved by Christ. Rubin discusses the discourse of bread and food, whereby Mary is seen as the provider of food to Christ, and Christ to all Christians. The Corpus Christi feast, established in the thirteenth century, is a further means of demonstrating the 'hegemonic sacramental world-view' of the Church, the teaching, doctrine and the overarching power of the Christian institution (1992, 51).

Martin Stevens

In 1978 Martin Stevens published a seminal essay, 'The Performing Self in Twelfth-century Culture', which encapsulated the performative nature of scholastic thinking and addressed its cultural production, incorporating an anthropological sensibility to the study of medieval drama. This model informs his work on the production of the Ellesmere manuscript and the Wakefield plays. The breadth of medieval British literature is reflected in his research – linguistics, Old English, Medieval Latin, Chaucer, ME drama,

Shakespeare and critical theory. His contribution to medieval studies lies not merely in developing new ways of conceptualizing its cultural products, but also in the related project of disrupting the traditional canon of great writers – primarily Chaucer – and addressing formerly marginalized texts like the English mystery plays. In *Four Middle English Mystery Cycles: Textual, Contextual and Critical Interpretations* (1987), Stevens confronts the difficulties entailed in a historicist analysis of medieval texts and provides a critically aware, historically grounded close textual reading of the plays which illuminates their cultural and ideological concerns.

Paul Strohm

Paul Strohm, now based at Columbia University, is the former J. R. R. Tolkien Professor of English language and literature at the University of Oxford. Strohm argues that texts are not mere reflections of history but that they are 'argumentative and interpretative documents' and 'objects of contestation' (1992, 167–72). Based on this theoretical concept, he reads *The Knight's Tale* and Maydistone's (Maidstone's) *Concordia: The Reconcilliation of Richard II with London* in the light of Richard II's and Queen Anne's activities in 1392. Strohm is concerned with the 'affiliated text', the connections between textuality, history, genre and social change. His *Politique: Languages of Statecraft between Chaucer and Shakespeare* (2005) is an innovative textual, linguistic and cultural analysis of political discourse in vernacular fifteenth-century English texts, read alongside continental writings, which explores interpretations of Fortune and uncovers a 'pre-Machiavellian moment' in politics. The impact of his books is manifested in a greater theoretical awareness in historicist approaches. (See Chapter 7: Marxism to New Historicism; Chapter 8: New Historicism and Blurring the History/Literature Divide; Chapter 10: Materialist Criticism.)

Study Questions

1. Define the following terms in your own words:

   - Agency
   - Gender
   - Heteronormative
   - Materiality
   - Monstrosity
   - Nationhood
   - Queer
   - Sodomy
   - Spectacle
   - Subjectivity

2. Outline three features of gender theory. Illustrate your answer with an example of how you might use this approach in literary analysis.

3. Describe two to three limitations of the biographical or textual/codicological approach in literary-critical studies. Why are codicological studies also essential to medieval literature?

4. Outline two strengths and two weaknesses of a psychoanalytic approach in literary-critical studies.

5. Discuss how the postcolonial perspective helps critics to understand individual behaviour. In you answer, refer to at least two texts that you have studied.

6. Explain the function of authorial agency in one of Chaucer's the *Canterbury Tales*. How might one use Kristeva's model of intertextuality to open up this text?

7. In your view, what does the introduction of race, gender and ethnicity studies do to your study and appreciation of medieval British literature?

8. In literary and historical studies of medieval culture, critics debate 'the pastness of the past' (*alterity*), the presence of the present in the study of the past (*presentism*) and 'the place of the past' in the present (*medievalism*). In your own words, try to define the differences in these critical positions. Identify one critic whom you would associate with each position and outline why you link your chosen critics with that particular position.

9. One criticism brought against current critical approaches is that supposedly they tend to favour the exceptional (the monstrous, magical, liminal and other) over the 'normal'. On the one hand, what are the merits of this criticism? On the other hand, what is to be gained by examining the more exceptional elements of medieval literature?

10. *Web Quest*: One way to gauge the degree to which an idea has permeated a broad area of study is to see if it has made its way into the classroom. Perform a web search using two keyword search terms: (1) the name of one of the scholars featured in this chapter (for example, Jeffrey Jerome Cohen, Carolyn Dinshaw or Louise Fradenberg) and (2) a concept detailed above (for example, alterity, the body, or the monstrous). Do this a half-dozen times to see how these scholars and their ideas are being used, criticized or developed further by other readers of ME literature. Which ideas and scholars seem to have the most currency? Which ideas are waxing and which are waning, if at all?

7   Changes in Critical
      Responses and Approaches

*John M. Ganim, University of
California, Riverside*

Chapter Overview

Literary Theory and Medieval Texts

The main theoretical developments of the past 30 years have been post-structuralism, New Historicism, feminism, gender and sexuality studies and postcolonial studies. This chapter provides definitions of these major currents and describes a typical or especially influential example of their uses in the study of Middle English (ME) literature. We will also consider how medieval literature itself has been fundamental to these new ways of thinking about writing, language and what literature itself is made of. We must also remember that the distinctions between and among these main currents are not hard and fast, and many approaches borrow from or build on other approaches. In addition, these new theoretical approaches are often inspired by a common roster of thinkers from many different disciplines. Some of these thinkers include Michel Foucault, whose interest in the history of power, punishment and control was one of the starting points of the New Historicism, and whose *The History of Sexuality* (1978), by highlighting the conventional and even constructed nature of gender roles, was one of the major influences on feminist studies and sexuality studies. Jacques Derrida (1976), the French philosopher associated with deconstruction, taught that the obvious and intended meanings of a piece of writing might be destabilized by their identity with that which they apparently oppose. The anthropology of James Clifford (1986 and 1988), Clifford Geertz (1973) and Pierre Bourdieu (1977 and 1990) has called into question the position of the observer, especially the privileged, Western, scientific observer interpreting the 'primitive' or non-Western world, and their critique of that position has been employed by some of these new theoretical movements to question how we understand the past and its mentalities.

We might ask ourselves why and what purpose these complex and often counter-intuitive approaches serve. After all, many of us are attracted to ME literature because of its accessibility. It seems to many beginning readers that, like children's literature or fairy tales, medieval literature is closer to an immediate, instinctive and uncomplicated view of life than that of more cynical, sardonic or depressing periods, such as the modern period. We are drawn to the romantic image of courtly love, to the untarnished heroism of chivalric romance or to the unembarrassed expression of religious devotion in medieval lyrics or plays. Nevertheless, the value of these theoretical approaches is to raise questions about why we are attracted to the apparent idealism and simplicity of this literature and to point out that both our response and the literature itself are more complex and contradictory than we would like to assume. Traditional literary scholarship has often made something of the same point, noting, for instance, that our picture of medieval literature would be quite different if we read the widely circulated *Prick of Conscience* rather than the uncertainly available *Sir Gawain and the Green Knight*. However, even traditional literary scholarship has modified its procedures and changed the questions it has asked because of pressure from theoretical advances.

It helps to understand the history of literary study and the place of ME literature in that history to appreciate the changes wrought by the theoretical revolution of the past 30 years. At the end of the nineteenth and the beginning of the twentieth century, to study English literature was to study Old and ME literature through its language. This was partly because the difficulty and antique appearance of ME literature seemed to equal the difficulty and antiquity of the literature of Greece and Rome, which had been for many centuries the only literature worth studying at the university level. At the same time, ME literature was a handmaiden of linguistic study, and the value of its texts was as evidence for early English language and, to some extent, early English life, an agenda inseparable from imperialism and nationalism in the nineteenth and early twentieth centuries. By the middle of the twentieth century, the rise of the New Criticism, with its formal emphasis, had displaced ME literature to the margins of the canon in favour of more amenable bodies of work such as metaphysical poetry. Medieval literary study fought its way back by attempting to prove that medieval literature manifested the qualities valourized by the implicit and explicit assumptions of the New Criticism. Thirty years ago, critics could point to Chaucer's poetic persona and his sophistication at manipulating narratives within narratives, the formal and verbal virtuosity of *Pearl* and *Sir Gawain and the Green Knight*, the metadramatic awareness of the *Second Shepherd's Play*, the imagistic intensity of the ME lyrics, all of which seemed to have added up to the rehabilitation of medieval English literature. By the middle of the twentieth century, especially after the Second World War, the rise of the New Criticism, with its formalist and aesthetic agenda, competed with Myth Criticism, with its psychological and anthropological agenda, as the primary ways in which students especially appreciated ME literature. (See Chapter 6: A History of Criticism.)

Challenging the Centrality of Chaucer

Now, however, a map of the study of ME literature would be very different. Chaucer is only first among equals, and his contemporary Langland, the author of *Piers Plowman*, is now at the centre of some of the most intense scholarship in the field. In the work of someone like Paul Strohm, Chaucer himself is now frequently thought of in terms of his struggle to maintain his patronage and privilege amidst the turmoil and shifting political fortunes of the late fourteenth century, particularly the factional struggles within Parliament and the clashes between Lancastrian and Ricardian forces during the last decade of the fourteenth century. This is a very different picture that of the ironically bemused aesthetic fashioner of an earlier phase of criticism, such as that of E. T. Donaldson. Now Chaucer finds himself discussed in the same language as his formerly lesser contemporaries and followers such as Thomas Usk, John Gower and Thomas Hoccleve, and William Langland, the last of whom he is sometimes compared unfavourably, at least in terms of his address to the social and political ills of his moment. Some scholars believe that for the last 15 years at least, the driving questions in late ME studies have not come from Chaucer or from medieval romance, the genres most associated with the period by those working outside the period, but from the study of medieval religious writings (medieval mystics, especially female, and the Lollards) and from the study of Langland's *Piers Plowman*. By drawing on his deep knowledge of Langland and his interest in how literary politics are real politics, John Bowers (2007) proposes nothing less than a rewriting of our understanding of the late medieval canon, replacing an idealized Chaucer as the father of English literature with a difficult and controversial work – *Piers Plowman* – that intervenes in literary tradition rather than serenely originates it. From Bower's point of view, the historical beginning point of the English literary canon is a virtual, and sometimes actual, battleground, where the stakes for supporting a particular idea of the literary can literally be fatal. In place of realism and irony, contemporary criticism has valourized an anxious and searching exploration of theological and political beliefs and institutions, and has not necessarily expected consistent or logical conclusions.

Even more fundamentally, the fifteenth century and the earlier ME period (Cannon 2004) have displaced the fourteenth century's former status as the Golden Age of medieval English literature. The revolution in gender studies, with its new appreciation of female authors and readers and a feminized spirituality, has canonized such works as *The Book of Margery Kempe* from the fifteenth century and *Ancrene Wisse* and other works of the so called *Katherine Group* from the early thirteenth and late twelfth centuries. Malory's *Morte d'Arthur* had always retained a wide popular readership, but criticism had relegated it to a shaggy missing link in the evolution of the novel. It is now being thought of in terms of the specific political conditions and literary discourses of the fifteenth century. Medieval drama, once thought of as a 'pre-Shakespearean' popular form, has been the subject of a thoroughgoing reconsideration of its origin, history, dating and performance practices, encouraged by the massive archival project known as *REED* (*Records of Early English Drama*). An entire new set of methodological and theoretical approaches, some of them grounded in the complex psychoanalytic theory of Jacques Lacan (1992) and the influential writings of French Feminists such as Luce Irigiray and Julie Kristeva (Marks and De Courtivron 1980), resulted in revised understandings of even early English texts by finding them implicated in changing notions of sexuality and gender. This chapter will suggest ways in which these sometimes mutually exclusive ways to read ME literature can be deployed to help students understand both the texts them-selves as well as the approaches and methodologies they will be asked to master in other courses. (See Chapter 5: Case Studies in Reading.)

Testing the Tenets of Theory

ME literature has always stood as something of a challenge to reigning critical paradigms. Not only has the scholarship surrounding the literature reflected attempts over the past 30 years to engage with the range of approaches that emerged in the wake of the New Criticism – feminist theory, New Histori-cism, postcolonial studies, poststructuralism and deconstruction, the study of queer, gay and lesbian sexualities, critical race theory – it also provides a test case for the limits or historical specificity of these approaches. This was no less true 30 years ago, when medievalists tested the New Critical tenets of an organic work of literature, the ambiguity and complexity of poetic imagery and the possibility of close reading as a key to all essential meanings of a text, against the almost intractable demands of medieval writing, with its complex status in manuscripts and its uncertain authorial intent, its historically alien language and diction and its apparent allegiance to an aesthetic that did not conform to the precision and balance advocated by the New Criticism. (See Chapter 10: Exegetical Criticism and its Critics.)

At the same time, it often comes as a surprise how much and how often the study of medieval literature and culture has been implicated in the conception or development of these many approaches that we usually think of as modern or postmodern (Holsinger 2005 and Labbie 2006). The trajectory of women's studies and feminist scholarship over the past 30 years would not have been the same without the impact of works such as *Jesus as Mother* (1982) and *Holy Feast and Holy Fast* (1987), both by Caroline Walker Bynum. At the same time that interest in medieval female mystics was being encouraged by Bynum's work, French feminist theorists such as Luce Irigiray and Julie Kristeva

(Marks and De Courtivron 1980) promoted medieval mystical writings as a unique form of female discourse, sparking debates about linguistic representation and gender. The rethinking of such classic studies as de Rougemont's *Love in the Western World* (1940), with its critique of romantic love, by Jacques Lacan (1992) in his seminars on courtly love helped shape his unique juncture of psychoanalysis and linguistic structuralism. If Eve Sedgwick (1985) pointed us to how the erotic and romantic conflicts of the English novel were really 'between men', she could not have done so without the earlier troubling of romantic plots in medieval romance noted by scholars of courtly love. In addition, one of the first articulations of what we now consider Queer Studies may well be the debate about the sexuality of the Pardoner in the *General Prologue* of Chaucer's *Canterbury Tales*. Similarly, the rise of the New Historicism, with its debt to Michel Foucault (1978), was inseparable from Foucault's many investigations into medieval mentality and sexuality, from the Church Fathers in the early Christian era to the reforms of the Fourth Lateran Council (1215) in the high to late Middle Ages. Even more specifically literary developments, such as the procedures of reader-response criticism as one of the first defections from New Critical orthodoxy, was formulated by medievalists such as Hans Robert Jauss (1982) with his definition of a 'horizon of expectation', first defined in terms of beast fables. (See Chapter 1: Theorizing the Texts.)

Structuralism and Poststructuralism

In 1975, Jonathan Culler published a book called *Structuralist Poetics* (1975). For many North American and some British scholars trained in the New Criticism or its offshoots, or, indeed, in the philological model that preceded the New Criticism, this book was a first introduction to what has become known as 'theory'. Culler in fact was describing a number of different developments, chiefly derived from French cultural thought in the 1960s. Some of these developments would more accurately be described as 'poststructuralist' rather than structuralist, and most of what we mean by theory today derives from poststructuralist developments. For Culler, the real promise of these new approaches was not that they led to a deeper understanding of an individual work or author, but that they sought to discover the general systems that governed the possible expressions of any given work, much as structural linguistics sought to describe the *langue* – the complete system of possible utterances – rather than the *parole* – the individual utterance within that system – of a language or language itself. (See Chapter 10: The Influences of Structuralism.)

Looking back on the changes of the past 30 years, it seems as if something other than what Culler advocated resulted from the discovery of 'theory'.

First, the new approaches were applied not to the *systems* of medieval literature, but as tools to understand *individual* texts and relatively limited groups
of texts. Second, poststructuralist theory transformed already existing
approaches to literature. For instance, stylistics was influenced by and even
transformed into semiotics. Marxism was synthesized with structuralism to
explain not so much how material conditions determine literary productions,
but how material conditions are represented in refracted form in literature,
indeed, in the form of literature itself. Psychoanalytic approaches to literature,
a staple of literary criticism since the 1920s, found itself reborn through the
work of Jacques Lacan, who described the workings of the unconscious mind
as akin to the system of language conceived in a poststructuralist format.
Lacan's theories, filtered through its powerful application in film theory, with
its emphasis on the subject position of the viewer, the gendered gaze of the
spectator and the construction of the image of the body, transformed a feminist criticism that had just started to revise a male-dominated canon and
search for the record of female experience in literature.

Questioning the Author

Many of these developments are paradoxical. They key nicely with new
developments in literary theory, but it is as if the criticism of medieval
literature paralleled on a separate track some of the most startling claims of
literary theory. That is, the criticism of medieval literature articulated what in
other fields would be avant-garde statements by means of a documentary and
historicist turn. Who or what is an author? The troubling of the concept of the
author, formerly a more or less naturally assumed position, can be traced to
the structuralist emphasis on the system of literature, and in poststructuralism, on the virtual autonomy of the discourse of writing, distinct, as it were,
from a person writing. The most famous statements of this reconceptualization of authorship are the wells know essays by Roland Barthes, 'The Death
of the Author' (1977) and Michel Foucault, 'What is An Author?' (1977).
Foucault and Barthes, among their other agendas, questioned the notion of a
heroic, autonomous self behind and within writing itself. While often
regarded by those outside the field as a reserve protected from the effects
of postmodern theory, medieval literary scholarship advanced claims that
were in their own way as striking. One was the well-documented medieval
tendency to defer to previous authority above and beyond an author's own
experience, a tendency often dramatized and perhaps parodied in Chaucer's
personae in *The Canterbury Tales* and *Troilus and Criseyde*. Another direction
was the study of the making of books and manuscripts, which over the past
few decades began to question the genetic model of descent and definable
authorial intention and paid new attention to such factors as scribal impro-

visation, patronage and traditions of miscellaneous compilations. Emphasis shifted, that is, to the way texts were written, read and understood by contemporary readers from a sole focus on the intentions of the author. Alistair Minnis (1988) referred to the medieval theory of *compilatio* to suggest that a medieval author was closer to that of a modern anthologist or editor. Sophisticated revisions of an older evolutionary notion of manuscript transmission gave new weight to the role of scribes, book collectors, and patrons in the shaping of what we think of as medieval literature.

Deconstructing the Text

While a certain amount of suspicion of theory was evident in the area of medieval literary study, rejecting presentist preoccupations and methods, in fact medievalists found themselves in grudging agreement with some of the tenets of poststructuralism. Structuralism had propounded the logic of language as a model for literary study, and some medievalists employed structuralist methodology to analyse the often anonymous and stereotypical outputs of so many medieval genres. Susan Wittig (1978), for instance, analysed the units and combinations of ME romance. As early as the mid-1960s, Paul Zumthor (1992) had described the semiotic system of Old French lyrics. By the time a generation of scholars was prepared to engage in such an enterprise, poststructuralism, with its interest in how rhetoric destabilizes and ironizes the apparent logic of language, had become the avant-garde of literary and cultural analysis. Critics who might have agreed with the allegorization and historicism of someone like D. W. Robertson (1962), a generation before, now found themselves interested in how a suspicion of decoration first established itself in the writings of the Church fathers, albeit in a highly rhetorical style. (See Chapter 10: Exegetical Criticism and its Critics.) The effort of poets such as Dante and Chaucer to forge a vernacular poetics, for instance, also meant grappling with a suspicion of the literary itself, as described in such studies as R. Allen Shoaf's *Chaucer, Dante and the Currency of the Word* (1983) or Jesse Gellrich's *The Idea Of The Book In The Middle Ages: Language Theory, Mythology, And Fiction* (1985). Both studies took a highly traditional medieval trope of how language obscures or occludes the truth it seeks to express, the 'fruit' lying under the 'chaff' of linguistic ornamentation and collocated it with the Derridean suspicion of the possibility of direct statement. The next step, a decade later, in the work of R. Howard Bloch (1991) and Caroline Dinshaw (1989), cast suspicion on the traditional denigration of rhetorical expression, noting that it was inseparable from the misogyny in early Christianity that regarded rhetoric and poetic imagery as seductive, female and fallen. A variant of linguistic analysis, sociolinguistics, which examines language in its social setting and context, has inspired Helen

Barr's analysis (2001) of some overlooked ME works, such as *Wynnere and Wastour, Mum and the Soothsegger* and *The Boke of Cupid*. (See Chapter 6: Language and Literature.)

It is difficult to find a full-scale attempt to read ME literature employing the ideas of Jacques Derrida and usually described as 'deconstruction'. An example of an influential work of Chaucer criticism that does call upon deconstruction is H. Marshall Leicester's *The Disenchanted Self* (1990). In contrast to an earlier criticism that celebrated the creation of fully rounded characters in Chaucer, who seem to be speaking directly to us, and that stressed the identity between Chaucer the poet and his narrator, Leicester invokes Jacques Derrida's critique that by privileging the spoken over the written word, we imbue the text with a presence that simply is not *there*. Structuralist and poststructuralist theories question whether an autonomous self can exist in any society. These theories attempted to replace the ideal of the *self* with the concept of the *subject*. We are not the conscious centres of awareness we think we are but are sites upon which various forces – psychological, sociological, economic and political – act and intersect. The Wife of Bath is constituted by the many antifeminist tracts and discourses that she argues against. Leicester's deconstructive reading of Chaucer reveals an investigation of the 'disenchantment' of the self and the recognition of the subject by emphasizing its radical textuality. (See Chapter 10: Deconstructionist and Psychoanalytic Approaches.)

Feminism and Gender Studies

The Women's Movement of the 1960s and 1970s encouraged interest in the history of women's writers and the record of women's experience as captured in literature. As feminism moved into an academic and theoretical phase, other questions began to be asked. To what extent can a male author accurately or fully capture female experience and to what extent is he projecting his own needs and desires on to his work? To what extent do the conventions of genre and narrative, of language itself, predetermine the representation of gender? Indeed, as feminist thought became influenced by and even helped shape postmodern and poststructuralist theory, the question of whether 'woman' could be found in literature shifted to the question of whether literature helps construct notions of gender and its cultural markings. Film theory, with its acute analysis of spectatorship and how the gaze of the camera replicates the visual control of males over females and the self-regard of females as if they were scrutinizing themselves, helped critique the apparent neutrality and coherence of a single point of view. Film theory itself was indebted to the complex juncture of psychoanalysis and structuralism in the work of Jacques Lacan, who pointed to the inescapably linguistic, textual, narrative and imagistic ways in which the psyche is constructed, especially in terms of gender identity. (See Chapter 9: Feminism.)

Feminists and Medieval Texts

The feminist revolution in literary study itself ran through a series of paradoxical developments, and these were accentuated in medieval studies. Here though, medieval literature and literary criticism was key to the study of other fields. A group of French feminist theorists, many of them associated with the key developments in poststructuralist thought, including Julie Kristeva and Luce Irigiray (Marks and De Courtivron 1980), turned their attention to the writings of medieval female mystics, arguing that these women forged a language of the body that represented both a critique of and a separate discourse than a male-dominated literary and theological culture. Meanwhile, Carolyn Walker Bynum produced two books that, while they only touch on English studies, were highly influential. *Jesus as Mother* (1982) explored a metaphor in male monastic pastoral care, one that depended on an analogy to gender and thereby allowing a certain point of contact for female piety. *Holy Feast and Holy Fast* (1987) explored the symbolic and somatic expression of the idea of food, feeding and self-denial in medieval piety, though it framed its agenda in ways that would seem to preclude the psychoanalytic and sexualized directions that French feminist theory was taking. Indeed, French feminist theory became increasingly interested in deconstructing patriarchal and self-limiting modes of perception, while Anglo-American feminists were concerned with rebuilding a lost female literary tradition and a positive history of female experience. Interestingly, such works as *The Book of Margery Kempe, The Showings of Julian of Norwich,* and *Ancrene Wisse,* soon to be included in widely assigned textbooks such as *The Norton Anthology of British Literature,* eighth edition (Greenblatt 2006), which first included Margery in its fifth edition, not only became canonical as a result of these new developments, but were links between a material and theoretical tracing of gender. (See Chapter 8: The Impact of Feminism and the Expansion of the Canon and Chapter 9: Feminism.)

As a result of their wide distribution on course syllabi, as well as their centrality to feminist thought and its wider articulation as gender theory, several feminist studies have influenced medieval scholarship. Chief among these have been Gayle Rubin's 'The Traffic in Women' (1975), Laura Mulvey's 'Visual Pleasure and Narrative Cinema' (1975) and Judith Butler's *Gender Trouble* (1990). These analyses have been employed to help us understand works written by medieval women, written for women or which take women ostensibly as their subject, as well as helping us to understand more deeply such stereotypically medieval forms as romance and its concomitant

construct, courtly love. Sarah Stanbury (1991) has employed theories of spectatorship and the gaze to demonstrate how pervasive visual imagery and its
associated sexual politics are in works ranging from medieval lyrics to the
Gawain-poet. Stanbury's use of the theory of the gaze is, of course, dependent
on Jacques Lacan's linguistic model of the psyche, which rendered psychoanalysis consistent with, rather than antagonistic to, feminism. As we have
seen, and as Erin Labbie (2006) has demonstrated in detail, Lacan's own theories developed in partial response to the idea of courtly love as described in
Denis de Rougemont's *Love in the Western World*. (See Chapter 3: Courtly
Love.)

The Feminine Other in Medieval Culture

Rubin's foundational article alerted us to the almost universal treatment of
women in various cultures as objects of exchange and, even more strikingly,
to the reification of this treatment in anthropological study. Students of
English literature will recognize this critique from Eve Kosofky Sedgwick's
Between Men (1985), which defined the structure of romance fiction and
plotting as 'homosocial', in that the female serves as an object to allow an
intercourse 'between men', especially obvious in the love triangle. Sedgwick
directly and indirectly builds on de Rougemont's analysis of the pathology of
the courtly love syndrome, especially as it is developed in Leslie's Fiedler's
widely known *Love and Death in the American Novel* (1960). Fiedler defined an
American variant on the European love plot, in which the American hero
escapes the constraints of life in the civilized and hence feminized town to live
in the wild with a male companion, usually a representative of the racial
Other. The influence of Sedgwick's readings have circled back to their point of
origin in medieval literature, especially in Susan Crane's *Gender and Romance
in Chaucer's Canterbury Tales* (1994), which demonstrates that romance and its
rituals are finally about the delineation of male subjectivity rather than a
particularly female address or narrative focus. Earlier, Elaine Tuttle Hansen
(1992) had critiqued Chaucer's implication in the discourse of gender, arguing
that Chaucer's apparent celebration of female characters was a way of
appropriating certain aspects of subjectivity associated with women,
including empathy, interiority and emotional range, for use by a male author.
Hansen argues that the Chaucerian narrator's identification with female
characters appropriates the slippery signification and relative lack of fixity
of the feminine other, the aspects of that projection most useful to poetic
discourse. Hansen's thesis not only questions the possibility of a feminist
Chaucer, it is also an attack on a humanist Chaucer, a Chaucer whose ironic
perspective transcends his age and reveals the timeless truths that inhabit his
fictions. At the same time, interestingly, Hansen's strategy itself is based on

a transhistoricized argument – that the nature of male poetic discourse by definition is self-limited in relation to the representation of its other.

In *The Romance of Origins*, Gayle Margherita (1994) is able to show both how medieval literature is of enormous importance to resolving our contemporary quandaries of theory and literary politics and also how and why this relevance has been systematically, if unconsciously, obscured. Her thesis is that medieval literary texts are marked by their fetishization of the female body, which functions both as metaphor and as contested ground within their narrative. Moreover, the modern criticism of medieval literature has in fact replicated precisely this drama, and this repetition has obscured the material experience of these texts, as well as the experience they represent. Feminist criticism often reads texts as allegories of gender, even when it supports that reading through copious attention to form and style. One of the most rigorous feminist readings of Chaucer's *Book of the Duchess*, for instance, is in Margherita's book. The poem frames literary discourse as part of bonding between two male figures, the narrator and the Black Knight. Their bonding is occasioned by the absent female, whom they recreate in literary language at the same time that she is literally dead. Their remembrances resurrect her in their and the reader's imagination, but in so doing they reveal a precarious relationship to a feminine that is erased as the same time that it is being written.

Gender, Identity and Queer Studies

As Robert Sturges has demonstrated in *Chaucer's Pardoner and Gender Theory* (2000), Chaucer's ambiguous character has been a starting point of some of the most contentious debates in the field of gender studies. The most famous example of gender theory in Chaucer scholarship is Carolyn Dinshaw's *Chaucer's Sexual Poetics* (1989). Her subsequent book, *Getting Medieval* (1999), is a highly influential example of queer theory in medieval studies. Thus, the progress of Dinshaw's work exemplifies the development of gender studies from its roots in feminism.

Dinshaw deals with some canonical ME texts – Chaucer's *Canterbury Tales*, the anonymous *Sir Gawain and the Green Knight*, and *The Book of Margery Kempe*. (See Chapter 5: Carolyn Dinshaw, *Chaucer's Sexual Poetics* [1989] and *Getting Medieval* [1999].) By considering the marginalized or erased 'queer' perspective on actions or characters within these works, Dinshaw proceeds to show how the representation of heterosexual sexuality is not only normative but essential to these works and to the cultural hegemony within which they operated. Without denying the importance of class or gender as base factors, Dinshaw demonstrates that heterosexuality itself is in many ways a matrix by which these other agendas find expression. Bringing her 'queer touch' to these texts, she shows how complicated, contradictory and insistent – even hysterical – is this emphasis on the heterosexual, and how fragile its construction turns out to be when faced with the sexual other. Dinshaw's readings uncover a self-conscious program, rather than an ideological assumption of the natural, behind the representation of heterosexuality in medieval literature, which insists compulsively on that very heterosexuality as 'natural.' Dinshaw seeks to reverse the lens of the perspective of the *General Prologue* and the *Wife of Bath's Tale*. Rather than accepting the normative stance of the narrator, with its marginalization of the Pardoner, Dinshaw asks what would happen if we read the *General Prologue* as the Pardoner would. Dinshaw points to the ways in which heterosexuality is represented as natural, even as identical to nature, and at the same time is elevated through high rhetorical language. Even characters like the Prioress and the Monk, whose vocations might seem to free them from being defined by their sexuality, are in fact characterized in terms of a functionally irrelevant heterosexual potential. Dinshaw points to the way that the Pardoner in turn, by interrupting the Wife of Bath's discourse, reveals the constructed and performed nature of the Wife's normative femininity. The Wife's recourse to romance is in fact required in order to reassert the heterosexual norm. Dinshaw's reading of the Pardoner is somewhat different here than in her *Chaucer's Sexual Poetics*, because here the arch tone of Pardoner's response is identified and placed. Dinshaw's disturbing thesis is that Chaucer, the classic liberal humanist, allows a voice for the marginalized Pardoner only to have normative heterosexual values reinscribed with even greater force, even though it requires the Host's threat of violence, and a police action by the Knight, to do so. (See Chapter 9: Gender Studies and Chapter 9: Queer Theory.)

Rereading Aristocratic Masculinity

Dinshaw also studies *Sir Gawain and the Green Knight*, and she artfully aligns the beleaguered hero of this poem with the unwilling lover-knight of the Wife's tale. Dinshaw revises the traditional thesis concerning courtly love (the unattainable lady of the castle surrounded by young adoring knights in training resulting in the 'courtly love complex') by pointing to the problem all Arthurian romance, and much late medieval court life has, with managing a large group of young, unmarried, heterosexual men. Taken as a mathematical formula, the result of the plot of *Sir Gawain* would be the coupling of the knight and his male host. Hence, the poem can be seen as a protracted effort to avoid just that, and a sublimation of this queer secret coding into various sorts of homosocial rituals. Dinshaw roots this reading in the context of the other poems found in the manuscript with *Sir Gawain and the Green Knight* and through the rumors surrounding Richard II and Robert de Vere. (See Chapter

5: Carolyn Dinshaw, *Chaucer's Sexual Poetics* [1989] and *Getting Medieval* [1999].)

Jeffrey Jerome Cohen is another critic who has fused the concerns of gender theory, especially with masculinity studies, body studies and identity studies. His book, *Medieval Identity Machines* (2003) continues this contribution. Scholars have worried extensively about the relative appropriateness of identity, subjectivity, the individual and the self as categories for understanding medieval social consciousness. Cohen shifts the debate from individual works to the entire system of medieval literature as a subset of medieval culture. He takes Deleuze and Guattari's anti-model of the human body and human identity (1977 and 2004) and demonstrates its surprising appropriateness to pre-modern culture, and in so doing questions our distinctions between the modern, pre-modern and postmodern. In each chapter, he takes some traditional categories of medieval literature and culture and rereads them in new contexts: race, gender, sexuality and nationality. The literature of chivalry and courtly love, canonically represented by Chretien de Troyes, is revealed to be a highly permeable construct, both insisting on and failing heterosexual normativity, representing an apparently fixed concept of masculinity that in fact turns out to be fluid. Cohen follows up this learned analysis (in terms of both medieval traditions and modern theory) with a definition of a complex he calls 'Masoch/Lancelotism'. The chivalric hero's impossible quest can only be achieved through a sort of fetishism. Chivalric heroism, gendered piety and monastic pacificism and abnegation are shown to be part of the same cultural matrix rather than polar opposites. His chapter on 'Saracen Enjoyment' demolishes what most of us have come to accept as received wisdom concerning medieval ideas of race and ethnicity, and he demonstrates the equivalence of medieval 'antisaracenism' with modern racial assumptions, rather than being a prehistory of racism. (See Chapter 5: Jeffrey Jerome Cohen, *Of Giants* [1999] and Jeffrey Jerome Cohen, *The Postcolonial Middle Ages* [2000].)

Gender and Religious Difference

In Lisa Lampert's *Gender and Jewish Difference* (2004), medieval Christianity defines itself by its difference from Judaism, but in so doing it inescapably genders the processes of interpretation, reading and ideological construction that underlie that difference. By demonstrating the complexities of this thesis through a wide range of texts, Lampert not only uses gender and feminist theory, on the one hand, and Jewish studies, on the other, to interrogate one another, she also deconstructs the exclusive binaries of particularist and universalist positions. This allows her to show how previously compartmentalized scholarly questions impinge on each other: how, for instance, debates on medieval heterodox movements such as the Lollards depend heavily on earlier discourses about a Jewish community that had been expelled over a century earlier; how anxieties about conversion in plays such as the Croxton *Play of the Sacrament* have as much to do with contemporary events in Spain as with a constant anti-Semitic stereotyping.

Marxism to New Historicism

The New Historicism continues the project of older historicisms, which is to place literary works in the context of the past. However, older historicisms saw literary works largely as *reflecting* the ideas and events of their time. The New Historicism regards literary works as agents as well as subjects in the making of their time. Older historicisms attempt to recover accurately how things were in the past. The New Historicism, influenced by new directions in anthropology, regards the literature of the past as part of a culture which can never be entirely recovered, but whose mentality concerning the relationship among aspects of that culture can be gleaned from its writings.

Even when many literary scholars were engaged in historical informed research in the 1950s and 1960s, the reigning critical orthodoxy, as we have seen, was a form of appreciative, idealizing criticism, usually referred to as the New Criticism, when stressing its analytic and intensely focused methodology, and sometimes referred to as Liberal Humanism, when stressing its larger intellectual allegiance, celebrating the works of great authors speaking universal truths to us across vast stretches of time. There were, however, two strains in critical approach that, while somewhat ossified by the early 1960s, had served as an opposition to the New Criticism and which were to receive startling reformulations through the impact of poststructuralism. One of these approaches was psychoanalytic criticism, to be discussed below, and the other was Marxist criticism.

Marxism Against New Criticism

The New Criticism had its chief antagonist in Marxist criticism, which it accused of replacing the aesthetics of the work with extrinsic and imposed contexts. Marxists, in turn, criticized the apolitical and mystifying aspects of the New Criticism. While the range of Marxist influenced critics is so broad as to defy easy categorization, it can be said that Marxist theory emphasized the social and political implications of a work, the relation of a work to the class status of its characters (and author and readers) and the degree to which a work revealed the process of historical reality as understood by Marxism. Some applications of Marxism could be criticized as 'vulgar materialism' even by other Marxists, but most earlier Marxist critics ascribed to Marx's famous dictum that it was 'not the consciousness of men that determines their being, but, on the contrary, their social being that determines their consciousness' (Marx 1977, 389). By the early 1970s, however, several directions in Marxist thought emerged to eclipse these debates. One was the belated impact of the so-called Frankfurt School, a group of émigrés, largely from Germany, who had developed a form of Marxist inflected analysis that accorded a complex and often counterintuitive influence to culture. These thinkers became part of as well as precursors to theory, and their names – Theodor Adorno, Hannah Arendt, Rudolph Horkheimer, Herbert Marcuse and their intellectual heir Jürgen Habermas – appear frequently in current theoretical discussions. Their ideas were introduced into the English-speaking literary world in a book called *Marxism and Form* (1971) by Fredric Jameson. Jameson himself has been the most important North American Marxist critic and his study of romance in *The Political Unconscious* (1981) has been the most influential statement on the genre since Northrop Frye. Jameson taught us how romance both expresses and controls desire, both personal and social, and how it allows a utopian impulse to be inserted into the everyday world. At the same time that these German theorists were being introduced to the English-speaking world, in France, Marxism met structuralism in a complex synthesis, notably in the work of Louis Althusser. Althusser proposed ways in which culture and other superstructural phenomena could be seen to mediate rather than merely reflect social and economic forces. The ideas of the Frankfurt School and of Althusser were fresh to American readers at least partly because the Cold War and McCarthyism had marginalized American Marxist traditions, and because the suppression of popular reform movements in Hungary, Czecho-slovakia and elsewhere had alienated Western intellectuals not only from a romance with communism but with the Marxism identified with it. (See Chapter 10: Materialist Criticism.)

British Marxism

While the impact of these continental ideas have been profoundly felt in American intellectual and academic circles, Britain always retained a more unbroken and independent strain of Marxist criticism. One earmark of British Marxism has been its investment in material culture and in analysing the ways in which the physical environment interacts with social and economic development. Even when British Marxism turned to a theoretical mode, as it did with the founding of *New Left Review* and the subsequent books by its editor Perry Anderson, whose *Passages from Antiquity to Feudalism* (1974) and *Lineages of the Absolutist State* (1974) influenced the award winning New Historicist studies by the medievalist David Wallace, such as his *Chaucerian Polity* (1997), it never lost these specifically British inflections. Another unique theme in British Marxism was its interest in unassimilable rebels, captured in the title of E. P. Hobsbawm's widely read *Primitive Rebels* (1963) and his later *Bandits* (1971). British Marxists cultivated a special interest in Robin Hood legends and literature, teasing out its various revolutionary and reactionary elements, and in the Rising of 1381, sorting out its cataclysmic events from the long-term consequences of its causes and effects. Indeed, New Historicist studies of the Rising, such as Steven Justice's *Writing and Rebellion* (1994), are indebted to this tradition, but emphasize the power and place of writing and texts in the events, rather than as a mere reflection of them. Similarly, Stephen Knight (1994) has reoriented the largely historical concerns – did Robin Hood actually exist? – of British Marxism to focus on the complexities of Robin Hood's literary and textual representations. (See Chapter 4: The 1381 Revolt.)

Mention of Robin Hood reminds us that some other strands in Marxist thought have also influentially shaped contemporary literary study. One is the unique thought of Antonio Gramsci (1988). As a leftist in fascist Italy, he sought to explain how and why workers and peasants would appear to vote against, in his view, their own interests. He elaborated a theory of *hegemony*, in which the cultural outlook of the ruling class becomes naturalized as the viewpoint of an entire culture. At the same time, he argued, popular culture could serve as a reservoir of resistance and subversion to this almost unrecognized domination. Coincidentally, the enigmatic Russian theorist M. Bakhtin (1968 and 1981) also had a belated impact on Western criticism through his widely influential concepts of the *carnivalesque* and the *dialogic*, wherein a holiday subversion of the normal social order offered a participatory response to the 'monologic' authority of 'official culture.' Bakhtin's ideas were rooted in what he took to be the folk culture of the Middle Ages and, as a result, have been widely applied to authors and works from Chaucer to the mystery plays.

Synthesizing the Political and Literary

By the late 1970s, Marxist ideas combined with the emphasis on material culture found in British Marxism and the emphasis on cultural hegemony developed in the writings of the Italian Gramsci to help shape the procedures of the New Historicism, though few Marxists would regard the New Historicism as Marxist and few New Historicists would identify as Marxists. An exception is the critic Sheila Delany (1990 and 1998), who has produced an extensive body of work often reflecting an unapologetic Marxist perspective, applied to writings as varied as Chaucer's *House of Fame* to the fifteenth-century author Bokenham's saints' lives. The New Historicism is, however, usually associated with the journal *Representations* and the work of its founders, especially Stephen Greenblatt, who also edited a book series called

'New Historicism'. Borrowing from anthropology as well as history, Greenblatt argued that texts were events as much as artefacts and that they embodied the circulation of power in the immediate culture that produced them. Medievalists sometimes feel that Greenblatt's appropriation of the linguistic category 'Early Modern' to apply to what we used to call Renaissance texts slighted the Middle Ages, but in fact medieval studies were well represented both in Greenblatt's journal and his book series, and Greenblatt was flexible as to when modernity begins, especially in regard to his ideas about identity and subjectivity in his influential *Renaissance Self-Fashioning*. The latest research in the field, embodied in *The Cambridge History of Medieval Literature*, edited by David Wallace (1999), which focuses mostly on ME literature, reflects this concern with the ways in which literary texts intervene in the byways and turning points of history, reversing the secondary role ME texts had played in the scholarship of a century before. (See Chapter 1: Extending the Medieval.)

Paul Strohm's books have been among the most influential syntheses of theoretical and historical scholarship. In *Hochon's Arrow* (1992), Strohm examines some apparently minor late ME literary texts and argues that they foreground the relation between history and textuality in special ways. These texts are 'open' to historical action, intervening in the very processes that would have seemed to create them. Strohm thereby seeks to make an important theoretical point, that historical background does not merely 'explain' literary texts, but that those texts are part of the history that produces them. Strohm studies Chaucer's short poems as part of Lancastrian apologetics, justifying the transition from Richard II to Henry IV. He discusses how Henry and his advisers sought to appropriate potentially apocalyptic prophetic language to the problematic of transition and order. In an influential chapter, 'Queens as Intercessors', he describes the 'intercession' of the allegorical queen in *The Legend of Good Women* as analogous to the actual intercession of royal women in conflicts between Richard II and John of Gaunt and between Richard II and the City of London, arguing that their symbolic role was more powerful than their actual influence. Gender, popular resistance, patronage and propaganda are thus brought into the same field of investigation. Indeed, Strohm's books move into the realm of historical study as much as literary criticism. It is tempting to compare his aims, methodologically at least, to books that break down the boundaries between literary and historical analysis, such as Natalie Zemon Davis' *Fiction in the Archives* or Robert Darnton's *The Great Cat Massacre*. He seeks to talk about historical actions, as they are presented in documents, as narratives, shaped by the demands of certain forms, and to talk about literary works as intervening, even interceding, in the shape of history.

Strohm's work focuses on precise moments in literary and political history, obliterating the difference between the two. In the work of others, post-structuralism and traditional literary history have converged to question the conventional periodization of the Middle Ages (or any historical period) on the basis of distinct centuries. Instead, recent studies have focused on some understudied stretches of time or have constructed literary *microhistories*. Frank Grady (2002) studies 'The Generation of 1399', tracing the influence of the events of that year on the writers of the late fourteenth and fifteenth centuries. Ralph Hanna (2005) writes a study of *London Literature 1330–1380*, focusing on the period before the so-called Golden Age of the late fourteenth century. Other studies question the border between medieval and early modern, such as James Simpson's volume in the Oxford English Literary History, *Reform and Revolution 1380–1520* (2002), instead emphasizing a commonality of concerns and longstanding tensions that predate the Reformation itself. An indirect and sometimes direct influence on this reconceptualization has been the *Annales* school of French historiography, named after the journal of that name, with its stress on *'la longue dureé'*. Associated with the work of Marc Bloch, Emanuel LeRoy Ladurie and Fernand Braudel, *Annales* emphasized strands of development that ran through apparently distinct cultural periods or arbitrary centuries and promoted geography and location as critical factors in understanding the development of cultures (Ganim 1992). An original example of such scholarship is David Wallace's *Premodern Places: Chaucer to Aphra Behn, Calais to Surinam* (2004), with its collocation of highly local microinfluences and sweeping temporal vistas.

Rather than being determined by or reflecting historical conditions, as an earlier scholarship had assumed, or transcending local and specific circumstances, as the New Criticism argued, medieval literary texts are now themselves regarded as agents and actors in the shifting cultural and political alignments of their time, often exposing tensions and contradictions (interestingly also New Critical values) in these events and contexts. (See Chapter 5: Lee Patterson, *Chaucer and the Subject of History* [1991].)

Postcolonial Criticism

Postcolonial theory began as an examination of the social and political challenges faced by countries that were formally colonies, especially of the European imperial powers. Its earliest writings were the searing manifestos like Franz Fanon's *The Wretched of the Earth* (1963) and Albert Memmi's *The Colonizer and the Colonized* (1965), as well as policy statements by anti-colonial nationalist political leaders. The introduction of these ideas to the sphere of literary and cultural identities and to representation in linguistic discourses is generally attributed to the massive influence of Edward Said's *Orientalism* (1978). Said's 'orient' was the Middle East, and his title derived from the academic discipline that defined the East from Suez to India (with less attention to Far Eastern Asia). Hence, for Said, the conflict between the West and the East was defined by French and English mercantile and imperial policy and often took the shape of an encounter between the Christian West and the Islamic East, but just as often between a supposedly rational, scientific and objective West and a passive and underdeveloped East, both a mirror of Western ambitions and desires and an absence. For Said, the simplistic and violent ignorance reflected in medieval anti-Semitism and the Crusades was a starting point that was often returned to again and again in later, apparently more subtle and sophisticated expressions of curiosity, dominance and contempt. Perhaps because of this dismissal of the medieval period and more obviously because the colonial model did not directly apply to medieval states and societies, medieval studies came late to the postcolonial debates, and it often did so in inverse ways, claiming, for instance, that the medieval past was often itself erased and intellectually colonized by the early modern European West. Primitive, backward, empty of objects and texts worth considering as anything other than negative examples or curiosities, the medieval past was sometimes thought of as a foreign country by many non-medievalist scholars and common readers. In some more specific studies, the complex local conflicts of regional language and culture and the layers of conquest resulting from feudal expansions created internal colonies within the West, such as Wales or Ireland in the British Isles. (See Chapter 8: Multilingualism, International Contexts, and Postcolonial Concerns.)

Premodern Postcolonialism

Medieval postcolonial studies was also crystallized by the influential collection of essays by Jeffrey Jerome Cohen, *The Postcolonial Middle Ages* (2003), and shortly after was fully developed in such books as Geraldine Heng's *Empire of Magic* (2003) and Sharon Kinoshita's *Medieval Boundaries* (2006), the latter covering medieval French literature. The colonial origins of some of the most apparently dominant themes in medieval literature, such as Arthurian legend, were analysed by Michelle Warren (2000) and by Patricia Ingham (2001). Ingham's thesis is that Arthurian literature has historically been a site of contest over crises in national identity, regional integrity, linguistic conflict and even matters of social life such as gender decorum and personal identity. She suggests that Arthurian literature has been employed to negotiate and even dissolve these crises in the service of a larger British rather than specifically English identity and policy. What seemed like puzzles and contradictions from Ingham's perspective now seem like part of the logic of the work in question. The place of Geoffrey of Monmouth, for instance, no longer seems like an egomaniacal aberration in a historical tradition; instead, she can read Geoffrey as externalizing the contradictions of an apparently Celtic figure being celebrated as an English hero. The interplay between high Arthurian literature and its Welsh and Irish analogues no longer are questions of source or origin, but become part of a larger struggle about regional versus national identity. When Ingham turns to canonical texts such as *Sir Gawain and the Green Knight* and Malory's *Morte D'Arthur*, she rephrases the personal quandaries of the protagonists as dramatizations of the problematic status of Arthurian literature.

Romance, Religion and Nation

Meanwhile, more and more attention is being paid to the interplay between Islamic, Christian and Jewish literary cultures in medieval Spain, most prominently in the work of Anna Maria Meñocal and the volume she edited as *The Literature of Al-Andalus* in *The Cambridge History of Arabic Literature* (2000) and in David Nirenberg's *Communities of Violence* (1998). Geraldine Heng's *Empire of Magic* proposes an original and striking reformulation of the place of romance. Where most studies, however much they may argue with a Hegelian tradition of regarding romance as an escape from the real, still conceive of it as a fantastic genre that accommodates history uneasily, as a contradiction or an intrusion, Heng sees a 'head on encounter with the very real', as Toni Morrison puts it. In the case of medieval romance, that 'very real' was the experience of the Crusades and the trauma both of Christian defeat and of admitted Western barbarism. By focusing on a few key themes, notably that of cannibalism, which appears as a bizarre and heretofore puzzling leitmotif in medieval romances (*Richard Coeur de Lion, Alliterative Morte D'Arthur*, and others), Heng argues for the seamlessness of the fantastic and the real in romance. The result is that she can read apparently absurd historical fantasies, such as Geoffrey Monmouth's *History of the Kings of Britain*, as powerful ideological statements, that stand in for the 'imagined communities' of later national identity. The odd symbolic intrusions of race, gender and nationhood in medieval romance, where they are not supposed to belong, are revealed to be quite central to the form, according to Heng. Suddenly these themes, instead of being some hallucinatory intrusions of modernity (a sort of premature orientalism), become the very function of romance itself. (See Chapter 9: Race Studies and Postcolonial Theory and Chapter 9: Postcolonial Studies.)

Heng also writes about *Mandeville's Travels*. Mandeville studies have recently acquired a new importance, partly as a result of the emphasis postcolonial studies have placed on medieval and early modern understandings of the East and partly because of a new scholarly interest in vernacularity and translation. The brief mention of Mandeville by Stephen Greenblatt (and earlier by Said in *Orientalism*) in his widely circulated essays and books about discovery and discourse in the Early Modern period (1980, 1990 and 1991) have brought Mandeville to the attention of a wide range of literary and cultural scholars working on different eras. It would seem that the *Book* of Mandeville is now taking the place that the *Book of Margery Kempe* has had for the past decade, with condescension being replaced by the application of an enormously sophisticated conceptual apparatus.

One of the key texts in the continued development of postcolonial studies was Homi Bhabha's *Nation and Narration* (1990). Issues of national identity, formerly considered as a distinct theme, are now often subsumed under postcolonial studies. The subject of Kathy Lavezzo's collection, *Imagining a Medieval English Nation* (2004) – the question of national identity and what Benedict Anderson (1983) calls an 'imagined community' – has taken its place as a leading theme of literary study from the Renaissance through the American literary tradition and finds its most complex formulations in the study of postcolonial and 'minority' literatures. As Lavezzo suggests, even paradigm-shifting thinkers such as Anderson and the industry that followed in the wake of his book *Imagined Communities*, nevertheless retain a question-able and quaint prejudice against extending their categories backward to the medieval period. Even the revolution wrought in early English literary study by the New Historicism proceeded partly by retaining a distinction between the Medieval and the Early Modern.

Psychoanalytic Theory

Traditional psychoanalytic criticism applied the ideas of Sigmund Freud, particularly his stress on the Oedipus complex and his taxonomy of dream symbolism, to works of literature, carrying on Freud's own belief that the works of artists and writers had the same access to the unconscious as dreams themselves. Freudian psychoanalytic criticism could also be strongly bio-graphical, studying the connection between the author's psyche and his or her writings. A variation on psychoanalytic criticism was the archetypal criticism associated with Freud's former follower Carl Jung, who promul-gated a theory that mythic archetypes and archetypal patterns captured uni-versal human experience. Applications of these psychological approaches often invoked medieval literature directly. Drawing upon Jung, Northrop Frye's archetypical scheme of genres related to seasons and cycles in – *Anatomy of Criticism* dominated the discussion of romance for several decades (1957). As the New Criticism disintegrated into an exploration of its former taboos, Norman Holland used psychoanalytic techniques to investigate one of them, the response of the reader. The New Criticism considered the response of a reader to be distinct from the meaning generated by the text, calling it the 'affective fallacy'. Holland considered affect to be an under-emphasized component of literary meaning, and in this he shared the perspective of what would be called Reader Response criticism, an influential movement in the early 1970s. Holland's *The Dynamics of Literary Response* (1968) included an investigation of the *Wife of Bath's Tale*.

City, Desire and Sacrifice

The most important work on ME literature informed by psychoanalytic theory are the books and articles by L. O. Aranye Fradenburg. Medieval Scots literature receives its most extended theoretical investigation in Fradenburg's *City, Marriage, Tournament* (1991). Fradenburg moves between the analysis of historical documents and literary texts (such as pageant descriptions, royal proclamations, the poetry of Dunbar and Foulis) on one level, and cultural theory (especially the work of Pierre Bourdieu, Elaine Scarry and feminist interpretations of Lacan) on the other. Her more recent books, such as *Premodern Sexualities* (1995), have questioned whether historical difference alone can account for the representations of sexuality in premodern culture, and have made a compelling case for the importance of theoretical claims, especially those indebted to psychoanalytic ideas. This is also the case with her influential articles about Chaucer, linked by the subject of memorialization and mourning. Fradenburg explores discourses of memory, pastness, elegy and nostalgia as key constituents of Chaucer's writing and of our response to it.

In *Sacrifice Your Love* (2002), Fradenburg draws upon such works as Slavov Zizek's *Enjoy Your Symptom* (1992) as well as the psychoanalytic theories of Jacques Lacan (1992). Fradenburg argues that the cultural injunction that we sacrifice our own wishes for a greater good is not a suppression of desire, but is in fact an expression of desire with its own pleasures. She examines such ritualized medieval ideals as courtly love and chivalry, as explored particularly in the work of Geoffrey Chaucer. A poem such as *Troilus and Criseyde*, for instance, represents Troilus' accession to the demands of Trojan society and his dedication to his heroic militarism as a tragedy. Criseyde's experience, however, is rendered as a betrayal at worst or an anticlimax at best. The sacrifice of the love-object dramatizes the sacrifice of the feminized other within the masculinized, heroic subject. Conversely, the frequent scene of mourning in Chaucer's works (such as *The Book of the Duchess*) recreates the other within the mourning subject as a way of retrieving the lost love. Fantasies of rescue abound in medieval narratives, underlining the dependence of the other on the subject. Thus, such typically medieval emphases as pity mask a form of enjoyment. As mentioned above, medieval scholarship has often formed a basis for some of the most daring theoretical formulations of the past thirty years or more, but scholars such as Fradenburg actually make original contributions to theory rather than merely applying theory to medieval works as way of rendering them relevant.

Emerging New Approaches

These new areas of inquiry have a history that predates the period covered by this chapter, but they have been revitalized by some of the theories and approaches described above, including feminism, deconstruction and post-structuralism. (See Chapter 1: Mapping New Approaches.)

Ecocriticism

A unique development in the study of ME literature can be understood as a species of ecocriticism. This may be surprising because we do not typically associate medieval literature with a celebration of nature, which we think of as specific to Romantic poetry above all. Furthermore, the largely symbolic and schematic representation of landscape in medieval art suggests to us that the Middle Ages did not look at nature in the almost deistic or transcendental way that many do now. Of course, the Romantics themselves found the medieval sense of landscape congenial, at least the bowers and forests of quest romance. Even Victorians such as William Morris imagined a medievalized landscape for the utopian future in his novel, *News from Nowhere*. In fact, the Middle Ages developed sophisticated ways of understanding natural creation as a divine system, particularly in the theology and philosophy of the School of Chartres. The life of St Francis, today still an icon of human identification with nature and the animal world, provided a model of the relationship between the human and non-human.

Descriptions of seasons and weather, while often highly conventional, can be memorable, such as the narration of time through seasonal variation in *Sir Gawain and the Green Knight* or the Harley lyrics where seasonal and natural imagery is integrated into the theme of the poems. Animals become significant characters in courtly works such as *Yvain*, where the knight is befriended by a lion, Chaucer's *Squire's Tale* with its eloquent bird, or Marie de France's fables and lays. The animal world is presented as a surrogate for the human world in the beast fable, most famously in Chaucer's *Nun's Priest's Tale*. Whether animals have souls, a parallel to the current debates about ethics and animal rights, was an important question in medieval theology. Thus, critics such as Gillian Rudd (2007) have asked us to consider the ecological perspective of medieval literature as a searching counterpoint to modern writing and thinking about the impact of humans on the natural world. The binary opposition between man and nature that governs ecocriticism, even as ecocriticism argues against such an opposition, is already questioned in medieval literature.

Theology and Theory

An earlier criticism, chiefly originating in the early twentieth century, was largely embarrassed by, or even hostile to, the pervasive religious orientation and content of medieval literature. When it did acknowledge religious themes, a largely Protestant academic establishment concentrated on overt criticism or subtle satire of medieval Catholicism, fostering, for instance, the appreciation of Chaucer's subversive criticism of clerical figures. More often than not, however, critics read back from a secular and sceptical cultural perspective, emphasizing the comedy and realism of even obviously devotional religious writings.

Criticism has only recently come to terms with the religious dimension of ME literature. This lack was partly due to the value that the New Criticism placed on irony and scepticism, so that only works that seemed to question religious orthodoxy were considered worthy of attention. Another reason, as Linda Georgianna (1990) has alerted us to in 'The Protestant Chaucer', was the embarrassment surrounding Catholic belief when viewed by secular, humanist or even mainstream Protestant scholars. When D. W. Robertson (1963), in the early 1960s and late 1950s, proposed an elaborate system of allegorical interpretation of medieval literature, the arguments against that system directly or indirectly objected to the totalized belief system propounded in Robertson's picture of the Middle Ages. (See Chapter 10: Exegetical (Historical) Criticism and its Critics.)

We do not ordinarily think of theology as a species of theory, but theory and theology are inescapably linked, even if deconstruction would question the metaphysical assumptions that underlay most theological speculation. The genealogy of theory can be traced to the natural supernaturalism of Romantic writers such as Samuel Taylor Coleridge and to the Higher Criticism of Christian scriptures in the nineteenth century, even if theory rarely acknowledges that past. The language of the scholars who led the conversion of American academia to theory, the so-called 'Yale School' of Harold Bloom, Geoffrey Hartman, J. Hillis Miller and Jacques Derrida, would be unimaginable without the widely read theologians of the 1950s and 1960s, including Martin Buber, Rudolph Bultmann, Paul Tillich and Thomas Altizer. These theologians and theorists wrestled with the difficult legacy of Martin Heidegger, upon whose thought so-called deconstructionists such as Jacques Derrida and Paul de Man both depended and struggled. Theory and theology have been in a mutually dependent relation.

Vernacular Theology

Over the past 30 years, however, the religious, even theological seriousness of ME literature has been given a new place of importance. An influential statement of this new importance is Nicholas Watson's argument (1995) that while official theological discourse was carried on in Latin, that there was such a thing as 'vernacular theology', constituting a rubric under which authors as disparate as William Langland and Julian of Norwich can be seen to be exploring religious experience and its implications in a deeply original, though usually orthodox, manner. Another voice arguing for the centrality of spiritual exploration inseparable from aesthetic and social concerns has been David Aers (2000), in a series of books and articles that span the period covered in this chapter. The spiritual dimension in ME literature, for Aers, is an instrument of social criticism and change.

Middle English literature is now seen not as distinct from or even merely reflective of the pervasive religiosity of medieval English culture, but as actively participating in spiritual exploration. Just as the New Historicism understood texts to construct rather than simply reflect historical events, so too are ME writings now often seen as complex sites of interaction among a multiplicity of religious and theological viewpoints. While not always explicit about their theoretical underpinnings, the studies of vernacular theology demonstrate the processes of practice within social fields described by Pierre Bourdieu (1977 and 1990), also a leading influence in New Historicist thinking.

Lollardy and Literacy

Nowhere is this emphasis on social practice and reading communities more evident than in the new importance accorded to Lollard writings in ME literature. Thanks to the groundbreaking account by Anne Hudson, in her tellingly titled *The Premature Reformation* (1988), Wycliffite and Lollard writings, and their suppression, have become one of the master narratives of late ME literary history. While Lollard writings receive attention in another chapter of this anthology, their relation to recent critical approaches to ME literature cannot be overemphasized. As Rita Copeland (2001) has demonstrated, Lollard writings intercede in complex debates about the role of language, translation and education in the late Middle Ages. Not only does Wycliffe's Bible translation have enormous cultural importance, it demonstrates the growth of literacy among the laity in the fifteenth century. Lollard movements thus exemplify of literary communities operating outside sanctioned religious institutions, cementing and creating new social relations and resisting repression through broadly popular networks.

If Lollard writings have been responsible for new theories of the connection between reading and social practice, and, in the study of their suppression by such figures as Archbishop Arundel and Henry V, a case study in the relation between authority and dissent, other religious writings, specifically mystical writings, have generated new thinking about the nature of authorship in the late Middle Ages. We have already seen how the importance of female mystics in this tradition became a fundamental issue in the development of feminist theory, specifically whether a certain kind of writing or language could be gendered as female, or when the emphasis on experience, and especially bodily experience, could be regarded as a form of writing, even when the female speaker was narrating her account to a male scribe, like Margery Kempe. The relation between narrating voice and recording scribe in fact foregrounded the question of authorship and authority.

Interdisciplinarity and the New Synthesis

If some medievalists rejected poststructuralism as a presentist imposition on the literature of the past, the rise of high theory did encourage thinking about literature in relation to, and even as a form of, philosophy. Such an approach was a longstanding one in relation to medieval literature, especially since the institution of medieval studies, as constituted in the US especially in the 1920s with the foundation of the Medieval Academy of America, was one of the first 'interdisciplinary' enterprises in American academic life. In practice, philosophy and theology held pride of place in the hierarchy of disciplines within Medieval Studies, and the New Critical analysis of medieval literature always had a tense relation to this enterprise. Here again D. W. Robertson, Jr., however much his colleagues debated against his specific schema, emphasized the moral and didactic aims of medieval writers, as in *A Preface to Chaucer* (1962). Variations on or reactions to his schema, such as Judson Allen's *The Ethical Poetic of the Later Middle Ages* (1982), pointed to ethical concerns roughly at the beginning of the period covered by this chapter. Yet, even Derrida, in his later works, turned to the question of ethics, and the belated but wide impact of the French philosopher Emmanuel Levinas, who influenced Derrida and who was championed by him, was widely embraced by scholars of medieval literature. (See Chapter 10: The Ethical Turn: From Discipline to Responsibility; Literature and Commentary; Violence and Religion: Toward Anti-Sacrificial Readings; and Midrash and Allegory.)

In much recent work on religion and ethics in ME literature, these various approaches – New Historicist, poststructuralist, feminist – form a new synthesis. Sarah Beckwith's *Christ's Body* (1993) was in many ways a breakthrough in bringing to bear the particularly materialist tendency of British cultural studies to the apparently insubstantial practices of medieval spirituality. As we have seen, Carolyn Walker Bynum books broke new ground, but Beckwith's study critiqued the hegemonic and fideistic limits of Bynum's famous books. By focusing on the symbolism of Christ's body, the ways in which it was represented and recirculated in medieval culture, she is able to stress how that symbolism was contested, rather than merely opposed on the one hand or absorbed on the other. From the point of view of feminist theory, Beckwith reinserts the problematic question of agency into a cultural history from which it had been erased. She surveys a wide number of texts and events, including Lollard texts, *The Book of Margery Kempe*, various English Franciscan writings, and Oldcastle's trial for heresy.

Furthermore, Beckwith's *Signifying God* (2001) also revives the interesting work on medieval drama that has been accomplished since the 1960s. Forty years ago, the study of medieval English drama underwent something of a revolution. As embodied in the volumes by E. K. Chambers (1903), medieval drama was assumed to have evolved out of liturgical drama, a religious ritual performed within the church. In this evolutionary paradigm, under the aegis of the guilds, processions of tableaux acquired dialogue and gradually grew into the elaborate cycles of the mystery plays. These plays, enacted on pageant wagons, flourished, but were maladapted to the more rational Reformation environment and ill-equipped to compete with the nascent Renaissance theatre, which appropriated its virtues of realism, character and comedy. By about 1970, no detail of this older paradigm withstood scholarly scrutiny. The publication of O. B. Hardison's *Christian Rite and Christian Drama in the Middle Ages* (1965) and V. A. Kolve's *The Play Called Corpus Christi* (1966) inspired a generation of scholars to reinvestigate every aspect, historical, editorial and theatrical, of medieval drama. The Chambers model, Hardison pointed out, was hopelessly Darwinian in its assumptions. According to Hardison, the Latin liturgical drama did not evolve into the cycle plays but maintained its own continuous history. The thesis that the mystery plays were suppressed acquired wide currency. Along with Hardison, V. A. Kolve exposed the Protestant and Whiggish denigration of the religious dimensions of the drama by earlier scholars and made a case for their aesthetic coherence and doctrinal sophistication. Even commonly accepted suppositions about outdoor staging on pageant wagons were subject to intense scrutiny, and scholars wondered whether entire cycles were staged at all, and if so, whether the wagons had any connection to actual staging. In the 1970s and 1980s, however, scholars of medieval drama turned to other projects, such as the laboratory staging of some of the cycles and the publication of archival documentation related to the drama, embodied in the massive *Records of Early English Drama* volumes. In contrast, Beckwith suggests a much more problematic relation of medieval drama to its cultural setting. By calling upon anthropology and political economy (and by exposing the functionalist sociology implicit in earlier studies), Beckwith proposes a model far more sensitive to disguised social conflict, implicit ideology, as well as explicit propaganda, and the deeply problematic dimensions of performance and spectatorship than heretofore acknowledged. Beckwith's work can be paired with the work of Jody Enders, who, while she works in French literature, has influenced the study of ME literature. While the rhetoric of medieval drama had been researched in traditional literary historical investigations and while the forensic origins of medieval rhetoric had been long acknowledged, in *Rhetoric and the Origins of Medieval Drama* (1992) Enders demonstrated a stunningly revealing deep structure – that the performative dimension of rhetoric, law and drama were linked both historically and structurally. Recent studies, such as those by Claire Sponsler (1997), emphasizing material culture as an aspect of medieval theatre, Susan Crane (2002), analysing court performances and display, and Ruth Nisse (2005), stressing the urban context of the political reception of the plays, continue to demonstrate the centrality of medieval drama to the field of ME literature. (See Chapter 8: Revising the New Orthodoxy.)

Metamedievalism

As fundamental shifts occurred in the way we think about medieval literature, a branch of scholarship has developed that in fact studies how we do think about medieval literature. A major impetus to this scholarship was a collection of essays by R. Howard Bloch and Stephen Nichols, *Medievalism and the Postmodern Temper* (1996). Another was the founding and continued publication of the journal *Studies in Medievalism*. This journal, and its associated conferences, dealt with the reinterpretation and reuse of the Middle Ages in general, but often touched on the history of its conceptualization in scholarship.

Reception Theory and Medieval Texts

Chaucer studies has been a special focus of this approach, with important contributions by Stephanie Trigg, whose *Congenial Souls* (2002) pointed to the assumption of a certain identity between critics and gentleman readers on the one hand and Chaucer on the other, which assumed that Chaucer and they shared the same clubby values. Similarly, Steve Ellis (2000) has chronicled the non-academic as well as academic uses of Chaucer in the modern period, underlining the differences between the two Chaucers who emerge. Richard Utz (2002) has detailed the important contribution of German scholarship on Chaucer, tracing its complex political history through the upheavals of the late nineteenth and twentieth centuries. Even the Middle Ages invented its own tradition. Seth Lerer's *Chaucer and His Readers* (1993) examines the reception of Chaucer by fifteenth century and early sixteenth-century writers and readers. Lerer writes a history of early Chaucerian reception that results in major revisions of some currently important topics in literary study: canonicity, authority, subjectivity, and how the 'literary' is constituted. 'Chaucer', that is, is invented and reinvented throughout the fifteenth century, but in ways that are already implicit in the fourteenth century texts, ways modern readers have avoided seeing or have denigrated.

David Matthews has described what he calls *The Invention of Middle English* (1999) with its connections to the changing nature of British national identity and the importance of ME literature to British and commonwealth educational policies. Bruce Holsinger's *The Premodern Condition* (2005) traces the impact of medieval studies and medieval ideas on the founders of structuralist and poststructuralist theory. The historian Kathleen Biddick (1998) provides with a sophisticated and startling investigation into how ideas about the Middle Ages are inextricably linked to ideas about empire and race, especially in the nineteenth century. These studies have alerted us to the possibility that the study of ME literature is not just an objective investigation of the texts and their archives, but a process intertwined with the social and political assumptions, and positions, of scholars and critics in particular and of readers in general.

Conclusion

The study of ME literature comprises a test case for some of the chief approaches to literary criticism over the past half-century. Its alterity and historical distance challenge the deployment of theoretical and conceptual methods and theories often developed in relation to modern and postmodern agendas. As a result, the study of ME literature has also demonstrated how richly detailed historical and generic contexts can lead to new insights both about method and theory and about the relation between the premodern and modern literatures.

Studies of ME literature can be seen to have informed the most dynamic directions in current scholarship, including the anthropological contextualization of the New Historicism, the related consideration of texts as performances and the difficult question of poetic subjectivity, particularly in terms of the position of the male author in relation to female characters and readers or audiences. Often segregated from the long history of English literature as minor or non-literary texts, ME writings have forced us to ask questions, as we have learned minor literatures do, about what constitutes a canon, an authorized text or a dominant critical approach. (See Chapter 1: Mapping New Approaches.)

Study Questions

1. Define the following terms in your own words:

   - New Criticism
   - Structuralism
   - Poststructuralism
   - Postmodernism
   - Feminism
   - Gender Studies
   - Queer Theory
   - New Historicism
   - Ecocriticism
   - Metamedievalism

2. Drawing upon your reading of this chapter, create a timeline based upon the publication date following works, offer a brief summary sentence for each, and identify the critical perspective(s) with which each critic is most readily associated:

   - Culler, *Structuralist Poetics* (1975)
   - Dinshaw, *Chaucer's Sexual Poetics* (1989)
   - Foucault, *The History of Sexuality* (1978)
   - Fradenberg, *Sacrifice Your Love* (2002)
   - Frye, *Anatomy of Criticism* (1957)
   - Holland, *The Dynamics of Literary Response* (1968)
   - Heng, *Empire of Magic* (2003)
   - Jameson, *The Political Unconscious* (1981)
   - Margherita, *The Romance of Origins* (1994)
   - Leicester, *The Disenchanted Self* (1990)
   - Robertson, *A Preface to Chaucer* (1962)
   - Said, *Orientalism* (1978)
   - Strohm, *Hochon's Arrow* (1992)
   - Simpson, *Reform and Revolution 1380–1520* (2002)
   - Wallace, *Chaucerian Polity* (1997)

   What patterns of overlap, association and influence can you detect in these works?

3. Compare and contrast the emphases two different theoretical approaches like New Historicism and psychoanalytic theory, queer theory and feminism, or Theology and Theory with postcolonial theory. What does each approach emphasize and/or minimize?

4. Look again at the ME texts discussed in Chapter 4 (Marie de France's *Lanval*, the texts of the 1381 Revolt, *The Book of Margery Kempe*, or *Mankind* and *The Tretis of Miraclis Pleyinge*) and describe the theoretical approaches used in each reading. How would the interpretations of each change if approached through a different theoretical lens?

5. Studies of Chaucer's Pardoner and Wife of Bath have been influential in the development of theoretical approaches to ME literature. From your reading of this chapter, outline the major studies that have examined either or both

of these characters. What do you think accounts for the popularity and importance of the Wife and the Pardoner in contemporary ME studies?

6. One way of thinking about the development of literary theory is to identify the types of 'data' that readers and critics bring to bear upon ME texts. Briefly identify the kinds of materials, theories, or extra-literary perspectives that each of the following theories utilize:

   • Deconstruction
   • Ecocriticism
   • Feminism
   • Gender Studies
   • Queer Theory
   • Metamedievalism
   • New Historicism
   • Postcolonial Criticism
   • Poststructuralism
   • Psychoanalytic Theory

7. Some readers are put-off by the technical language (or *jargon*) of literary theory, yet contemporary literary theory is part of the 'tool box' of professional literary study. On one hand, what are some of the reasons why readers dislike theory? On the other, why is literary theory so important to the study of literature? Is a 'theory-less' form of reading even possible? Why or why not?

8. *Web Quest*: Although Freudian psychotherapy has fallen out of favour as a popular mode of psychology, Freud is alive and well in the academic study of literature, especially as inflected through Freud's self-appointed heir in France, Jacques Lacan. Investigate the differing Freudian and Lacanian definitions of the following psychoanalytic concepts:

   • Desire
   • The Ego
   • Fetish
   • The Oedipal Complex
   • The Unconscious

   How have these terms been deployed by ME critics?

9. *Web Quest*: In many surveys of literary and cultural theory, 1968 is a watershed year, especially in France (student protests in May 1968) and in the US (the infamous 'summer of love'). Beginning with 'May 1968', investigate through an online search the international events of the late 1960s to identify the links between those events and the development of different forms of literary theory.

10. *Web Quest*: Take several of the book-length studies discussed in the chapter and, after identifying the date of their publication, research online some of the important historical, social, cultural and political events in the 5–10 years prior to their publication to see if you can identify any connection between historical events and the development of literary theory. How does this kind of investigation parallel the New Historicist approach to ME literature?

Changes in the Canon

Nancy Bradley Warren,
Florida State University

Chapter Overview

'Authoritative' Texts

The well-known literary critic Harold Bloom defines canonical authors or writers as those who are 'authoritative in our culture' (1994, 1), though the medieval understanding of 'author' was quite different from the contemporary view (Symes 2007, 13). In the past 30 years, the body of material written in Middle English (ME) deemed 'authoritative' and hence worthy of scholarly attention has changed dramatically. The object of study, which had historically been defined as 'the literary work', has shifted since the 1970s to the more encompassing category of 'the text'. The broadening of the field of study was largely influenced by the emergence of feminist and New Historicist critical methodologies in the 1980s and 1990s. It has been further driven by the influential role played by postcolonial theory in ME studies as well as by more recent moves to rethink the methods of New Historicism. Important dimensions of canon change driven by these critical trends include introducing into the critical mainstream of ME works by and for women; privileging the political, social, practical and historical over the narrowly aesthetic; re-evaluating the canonical place of fifteenth-century writing; internationalizing ME texts and attending to their (somewhat paradoxical) multilingualism; and revising the very category of 'the medieval'. These changes have brought such works as conduct books, accounts of mystical and visionary experiences, saints' lives and chronicles (just to name a few genres now solidly in the mainstream of ME studies) into the canon alongside long privileged works by such 'authoritative' writers as Chaucer, Langland, and the *Gawain*-poet (also known as the *Pearl*-poet).

The Traditional Canon of Middle English Literature

Let us begin with a few snapshots, somewhat unscientific but revealing nonetheless, of the way things stood 30 years ago, in 1977. The *MLA International Bibliography* conveniently demonstrates what ME writing received scholarly attention and what literature was deemed a legitimate object of scholarship by the forces that control academic publication. Searching this database for Chaucer, Langland and the *Pearl*-poet reveals the strong dominance of Chaucer, with 156 entries for the year 1977 alone. This dominance is not surprising, since Chaucer's place in the ME canon was arguably assured as early as the fifteenth century; as Carol Symes observes, 'In 1476, the inaugural year of his press's operation in London, William Caxton (c.1422–1491) made a signal contribution to the modern canon of medieval literature when he published a first edition of Chaucer's *Canterbury Tales*' (9). Notably, Chaucer is also one of the four pre-modern writers whom Bloom labels 'canonical'; the others are Shakespeare, Dante and Cervantes. Alongside the more than 150 publications appearing in 1977 concerning Chaucer, we find a less voluminous, but still relatively healthy, numbers of entries for Langland (7 entries – with a search for the title *Piers Plowman* yielding 11) and the *Pearl*-poet (15 results).

By way of comparison, a search for work on Margery Kempe, whose *Book*, as we shall see, becomes by the last decade of the twentieth century a canonical mainstay of ME teaching and scholarship, provides no entries at all for the year 1977. Similarly, a search for work on Julian of Norwich, a figure whose writings also become canonically central by the 1990s, reveals only 2 entries for 1977. More revealing still is to compare results for searches for the three 'mainstream' authors mentioned above (Chaucer, Langland and the *Pearl*-poet) and searches for Margery Kempe and Julian of Norwich for a slightly longer period, the 3 years at the beginning of our 30-year span: From January 1977 through December 1979, there are 489 entries for Chaucer, 23 for Langland, 54 for the *Pearl*-poet, 5 for Margery Kempe and 6 for Julian of Norwich.

A glance at the table of contents for the *Norton Anthology of English Literature*, vol. 1, that collection so often used in undergraduate survey classes, is similarly revealing. The third edition, published in 1974, highlights the dominant place of Chaucer in the ME canon in the early 1970s. This edition contains more selections from Chaucer than any edition of the anthology before or since, including numerous excerpts that appear only in that edition (for instance, the *Merchant's Tale* complete with Introduction and Epilogue and the *Franklin's Tale* complete with Introduction and Epilogue as well as an excerpt from *The Parliament of Fowls*). It also incorporates Chaucerian excerpts that had been introduced in the second edition of 1968 and were subsequently dropped in the fourth edition of 1979 (for instance, an excerpt from the *Knight's Tale* given the title 'A Thoroughfare Full of Woe' and snippets from the *Monk's Tale*). These statistics from the *MLA International Bibliography* and the *Norton Anthology* bear witness to the continuing value placed in the third quarter of the twentieth century on what had since the early days of professional ME scholarship been judged as 'literature'. This state of affairs undoubtedly owed much to the influential role played by New Criticism, which privileged the literary work as an idealized aesthetic object, in Anglo-American higher education.

The Impact of Feminism and the Expansion of the Canon

However, by the late 1970s and early 1980s, change was already on the horizon, as the appearance of fewer Chaucerian excerpts in the fourth edition (1979) of the *Norton Anthology* suggests. The convergence of political and literary feminism in this period animated the scholarly work of rehabilitating ME texts by and for women that had largely been tacitly ignored or overtly dismissed as unworthy of study (the very negative early critical reception of *The Book of Margery Kempe* provides a case in point of the latter phenomenon) (Warren 2007, 1–19). Tellingly, a keyword search in the *MLA International Bibliography* for 'women and ME' yields 62 entries for the period 1970–79 (with 41 of those 62 appearing in 1975 through 1979), and nearly exactly three times that many (187) for the period 1980–89.

The Development of Feminist Criticism

In the later 1970s and early 1980s, feminist medievalists created new publishing venues like *Mystics Quarterly* (initially founded in 1974 under the title *Fourteenth Century English Mystics Newsletter*) where they could present their research. Such scholarly publications proved a vital force for canon change; they introduced an ever-growing number of students and scholars to a wider range of ME texts, a range with a new emphasis on material by, for and about women. The *MLA International Bibliography*'s entries on Margery Kempe and Julian of Norwich in the first half of the 1980s demonstrate the impact of feminist scholarship. During this period, 22 entries appear for Margery Kempe and 35 for Julian of Norwich. Of course, not all works published on these figures, nor on other emergent ME texts by and for women, are feminist in orientation. The very existence, however, of a work like Michael E. Sawyer's *A Bibliographical Index of Five English Mystics* (1978), which situates Margery and Julian alongside Richard Rolle and Walter Hilton, suggests that the canonization of Julian's *Showings* and *The Book of Margery Kempe* as legitimate works to which scholars and students of ME might direct their attention was well underway.

At the same time, the work of scholarly editing, a key dimension of canon formation, bears witness to the emerging interest in and legitimation of ME texts authored by or associated with women. The case of Julian of Norwich is emblematic here. The second half of the 1970s saw editions of Julian's writings from manuscripts (rather than the 'versions' or 'modernizations' that had dominated earlier offerings) beginning to appear. Marion Glasscoe's edition of MS BL Sloane 2499 appeared in 1976, and Francis Beer's text of the short version in 1978. That was the era, too, of the Colledge and Walsh two-volume edition (1978) including both texts, a comprehensive introduction, and a critical apparatus that provides the base for other students of Julian (Crampton 1994, 18).

In the 1980s, a true sea change in ME studies occurred, one that dramatically advanced the expansion of the canon that feminist scholars had begun to inaugurate in the late 1970s and early 1980s. Indeed, in the 1980s feminist scholarship converged with what proved to be an extraordinary paradigm shift in the field. In 1987, Caroline Walker Bynum's *Holy Feast and Holy Fast* was published as the first work in Stephen Greenblatt's series 'The New Historicism: Studies in Cultural Poetics', a publication that serves to signal the so-called 'cultural turn' in medieval studies. With this book, Bynum continued the process she had begun in her 1982 book *Jesus as Mother*, doing nothing less than bringing female spirituality and the female body to the centre of ME studies. In her preface Bynum rightly claims that she 'advance[s] theories about the nature of asceticism and about women's use of symbols that are far-reaching in their implications for women's history and for the history of religions' (1987, xv). She further observes, 'Both to knowledgeable medievalists and to committed feminists – although for different reasons – these theories will seem to be audacious reversals of received wisdom' (xv). Bynum's theories and 'audacious reversals' helped irrevocably to open up the range of texts available as legitimate objects of study for ME scholars.

Rita Copeland's review of *Holy Feast and Holy Fast*, published in the influential medieval studies journal *Speculum* in 1989, makes clear the book's impact. Copeland notes that in the 2 years since its publication, *Holy Feast and Holy Fast* 'already found a large audience both within and beyond medieval studies, among historians of sexuality, feminist historians and critics, and, more generally, literary scholars regardless of field and period, whose work is invested in the relationships between texts and social practice' (1989, 143). Bynum's scholarship, along with New Historicism's interests in 'self-fashioning' (to take up Stephen Greenblatt's influential term), the operations of ideological systems, and the cultural work done by previously ignored categories of texts, bolstered the increasing inclusion of texts by and for women in the ME canon.

Julian of Norwich and Margery Kempe

That this category of previously marginalized texts had made significant inroads into the canon is signalled by the fact that it is in this period that excerpts from *The Book of Margery Kempe* and Julian's *Showings* made their debut in the *Norton Anthology of English Literature*, that iconic representation of canonical literature in the American academy. Excerpts from *The Book of Margery Kempe* first appeared in volume one of the fifth edition (1986), and selections from the *Showings* were first included in volume one of the sixth edition (1993). Subsequently, Margery and Julian's writings have only become more canonically central. Between 2000 and 2006, 29 entries on Julian of Norwich appeared in the *MLA International Bibliography*. In 2005, the Norton Critical Edition of *The Showings of Julian of Norwich*, edited by Denise N. Baker, appeared, increasingly the accessibility of this text, particularly for undergraduate teaching; Nicholas Watson and Jacqueline Jenkins also published a new scholarly edition of the Short and Long versions of Julian's text in 2006, including previously unedited material from seventeenth-century manuscripts associated with the Cambrai Benedictine nuns whose community was largely responsible for preserving Julian's text. Even more strikingly, since the year 2000 the *MLA International Bibliography* features 97 entries on *The Book of Margery Kempe*, including an entry for Lynn Staley's Norton Critical Edition of this text (2001). (See Chapter 4: Margery Kempe, *The Book of Margery Kempe*.)

Websites devoted to both Margery and Julian also abound; Julia Bolton Holloway's site called 'The Mystics' Internet' (http://www.umilta.net/mystics.html) provides extensive information on both figures, and an excellent site entitled 'Mapping Margery Kempe' (http://www.holycross.edu/departments/visarts/projects/kempe/) presents copious contextualizing material. Such sites attest to the popular, as well as the academic, interest in these representatives of ME women's religious writing, as do publications like Robert Gluck's novel *Margery Kempe* (1994) and contemporary devotional works like John Kirken and Richard Chilson's *All Will be Well: Based on the Classic Spirituality of Julian of Norwich: 30 Days with a Great Spiritual Teacher* (1995).

Furthermore, Margery Kempe's *Book* and Julian's *Showings* are by no means the only representations of women's writing in ME. Early on in the history of scholarship on *The Book of Margery Kempe*, Hope Emily Allen proposed that Margery should be understood in the context of such Continental holy women as St. Birgitta of Sweden, Marie of Oignies and St. Catherine of Siena, among others. The writings of many of these women circulated in ME translations, and these figures have benefited from a comparativist impulse often found in New Historicist scholarship as well as from feminist work of textual recovery. Scholarship on Continental women's texts has become commonplace in recent years among scholars working and teaching in English departments, and Alexandra Barratt's volume *Women's Writing in Middle English* (1992) made excerpts from the ME texts of many female writers available to students, containing as it does excerpts from such figures as Mechtild of Hackeborn, Elizabeth of Hungary, Catherine of Siena, Birgitta of Sweden and Marguerite Porete. The introduction of these texts into the ME canon resonates not only with aims of feminist and New Historicist critics but also with other important canonical trends, especially an increasing awareness of the internationalism of ME literature (see discussion below).

New Historicism and Blurring the History/Literature Divide

The expansion of the canon sparked at least in part by the critical concerns of New Historicism goes far beyond the upsurge in interest in texts by and for women. In the 1980s, and increasingly in the 1990s, we see growing interest among scholars of ME in texts previously considered the purview of linguists, historians and theologians. Indeed, the fact that Bynum's influential *Holy Feast and Holy Fast*, the work of a historian, was and is, as Copeland observes in her review, of such interest to literary scholars is revealing, as is Copeland's reference to the significance of work 'invested in the relationships between texts and social practice' (143). We could accurately say that a shift towards the social, the practical and the historical characterizes another important feature of canon change in the later 1980s and early 1990s. Indeed, as Stein points out, 'Techniques of close and extremely attentive reading that historically were elaborated to come to grips with the complex, evocative and highly self-conscious linguistic procedures of the great artistic works of high culture have, since the linguistic turn throughout the human sciences, been brought to bear with extremely fruitful results . . . on linguistic and symbolic material of all sorts' (2007, 35). Paul Strohm's *Hochon's Arrow: The Social Imagination of Fourteenth-Century Texts* (1992) stands as an illustrative exemplar of such critical methodology. As Peter W. Travis writes in his review of *Hochon's Arrow* in *Speculum*, Strohm 'react[s] against a tradition that views historical records as two-dimensional backdrops to transcendent works of art' and finds in archival sources 'a literary richness, tension, and ambiguity equaled only by the historical complexity of certain, often minor, contemporary works of literature' (1995, 432). (See Chapter 7: Marxism to New Historicism.)

Wycliffe and Lollardy

The upsurge in publications on Lollard texts, which were previously studied primarily by religious scholars or historians, reveals the newly canonical status of non-literary texts. To use the *MLA International Bibliography* once again as a touchstone for literary trends, one notes that a search for 'Lollard' or 'Lollardy' produces 8 results in the 1970s, 29 in the 1980s, 47 in the 1990s and 61 for the period 2000–06. Such essays as Ruth Nissé's 'Reversing Discipline: *The Tretise of Miraclis Pleyinge*, Lollard Exegesis, and the Failure of Representation' (1997) and Rita Copeland's 'Why Women Can't Read: Medieval Hermeneutics, Statutory Law, and the Lollard Heresy' (1994) emblematize the emergent interests of ME scholars in previously little known texts as well as in the intersections of textual operations and politics. These trends also influence the kinds of scholarship undertaken on traditionally canonical writers from the 1980s onwards. For instance, a search in the *MLA International Bibliography* for 'Chaucer and Lollard' yields 14 results, with 12 of those 14 seeing publication in 1984 or later. A representative example, the title of which again manifests the concerns of the New Historicist inflected 1990s, is Paul Strohm's 'Chaucer's Lollard Joke: History and the Textual Unconscious' (1995). Similarly, a search for 'Lollard and Langland' provides 17 references to books and essays, all of which have been published since the mid-1980s.

Interestingly, a search in the *MLA International Bibliography* for Wyclif/Wycliffe/Wycliffite does not reveal the same exponential expansion in interest as do searches involving some variation of the term 'Lollard'. A search for variations of 'Wyclif' yields 35 results for the 1970s, 49 for the 1980s, 41 for the 1990s and 46 for 2000–06. Perhaps this difference stems from a steady interest since the 1970s in the more 'academic' (and hence more readily accepted as a legitimate topic for scholarly inquiry) version of the heresy in contrast to the more recently enhanced interest in the more 'popular' version fuelled by the concerns of New Historicism. This is a distinction marked the choice of descriptive terminology; using forms of the name of the Oxford theologian John Wyclif tends to indicate the more academic form of the heresy, while using variations on 'Lollard' typically signals the more popular version, something more in harmony with what Copeland terms the 'relationship between texts and social practices.' (See Chapter 3: Lollardy and John Wyclif.)

From Literature to Texts

From the 1990s through the early twenty-first century we also find growing numbers of student editions of 'non-literary' (at least as the term 'literary' was construed through the 1970s) ME texts emphasizing the social, historical and practical aspects of medieval culture. This development foregrounds a shift in what teachers value and what students encounter in the classroom. For instance, in 1990 Oxford University Press published Bella Millett and Jocelyn Wogan-Browne's *Medieval English Prose for Women: Selections from the Katherine Group and Ancrene Wisse*, and Clarendon issued a revised paperback edition in 1992. Millett and Wogan-Browne's edition includes didactic religious treatises, saints' lives and religious rules for women. Their incorporation of facing-page translation helps to bring these linguistically difficult, though culturally and religiously influential, ME texts within the horizon of possibility for study by graduate and undergraduate students alike.

Additionally, publications in the TEAMS Middle English series of editions from the later 1990s and early twenty-first century demonstrate the acceptance of historical, political and social texts into the corpus of ME texts in American academia. The TEAMS series, published by the Medieval Institute of Western Michigan University, is designed, as their website states, 'to make available to teachers and students texts which occupy an important place in the literary and cultural canon but which have not been readily available in student editions'. Publications in this series accurately indicate what texts have gained sufficient scholarly acceptance to be regularly taught and studied in university classrooms. The TEAMS list of publications reveals a tellingly strong political component from the 1990s onward; witness, for instance, James M. Dean's 1991 edition of *Six Ecclesiastical Satires*, Dean's 1996 volume *Medieval English Political Writings*, and David Carlson's 2003 edition of *Richard Maidstone: Concordia (The Reconciliation of Richard II with London)*.

Additional evidence for the expansion of the ME canon into social, historical, political and practical texts rather than traditional 'literature' comes from a comparison of the tables of contents of the sixth and seventh editions of volume one of the *Norton Anthology of English Literature*, published in 1993 and 2000 respectively. The seventh edition contains excerpts from chronicles and 'legendary histories of Britain' not present in the sixth edition or, for that matter, in other previous editions, and it also includes an excerpt from the *Ancrene Riwle* (or *Ancrene Wisse*). The *Norton Anthology* is by no means alone among student anthologies in representing this trend. The most recent edition of the Blackwell anthology *Old and Middle English c. 890–1400* (2004) similarly reflects this shift. In addition to the expected ME lyrics and works by Chaucer, Langland, and the *Gawain*-poet, it contains numerous saints' lives, homilies, excerpts from chronicles, and selections from both the *Ancrene Wisse* and the didactic treatise on virginity entitled *Hali Meidhad*.

Rethinking the Boundaries and Fifteenth-Century Literature

Still another manifestation of canon change driven at least in part by New Historicists' interests in the social, historical, political and practical is the reevaluation of and concomitant serious, sustained attention given to fifteenth-century texts, which had been all but ignored by the New Critics and previous literary scholars, over the course of the 1990s. In his seminal essay 'Dullness and the Fifteenth Century' (1987), David Lawton begins by characterizing longstanding critical attitudes towards such fifteenth-century writers as John Lydgate, Thomas Hoccleve and Osbern Bokenham. He opens by observing that some may see his essay's 'title as self-explanatory and self-justifying, in line with the English fifteenth century's received reputation: the very scholars who have found it interesting enough to work on have been the first to assure us that it is dull' (761). He points out that scholars have, mistakenly in his view, tended to concentrate on matters of style in discussing fifteenth-century texts. He argues, 'Critically and historically, the view distorts. It ensures both that we encounter great difficulty in reading any fifteenth-century poem, and that we fail to acknowledge the fifteenth century in our literary history, so that for all practical purposes the sixteenth century is regarded as the period in which English poetry has the sense to begin all over' (774). Lawton further notes that a 'fundamental assumption of the English literary canon' has historically 'doomed the English fifteenth century' – the assumption 'that what makes literature interesting is individualism, preferably bourgeois individualism' (762). In contrast, Lawton claims that 'a major interest of fifteenth-century writing is its lack of individualism . . .; historically . . . the fifteenth century authoritatively consolidates the public voice and role of English poetry' (762). He goes on to state, 'There is little theoretical room in the fifteenth century . . . for a distinction between literature, society, and history.' (771).

It is thus not surprising that fifteenth-century texts, texts that Lawton sees as constructing the 'public sphere' (1987, 793), would appeal to a generation of scholars preoccupied with the public and cultural work that texts perform. TEAMS editions published in the last 15 years highlight the newly central place of fifteenth-century texts in the ME canon. Charles R. Blyth's edition of *Thomas Hoccleve: The Regiment of Princes* appeared in 1999, for example, while Robert R. Edwards's *John Lydgate, Troy Book: Selections* came out in 1998, followed by his *John Lydgate, The Siege of Thebes* in 2001.

Osbern Bokenham and Thomas Hoccleve

Publication statistics on two of the fifteenth-century writers that feature in Lawton's essay, Osbern Bokenham and Thomas Hoccleve, make even clearer the canonical establishment of fifteenth-century ME writing in the course of the 1990s. For Bokenham, no publications at all are recorded for the entire decade of the 1970s in the *MLA International Bibliography* and only one each for the 1940s, 1950s and 1960s respectively – even though the Early English Text Society, which since the nineteenth century has published scholarly editions of medieval English texts, had made a scholarly edition of Bokenham's *Legendys of Hooly Wummen* available in 1938. Two items on Bokenham appeared in the 1980s, one of which, a PhD dissertation, tellingly, explicitly focuses on style, confirming Lawton's assessment of scholars' typical interests in fifteenth-century texts. In the 1990s, six critical essays appeared, and, significantly, Shelia Delany published both a monograph on Bokenham, the title of which gestures towards the social concerns of the era's literary scholars (*Impolitic Bodies: Poetry, Saints, and Society in Fifteenth-Century England: The Work of Osbern Bokenham* [1997]) and a translation of Bokenham's collection of female saints' lives (*A Legend of Holy Women: A Translation of Osbern Bokenham's Legends of Holy Women* [1992]). An additional six essays on Bokenham appeared between 2000 and 2006, demonstrating continued interest.

In the past decade and a half, Hoccleve's work has become even more canonically mainstream than Bokenham's, though arguably it had something of a head start. There were a respectable 15 items on Hoccleve published in the 1970s, according to the *MLA International Bibliography*, but the number nearly doubled to 27 in the 1980s, and then expanded more dramatically still in the 1990s to 46, with an additional 29 items seeing publication between 2000 and 2006. The appearance of Ethan Knapp's *The Bureaucratic Muse: Thomas Hoccleve and the Literature of Late Medieval England* (2001), according to the University of Pennsylvania Press 'the first full-length study of Hoccleve since 1968', highlights Hoccleve's current status.

Multilingualism, International Contexts and Postcolonial Concerns

The table of contents of the eighth edition of the *Norton Anthology of English Literature* (2006) reveals an additional legacy of the critical concerns with the historical, political, practical and social that did so much to change the canon of ME literature. Many of the politically and historically oriented texts added from the sixth edition are grouped in a section labelled 'Anglo-Norman England', where they appear alongside Celtic texts as well as the *lais* and fables of Marie de France (the latter a writer whose texts were also translated into ME). The creation of this category gestures not only towards the politics of the Norman Conquest and its textual consequences but also towards another key development in the ME canon in the last 15 years – what might be called the 'internationalization' of ME. Scholars are increasingly aware that the literature of the medieval British Isles was far from insular, and in fact, somewhat paradoxically given the focus on the ME canon, not always written in English. As Stein observes, 'Even before the Norman Conquest introduced a significantly large population of French speakers to the Island of Britain, England was polyglot' (2007, 23). He further notes, 'A very large number of twelfth- and thirteenth-century manuscripts produced in England cross-linguistic boundaries in their contents' (31).

The trend towards acknowledging the international and multilingual dimensions of the ME canon is further advanced by the growth of post-colonial theoretical approaches to medieval literature in the 1990s. As Jeffrey Jerome Cohen, one of the foremost postcolonialist medievalist scholars observes, 'Postcolonial theory typically analyzes the conflict and accommodation that unfold in the wake of conquest and other kinds of cultural admixture. . . . Postcolonial criticism has therefore developed a sophisticated vocabulary for describing hybridity, the conflictual interpenetration of cultures that results from colonial contact and that transforms both colonizer and indigene' (Postcolonial Theory). The topics and texts considered by contributors to Cohen's *The Postcolonial Middle Ages* (2000) writing on the English Middle Ages are illustrative. Consider, for instance, the implications of Geraldine Heng's essay in the collection: 'The Romance of England: *Richard Coer de Lyon*, Saracens, Jews, and the Politics of Race and Nation'. The essay focuses on the ME versions of a crusade romance that exemplifies what Christopher Baswell terms 'multilingualism on the page'. *Richard Coer de Lyon* features 'brief but intense emergences of the Anglo-French language of aristocratic authenticity' (Baswell 2007, 43); Heng's essay considers, as Kathy Lavezzo notes in her review of Cohen's volume, 'the gruesome means by which the romance imagines the English crusader's conquest of the "Infidel" ' as a means of constituting a Christian, English community (Rev. of *The Postcolonial Middle Ages*). Michelle R. Warren's book *History on the Edge:*

Excalibur and the Borders of Britain 1100–1300 (2000) similarly reveals the international, multilingual trend in medieval English scholarship as shaped by postcolonial approaches. Warren, who, at the time of the book's publication, was on the faculty of the French department at University of Miami and who currently teaches in the department of Comparative Literature at Dartmouth (facts that themselves point to the internationalization of the ME canon), states that the 'book pursues an encounter between medieval narratives of British colonial history and postcolonial theories' (2001, 152). Significantly, she considers insular and Continental texts written in Latin, Anglo-Norman and ME.

England and the Continent

Such work emblematizes a move towards seeing ME texts and medieval English culture in dialogue with Continental trends and developments, one not confined to the realm of postcolonial approaches. Indeed, Elizabeth Salter's work in the late 1980s pointed field in this direction prior to her untimely death, and Kathryn Kerby-Fulton's recent study *Books Under Suspicion: Censorship and Tolerance of Revelatory Writing in Late Medieval England* (2006) signals potential future implications for the canon of understanding ME as a non-insular, multilingual literary culture (see Salter, Pearsall, and Zeeman [1988]). In this groundbreaking book, Kerby-Fulton takes a major step in realizing what Stein has called the 'literary consequences' of post-conquest trilingualism in England (2007, 24). As Stein states, 'The polyglot reality of medieval life, while often acknowledged, has barely received its due as a literary phenomenon', and the reasons for this neglect involve 'the historical development of literary studies during the nineteenth and twentieth centuries and . . . the ghosts of earlier moments in their history that still haunt current academic configurations. Although medievalists study a period prior to the state, they do this, if they are literary scholars, as part of the historical study of national literatures' (28). Such trilingualism appears, for instance, in the work of John Gower (one of the figures brought into the mainstream of the medieval English canon by recent work on the fifteenth century), who wrote in Latin, Anglo-Norman and ME.

Books Under Suspicion includes a great deal of sophisticated work on heretofore unedited and unpublished manuscripts, and Kerby-Fulton uncovers previously unrecognized histories of texts long assumed not to play significant roles in the religious and literary cultures of fourteenth- and fifteenth-century England. For instance, she reveals a fascinating pattern of heterodox and heretical texts from Continental Europe being distributed in England as part of widespread English interest in and concern with Continental religious trends.

Similarly, Kerby-Fulton provides a new angle on Margery Kempe's relationship to Continental female spirituality. Rather than focusing just on such hagiographical and mystical Continental 'role models' for Margery as Birgitta of Sweden and Marie of Oignies (role models that she by no means discounts), Kerby-Fulton argues that 'one of the key motivations for Margery's public teaching and mysticism may have come from alternative European models of urban devotion' (2006, 249). Kerby-Fulton also makes a persuasive case for connections between Julian of Norwich's *Showings* and the Continental mystic Marguerite Porete's *Mirror of Simple Souls* (a text judged to be heretical and one for which Marguerite was burned at the stake in 1310). We can well imagine ME texts associated with these groups, heretical and representatives of what Kerby-Fulton calls 'left-wing orthodoxy' alike, making their way into the ME canon as their importance for such already canonical writers as Margery Kempe, Julian of Norwich and even Chaucer, Langland, and the *Pearl*-poet, becomes understood, a task Kerby-Fulton has done much to advance with her study.

Revising the New Orthodoxy

In the new millennium, scholars have begun to revise methods and assumptions associated with the New Historicism that so strongly characterized the last decade of the twentieth century in medieval studies. In particular, scholars are moving away from a focus on textual micro-contexts and brief historical snapshots. The ME canon is in the process of expanding still further as the very definitions of what constitutes the 'Middle' aspect of the label shift along with definitions of what constitutes 'English'. The category 'medieval' itself is being rethought. Unlike New Historicist criticism, which tends to focus on relatively localized textual environments and relatively short periods of time, recent work by some medieval scholars increasingly considers longer historical periods and the importance of continuity, as well as change, over long spans of time. In other words, the world of ME not only *exceeds* the geographical boundaries of England, but it is also *exceeds* the period that has conventionally been defined as the Middle Ages. In her call for still more revision of the medieval canon, Symes argues that 'Nearly everything that we take for granted about the identification, classification, and evaluation of texts must . . . be subjected to rigorous scrutiny in the twenty-first century' (2007, 21). Work currently being done by David Wallace provides an ideal example of such rethinking and admirably illustrates the potential of such work to act as a catalyst for canon change. In his essay 'Periodizing Women: Mary Ward (1585–1645) and the Premodern Canon', Wallace 'considers the misalignment of pre-modern women's experiences and textual remains' with the 'developmental narratives' of 'periodization paradigms' (2006, 398). His test case is

Mary Ward, a woman 'at once unknown and a figure of European stature; an epical traveller inspired by saints' lives a la Margery Kempe' (398). He argues that the absence of Mary Ward's texts (which survive primarily in Italian versions) from the pre-modern English canon 'speaks both to long-running struggles within Roman Catholicism and to assumptions of Protestant historiography complicit with such absenting. The habilitation of Mary Ward wins new points of observation upon long histories of English women and writing that ride out medieval/Renaissance, Catholic/Protestant divides' (398–99). Wallace's essay, along with manuscript-based scholarship like that of Kerby-Fulton and editing work such as that undertaken by Watson and Jenkins, signal new developments in the new millennium in the ongoing efforts of feminists and others alike to recover little known texts and to open new fields in which academic innovation and creative pedagogy can occur.

Study Questions

1. Define the following terms in your own words:
   - Canon
   - New Criticism
   - New Historicism
   - Feminism
   - Postcolonial theory
   - Mysticis
   - Hagiography
   - Heresy
   - Multilingualism

2. What are the chief theoretical developments that influenced the expansion of the ME canon over the past 30 years? Summarize the impacts of each development on the canon.
3. What are three central concerns of feminist criticism in relation to canon formation?
4. Compare the sorts of writings privileged by New Criticism and New Historicism. Then, outline a New Critical and a New Historical reading of a single ME text.
5. What are some of the shared interests of feminist and New Historicist critics, and how did these interests help to transform the canon of ME literature?
6. What are some of the shared concerns of feminist and postcolonial theorists? How did these shared concerns help to shape the canon of ME literature?
7. Why were fifteenth-century English writings largely ignored prior to the 1990s? What arguments does David Lawton make concerning the need to revisit fifteenth-century English literature?
8. Describe three trends in scholarly publication over the past 30 years that reflect changes in the ME canon.

9. How are ideas about historical periods and the boundaries between them changing? What implications might such scholarship have for future developments in the canon of ME literature?
10. *Web Quest*: While the study of ME literature has expanded in scope and date, expanding the traditional canon, not everyone is pleased with these changes. Perform a web search on 'the canon' to see what kinds of discussion you can find about changes not only in the medieval period but throughout the study of British and American literature in the last 30 years. How do people on different sides of the question account for these changes? If you want to make your search even more interesting, try 'canon war(s)' and you will likely find even more heated rhetoric on all sides of the question.

9

Issues of Sexuality, Gender and Ethnicity

Diane Cady, Mills College

Chapter Overview

Christine de Pizan and the *Querelle de la Rose*

Feminist literary theory emerged in the 1960s and 1970s, during what is sometimes called 'second wave feminism'. However, some scholars have located feminism's practice in much earlier periods, including the Middle Ages. Take, for example, Christine de Pizan, one of Europe's first professional women of letters. Widowed at the age of twenty-four, Christine turned to writing to support her young family. Writing was an exceedingly rare career choice for a woman living at the beginning of the fifteenth century. Perhaps even more unusual was Christine's willingness to use her writing to challenge the misogynistic tradition. She participated in the *Querelle de la Rose*, the fervent debate surrounding the popular *Romance de la Rose*. She reprimanded one of the authors, Jean de Meun, for his depiction of women as weak-willed creatures, prone to lasciviousness, fickleness and greed. Rejecting the adage that there must be some truth to the stereotype, Christine offers a much simpler explanation for the misogyny she encounters so frequently in the books she reads:

> And if someone tells me that books are full of their vices,
> Here is my response to those about whom I complain;
> I answer that women did not write books
> Nor put in them what is said
> Against them and their behavior. . . .
> But if women had written books,
> I know for certain that things would be otherwise,
> Because women know that they are wrongly accused. (2000, 4–5)

A few years later, Christine pens a more direct riposte in her *Book of the City of Ladies* (1405). Drawing on Augustine's trope of a 'city of God', she constructs a city populated with mythological, historical and contemporary women whose characters and achievements call into question misogynistic stereotypes. Christine's city is heavily fortified, suggesting that she sees women needing protection from the slings and arrows of misogynistic discourse. (See Chapter 3: Christine de Pizan.)

The Place of Chaucer's Wife of Bath

While some scholars have located feminist literary practice in actual medieval women like Christine de Pizan, still others have turned to fictional female characters for example. Perhaps one of the most frequently cited examples (and one of the most controversial) is Chaucer's Wife of Bath. Like Christine, Alisoun observes that the negative depiction of women in literature has everything to do with who is holding the pen:

> By God, if women hadde written stories
> As clerkes han withinne hire oratories,
> They wolde han writen of men moore wikkednesse
> Than all the mark of Adam may redress. (III.693–6).

The Wife of Bath asserts that her experience trumps the 'auctoritee' of clerks, she exposes clerks' penchant for massaging meaning out of texts in order to advance certain agendas, and she insists on the right to engage in sex for pleasure and for profit. For many modern readers, such assertions reflect a feminist stance.

However, upon closer scrutiny, both Christine and Alisoun serve as ambiguous examples of feminist literary practice. First, there is the simple fact that 'feminism' as the term is understood today did not exist in the Middle Ages. Indeed, the word does not appear in English until 1894. Can we ascribe feminist motivations to women or literary figures that lived or were conceived of before the concept had even come into being (Gottlieb 1985)? Do such assignations smack of what some scholars call 'presentism': that is, the practice of reading the past based on the values and beliefs of the present day and the particular desires of the scholar or scholars who are doing the reading? Even if these questions could be answered satisfactorily, difficulties remain. Sheila Delany, for example, argues that Christine's circumscribed view of women's abilities, as well as her class biases, mitigate the power of her defence of women (Delany 1987; 1992). Or, take a figure like the Wife of Bath. Both students and scholars alike gravitate towards Alisoun in part because there is a dearth of extant women's voices from the period. Yet what does it mean to call a literary construct 'feminist', particularly one conceived by an author whose work reflects, at best, an equivocal view of women? Indeed, while from a modern perspective the Wife of Bath's insistence on the right to pursue sexual pleasure or to use her body for economic gain may sound like feminist positions, the link between a woman's economic and sexual insatiability is one of medieval misogyny's most hackneyed complaints. Thus, what we might interpret as a feminist attitude from a modern perspective, may, from a medieval perspective, read as misogyny.

Christine and Alisoun, like so many figures we find in medieval literature, reflect and refract the period's complicated and contradictory attitudes towards women. They make manifest both the rich complexity of medieval literature and its interpretive challenges. They also demonstrate why feminist literary theory is itself such a diverse and complex critical approach. As we will see, these complexities are not only at issue in feminist approaches to the Middle Ages, but also in discussions of gender and race. Far from comprehensive, this essay will sketch with broad strokes the historical context of feminism, gender study and race theory, outline some of the work medievalists have done in these areas, and explore the interstices among these theoretical approaches.

Feminism and Feminisms

Given the vast range of approaches, methods and concerns present in feminist literary theory, it might be more accurate to speak of 'feminist theories', rather than a single, unified feminist theory. Nonetheless, there are certain precepts that most feminists accept. One of the most important is the distinction between sex and gender. Sex refers to biological sex, based on the sex-specific physical characteristics that mark a person as male or female. These characteristics include genitalia, body hair, and breast, muscle and fat distribution. (Of course both men and women can share some of these physical characteristics, making biological sex a much less stable category than we might at first imagine, an issue I will return to in the gender studies section, below). Gender, on the other hand, might be thought of as the social side of sex: it includes the behaviours and qualities that a society expects men and women to display because they are a certain biological sex. Men and women who do not behave in these prescribed ways are often labelled as 'unnatural' by society. However, many feminists would argue that nature has little to do with gender. What constitutes masculine and feminine behaviour varies widely, depending on historical and cultural context. If ideas about masculinity and femininity were, indeed, based on an unchanging natural order, they would not change over time and across societies. Sexual behaviour and gender roles play a crucial part in a number of cultural institutions, practices and values. Therefore, most societies are invested in blurring the differences between sex and gender in order to imply that a 'natural' link exists between them. The feminist anthropologist Gayle Rubin notes that all societies have a 'sex/gender system', 'a set of arrangements by which the biological raw material of human sex and procreation is shaped by human, social intervention and satisfied in a conventional manner, no matter how bizarre some of the conventions may be' (1975, 159). By analysing the sex/gender system, scholars gain insight into the investments, fantasies and anxieties of particular cultures and societies. (See Chapter 8: The Impact of Feminism and the Expansion of the Canon.)

Until quite recently, scholars divided feminist literary theory into two groups: Anglo-American and French. These divisions are not free from problems. The term 'Anglo-American', for example, glosses over some of the real methodological differences between English and American feminist scholars. Nor are all the 'French' feminists French: Two of the most important scholars in this group, Hélène Cixous and Julia Kristeva, are from Algiers and Bulgaria respectively. In addition, with the increasing influence of poststructuralist theory in the US, differences between the two groups have decreased. Nonetheless, references to 'Anglo-American' and 'French' feminism continue in discussions of feminist literary theory, making it useful to have a sense of the characteristics of each group and how medievalists have worked within and responded to their ideas. (See Chapter 7: Feminism and Gender Studies.)

Anglo-American Feminism

The project of early Anglo-American feminist theory was twofold. Initially, feminist scholars set about uncovering the sexist assumptions found in canonical American and British works. Perhaps the most influential work in this regard is Kate Millett's *Sexual Politics* (1969). Millett's study exposes the sexist and heterosexist assumptions found in the works of such major authors as Norman Mailer, D. H. Lawrence and Henry Miller and lauds authors like Jean Genet, whose writing she claims serves as a counterpoint to such assumptions. Looking back on her work from a contemporary vantage point, the claims of *Sexual Politics* might seem far from revolutionary and perhaps even a little naïve. Is it really so revelatory to observe that the work of major authors can be sexist and heterosexist? Nearly 500 years earlier, both Christine de Pizan and Chaucer's Wife of Bath observed that what a reader sees or does not see in a text depends greatly on the reader's subject position. Yet clearly the point still needed to be made in 1969, since at that time literary scholars had hardly commented upon the presence of misogyny and homophobia in canonical literature.

Gynocriticism

If the first project of early Anglo-American feminist criticism was to reread texts written by men, its second project was to uncover the often-marginalized work of women writers and to incorporate their texts into the canon. Elaine Showalter coined the term 'gynocritics' to describe this new focus on women not as the subject of writing, but as writers themselves: 'its [gynocriticism's] subjects are the history, styles, themes, genres, and structures of writing by women; the psychodynamics of female creativity; the trajectory of the individual or collective female career; and the evolution and laws of a female literary tradition' (1981, 184–5). Another project written in the vein of gynocriticism is Sandra M. Gilbert and Susan Gubar's influential *The Madwoman in the Attic: The Woman Writer and the Nineteenth-Century Literary Imagination* (1975). Gilbert and Gubar argue that in Western literature women are presented in one of two ways: as either the patriarchal ideal – docile, passive and selfless, 'the angel in the house' – or, as the patriarchal nightmare – assertive, seductive and duplicitous. We find a similar binary in medieval literature as well, which is populated with 'patient Griseldas' (self-sacrificial martyrs) on the one hand, and 'likerous' women (lecherous, man-eating harpies) like the Wife of Bath on the other. Women writers of the nineteenth century not only had to grapple with these, but also with the belief that writing was primarily a male activity. Thus, women find themselves in a double bind: Either forced to use a language that does not reflect their experience or be rendered unintelligible or silent in the public sphere.

Today, feminist literary theory is a vital and important critical approach in medieval studies. However, this was not always the case. Even as recently as 1993, Judith Bennett observed that in the minds of many, medievalism and feminism were 'an odd and unwelcome couple'. This belief existed even though there is a long history of women medievalists, many of whom wrote about women's history and writing (Bennett, 9). Speaking before the Medieval Academy in 1983, David Herlihy noted that one-third of the Academy's members were women. Although not amounting to parity, this figure certainly surpassed many other academic fields at the time. Yet the role of women in the field has traditionally been downplayed. Historically, many women medievalists were isolated professionally because they were trained separately from men in single-sex institutions, and while male medievalists lauded early pioneers like Eileen Power, Nellie Neilson, Bertha Putnam and Hope Emily Allen, some of the major histories of the field made little if any mention of their work. A glance at the publication record of one of medieval studies premiere journals, *Speculum*, demonstrates the marginality of feminist theory in the history of medieval studies. From 1971 to 1990, the journal published an average of only one article related to medieval women, and this at a time when feminist theory was at its height in other disciplines (Bennett 1993).

Medieval Women's Writing

Despite these slow beginnings, by the mid-1980s a wellspring of feminist work began to appear in medieval studies. New anthologies and editions expanded the canon and, in some cases, made available for the first time new writings by medieval women (see, for example, Dronke 1984; Wilson 1994; Petroff 1986; Thiébaux 1994). New scholarship renewed interest in medieval women like Christine de Pizan, Hrotsvit of Gandersheim and Margery Kempe, as well as texts written specifically for women, such as the *Katherine Group*. *Signs* (1989), *Exemplaria* (1992) and *Speculum* (1993) all published special issues on medieval women. The *Medieval Feminist Forum* (formally called the *Medieval Feminist Newsletter*) was founded in 1984, with the goal of providing a venue for what was then very new work in medieval studies. Other feminist work in the field included studies on the body, gender and issues of concern to medieval women (for example, see Ferrante 1975, Gravdal 1991, Lomperis and Stanbury 1993). More recently, essays in *Women Medievalists and the Academy* (Chance 2005) have explored the role that women medievalists have played in the formation of medieval studies. (See Chapter 8: The Impact of Feminism and the Expansion of the Canon.)

During the 1980s and 1990s, feminist scholars also undertook re-examinations of canonical writers. While in some cases analysing the same literary material, these feminist re-examinations often reached different interpretations of the texts they read. In contrast to Carolyn Dinshaw's argument that Chaucer's women 'envision the place of the Other in patriarchal society' (10), Elaine Tuttle Hansen reaches quite different conclusions. While she admits that initially she saw Chaucer's portrayals of women as sympathetic, and perhaps even as an articulation of an embryonic feminism, but as time passed she began to have doubts because:

> What often sounds like a woman's voice [in Chaucer's texts], what is spoken in the name of women, inflected by different and highly realistic, sometimes subversive dialects, always enters and leaves Chaucerian story not as the enunciation of an autonomous speaker, but as urgent problems for male characters, male narrators, and (?male) readers. (Tuttle Hansen, 1992, 12)

The fact that Dinshaw and Tuttle Hansen can examine the same evidence and reach quite different conclusions about it is a reminder of why it might be more accurate to refer to *feminisms*, rather than a monolithic, singular feminism. Like most critical modes, feminism does not render homogenous outcomes. (See Chapter 5: Carolyn Dinshaw, *Chaucer's Sexual Poetics* [1989] and *Getting Medieval* [1999].)

French Feminism

Perhaps one of the biggest differences between early Anglo-American feminism and French feminism is its attitude towards traditional literary theory. Early on, many Anglo-American feminists (although certainly not all) were suspicious of traditional literary theory, viewing it as a product of patriarchal culture. However, many of the French feminists were heavily influenced by theory, particularly the work of poststructuralists like Jacques Derrida and Jacques Lacan. This influence also accounts for another major difference between second wave Anglo-American feminism and French feminism. While the former group analysed literary representations of women and the work of individual women writers, the latter group focused on language and its role in producing knowledge. Specifically, French feminists like Hèléne Cixous, Julia Kristeva and Luce Irigaray analysed the links between discourse and patriarchal ideology. They note that in order to speak and act publicly, women must adopt patriarchal discourse, a language that, according to many French feminists, curtails women's expression because it does not reflect their experience or epistemology. Much like the 'anxiety of authorship' identified by Gilbert and Gubar in the work of nineteenth-century female writers, the patriarchal quality of language leaves women in a double bind. Women are either forced to use a language that does not reflect their experience or be rendered unintelligible or silent in the public sphere.

Écriture Féminine

For many of the French feminists, the solution to breaking out of this linguistic double bind is, perhaps paradoxically, language itself. In 'The Laugh of the Medusa' (1976), Hèléne Cixous advances an alterative to patriarchal language that she calls *écriture féminine* ('feminine writing'). Unlike patriarchal discourse, which is analytical, linear and bound by rules, écriture féminine is stream-of-conscious, circular and free from rules. According to Cixous, men can be practitioners of écriture féminine (she offers James Joyce as an example). However, it is a form of expression she associates specifically with women's bodies:

> Women must write through their bodies, they must invent the impregnable
> language that will wreck partitions, classes, and rhetorics, regulations
> and codes, they must submerge, cut through, get beyond the ultimate
> reserve-discourse, including the one that laughs at the very idea of
> pronouncing the word 'silence', the one that, aiming for the impossible,
> stops short before the word 'impossible' and writes it as 'the end'.
> (Cixous 1976, 886)

In somewhat similar terms, Cixous' contemporary, Julia Kristeva, differentiates between traditional language and écriture féminine. Traditional language, she argues, is *symbolic*. It is associated with the conscious mind and is marked by authority, repression and what Lacan calls 'the Law of the Father'. It assumes a fixed, unified and masculine speaker. Associated with the unconscious mind and femininity, on the other hand, *semiotic* language is marked by displacement, fragmentation and slippage. For Kristeva, symbolic language is more likely to be prose, whereas semiotic language is more likely to be poetry (Kristeva 1980).

Like Cixous and Kristeva, Luce Irigaray pays particular attention to the masculinist qualities of traditional language. Irigaray views women's adoption of male discursive forms as a type of mimicry, which she reads as a form of hysteria. There are a few instances, however, when women have been able to speak both publicly and in a way that allows them to escape the traps of patriarchal discourse. Irigaray sees the mystical experiences of medieval women as one instance. She reads in the erotic and ecstatic qualities of their visions a *jouissance*, a pleasure that extends beyond the confines of traditional discourse and representation. Despite adopting a language that flies in the face of the mandates of patriarchal discourse, many of these female visions were widely circulated and, in some cases, the visionaries were able to wield a great deal of political and social influence. Irigaray sees mysticism as 'the only place in Western history where woman speaks and acts in a public way' (1985, 191).

Authorship, Audience and Authority

For medievalists, Irigaray's claim about the public nature of mystical discourse and its potential as a site for agency evokes complicated the questions surrounding authorship, audience and authority. In the vast majority of cases, female mystics in the Middle Ages did not write down their visions; rather, they dictated them to an *amanuensis*, a scribe or secretary. The visions of Bridget of Sweden provide an instructive example. Bridget recounts her visions in Swedish to Petrus of Alvastra; he, in turn, translates them into Latin, adding explications. Later, wanting to improve Petrus' rather crude Latin, Bridget gives the text to Alfonso of Jaen. He 'corrects' Petrus' Latin and divides the *Revelations* into eight books. These eight books were then translated into Middle English in the fifteenth century and condensed into a much shorter version by two different scribes. (See Chapter 3: Birgitta of Sweden.) In which text would Irigaray locate Bridget's 'voice'? Certainly it could not be the original visions before they were recorded, because at that point they were still private. Indeed, the very act of putting her visions into words constitutes a form of translation, since the mystical experience is an ineffable one. Is

Bridget's female voice located in the first translation? Or is it in the second? Or the third? Indeed, like all mystical texts, Bridget's is *polyvocal*, with layers of voices that make it impossible to uncover fully any kind of authentic voice (if such a phenomenon ever does exist). Complicating these issues further is the fact that today only a small group of people can access Middle English and an even smaller group Latin. The rest of us must rely on translations, which, while often carefully prepared, serve as yet another level of mediation. Translation and editing are important tasks, ones that always require interpretation and editorial judgment. Julia Bolton Holloway chooses to summarize portions of Bridget's visions in her edition (1992), rather than translating them. While Holloway explains her reasons, not all editors are so transparent with their decisions, leaving most readers unaware of the silent omissions, emendations and additions that are made to a text. (See Chapter 6: Marginal Voices.)

In most cases, the role of the amanuensis extends well beyond that of simple scribe. Many amanuenses were also the male confessors of the women whose visions they wrote down. Caroline Walker Bynum notes that the influence of important mystics like Catherine of Siena, Bridget of Sweden and Joan of Arc 'depended almost wholly on the success, in ecclesiastical and secular politics, of their male adherents' (1987, 23). Nor was this dependency unilateral. If a penitent under a confessor's spiritual care was found to be heterodox, the situation could be not only politically damaging but also personally dangerous to him. A case in point is found in the opening pages of *The Book of Margery Kempe*. Margery's amanuensis explains that he is the second scribe to take a shot at writing down her visions, the project having been started by a German acquaintance of Margery's. The second scribe claims that the first scribe's handwriting was so poor he was initially unable to read the book. Through Margery's prayers, he later gains the ability to read this illegible handwriting. However, the second scribe's difficulties might have less to do with sloppy penmanship and more to do with his concerns about his political and personal safety. Referring to himself in the third person, he confesses that 'there was such evil talk about this creature and her weeping that the priest out of cowardice dared not speak with her but seldom, nor would write as he had promised the said creature' (36). (See Chapter 4: Margery Kempe, *The Book of Margery Kempe*.)

Legitimizing Mysticism

Perhaps due in part to these larger concerns about personal and political safety, mysticism becomes so codified by the fourteenth century that women's visions were expected to take a very specific form if they hoped to be considered orthodox. *The Book of Margery Kempe* again offers an instructive example. A desire to legitimize Margery's visions might have been one of the motives behind the construction of the *Book*. Part of the text's legitimizing strategy involves framing Margery's experiences in the context of medieval mystics whose visions have already been deemed orthodox by the Church. While Margery's penchant for breaking out into uncontrollable tears vexes almost everyone around her (including, as noted above, her amanuensis), he finally accepts that they are a gift from God when he, too, experiences the gift of tears while performing Mass. Margery's amanuensis may be worried, however, that his experience alone is not enough to convince the reader that God is the source of her tears. Therefore, he recounts a similar story that he finds in Marie d'Oignes *vita*, which not only confirms the orthodoxy of such crying, but also legitimizes his own experience, which parallels those of Marie's confessor, who also had doubts about the authenticity of his penitent's tears until God bestowed the gift of tears onto him. Of course, it is also possible that Margery's amanuensis first read the story of Marie's confessor's uncontrollable tears and then constructs a similar narrative for himself. While it is possible that Margery included the story of Marie in her dictation, Margery's amanuensis cites the specific chapters of the *vita* he is quoting (191–2), perhaps suggesting a clerical insertion of an authoritative text.

As a result of these complications, Laurie Finke advocates approaching mystical texts with a 'theory of complexity' that allows the reader to recognize both the potentially dissident qualities of these texts and, at the same time, the historical and cultural context in which they developed. For Finke, mystics carve out a tenuous space for themselves through the manipulation of social codes, rather than through the use of a feminine form of language: 'The discourse of the female mystic was constructed out of disciplines designed to regulate the female body, and it is, paradoxically, through these disciplines that the mystic consolidated her power' (Finke 1992, 78).

Third Wave and Third World Feminism

Starting in the late 1970s, new questions emerged about feminism's assumptions. Many of these questions centred around the issue of essentialism. *Essentialism* is the belief that women possess an innate, natural, feminine essence that exists outside social and cultural controls. In other words, gender may be a social construct, but women, by virtue of being women, share certain characteristics. Certainly some were early feminists rejected this idea. Simone de Beauvoir declared that 'One is not born a woman but becomes one' (1952, 249). However, concepts like *écriture féminine*, which ascribes femininity to a certain style of writing, or gynocriticism, which privileges a writer's biological sex over other locations (such as race, class, sexual orientation, nation and historical period), have at their core essentialistic assumptions.

Critiquing Essentialism

The critique of essentialism came from two directions. One was from post-structuralism, which criticized universalizing, ahistorical concepts. For a poststructuralist, concepts like 'woman' are not natural, but rather socially constructed and products of a particular historical and cultural moment. While feminism's theorizing of women and women's experience can offer a counterpoint to patriarchal definitions of women and their experience, theory can still confine women to an equally narrow and ahistoricizing definition. This narrow definition of what it means to be a woman was also the source of criticism from another group of scholars and activists. In its early years, feminism was formed and informed primarily by white, heterosexual, upper-class women. Many women who did not identify with these subject positions wondered if the feminist movement also represented their interests as well. What did it mean that such a small, privileged group of women were defining a supposedly universal feminine essence? Women of colour, lesbians and working-class women found themselves doubly marginalized, both as females and as minorites. They began to question whether being a woman was their primary identification. As Toni Cade Bambara explains in her foreword, the essays in *This Bridge Called My Back: Writings by Radical Women of Color* (1983) reflect the need to 'protest, complain or explain to white feminist would-be allies that there are other ties and visions that bind' (1983, vi). Chela Sandoval coined the term 'US Third World Feminism' to describe feminism that sets itself in opposition to dominant feminism and suggests that feminists whose experiences do not fit mainstream feminism's categorization of gender and sexuality function as a third gender (Mills 1998, 108).

These questions about position and privilege also extend to literary analysis. In her essay 'Three Women's Texts and a Critique of Imperialism' Gayatri Chakravorty Spivak argues that a desire to locate and laud feminist qualities in women's writing has led other issues to be overlooked. For example, she wonders what it means that the 'mad woman in the attic' in *Jane Eyre* is a woman of colour and a colonized subject. She argues that Gilbert and Gubar fail to see Bertha as a separate person with her own history and needs, and therefore more than just Jane's 'truest and darkest double'. Rather than reading Bertha as a device through which the female writer struggles against social and literary constraints, Spivak reads her as the sacrificial lamb through which Jane achieves individuality:

In this fictive England she [Bertha] must play out her role, act out the transformation of her 'self' into that fictive Other, set fire to the house and kill herself, so that Jane Eyre can become the feminist individualist heroine of British fiction. I must read this as an allegory of the epistemic violence of imperialism, the construction of a self-immolating colonial subject for the glorification of the social mission of the colonizer. (Spivak 1985, 245)

Critiques such as these have left some feminists worried that feminist theory is now hopelessly fragmented. Nancy Miller laments that 'between the indictment of the feminist universal as a white fiction bought by women of colour and the poststructural suspicion of a grounded subject, what are the conditions under which as feminists one (not to say "I") can say we?' (qtd. in Gezari 2006, 270–71). However, as Avtar Brah argues, 'Woman may no longer be thought of as a unitary category, but it might still possibly be a unifying one' (qtd. in Jackson and Jones 1998, 6). The key to such unification might lie in not simply folding ever more feminisms into the larger rubric of feminist theory but to allow alternative feminisms to transform feminist theory in new and productive ways (Mills 1998, 106).

We might make the same argument about the role of medieval studies in feminist theory. While the medieval period shares more in common with the modern period than most realize (or perhaps are willing to acknowledge), gender and sexuality do look different in the Middle Ages (a point I will return to below). Thus, an exploration of the Middle Ages through the lens of feminist theory not only supplements our understanding of the period, but also provides insights into the history of women's oppression and their resistance to that oppression. (See Chapter 7: Feminism and Gender Studies and Chapter 10: Violence and Religion: Toward Anti-Sacrificial Readings.)

Gender Studies

Many view gender studies as the latest manifestation of feminist theory (Schor 1992, 275). Certainly the two fields share a number of similarities. Like most feminists, gender studies scholars differentiate between biological sex and gender. Both fields tend to be interdisciplinary in approach and they share a number of critical influences, including poststructuralism. However, while feminist literary theory focuses on women's writing, women's place in society, the social construction of femininity and how social and cultural institutions reflect that construction and effect women's lives, gender studies has a broader focus and includes not just the study of women and femininity, but also the study of men and masculinity, as well as sexual orientation. Everyone bears a gender, but given that historically the world has been read through a masculinist lens, women tend to be the ones marked as gendered, as 'Other' from men. As we will see below, such marking is very similar to the way racial identity is socially constructed. While everyone possesses a racial identity or identities, only certain people are marked as having a race.

The Sex/Gender System

Gender studies scholars are quick to point out that the relationship between gender and biological sex is much more complicated than it might at first seem. Take, for example, biological sex. We might assume that, given biological sex's location on the body, it is relatively fixed. However, bodies certainly can be changed, not only through dress or discipline, but also through surgery. Indeed, what used to be called a 'sex-change operation' is now called 'gender reassignment surgery', a change that recognizes that for many who undertake this surgery an identification with a particular gender is as important as a desire for a particular body. Nor does changing the physical body necessarily change how that body is understood socially. In England, for example, a person cannot change her birth certificate after gender reassignment surgery to reflect his new sex and gender (Glover and Kaplan 2000, xxvi). In the end, then, are sex and gender primarily legal categories? Such questions are of great interest to gender studies scholars, who see gender as an ontological category that operates well beyond issues of sexuality or reproduction.

Medieval Bodies

The medieval notion of the gendered body is surprisingly similar to these contemporary gender studies perspectives. The two most influential classical writers on medieval medicine, Galen and Aristotle, both imagine women and men to have basically the same anatomy; women are men turned inside out. According to Galen, 'you could not find a single male part left over that had not simply changed its position [in women]' (qtd. in Laqueur 1990, 26). As Laqueur explains Galen, it is as if 'the womb, vagina, ovaries, and external pudenda remain forever as if they were still inside the womb. They cascade vertiginously back inside themselves, the vagina as an externally, pre-cariously unborn penis, the womb as stunted scrotum and so forth' (28). We see the blurring between male and female bodies in Aristotle's language as well. The word Aristotle uses for penis and scrotum (*perineos*) is the same word he uses to describe the inside of a woman's thighs and buttocks. The word *aidoion*, which means penis when in its singular form, is translated as 'shameful parts' in its plural, and is equivalent to the Latin *pudenda*, which can refer to the genitalia of both sexes. While this conflation of anatomical parts might seem sloppy and confusing to the modern reader, Laqueur observes that Aristotle and Galen had no need to develop a more precise vocabulary 'because the female body was a less hot, less perfect and hence less potent version of the canonical body ... Distinct organic, much less genital, landmarks mattered far less than the metaphysical hierarchies they illustrate' (35).

Although the male body was imagined to be, as Laqueur puts it, 'the canonical body', the similarities between male and female bodies evoked a great deal of anxiety in late medieval culture. Joan Cadden identifies a tension between medical and religious discourse in the Middle Ages: While scientific explanations existed for hermaphrodites, the possibility of their existence posed a threat to the gender dichotomies that undergird Christianity (Cadden 1993). It was for this reason that hermaphrodites and other 'disorderly' bodies (cross-dressing women, men who have sex with men and other bodies that did not fit the dictates of sexual and gender norms in the Middle Ages) had to be contained and regulated through law, medicine, religion and other social and cultural institutions. Despite the attempt to discipline the body through these regimes, there was always the possibility that they (and thus all bodies) could slip these constraints: 'there was an ontological awareness that these were social conventions masking for more powerful and threatening states of being untouched by the ordering power of institutions, states of being that confronted medieval people, as they do us, with their breathtaking challenges – challenges that are also possibilities' (Rubin 1996, 26–7).

Medieval Drag

Judith Butler's work on gender as drag has been particularly important in the development of gender studies. The term 'drag' often evokes an image of a person performing (through dress, behaviour, and actions) in a way that society deems does not correspond to her or his biological sex. Thus, a man dressing as a woman or a woman 'acting' as a man are readily recognizable forms of drag. Butler, however, argues that all men and women are in drag. That is, both men and women perform their gender on a daily basis by conforming their physical appearance, dress, behaviour and desires to their society's expectations of what it means to be a man or a woman. What constitutes a normative gender performance depends greatly on a person's historical and cultural context: 'gender is an identity tenuously constituted in time, instituted in an exterior space through a *stylized repetition of acts*. The effect of gender is produced through the stylization of the body and, hence, must be understood as the mundane way in which bodily gestures, movements and styles of various kinds constitute the illusion of an abiding gender self' (Butler 1997, 402). One sees the performative quality of gender in the romance *Silence* (ca. mid-thirteenth century) in which the female protagonist successfully performs masculinity from childhood into young adulthood. Certainly, many medieval texts depict cross-dressing figures. There is, for example, a long tradition of cross-dressing saints in medieval hagiography. However, the narrator of *Silence* seems both comfortable with the idea of gender as a performance and calls the reader's attention to it by sometimes referring to the protagonist as a man and sometimes a woman – and sometimes as both, within the same line. (See Chapter 6: Performance and Spectacle.)

Butler cautions that just because gender is a performance does not mean that we can wake up on a given morning and decide which gender to don. Such a belief assumes that a person freely chooses her gender. On the contrary, a person is *interpellated* (that is, 'hailed' or 'called into') gender at a very early age. The acquisition of gender is similar to the acquisition of language as described by the linguist Ferdinand de Saussure. (See Chapter 10: The Influences of Structuralism.) Most people do not recall learning their first language as young children. Likewise, they do not recall learning a gender, but soon (and at a very early age) they are performing it. It is this forgetting that leads many to conclude that gender stems from nature, rather than from society. Nonetheless Butler, like the French feminists who imagine a language unencumbered by the constraints of patriarchal language, imagines the possibility of 'a queer poststructuralism of the psyche' (Butler 2004, 44). (See Chapter 7: Gender, Identity, and Queer Studies.)

Queering Theory

Sexual orientation is another important area of study for gender studies and medieval scholars. Society often makes assumptions about a person's sexual orientation, much like gender, based on his or her biological sex. Feminists early on drew attention to what Adrienne Rich called 'compulsory heterosexuality' (1981, rpt 1993). However, just as women of colour and of various classes began to wonder if mainstream feminism spoke for them, women (and men) of various sexualities and genders began to ask similar questions. What if one's sexual desires or psychological identity does not conform with the way the feminist movement initially imagined women and femininity? Is a 'masculine' woman 'male-identified', as the feminism of the 1970s would suggest, or does such a person simply reflect the wide range of possible genders and sexualities? Does the general category 'woman' conceal and suppress real differences between women in terms of their sexual desires, sexual practices and psychological identities (Rivkin and Ryan 2004, 836)? For gay men in particular, the need for a political voice became increasingly urgent in the wake of the AIDS epidemic. In the early years of the disease, gay men were disproportionately infected, at least in the US and western Europe, and many gay activists argued that the government's lethargic response was in large part due to the popular belief that AIDS was primarily a 'gay disease'.

Organizations like Act Up and Queer Nation pushed for better research and health care for those with HIV and better education to counteract public ignorance about the disease and its transmission.

Queer theory developed in the early 1990s in the wake of this activism. Queer theorists are interested in sexuality, for just as gender is socially constructed, so, too, are categories defining 'normal' or 'deviant' sexualities. And much like the blurring between socially constructed gender and biological sex discussed above, the role that sexuality plays in the maintenance of social and cultural institutions motivates that blurring. While gay and lesbian studies focus primarily on homosexuality, queer theory focuses on all forms of sexuality that are deemed non-normative by a particular society, including practices that heterosexual men and women might engage in, such as S/M, fetishes and bisexuality, to name a few. The adoption of the term *queer* is usually viewed as strategic; it refuses to identify whether or not the person speaking is gay, lesbian, bisexual, heterosexual or some other orientation. The scholar Eve Sedgwick, for example, is married to a man and identifies as queer. Some have worried that the term has become too inclusive, perhaps imposing a false unity around practices and communities that are very different and whose political motivations might be quite different as well. However, as Elisabeth D. Däumer has suggested, the power of the term is that it recognizes 'the queer in all of us' (1992, 20).

Foucault's 'Repressive Hypothesis'

Perhaps more so than any other scholar, Michel Foucault influenced the development of gender studies. In the first of his three-volume *History of Sexuality* (1978), Foucault questions what he calls the 'repressive hypothesis'. According to this hypothesis, starting around the nineteenth century and corresponding with the rise in capitalism and industrialism, sex became a taboo topic. We can see evidence of this sexual repression particularly in the Victorian practice of covering table legs so as not to inadvertently summon the image of a woman's legs. Today, the hypothesis continues, even though Western society appears to be much more sexually liberated. People talk about sex all the time: with their friends, their therapists, in books and on talk shows. People are encouraged to 'come out of the closet' and to announce their sexual desires and pleasures. Such sexual liberation is a mark of modernity and a sign of contemporary freedom and progress, right?

In a word, Foucault would say *no*. He argues that power does not *repress* sexuality, but rather *produces* it. What in the past were undefined pleasures of the body became in the nineteenth century specific acts that were defined, codified and analysed institutions like law, medicine, religion and psychology. People were mandated to confess their sexuality, and what they had to say about it was taken as evidence of who they were, a mandate that continues today. In Foucault's often cited formulation, 'The sodomite has been a temporary aberration. The homosexual was now a species' (1990, 43).

Foucault's work has both intrigued and vexed medievalists since its publication. On the one hand, Foucault's claim that in sodomy was an 'utterly confused category' in the Middle Ages is an apt one. In medieval discourse, *sodomy* encompassed a wide range of acts including (but not limited to) oral and anal sex, bestiality, masturbation (alone or with others), femoral fornication, adultery, sex between married partners in any position besides the missionary position, sex on Sundays, holy days of obligation, or Lent, and when a woman was menstruating, to name a few. In addition, 'sodomy' denoted a whole range of behaviours seemingly outside the sexual realm, including heresy and treason (Goodrich 1979, 7–10; Boswell 1980, 283–6; Dinshaw 1999, 55–99) and usury and simony (Vance 1986, 230–55; Jordan 1997, 64; Leyser 1995, 191–211).

Yet, as a number of medievalists have noted, Foucault tends to oversimplify medieval sexuality, arguing that is was a unitary discourse tied to penance, in contrast to the modern situation when 'this relative uniformity was broken apart, scattered, and multiplied in an explosion of distinct discursivities' (1990, 33). Against this view, Karma Lochrie argues Foucault simplifies medieval sexuality and its disciplining networks to form a unified backdrop against which modern sexuality and its distinct discursivities can explode (1999). (See Chapter 5: Karma Lochrie, *Covert Operations* and *Heterosyncracies*.) Nor can the Middle Ages be divorced from the disciplinary regimes of modernity. As Mark Jordan demonstrates in the *Invention of Sodomy* (1997), theological works like Peter Damian's *Book of Gomorrah* (ca. mid-eleventh century) establish the groundwork for later constructions of the sodomite as an identity. Foucault's presentation of medieval sexuality, however, makes sense if one considers the political motivations behind his argument. Carolyn Dinshaw suggests that we can read in Foucault's theories an ethical and aesthetic vision for a utopian world before sexual pleasure was so vehemently policed (Dinshaw 1999, 191–206). Thus, for Foucault, the Middle Ages function as a site of nostalgia and an 'other' against which modern sexuality can be defined. (See Chapter 5: Carolyn Dinshaw, *Chaucer's Sexual Poetics* and *Getting Medieval*.)

The Place of Chaucer's Pardoner

Just as Chaucer's Wife of Bath has been a touchstone for feminist literary theory, the Pardoner has been a touchstone for medievalists interested in queer theory. Michael Calabrese describes the Pardoner's sexuality as 'one of the great mysteries of Chaucerian criticism' (1993, 269). Over the years,

Chaucer's narrator has been described variously as 'homosexual or gay' (McAlpine 1994; Kruger 1994); as 'feminoid' (Howard 1976); as 'normal' (which translates as heterosexual in these studies) (Benson 1982; Green 1982); as a literal or metaphoric 'eunuch' (Curry 1960; Miller 1960; Dinshaw 1989); and in language that echoes the pathologizing discourse of nineteenth-century forensic medicine, as 'a testicular pseudo-hermaphrodite of the feminine type' (Rowland 1964, 58); as 'a manic depressive with traces of anal eroticism; and a pervert with a tendency towards alcoholism' (Stockton 1961, 47). However, the evidence for the Pardoner's sexual identity is notoriously inconclusive. On the one hand, the Pardoner has physical characteristics that some scholars have associated with effeminacy in the Middle Ages, according to the *General Prologue*: shoulder-length hair (I.675); a fondness for stylish clothing (682); glittering eyes like a hare (684); a voice like a goat (688) and a smooth, beardless face (689–90). In addition, there is also something suggestive about the Pardoner's relationship with the Summoner, who is described in the *General Prologue* as the Pardoner's friend and companion (I.670). The Pardoner sings a love song ('Come hither, love, to me' [672]) and the Summoner accompanies him with 'a stif burdon' (672) – with a 'strong bass', as the *Riverside Chaucer* notes, but perhaps also with a sexual pun.

Nonetheless, just as it is anachronistic to ascribe feminist motivations to persons and characters that exist before the invention of feminism, it is equally problematic to attribute a specific sexual identity to a character before that sexual identity has been defined. Even if we set this issue aside, the evidence offered in arguments about the Pardoner's sexuality and body are far from conclusive. Take, for example, the Pilgrim-Narrator's observation that he has the glittering eyes of rabbit (I.684). John Boswell notes that in medieval bestiary lore (encyclopaedic compendia of different animals, both realistic and fantastic), the hare was thought to grow a new anus every year and thus often was associated with male-male desire and anal sex in particular (Boswell 1980). However, as Larry D. Benson argues, the hare was more frequently used as a symbol of lechery in general (1982). In addition, while there may be a suggestion of a sexual relationship between the Pardoner and the Summoner, the Pardoner also expresses heterosexual desires – he claims to have a lover in every town (VI.453) and tells the Wife of Bath that he was contemplating getting married, but her description of the difficulty of marriage has made him think twice (III.165–7). Perhaps the Pardoner's statements are efforts to *perform* heterosexuality to foreclose any speculation about his sexual proclivities or his possible deformities. Nonetheless, Chaucer seems unwilling to provide a definitive answer, for the Pilgrim-Narrator himself cannot tell if the Pardoner is 'a gelding or a mare' (I.693).

Despite these interpretive difficulties, Steven Kruger observes that many of his students, like a number of scholars, read something queer in Chaucer's presentation of the Pardoner (1994). The question becomes, then, what does that *queerness* mean? Gregory Gross suggests that rather than focusing on the meaning of the Pardoner's body, readers should explore more broadly the interpretive possibilities in Chaucer's portrait of the pilgrim. The Pardoner, whose tongue, the reader is told, is sharper than a file, skilfully wields his weapon to extract every penny he can from his naïve audience. There is a long tradition of linking manipulative rhetorical practice with sexual impropriety (Gross 1995), and this tradition is buttressed in part by the ability of the Latin *impropria* to signify both sexual and linguist impropriety. Perhaps one of the most famous and most extended examples of this sexual and linguistic conflation is in Alain de Lille's *The Complaint of Nature* (ca. 1160–70). Alain complains that the 'barbarians of grammar' have broken both the rules of good linguistic practice and the rules of normative sexuality. It is unclear which practice is at the heart of Alain's criticism – that is, whether Alain is principally concerned with sexual or linguistic practice. In the end it may not matter given the ways in which *sodomia* covers a multitude of sins – linguistic, sexual, religious, civil and economic. But another way of reading Chaucer's Pardoner is as a critique of the legislating practices of linguistic and sexual regimes. The Pardoner's body, like that of the hermaphrodite, slips outside the binary of 'normal' and 'abnormal' sexuality and of clearly-assigned male and female bodies. Because it is unclear whether the Pardoner is a 'geldying or a mare', it is in this 'in-between' space of sexuality that he deconstructs the disciplinary mechanisms that insist upon neatly categorizing people and their desires. (See Chapter 5: Carolyn Dinshaw, *Chaucer's Sexual Poetics*.)

We might think of queer theory more broadly as a deconstructive tool for exploring the Middle Ages. As Glenn Burger observes in *Chaucer's Queer Nation* (2003), queer theory troubles essentializing readings of canonical writers like Chaucer, which not only delimit subjects but also replicate the practices of regulatory regimes in its work. In turn, the history of sexuality, which tends to begin with the nineteenth century, can benefit from the intervention of medievalists, whose work deconstructs the binary between the medieval and the modern.

Race Studies

In many ways, the study of race and ethnicity in the US has followed a trajectory similar to that of feminist theory. Like women, African-Americans, Latinos and Latinas, Native Americans and Asian Americans had been writing literature long before their work gained recognition and canonical status. The Civil Rights Movement brought renewed attention to African-American literature and, subsequently, attention to the work of other racial minorities. As in early feminism, one of the initial projects of race studies was to recover lost or marginalized texts and bring them into the canon. While many of these texts were plays, novels and poetry, they also included slave narratives, journals, oral traditions and others. Another early project was to expose the racism prevalent in a number of canonical works. In *Playing in the Darkness*, for example, Toni Morrison explores how blacks, much like *Jane Eyre's* madwoman of colour described by Spivak, enable white characters to enjoy individuation and freedom (Morrison 1993).

Just as feminists and gender studies scholars have problematized the categories of gender and sexuality, scholars working in the field of race studies have problematized the category of race. As Henry Louis Gates, Jr., explains, like gender, race is not a concept that is solely biological or tied to an unchanging nature. Rather, it is a form of classification that pretends to be objective, but actually is wielded in an effort to mark and reduce as inferior the bodies of others (1986). In his definition of race, Ian F. Haney López emphasizes race's status as a social construction. *Race* is 'neither an essence nor an illusion, but rather an ongoing, contradictory, self-reinforcing, plastic process subject to the macro forces of social and political struggle and the micro effects of daily decisions' (2000, 966). López's observation that there are more similarities between the races than there are differences echoes Gayle Rubin's observation that women and men have more commonalities than differences. Just as the social construction of race obscures the similarities among racial groups, the 'sex/gender system' obscures the similarities between men and women. López argues that the anthropological view of the world being divided into three races, 'Caucasoid', 'Negroid' and 'Mongloid', 'is rooted in the European imagination of the Middle Ages, which encompassed only Europe, Africa and the Near East' (967).

However, the 'plastic process' that López ascribes to modern notions of race is certainly in operation in the Middle Ages as well. Both of the primary explanations of racial difference circulating in the Middle Ages point to the social construction of race. The first medieval theory of racial difference held that race was primarily a matter of climate. Those who lived in cold environments tended to be lighter skinned than those who lived in warmer climates. The second prominent theory deemed race a product of custom, language, law and lineage. These first three qualities are markers of culture; only the last might be read primarily as a marker of biology. Thus, a Jew and a Christian living side by side might share the same skin colour and language but be viewed as racially different in the Middle Ages. Bartlett notes that contemporary sociology sometimes draws a distinction between race and ethnicity, giving preference to the term *ethnicity* because, ethnicity it is argued, is a social construct, unlike race. However, Bartlett also argues that race is not to biological sex as gender is to ethnicity. Rather, in the Middle Ages, we can see both race and ethnicity as socially constructed. It is for this reason that Bartlett uses the terms interchangeably and somewhat controversially in his work (2001).

Medieval Race and Cultural Difference

Although these explanations of racial difference seem to place culture above biology, bodily difference is used as a way to signify cultural distinction during the Middle Ages. For example, while St. Jerome seems to be taking an egalitarian stance when he claims that in sin 'we are all Ethiopians' until washed with the water of baptism, dark skin is the signifier of a sinful spirit. As a number of scholars have noted, dark skin is also the signifier for Saracens and pagans in a wide variety of medieval texts (Verkerk 2001; Kinoshita 2001; Cohen 2001). Thus, while race may read differently in the Middle Ages than it is in the modern era, race still serves as what Henry Louis Gates Jr. calls 'the ultimate trope of difference' (qtd. in Hahn 2001, 6).

Crusaders and Conversion

However, as is the case of gender and biological sex, this trope of difference is far from stable. Crusading romances offer another telling example of the instability of race. On the one hand, crusade narratives deploy the trope of race in all the stereotypical ways that one might imagine. Muslims are marked as different not only by the colour of their skin, but by their grotesque appetites, their bad tempers and their penchant for lust and greed, and yet in a romance like the *King of Tars* (fourteenth century) a Muslim's skin colour changes from black to white upon conversion:

His hide, þat blac & loþely was,
Al white bicom þurch godes gras
& clere wiþ outen blame.
& when þe soudan seye þat siyt,
þan leued he wele on god almiyt . . .

His skin, that had been black and loathsome, became all white, through God's grace, and was spotless without blemish. And when the sultan saw that sight, he believed on almighty God. . . .

'Lo, dame', he gan to say,
Certeyne, þi god is trewe'.
þe leuedi þonked god þat day,
For ioie sche wepe wiþ eyyen gray,

'Lo, lady', he began to say, 'certainly your God is true'. The lady thanked God that day, and her gray eyes wept with joy.

Vnneþe hir lord sche knewe.
þan wist sche wele in hir þouyt,
þat on Mahoun leued he nouyt,
For chaunged was his hewe.
(Krause, 1888, ll. 923–6, 932–9)

Scarcely did she (his wife) recognize her lord. Then she well knew in her mind that he did not believe at all in Mohammed, for his colour was entirely changed).

While some medieval readers might see such a change as evidence of the power of Christianity, it also evokes the instability of race, perhaps leaving a medieval English audience with this question: If a Saracen can turn white, why can't a Christian turn black? And if such inversions are possible, is there any real difference among the races?

Written in French but known in medieval England, *The Chanson de Roland* (ca. late eleventh century) offers yet another striking example. It is hard to imagine a phrase that more succinctly articulates the supposed difference between Muslims and Christians than Roland's rallying cry, 'Pagans are wrong and Christians are right'. (See Chapter 3: *Chanson de Roland* and the 'Matter of France'.) Yet despite this straightforward proclamation, the text continually calls attention to the similarities between Christians and Muslims. Both groups, for example, speak the same language (thus making unnecessary the use of translators, which one finds in other *chansons*), and the narrator of *Roland* praises the military prowess of both groups. In a striking alteration of Muslim theology, the author even constructs a false parallel between Christianity and Islam by creating a Saracen 'trinity' of three gods: Mahomet, Apollin and Termagant. Alongside these similarities is the historical reality that to many western Christians the cultural practices of their co-religionists seemed as foreign to them as those of the infidels they came to fight. In turn, the groups of unruly western Christians descending upon their land during the Crusades alarmed many eastern Christians. In the contemporary context of the Crusades, the reader of a romance like *Roland* is left with the uneasy realization that western Christians may have more in common with Saracens than they do with their eastern counterparts. Perhaps it is for this reason that *Roland*, unlike later *chansons de geste*, does not offer the possibility of Saracen conversion to Christianity. The 'trope of difference' that undergirds religious identity during the period is so radically unstable: 'If the possibility of conversion is held open, than any sense of identity which depends on the opposition between self and other is intrinsically unstable' (Kinoshita 2001, 86).

Postcolonial Studies

Until quite recently, postcolonial theory played a marginal role in medieval studies. As Benedict Anderson famously remarked 'medieval colonialism [is] oxymoronic, indeed anachronistic' (qtd. in Cohen 2000, 4). One reason for this belief may lie in postcolonialism's tendency to focus on nineteenth- and twentieth-century western colonialism. For example, postcolonial theory's most influential text, Edward Said's *Orientalism* examines the construction of 'The Orient' during nineteenth-century British expansion. Said argues that what western European cultures know about the East says more about the West's fears and fantasies than it does about the East itself (1978). Post-colonialism's attention to the previous two centuries parallels queer and feminist theorists' focus primarily on the nineteenth and twentieth centuries as the historical moment in which homosexual identity was invented. However, just as an examination of sexuality before the nineteenth century helps to uncover the shadowy history of sexuality, so an exploration of premodern postcolonialism helps excavate the history of colonialism. Indeed, as several scholars have noted, the Middle Ages haunt the theories of postcolonial scholars like Said, much as it does the sexual theories of Foucault and racial ideas of López. Said evokes the Middle Ages as the foundation of modern Orientalism and, simultaneously, closes it off from modernity (Biddick 1998; Cohen 2000; Davis 2000).

Saracens and Others

The ME *The Sultan of Babylon* provides a telling example of the psychodynam-ics of Orientalism. Like *The King of Tars* and other crusading romances, the *Sultan of Babylon* delineates in great detail the imagined excesses of the Sara-cens – they enjoy rich food (including serpents fried in oil); they consume too much wine (although Islam's prohibition against drinking was well-known to Christians) and they engage in various 'perverse' sexual practices, including pederasty, same-sex relations and orgies. One way to interpret these descrip-tions is to say that they serve to demonize non-Christians. However, as Jeffrey Jerome Cohen notes, these depictions of Saracens also fulfil another pressing need for western medieval culture. The Saracen serves as:

> a figure who consumes and hoards the enjoyment that 'we' as Westerners have renounced in order to be Westerners. Orientalist dreams of distant, copious indulgence provide a necessary support for the West's sacrificial systems of nationhood and identity in that they maintain the fantasy that a potentially recoverable full enjoyment is in fact located somewhere, even if it is not possessed by 'us'. (Cohen 2001, 125)

The profligate Saracen, then, provides a fantasy that while sacrificing pleasure is the price Western Crusaders must pay for their Christian identity, exuberant *jouissance* still exists 'out there' and is therefore still potentially within reach.

Rather than serving as a historical 'Other', the Middle Ages can serve as a tool for exploring current questions postcolonial scholars are posing about their field. Specifically, scholars like Anne McClintock and Ania Loomba have questioned the 'post' in postcolonialism. Among other concerns, both fear that 'post' intimates that colonial oppression was a blip on the historical timeline, one that has now passed. Such thinking fails to acknowledge the oppression that lingers after colonial powers have pulled out, not to mention the various forms that colonialism can take. (Hong Kong at the end of the twentieth century and slavery in nineteenth century America are both situations that can be described as colonial, although what that colonialism signifies is radically different.) Thus by taking postcolonialism back to the Middle Ages, scholars have a historical field for working through these ideological questions. In turn, while it might seem comforting to imagine the Middle Ages as free from the scourge of colonialism, medieval England was, among other things, both a colony as well as a colonizer. Any scholarly examination that does not take up colonialism in the Middle Ages effaces an important part of medieval history. Moreover, as Kathleen Biddick observes, the rise of medieval studies as a discipline is itself imbricated in the colonial project, making even more urgent the need to examine the colonial Middle Ages and the role of colonialism in the construction of our field (Biddick 1998). (See Chapter 5: Patricia Clare Ingham and Michelle Warren, *Postcolonial Moves* (2003) and Jeffrey Jerome Cohen, *The Postcolonial Middle Ages* (2000); Chapter 7: Postcolonial Criticism; See Chapter 8: Multilingualism, International Contexts, and Postcolonial Concerns.)

Intersections: Race, Gender and Sexuality

As the discussion above makes clear, race, gender and sexuality are not independent realms hermetically sealed from one another, either in medieval studies or modern literary theory. Indeed, some of the most interesting work currently being done takes up the interstices among these fields. To return to *Roland*, as noted above, despite its claim that 'Pagans are wrong and Christians are right', the text is haunted by the possibility that the supposed difference between Christian and Saracen men is radically unstable. However, the differences between Saracens and Christians become acute when the text turns its attention to women. The domineering Saracen queen, Braminonde, is portrayed radically differently from Roland's mild-mannered love interest, Aude, and although women seem to play a marginal role in *Roland*, they play a pivotal role in the transmission of the *Roland's* racial ideology. The instability of racial difference that the text tries, unsuccessfully, to navigate by removing the possibility of conversion is stabilized only by bringing into the discussion another cultural construct, gender (Kinoshita 2001).

Kinoshita's observation of the role gender ideology plays in the formation of racial difference points to a crucial contribution that medievalists can make to the analysis of the intersections among race, sexuality and gender. The Enlightenment, with its penchant for dividing and codifying ontological categories, places race, sexuality and gender into separate fields, and recent academic work in feminist theory, gender studies and postcolonial theory traces these linkages in post-Enlightenment texts. However, the Middle Ages exist at a time well before that separation, when ontological categories, much like biological bodies, slipped from one form and into another. Examining these slippages in the medieval context thereby historicizes the categories of race, sexuality and gender. Such historicization deconstructs disciplinary regimes by excavating their cultural – and revealing their 'unnatural' – origins.

Study Questions

1. Define the following terms in your own words:

   - Ahistorical
   - Essentialism
   - *Écriture Féminine*
   - Feminism/Feminist
   - Gynocriticism
   - *jouissance*
   - Misogyny
   - Natural
   - Other
   - Sex vs. Gender

2. Using the discussion above as a springboard, briefly define the following three forms of feminism and identify their distinguishing characteristics:

   - Anglo-American Feminism
   - French Feminism
   - Third Wave and Third World Feminism

3. Based upon your work on Question 3 and your reading of the chapter, do you think it is valid to speak of *feminism* (in the singular) or *feminisms* (in the plural)? Why or why not? What factors play into your answer? What are the advantages and disadvantages of each position?

4. The distinction between different theoretical orientations can sometimes be confusing. Review the sections on Feminism(s), Gender Studies and Queer Theory above and (1) identify areas in which they overlap and (2) distinguish their particular areas of interest. In other words, what specific ideas, concepts and areas of interest unite and distinguish them?

5. Taking Foucault's 'Repressive Hypothesis' as a starting point, identify specific examples from medieval texts in which speaking about sexuality is explicitly linked to identity. *Sir Gawain and the Green Knight* might be a good place to start. Likewise, can you identify contemporary situations where the 'Repressive Hypothesis' appears to be in effect?

6. Review the critical opinions concerning Chaucer's Pardoner. First, which one is most congenial to your perspective and why? What evidence from the Pardoner's Portrait in the *General Prologue* and the *Pardoner's Prologue*

and Tale would you summon to support your position? Second, review the publication dates of each article mentioned in the chapter to see if you can discern either a historical or cultural pattern in the emergence of these varied opinions.

7. In contrast to Question 6, think about the Pardoner in a slightly different way. Instead of claiming a particular 'subject position' for the Pardoner, think about what different claims about the Pardoner achieve *theoretically*. Put differently, what are the potential effects on the academic study of the Pardoner (and, by extension, of Chaucer as well) of arguing that the Pardoner is 'gay', 'queer', 'feminist' or even 'normal'?

8. Although Race Studies and Postcolonial Theory is most often applied to more contemporary literatures, medieval Britain itself was beset by invaders and colonizers throughout its history, going back at least to the Romans. Why is it so difficult to think of Britain as a 'postcolonial' domain? What medieval linguistic and literary evidence betrays this colonized past, and what social, cultural or historical currents account for the seeming erasure of Britain's history of being *colonized* rather being a *colonial* power?

9. Thinking through subjectivity and subject formation in terms of gender, sexual orientation, class, race, ethnicity or other factors is often decried as 'identity politics'. Without necessarily taking sides on the truth or falsity of this position, analyse the pros and cons of such analysis. What does this kind of analysis reveal, and what does this kind of analysis obscure? How then might readers and critics minimize the negatives and emphasize the positives?

10. *Web Quest*: Using the *Song of Roland* as a backdrop to your investigation, particularly the Christian rallying cry that 'Pagans are wrong and Christians are right', conduct an internet search concerning religious truth-claims (that a particular religion, doctrine or practice is true) and their function in justifying other beliefs and practices related to (for example) gender roles, sexual orientation, racial identity, ethnic communities and so on. Then, ascertain competing truth-claims concerning the same beliefs and practices? The point here is not so much to argue a particular position as it is to identify how each side makes its claim and what religious evidence is summoned to support the respective position.

10 Mapping the Current Critical Landscape

Sol J. Neely, Purdue University

Poststructuralism and Post/structuralism

Mapping the critical landscape of current medieval literary theory presents sure difficulties that emerge largely from institutional pressures and the critics around which these pressures have reified. As such, it requires a kind of structuralist endeavour to account honestly for the origins of different critical schools, the relations between theorists and the critical dialogue between critics and schools. We should remember, however, as the French cultural theorist and postmodern philosopher Jean Baudrillard observes, that we should not mistake the map for the territory. This map of the current critical landscape begins with a debate within medieval studies concerning the work of D. W. Robertson and progresses through the schools of thought most directly concerned with history and historicism. Although the chapter de-emphasizes other critical endeavours addressed in more detail throughout the *Continuum Handbook* – like psychoanalysis, feminism, queer and gender studies, race and ethnicity studies and postcolonialism – this is only to say that they anticipate the recovery of ethical exegesis.

As an opening caveat, then, we must note the confusion that often occurs between the terms *structuralism* and *poststructuralism*. Many important critical theorists, scholars and philosophers who are associated with these approaches readily resist such classification, and theorists like Roland Barthes, Michele Foucault and Julia Kristeva eventually changed in their understandings of the relationship between history and literature. I deliberately use the expression *post/structuralism* to signify the ambiguity and slippage between the terms, concepts, and practitioners associated with structuralism and poststructuralism. For this essay, I highlight the distinction between the *synchronic* and *diachronic* as more suitable to the task of describing post/structuralist approaches that emerged during the debate between New Criticism and patristic exegesis. In their broadest definitions, the synchronic relates to a *moment* in time; it is ahistorical and is often described in spatial rather than temporal categories. The diachronic, in contrast, is sequential rather than spatial, and it is robustly historical. As Sandor Goodhart reminds us, however, the synchronic and diachronic distinction should not pose an absolute difference between respective jurisdictions; rather, they are continuous with each other in a way that understands the synchronic as a moment *within* the sequentiality of the diachronic, even if the diachronic escapes the restricted economies of historical representation (1996, 258–9). Goodhart's point is integral, as we will see, to the ethical transformations of post/structuralism, because in the critical studies that we draft, commission, study or deploy, there is always some component of the literature that resists narratization – some element that cannot be contained by the text or made visible in our genealogies.

Exegetical Criticism

When situating the emergence of the exegetical criticism of Middle English (ME) literature – also referred to as patristic exegesis or historical criticism – scholars often foreground its development in contrast to New Criticism, embodied in the critical tensions between D. W. Robertson, the advocate of patristic exegesis, and E. Talbot Donaldson, exemplar of New Criticism (See *Speaking of Chaucer*, 1970). In *A Preface to Chaucer*, Robertson argues for an allegorical approach to Chaucer, one approximating a medieval exegetical understanding of the divine. Robertson thus argued that medieval artists were well trained in a sophisticated technique, the four-fold system of medieval exegesis consisting of the literal level, the tropological level, the allegorical level and the anagogical level. For Robertson, all medieval literature was didactically and allegorically structured as an attempt to promote charity and censure cupidity, as in the Augustinian tradition. Robertson argued that the problem with medieval critical approaches contemporary to his time were too heavily influenced both by the Hegelian theory of tragedy and by a romantic notion of allegory that emphasized 'feeling brought about by a new concept of "humanity" ' (44). Arguing that medieval tragedy promoted the 'triumph of Divine Providence, just as the outcome of an early Greek tragedy was a triumph of *Dikê* [justice]', Robertson aimed to recover an understanding of allegory prior to its distortion by Hegel's theory of tragedy, its appropriation by romantic thinkers and its misuse by those who offered a morality based on 'sympathy and sentiments of humanity' such as David Hume and Jean-Jacques Rousseau. Reading medieval texts from such modern notions of self and consciousness weakened 'the medieval hierarchy of values' (43). While Robertson's critique against applying modern critical assumptions to medieval literature was groundbreaking, it nevertheless seemed no less limiting in its insistence on the didactic role of allegory. Nevertheless, the recent 'ethical turn' in literary criticism takes its cue, in some sense, from at least three important manoeuvres initiated by Robertson: (1) the unconditioning of our critical approaches from a sublimated Hegelianism, (2) an even more vigorous attempt to recover the dynamics and ethical value of allegory (3) and an emphasis on moral didacticism (*caritas* vs. *cupiditas*).

Donaldson's Critique

Prior even to the publication of Robertson's *A Preface to Chaucer*, E. Talbot Donaldson had already initiated his critique against the historical positivism that came to characterize 'Robertsonianism'. New Critics like Charles Muscatine, F. R. Leavis, I. A. Richards and William Empson turned their backs on what seemed to be an arbitrary and capricious historicism and engaged instead on close readings of the texts themselves. New Criticism thus promoted an interpretive system that identified the internal tensions of any given text and focused on literary artistry and technical mastery. Perhaps one of the more ironic qualities of New Criticism is that while such an approach often bracketed out historical concerns, it was itself a product of difficult historical times: After the Second World War, the mid-twentieth century was pervaded by what Muscatine described as a feeling of 'an unresolved dialectic' (9–10). Terry Eagleton notes that New Criticism found place in academia due, in part, to the fact that its Hegelian 'view of the poem as a delicate equipoise of contending attitudes, a disinterested reconciliation of opposing impulses, proved deeply attractive to skeptical liberal intellectuals disoriented by the clashing dogmas of the Cold War' (1996, 43). To the New Historicist and Marxist inflected theory that emerged later, New Criticism was both a symptom of the desire to find stability and value in a world devastated by war and the worse kind of conservative indifference towards political turmoil and historical forces.

The Influences of Structuralism

Responses to the debate between Robertsonian historicism and New Criticism opened into other critical responses, and by the 1960s scholars became interested in the literary background as well as cultural and social contexts of medieval writers. Patristic exegesis renewed interest in historical context, for instance, as structuralism focused upon the structures underlying human relations and culture. The terms of structuralism were primarily introduced by the Swiss linguist Ferdinand de Saussure (1857–1913), whose posthumously published set of lecture notes, collected by students and titled *Course in General Linguistics* (1915) advocated a science studying 'the role of signs as part of social life' and investigated 'the nature of signs and the laws governing them' (*semiology*) (1986, 15–6). Sausurre's science aimed for what he called a *synchronic linguistics*, which he opposed to a *diachronic* study of *historical linguistics*. To the synchronic, Saussure argued, belonged all the essential principles of a general, even universal, grammar; synchronic linguistics thus brackets out the historical evolution of particular languages, with an emphasis on sequential connections and changes through time, to understand the fundamental principles and structures that made such evolution possible. In short, Saussure refocused linguistic study away from actual utterances (*parole* or speech) and towards the underlying structures that makes such utterances possible (*la langue* or languages). One of Saussure's primary contributions to structuralist terminology is his reevaluating of the term *sign*. Traditionally, *sign* is taken to mean the 'sound pattern' (*signifier*) which points to a concept (*signified*). However, Saussure understood the sign as the combination of the *signifier* with the *signified* in the process of *significa-tion*, leading to two key principles. First, the relation of *signifier* and *signified* is entirely *arbitrary* (67ff.); that is, there is no internal or natural connection between the concept and the signifier that points to it. Second, because signifi-cation is arbitrary, the mechanism of language turns on the *relation* between identity and difference; that is, meaning is determined not by fixed terms but by the *function* of such terms within the overall system. In other words, any particular utterance (*parole*) has value only within the broader self-sufficiency of the general system (*langue*).

The Subject and Subjectivity

Structuralism gained prominence in the first half of the twentieth century due in large part to collaboration among prominent intellectual émigrés who fled to New York from the Continent during the Second World War. At the *École Libre des Hautes Études*, a university-in-exile located at the New School for Social Research, Russian-born linguist Roman Jakobson partnered with French anthropologist Claude Lévi-Strauss, and together they helped to shape the structuralist principles that radically influenced the theorists who became so important to contemporary medieval criticism: Louis Althusser, Roland Barthes, Helene Cixous, Jacques Derrida, Michel Foucault, Julia Kristeva, Jacan Lacan and others. For example, one of structuralism's important contributions is to understand the individual as a 'subject' of such signifying and structural relations, as Kaja Silverman discusses (1983, 130). This understanding of the 'subject' decentred not only how we conceive of the stability attributed to individuals, but also to texts. One reason, of course, that medieval literary theory is so attracted to these developments is because medieval literature in general *already* questions the stability of the author, text and hermeneutics. In many ways, medieval literature already anticipates the belated arrival of contemporary theory, and we discover that much of the great medieval literature has already raised the spectre of the resistant subject in relation to the multiple registers of power and textual constitution.

In light of shifting emphases in the synchronic priorities of structural linguistics, new theoretical approaches like semiotics, ethnology, cultural anthropology and Lacanian psychoanalysis organized themselves around the critical question of the 'subject'. Key here is the work of Michel Foucault, who in some sense exhausted the logic of structuralism only to shift focus from his early synchronic studies – what Foucault called his *archeological* work (for example, *The Archaeology of Knowledge*, Engl. 1972) – to broader questions of diachronic historical transformations, which he called his *genealogical* work (for example, *Discipline and Punish*, Engl. 1977). Foucault described this shift as seeking a 'history of the present', and his genealogical work questioned what constitutes historical narratives, how they are legitimated, whose interests they serve and how historical subjects, as readers of history, are *interpellated* into their ideological regimes. In short, many approaches to medieval literature in the last 30 years have become intensely interdisciplinary, drawing from feminism and gender/queer theory, ecocriticism, postcolonialism, anthropology, economics or the recovery of a complex and profoundly critical post/structuralist theology.

Materialist Criticism

We can loosely relate together three critical approaches, all of which employ a more dynamic understanding of (structural) historical forces than Robertson's patristic exegesis. Marxist criticism, New Historicism and Cultural Materialism all emphasize the material and diachronic forces of culture as they shape and are in turn shaped by dominant social forms and basic economic conditions. Importantly, all three of these approaches should be understood as *forms of critique* and critical *practices* rather than static ideologies or doctrines that *de-center* the subject of history, whatever that subject might be. Questioning the privileged 'subject' of history shifts analysis from the desire to unpack patristic allegory and moves towards exposing patriarchal discourse through which unexamined economic, domestic, geographical and carceral (or bodily) relations of force are disseminated. In other words, we move from an allegorical understanding of history into an historical understanding of allegory. Such critical modalities recognize that no individual is entirely isolated from social systems and no text is entirely separate from overlapping systems of thought.

Marxism

Karl Marx and Friedrich Engels did not necessarily develop a comprehensive approach to literature, but their attempt to situate cultural artefacts as products of economic and class relations presents an early, almost protostructuralist, attempt to understand the 'subject' and its relation to historical material forces. Famously asserting in the *Communist Manifesto* that 'the history of all hitherto existing society is the history of class struggles', Marxism takes its broader structural approach from what is described as a 'materialist conception of history' – also know as *dialectical materialism* or *historical materialism* (473). The relevant structural distinction to be made here is the difference between what Marx calls *the base* and the *superstructure*. According to Marx and Engels, economic relations and the forces of production – including the material means of production, distribution and exchange – serve as the foundational *base* upon which all cultural, social

231

and political forms of life – including ideology, art, religion, law and even consciousness – are mere *superstructures* added to the material base. Ideology and consciousness do not so much produce social and economic relations as the latter determine the superstructure.

Marxist critic Raymond Williams later reevaluated the relation between base and superstructure by which cultural forms of life (*superstructure*) also determine its productive forces (*base*): 'We have to revalue "the base" away from the notion of a fixed economic or technological abstraction, and towards the specific activities of men in real social and economic relationships' (492). Williams' revaluation critiques Marx's *vulgar* (or simplistic) materialism and understands the ways cultural forms of life (re-)produce hegemonic consent among subjects. *Hegemony*, a term coined by Italian Marxist critic Antonio Gramsci, refers 'to the process of consensus formation and to the pervasive system of assumptions, meanings and values – the web of ideologies, in other words – that shapes the way things look, what they mean and therefore what reality is for the majority of people within a given culture' (1988, 154). Such a complex understanding of the dynamics of hegemonic consent are further complicated by Marxist literary critic Terry Eagleton who recognized that texts do not so much shape ideological forces as much as they are shaped by such forces of consent. He argues in *Criticism and Ideology* that the task of criticism is thus 'to show the text as it cannot know itself, to manifest those conditions of its making (inscribed in its very letter) about which it is necessarily silent' (1976, 43). While Marxist literary criticism can thus be driven by the critical impulse to recontextualize literary production within broader economic relations of hegemony and consent, Eagelton's concern to show the text *as it cannot know itself* has also proven productive in other approaches such as psychoanalysis, as seen in Lacan and Althusser, in which the subject cannot ever know him or herself fully.

New Historicism and Cultural Materialism

New Historicism developed in the 1980s largely as a response to the ahistorical, text-centred formalism of New Criticism. New Historicist analysis was motivated in part by a radical new understanding of history and its ideological function in maintaining hegemonic consent. The radical new understanding of history was influenced by the work of Michel Foucault, who argued in *The Archaeology of Knowledge* that the old questions of traditional analysis was giving way to 'the phenomena of rupture, of discontinuity, of interruption' (4). In short, Foucault criticizes the history of Hegel and even of Marx, understood as 'the metahistorical deployment of ideal significations and indefinite teleologies' ('Nietzsche' 1994, 352). (See Chapter 5: Lee Patterson, *Chaucer and the Subject of History* [1991].)

In contrast to history in the Hegelian sense, then, Foucault – especially in his later writings – promotes a descriptive, genealogical approach, which 'opposes itself to the search for "origins" and contests "describing the history of morality in terms of a linear development – in reducing its entire history and genesis to an exclusive concern for utility" ' ('Nietzsche' 352, 351). Instead, Foucault shifts to a genealogical, diachronic, micropolitical sense of the historical that he borrowed largely from Nietzsche's influences. In an aptly medieval, palimpsestic image, Foucault notes that genealogy 'requires patience and a knowledge of details, and it depends on a vast accumulation of source material'; it is 'gray, meticulous, and patiently documentary. It operates on a field of entangled and confused parchments, on documents that have been scratched over and recopied many times' ('Nietzsche' 351). Importantly, Foucault's diachronic shift does not negate the synchronic, structuralist approaches of his earlier archaeological work; rather, the diachronic emphasis situates the synchronic endeavour as a rigorously self-defining moment ('Nietzsche' 359). Ideas, then, are never ahistorical.

New Historicism thus emerged from the confluence of Foucault's later writings on genealogy, the anthropological work of Clifford Geertz and Victor Turner, and the historiography of Hayden White. The so-called 'Berkeley School' – which included Stephen Greenblatt, Jonathan Goldberg, Stephen Orgel and Joel Fineman – radically challenged the older notion of history oriented towards the grand narratives and the self-movement of Hegel's dialectical idealism. New Historicists such as Greenblatt, H. Aram Veeser argues, 'dismantle the dichotomy of the economic and the non-economic – that is, 'New Historicists will try to discover how the traces of social circulation are effaced' (xii–xv). The collapse of distinction between literary and non-literary, aesthetic and cultural, non-economic and economic, boldly questions the sacralization of literature in our culture and how such sacralization functions in the broader academy. Questioning the relationship between art and society – and foregrounding the methodological self-consciousness of New Historicism – Greenblatt insists that 'the work of art is the product of a negotiation between a creator or class of creators, equipped with a complex, communally shared repertoire of conventions, and the institutions and practices of society' (1989, 12). Collapsing the historical, critical and disciplinary divisions between the economic and non-economic moves New Historicist analysis towards the systems of exchange and the relations of force that manipulate and adjust the relative systems of which they are a part. Although it is an over simplification, New Historicism, dominant in American criticism, tends to analyse the discourses at the apex of society (the church and aristocracy, for example), while Cultural Materialism, more pronounced among British practitioners, tends to examine the lower end of the social hierarchy (such as the lower-classes, women and others at the margin). Indeed, what is most exciting is that the genealogical descriptions uncannily anticipate some of the dramatic, literary critique of such allegorizing and reductive tendencies in criticism of medieval literature. What we learn, as Terry Eagleton acknowledges, is that what is true of the subject is true of the text: that often we cannot even know ourselves. Such insights have proven remarkably appropriate to Chaucer studies, for instance, as contemporary readers approach the pilgrims with a sense of the subjective complexity that Chaucer already dramatized.

Deconstruction

Genealogy – and the detailed, descriptive and archival work it entails – is not the only post/structuralist critique of totalizing systems, especially those beholden to Hegelian idealism. Deconstruction also critiques the ethical transgressions of historiography that draws into its narrative and epistemological assumptions a problematically modern and deeply sublimated Hegelian conception of the self and of representation. However, while New Historicism has offered tremendous insight and energy to medieval literary studies, scholars have given less sustained attention to the contributions of deconstruction, partly because of simplistic 'deconstructive' readings that lost sight of ethics and simply reduced everything to difference and indeterminacy. Still, Jacques Derrida and the early proponents of deconstruction – including the so-called 'Yale School' of Paul de Man, Geoffrey Hartman, J. Hillis Miller and Harold Bloom – have contributed to the ethical turn made by recent critical theory.

Derrida: Interpreting Interpretations

The origins of post/structuralism bear an appropriate irony: At the time when structuralism was beginning to emerge with particular interest within American universities in the 1960s, its limitations were being criticized in Europe. Derrida's famous 1966 lecture at Johns Hopkins, 'Structure, Sign, and Play in the Discourse of the Human Sciences' (See Chapter 1: Theorizing the Texts), which some consider to be the origin of post/structuralism, was later published in *Writing and Difference*. It opens with an epigraph from Montaigne, which reads, 'We need to interpret interpretations more than to interpret things'. Deconstruction shares the New Critical affinity for close reading; however, much more like New Historicism, deconstruction radically reevaluates what we mean by a *text* (See Chapter 8: New Historicism). The notion of *interpreting interpretations* is consistent with Derrida's opening observation in 'Structure, Sign, and Play' that 'something has occurred in the history of the concept of structure'; this occurrence, Derrida adds, could be called an 'event', which Derrida opposes to the idea of 'structure' (1978, 278). While Derrida acknowledged the importance of Saussure to the development of cultural anthropology, he nevertheless remained critical of the systems of difference it posited. Specifically, Derrida believed that if all meaning was constituted through relations of difference, then where does the endless chain of signification end? Derrida's critique of structuralism hinges on the idea that each signifier never points *decisively* to a signified; rather, signifiers only point to other signifiers. The endless play of signification can come to any decisive end only when a *transcendental signified* is posited, like God or Truth, which is an impossibility for Derrida. Furthermore, any notion of a *transcendental signified* presupposes a *metaphysics of presence* – the idea that we can access an absolute pre-expressive truth, or that we can somehow have access to the world prior to its discursive organization, in its im-mediacy (lit. *without mediation*).

Il n'y a pas de hors-texte

What we discover through Derrida is that truth does not exist before the text; rather, truth is *subject to* the text (in Derrida's famous phrase, *il n'y a pas de hors-texte* [lit. *'there is no outside (of a) text'*]). Again, the notion of the 'subject' from structuralism emerges, but now it is read in terms of *subjection* to the governing principles of the system. The problem is that structuralism does not take into account the structure of the structure. Derrida's important neologism, *différance*, expresses the impossibility of a transcendental signified in this way. Playing on the ambiguity of the French word *différer* – which can mean both *to differ* and *to defer* – Derrida argues that any resting point or final meaning in a system of differences is always itself deferred to another text or signifier. Whereas deconstructive undecidability within a text is something at which one arrives – through a close, careful exposition of the governing binaries and assumed hierarchies that organize meaning within any textual structure – by the early 1990s there was a tendency to simply begin with this assumption, much to Derrida's chagrin. H. Marshall Leicester's *The Disenchanted Self: Representing the Subject in the Canterbury Tales* (1990) suffers from this reductive understanding of Derrida's outside–inside distinction and is therefore unable to reconcile his reading with any concrete ethical or political concerns. Derrida's important later work on mourning, forgiveness, democracy and theology reinstated ethical concerns and has regained substantial interest in light of the postsecular turn in Continental philosophy.

Gender and Politics

Terry Eagleton closes his book *Literary Theory: An Introduction* with the chapter 'Political Criticism', which has place of privilege as a concluding section rather than as one more approach among others because all criticism is, in some sense, political. In this manner, Eagleton defines *the political* as the general coordination of social relations. In some sense, we could say the same about the political role of feminist criticism and the insights of gender/queer theory in that they have also problematized logocentric, synchronic, representational and allegorical modes of thinking. To this extent, contemporary feminist approaches bring theoretical insight to bear upon concrete economic, political and historical violences against women (and others) to reveal the cultural and theoretical apparatuses that normalize such relations of difference and force. Contemporary feminist approaches have likewise helped to expose the organizing phallogocentrism disseminated through academia as an institution dominated, in large part, by a masculine positivism and eschatology that contributes to the very logic of reading adopted from Aristotle through Hegel.

If Robertson attempted to return to an Augustinian understanding of allegory before its modernization by Hegel, Gayle Margherita notes, in her essay 'Originary Fantasies and Chaucer's *Book of Duchess*', that Robertson nevertheless commits to a Hegelian dialectical recuperation of meaning by positing allegory as the 'dialectical synthesis of the particular and the universal' (1993, 117). Such 'first wave' historicism, Margherita argues, couples 'an insistence on the alterity of the past with a belief in its recoverability'; such a move, she claims, makes an appeal to a theological apparatus – a transcendental signified – that remains as blind to what it suppresses as it is insightful about what it recovers. To the extent that Margherita combines a feminist critique with Lacanian psychoanalysis, we can discern an important critical salvo that stages *from the perspective of the subjugated* the dramatic implications of the critical blindness endemic to Robertsonianism and still prevalent in contemporary criticism. In a similar vein, Karma Lochrie admonishes critics employing a Foucaultian notion of desire in their critical excavations of power relations, at the same time she critiques Foucault's own understanding of the Middle Ages. Lochrie's readings are not simply a feminist appropriation of post/structural critical theory; rather, they provide important correctives from the perspective of the literature itself that opposes totalizing critique. (See Chapter 5: Karma Lochrie, *Covert Operations* and *Heterosyncrasies*.)

The Ethical Turn: From Discipline to Responsibility

Where, then, do the various critical emphases of post/structuralism lead in our approach to medieval literature, and how can we preserve a sensitivity to the violences of representational thinking and a privileged concern for the victims of its critical exposition? Put more broadly, does literary theory have a political potential? One approach emerging with special rigor might be called *the ethical turn*, which offers robust new insights into the functions of allegory, text, violence and community. Inspired as much by postsecular Continental philosophy as it is by ancient modes of biblical, prophetic and rabbinic reading, the ethical turn attends to the political, economic and historical concerns of post/structuralism, but it intensifies them in a way that radically reevaluates the long-standing critical privileging – from Aristotle to Hegel and beyond – of philosophy over the poetic, of commentary (or criticism) over literature. The ethical turn accordingly expresses a profound new mode of what it means both *to read* and *to read in community*, which is exactly the problem that ME literature so often stages.

The ethical turn reaches towards non-dialectical reading that nevertheless establishes a continuity between the medieval and the post/modern without resorting to the reductively allegorical theology of patristic exegesis, as Margherita avers, or to the fetishizing of the subjugated that too often occurs in the 'identity politics' of contemporary critical approaches. Such an ethical turn, moreover, recovers the materiality of post/structuralist approaches – in their attempt to recover subjugated knowledges – by understanding critical situatedness as an inherently material endeavour in itself. Thus, the ethical turn approaches great literature as already performing a prophetic, critical function as it dramatizes an awareness of its own metonymical deferrals, diachronic blindnesses and attention to the violences harboured within the limits of its own representational modes.

While such an ethical turn is already marked out in some of the earliest works of the Yale school, feminism, psychoanalysis, and critical race, ethnicity, and gender studies, much of the contemporary ethical exegesis also has its origins in Continental philosophy and the phenomenological traditions from which philosophers such as Emmanuel Levinas and Jean-Luc Marion work, both of whom redirected phenomenology away from the positivist and eschatological characteristics criticized by Foucault. Instead, Levinas, Marion and others orient their phenomenological attention towards what cannot be contained within representational narratives, positivist historicism or reductionistic allegory, like the irreducible datum of suffering or the lived experience of paternity and filiation (See Levinas 1998, 1969). From this perspective, the text is *saturated* with meaning and always resists the totalizing gaze of the critic. Levinas and Marion centre their analyses in essential questions regarding ethics, mourning, forgiveness, sacrifice and justice, which are not simply literary or analytical categories. The work of Emmanuel Levinas has been especially important here, as he has made a powerful appeal to an ethics that comes before ontology or epistemology and that commands our *response* as *responsibility*. The ethical, for Levinas, is issued in the *face* of the Other – expressed in the 'Thou shalt not kill' – but it is also expressed in the *text* and even in *nature*. We therefore have access to the ethical from these three perspectives (face, text and nature), and for this reason Levinas' revolutionary work insists on responsibility for the Other and a careful evaluation of the ways in which a representational thinking – what we have been calling mythic or sacrificial – undermines the more radical task of ethical exegesis and praxis. These emphases parallel the later Derrida wherein deconstruction runs against its own limits – which is to say, as deconstruction begins to approach that which cannot be deconstructed.

Therefore, a key question is how do such methodologically atheistic and secular reevaluations of history, authority and the production of knowledge coordinate with a medieval literature that reserves for itself an unembarrassed commitment towards the religious, the theological and the moral? In response to the tendency of medieval studies after Robertson to eliminate religion as a category of analysis, David Aers offers a critically nuanced approach to questions of faith and reason as played out across disparate and conflicting literary accounts. He suggests that we bring 'theological, ecclesiological, social, and political' correctives to literary approaches (*Chaucer* 1998, 349). Just as importantly, Aers exposes the sublimated assumptions of liberal humanism that uncritically inform many approaches to medieval literature. Aers thus appeals to previously ignored late-medieval religious writings and attempts to uncondition literary criticism from the fixed scholastic terms of a neo-Aristotelianism, which, for our purposes, culminate in the Hegelianism of representational thinking and the self-moving dialectic of consciousness.

Literature and Commentary

In short, we are beginning to discover how so much of great medieval litera-ture already responds to the violent dangers inherent in representational thinking that asserts itself in the institutions and economies of sacrificial difference, which our traditions of commentary miss precisely because they are still beholden to the same sacrificial economy. It is important, then, to understand that the ethical turn in literary criticism does not overturn criticism that comes before it; rather, it aims to deepen, intensify and correct these commitments by bringing them to an awareness of their own failings, which paradoxically are often already anticipated by the literature itself (See Goodhart). Foremost, the ethical turn in literary theory takes seriously the instructive power of the literature by first deconstructing the hierarchy of commentary over literature. Recovering the critical work of the literary by way of the ethical finally presents radical new means of diagnosing and responding to the problems of mimeticism, sacrifice and theodicical accounts of violence – all of which are shared though differently expressed across historical distance. Many scholars are thus discovering important critical insights regarding the ethical that are contemporary with the unalterable *otherness* of the Middle Ages (for example, see Cohen 2003, 1999, 1996; Copeland 2001; Dinshaw 1999; Fradenberg 2002; Holsinger 2001; Kerby-Fulton 2006; Rudd 2007). Simply put, the ethical turn first recognizes that critical commentary is inextricably linked to the systems of oppression and violence which it criticizes and, second, with that recognition attempts to create new forms of reading that remain under the tutelage of literature rather than its putative master, philosophy.

The relationship between the literary, or even the religious, and economies of violence is taken up with urgency by contemporary literary theory. Since Plato, philosophy has traditionally reserved for itself the synchronic task of determining difference – primarily distinguishing truth from non-truth. Plato's *Republic* considers poetry as an imitation (*mimesis*) of reality, which is itself an imperfect reflection of the ideal forms of truth. Poetry, as such, has traditionally been understood as an episode within philosophy: The philosophical reader (or critic) is the one who evaluates, studies and masters the dramatic surplus of the literary through commentary. For scholars such as Sandor Goodhart, European epistemology is thus governed by an idolatry of Platonic reasoning, but precisely because such idolatry constitutes the philosophical endeavour, philosophy remains blind to the violences of its decision to expel the poetic. Philosophy (and thus commentary) is guilty of the sacrifice of literature. Such a privileging of the philosophical over the poetic has engendered one of the more stubborn critical distinctions between *literature* and *commentary*: determining what is *inside* the text versus what is *outside* the text. The problem of separating the *outside* of the text from the *inside* is precisely the problem of separating commentary from literature and privileging the former over the latter.

Chaucer's Boethius and the Violence of Philosophy

At the heart of philosophical thought is a fundamental assertion of difference that is *sacralized, mythologized* and uncritically *appropriated* in the traditions of critical analysis and commentary, but literary and poetic texts are already aware of these difficulties. Consider, for instance, Chaucer's translation of Boethius' *Consolation of Philosophy*. Though Boethius served as perhaps the most influential writer for Chaucer and the Middle Ages, much of the power of Chaucer's poetry emerges from his ability to render explicit the violence implicit in rigid epistemological systems, as when Lady Philosophy's seamless garb is torn by the hands of impatient men in Book I, Prosa 1 of *Boece*: 'Natheles handes of some men hadden korve that cloth by violence and by strengthe, and everich man of hem hadde boren away swiche peces as he myghte geten' (ll. 37–41). The torn hem, as a mark of violence in the human struggle to impatiently secure truth, indicates already in the struggle of

239

comprehension against (understanding) the proclivity for *apprehension* (as a grasping or seizing). Second, there is a subtle sacrificial gesture evident in Philosophy's expulsion of the poetic muses upon her appearance: 'And whan she saugh thise poetical muses aprochen aboute my bed and enditynge wordes to my wepynges, sche was a litil amoeved, and glowede with *cruel eighen*' (ll. 44–7, my emphasis). Philosophy's banishing of the poetic muses is not unlike Plato's banishing of the poets from his republic; like Plato, Lady Philosophy is concerned that the narrator will not recognize, and thus *know*, the truth because of the imposition of the poetic muses. In Book I, Prosa 2 she asks, 'Knowestow me nat?' (ll. 11–2), and with this question she wipes his eyes clean: 'He hath a litil foryeten hymselve, but certes he schal lightly remembren himself yif so be that he hath knowen me or now; and that he may so doon, I will wipe a litil his eien that ben dirked by the cloude of mortel thynges' (ll. 21–6). The muses of 'fool erthe' have kept his 'nekke [. . .] pressyd with hevy cheynes' (Book I, Metrum 2, ll. 26–32), and Philosophy aims to relieve the narrator from his exile from truth (Book I, Metrum 1, ll. 9–10). The privileging of philosophy, of truth, engenders its own exile of (and from) the poetic: Truth is contaminated by the mimetic seductions of poetry, in which the narrator has taken sorrowful refuge as represented by the platonic cave. From the perspective of philosophy, the mimetic crisis occurs when the narrator gives himself to the habit of the world, those concerns of the muses who confuse desire and affectations with truth.

In a close reading of Philosophy's raiment, the relation between epistemological claims and representation emerges culturally as a mediation of violence. It is not, of course, that Chaucer offers a wholesale critique of Platonic rationality; nonetheless, Chaucer avers a sophisticated concern for the tendency of violence to emerge from out of such representational thinking, and just as Plato did not think all mimesis was wrong, Chaucer remains indebted to Boethius and the Platonic tradition in this regard. The critique Chaucer offers, however subtly, seems to lie at the limits of the ethical – which is a concern for the impatience of appropriation in its struggle to *apprehend*, rather than *comprehend*, truth. It is a concern for the torn hem of Philosophy, a *raptus* of proximity transformed aggressively into the seizure of *rape*. In fact, the *Consolation of Philosophy* is written in both prose and poetry. But yet here is an image of the poetic in internal exile to philosophy, for how is Boethius read in medieval studies? As philosophy, not poetry. However, Chaucer's translation of Boethius reserves for itself the instructive power of the literary, so that rather than separating philosophy from the poetic in a synchronic system of difference, philosophy finds itself *translated* rather than *represented* by the literary. The act of translation itself allows philosophy to read itself as a moment within the instructive power of the aesthetic – which is to say, philosophy reads itself from the point of view of that which it would expel.

Violence and Religion: Towards Anti-Sacrificial Readings

Of course, what we are concerned with here are tendencies within contemporary medieval criticism – or, if not tendencies, at the very least the risk – of epistemic violence. The ethical turn in literary criticism thus becomes intensely self-reflexive of its own motivations and consequences by reading itself from a perspective within the literary. To paraphrase Goodhart, rather than reading literature from the point of view of philosophy, we should read philosophy from the point of view of literature, for what is at stake in the ethical turn is nothing short of exposing the sacrificial tendencies of a literary criticism derived from the Platonic response that separates the 'violence' of literature from the 'truth' of criticism. However, this is not to say that we ever arrive at a moment that is entirely free of violence; rather, we reckon with it by exposing and situating it. Goodhart thus insists that there are 'only two distinct readings or interpretations in this domain: those that are sacrificial, and those that are aware of their sacrificial dimensions and to which we accordingly give the name "anti-sacrificial". There are no non-sacrificial readings, although some sacrificial readings are more cognizant of the constraints or limitations or repetitions in which they work than others' (1996, 258). The instructive power of the literary lies in precisely its occurring before and after criticism – of our approach to the literary not from a point of view outside the text, but to read our commentary from a perspective within the text.

Among others, Ann W. Astell has made much of Goodhart's work in applying these concerns to medieval literature, especially the work of Chaucer. Astell notes that at the closing of the *Canterbury Tales*, 'Chaucer becomes intensely self-reflexive'. She adds: 'He speaks not only as an artist, but also as a critical theorist, a profound commentator on his own art, its mythic [sacrificial] origins, and its end' (2005, 323). The ethical turn is not a religious experience predicated on the sacrificial, but one that is profoundly anti-sacrificial in its exposition of the sacrificial mechanisms that govern culture. Astell, here, draws her critique from the work of René Girard and Eric Gans. Girard argues that Western culture has misread the Gospel text as promoting a sacrificial vision of Christendom; to the contrary, Girard argues, '[t]he Gospels only speak of sacrifices in order to reject them' (1978, 180). That is, the underlying sacrificial logic of culture can be subverted only to the extent that it is exposed, and it is precisely this critical exposition against the sacrificial vision that great literature preserves. Citing Goodhart's work in this area, Astell thus asks an important question: 'If we choose for ourselves a mythic [. . .] reading of the *Canterbury Tales*, "we give up the anti-mythic perspective that [Chaucerian] literature offers us for another myth by which its challenges may be domesticated" ' (338, citing Goodhart). Astell writes:

> In Chaucer's own time and in ours, the *Canterbury Tales* 'participates in
> the Judeo-Christian deconstruction of sacrifice.' If we do not read Chaucer
> that way, is it because 'we are no longer able to appreciate the difference
> between sacrifice and the critique of sacrifice,' or is it, as Eric Gans has
> argued, because 'we have reached the point in the historical unfolding of
> this critique at which there is no longer any ethical value, which is to say,
> any further deferral of violence, to be derived from it'? (338; internal
> quotations from Gans)

Astell brings a radical perspective to the ethical turn in medieval literary
theory. From the perspective of our own 'precarious, post-Holocaustal
existence', we cannot separate the aesthetic from the ethical, and it is precisely
by reading philosophy from the perspective of the literary – rather than the
other way around – that we 'make *ernest* of Chaucer's *game*', as Astell writes,
and thus commit to the anti-sacrificial, anti-mythic as important ethical
correctives to our critical tasks (338).

Midrash and Allegory

As is evident by now, the ethical turn in literary theory calls for a radical
reevaluation of the terms foundational to post/structuralism. Among these
we can reformulate our understanding of the synchronic and diachronic, and
we can renew our sense of allegory. A synchronic approach to understanding
allegory reads it, as is the case with patristic exegesis, as a mode of *representation*. A diachronic approach, in contrast, reads allegory as a mode of
translation.

The ethical turn in literary criticism is thus especially beholden to a Judaic
experience of reading known as *midrash* – what Levinas describes as
'exposition or research, or interrogation'. Levinas notes that the 'invitation to
seek, to decipher, to the *midrash*, already marks the reader's participation in
the Revelation, in the Scriptures' (1989, 194). Scholars like Emmanuel Levinas,
Geoffrey Hartman, Michael Fishbane, Gerald Bruns, Sandor Goodhart and
others extend this ancient form of scriptural interpretation to avoid the
trap of representation precisely because it reads commentary as a *material*
extension of the text itself. There is no longer the synchronic distinction
between literature and commentary; instead, the two are continuous with
each other. Interpretation is a material extension of the text in this robust
sense. In his important essay, 'Midrash and Allegory', Gerald Bruns observes
that:

> the structure of the Bible as a redacted, self-interpreting text has this
> important exegetical consequence: the Bible effectively blocks any attempt

to understand it by reconstruction of its textual history and a working back to an original, uninterpreted intention. This self-interpreting text is also self-effacing with respect to its origins. The whole orientation of Scripture is toward its future, not toward its past. The Bible is prophetic rather than expressive in its structure. (1987, 627)

It is important here to separate the prophetic (as a form of speaking truth to power) from the eschatological (as understood in traditional Christianity). Moreover, in contrast to patristic exegesis that finds a philosophical truth that must be *extracted (and abstracted) from* the poetic text, Bruns notes that 'the basic historical task of biblical hermeneutics is not simply to describe the techniques of exegesis that have been applied to the Scriptures, but also to elucidate the conditions in which the understanding of these texts has occurred' (625). Rather than approaching the text from some presumed and privileged outside perspective, we discover that we are contemporary with the text, but not in the sense that we have access, as Bruns notes, to some self-effacing origin of the text. Rather, ethical readings are contemporary (or contemporaneous) with the text precisely to the extent that they are oriented towards a non-teleological future. Such an (ethical) interpretative approach we can now call, alternatively, the *midrashic*, the *diachronic*, the *symptomatic*, the *anti-mythic* or the *prophetic*. It is continuous with the text, not as a representation of the text or its truth, but in its translation of the text into other contexts. As translation, it is a material extension of the text, but it preserves within its materiality the very tensions, redactions, questions, aporias and mysteries of the original rather than mastering the text through reference to a philosophical truth or transcendental signified.

The ethical turn of this midrashic approach – of this recovered sense of the allegorical – recovers another kind of materiality. In his article 'Reflections on D. W. Robertson, Jr., and 'Exegetical Criticism', Alan T. Gaylord outlines the important correctives of 'exegetical criticism' as developed by scholars such as Ann Astell and Larry Scanlon. For instance, Gaylord notes that Astell's recent work brings a sensitivity to feminist issues and helps to 'provide a supplement and corrective to that part of the Robertsonian legacy that is dismayingly misogynistic' (2006, 325). In effect, the ethical turn offers a radical recovery of the material within allegory; that is, we aim to recover that which has been excluded by representational modes of allegory – its pointing outside of the text – from the marginalization of children, the depleted environment, transgendered bodies, sacrificial bodies or dead infants. For this reason, the ethical turn proves not only appropriate but necessary as a correction to the traditions of commentary that harbour within them the remnants of a sacrificial vision of hermeneutics: the triumph of philosophy over literature. Thus, from such initial attempts at invigorating an ethical approach to understanding medieval allegory, Gaylord hints that '[p]erhaps some Neo-Exegetical Criticism has yet to be completely formulated' (326). Indeed, it is not so much that an ethical exegesis such as this is being formulated as it is being recovered. What we learn, as Sandor Goodhart is fond of reminding us, is that the very oldest texts become the most new.

Reading in the Shadow of the Shoah

In recent years, we have seen a number of essays published that draw the insights of the ethical turn into considerations of medieval literary criticism, and many of these approaches specifically pull from Levinas's influence in phenomenological, pedagogical and literary circles. It is important, therefore, to offer a final consideration. The ethical turn should not become reified into a critical approach that would dare to understand ethical exegesis as one more critical approach among others, as happened to deconstruction in the 1980s as it became simply another predictable critical manoeuvre. The ethical turn does not promote a standard prescriptive or thematic set of concerns, questions, or distinctions; rather, it opens a new way of understanding the literary as contemporary with our own critical struggles, but in a way that no longer privileges the representational totality of ontotheology. As Monica Osborn observes of the ethical turn, it is the desire 'to witness that tradition transformed into something significant to our contemporary lives' (2006). If we return to the broader genealogy of the ethical turn, we see that Robertson's important critical contribution was his attempt to uncondition our under-standing of allegory from its Hegelian and Romantic receptions. By returning to an Augustinian emphasis on charity and cupidity, however, Robertsonian-ism substituted one reductive approach to allegory with another that was no less limited by the pitfalls of representational thinking. In light of the ethical turn, contemporary critical theory approaches a robust, diachronic notion of allegory that moves from allegory as *representation* to allegory as *translation*. From the point of view of the anti-sacrificial, then, our work still must aim for a deeper and more intense recovery of the prophetic if we are to develop a form of literary response capable of situating, exposing and thus subverting the sacrificial dynamics and mythic fallout of culture.

After all, we are not only reading medieval literature, but we are reading medieval literature in the wake of the most egregious deployments of repre-sentational, mythic thinking in history, culminating in the devastations of the Holocaust (Levinas 1989). Recovering the prophetic mode of reading opens medieval literature to questions of ethics and the demands of responsibility. These urgent questions intensify rather than compromise the important con-cerns raised by post/structuralism. Exposing the operations of the sacrificial logic at the heart of so many critical approaches allows for a sober approach to problems of violence and the sacred addressed in medieval literature, and are guided by such concerns. More importantly, the ethical turn provides the possibility to understand how medieval literature already responds to questions of gender, ecology, ecclesiastical authority, theological violences and subjectivity within the dominate relations of power and force. To read literature prophetically is to deconstruct the implicit hierarchal assumptions of what is in the text and what is outside the text: We are moved, seduced and transformed by the text as much as the text is moved, seduced and transformed by our critical operations.

Study Questions

1. Define the following terms in your own words:
   - Synchronic vs. diachronic
   - Four-fold system of exegesis
   - *Parole* vs. *la langue*
   - Signifier vs. signified
   - Dialectical materialism
   - Base vs. superstructure
   - Hegemony
   - Transcendental signified
   - *Différance*
   - The political
   - The ethical turn

2. Compare different accounts of a particular theoretical approach with a comparable section in another chapter of the *Continuum Handbook*, and identify the similarities and differences in the two accounts. Here are some possibilities:
   - Chapter 10: The Influences of Structuralism (Neely) vs. Chapter 7: Structuralism and Poststructuralism (Ganim)
   - Chapter 10: Materialist Criticism: Marxism Criticism, New Historicism and Cultural Materialism (Neely) vs. Chapter 7: Marxism to New Historicism (Ganim)
   - Chapter 10: Feminism and Gender Theory (Neely) vs. Chapter 9: Feminism (Cady)
   - Chapter 7: Gender, Identity, and Queer Studies (Ganim) vs. Chapter 9: Queer Theory (Cady)
   - Chapter 9: Race Studies and Postcolonial Theory (Cady) vs. Chapter 8: Multilingualism, International Contexts, and Postcolonial Concerns (Warren)
   - Chapter 10: The Ethical Turn: From Discipline to Responsibility vs. Chapter 9: Intersections: Race, Gender, and Sexuality (Cady)

   What accounts for the differences? What kinds of similarities do you see?
3. Neely uses the term 'violence' in a number of different ways. Identify and define at least three to four different inflections of the term in the chapter.

4. What is the relationship of violence to ethics? Of violence to philosophy and theory?
5. What are the theoretical emphases and conceptual trajectories that have led to 'the ethical turn', according to Neely?
6. What sort of discursive characteristics would an ethical reading have in Neely's conception? How does such a reading differ from more traditional interpretations?
7. Why would literary criticism become concerned with the problem of violence and the question of ethics at this particular point in history? What social, political or cultural aspects of the early twenty-first century could motivate such an emphasis and give the possibility of 'ethical reading' such urgency?
8. *Web Quest*: The practice of midrash is old and well established in Judaic tradition. Conduct a web search on 'midrash' and collect examples that seem to uniquely embody midrash as an ethical interpretive practice. What, typically, does midrash concern itself with? Who practices (or practiced) it, for what purposes, and in what kind of institutional contexts? What kind of writings or textual practices does midrash yield, and how is midrash used or interpreted?
9. *Web Quest*: The ethical turn is often associated with 'negative theology' and 'post-Holocaust theology'. Investigate both ideas (and associated terms) to discover (1) what negative theology investigates and (2) how some thinkers believe that theology (and philosophy) can no longer be the same after the Holocaust as before.
10. *Web Quest*: Emmanuel Levinas is not as widely known in the United States and the United Kingdom as he is in Europe, though he is widely acknowledged to be one of the most important philosophers of the second half of the twentieth century. One way to judge a thinker's impact is to investigate who s/he influenced. Do a thorough web search on Emmanuel Levinas (1) to discover his key concerns, (2) to identify his most important texts and (3) to ascertain whom he influenced through his writing and teaching. Put simply, who quotes Levinas, what do they quote, and when did they quote him?

Glossary

Ahistorical/Universal: The characterization that a belief or idea transcends history and is applicable in all places and at all times.

Binary/Binary Opposition: Mode of Western thought since the Greeks that the world is organized according to 'natural' oppositions like male/female, white/black, good/evil, reason/passion, west/east and so on. Deconstructive thought considers these binaries not as equally distributed aspects of reality but instead a hierarchy in which one of the terms is more valued (male over female, for example) and requires the denigration or elimination of the other for its success.

Essentialism: The idea that humans of all ages and cultures share an unalterable and shared universal essence that transcends the vagaries of history and culture. In the case of women, according to Diane Cady, essentialism 'is the belief that women possess an innate, natural, feminine essence that exists outside social and cultural controls'.

Discourse: More than a synonym for 'language', discourse describes the simultaneously systemic and shifting relationship between individual subjects, social systems, power operations and textual productions. Drawn from Foucault, in this sense discourses are also seen genealogically to arise from and shape specific institutions such as religion, medicine, politics, the sciences and other social formations and groups.

Feminism and Gender Studies: In John Ganim's formulation, beginning with the recovery of women's experience and the rediscovery of women writers and readers, feminism develops into a critique of ideal or essential categories of gender and questions whether the representation of the feminine is inextricably linked to a defense of patriarchy. The female mystics, including Margery Kemp and Julian of Norwich, and characters such as the Wife of Bath and Criseyde, play a role in these debates.

Hegemony/Hegemonic: The social conditions established by, and reinforcing, the dominant social, political and cultural systems and the further discursive mechanisms deployed to render these conditions normal, 'natural' or God-given. In John Ganim's words, hegemony as derived from Antonio Gramsci denotes when 'the cultural outlook of the ruling class becomes naturalized as the viewpoint of an entire culture'.

Heteronormative/Heteronormativity: Describes the social expectation and cultural pressures designed to confine intimate relationships to those between heterosexual couples and, in contrast, to discourage, inhibit or demonize same-sex relationships.

Interpellation: The concept that subject-individuals are 'hailed' or called into being by the social structures in which they are embedded. Most often associated with the work of Louis Althusser, particularly 'Ideology and Ideological State Apparatuses: Notes Toward an Investigation', the cardinal example of the power of 'being interpellated' is to think that you hear your name called across a room. The experience stops you in your tracks and calls your to attention to that voice, even if you are not sure of what you heard. Althusser divided the social structures to which one is subjected into RSAs (Repressive State Apparatuses like the police, the legal system, the military etc.) and ISAs (Ideological State Apparatuses, like the family, religion, education etc.).

Gender, Identity and Queer Studies: For John Ganim, as feminism questioned the accepted norms of what it means to be 'woman', so too other categories or sexual roles were seen as malleable and constructed: masculinity, heterosexuality and homosexuality. The recovery of the experience of gays and lesbians was eclipsed by the redefinition of the term 'queer', a category meant to trouble the normative definitions of gender and sexuality. Chaucer's Pardoner is a key figure in Queer Studies debates.

Jouissance: Usually rendered as 'enjoyment', especially that associated with sexual orgasm, *jouissance* indicates a pleasure so extreme that it becomes suffering. For Lacan, this paradoxical pleasure/pain transgresses the normal boundaries of Freud's 'pleasure principle', which seeks to limit *jouissance*. Lacan also described a distinctly feminine *jouissance*, a *jouissance* of the other.

Modesty Topos: Common rhetorical trope of self-effacement in medieval texts, especially from an author to a patron or supplicant to a lady, as when Gawain tells the Lady in *Sir Gawain and the Green Knight* that 'I am not that Gawain of whom you speak'.

Marxism and New Historicism: As John Ganim describes, traditional historicisms attempted to place literary works firmly within the context of their own time, viewing them as reflecting the outlook of their age. Newer historicisms, including the New Historicism itself, cultural materialism and neo-Marxism, see literature as having an active role in shaping political and social events, and even regard historical events as a sort of text to be interpreted. Crises such as the Rising of 1381 and Henry IV's coup d'etat against Richard II play an important role in these debates.

Other/other: The Other (or other), a term often used in contemporary literary and cultural theory, has different denotations according to the theory that employs it. Generally, the Other indicates those persons, groups or characteristics against which the majority culture defines itself, so that 'homosexuality' is the Other to heterosexuality and so on. This process of 'Othering', or positing the characteristics of an opposing group for one's own purposes, inevitably introduces ideological distortions, as uncovered by postcolonial theory's recognition of how 'Orientalism' serves the ideological uses of Western colonial powers.

Palimpsest: Medieval texts were generally copied on specially prepared animal hide (parchment), and the parchment could be reused for a new text if the old ink was scraped off. A palimpsest is this reused text in which the vestiges of the previous text are visible beneath the lettering of the newer text.

Postcolonial Criticism: For John Ganim, the end of the colonial empires dominated by Western Europe resulted in new nation-states in the third world, but the cultural weight of Europe remained strong, resulting in 'hybrid' identities, as well as in reverse migration to the home countries. Debates concern whether the Crusades are an example of early European colonialism. The relation of England to its Celtic fringe is sometimes seen to be a colonial relationship. Romances of the Crusades and narratives such as Mandeville's *Travels* have been the subject of postcolonial analyses.

Psychoanalytic Theory: In John Ganim's formulation, an older Freudian criticism treated literature as an expression of the author's unconscious, revealing repressed sexual desires, often related to incest. Jacques Lacan revised Freud using the models of linguistics and poststructuralism, and his followers have used his ideas to demonstrate how psychosexual development is implicated in the reproduction of domination and power. The concept of courtly love plays a role in Lacan's theory, and his ideas have influenced feminist approaches to medieval literature.

Repressive Hypothesis: Foucault's thesis from *The History of Sexuality, vol. 1* that rather than leading to liberation, talking, discussing and writing about sexuality leads towards repression as those discourses are institutionalized or as they emerge from and are controlled by different institutions like religion, medicine and law. As a form of confession, these enunciations are then equated to the subject's identity.

Structuralism and Poststructuralism: According to John Ganim, in the mid-1970s, the study of literature was transformed by theories known as structuralism and poststructuralism. Structuralism emphasized the system of literary meanings and productions, rather than the individual work or author. Semiotics regarded literary works as part of a larger system of signs that included popular culture. Deconstruction questioned the intended and overt meanings of a work and stressed the slipperiness of signification and the multiple meanings of written language.

***Trivium* and *Quadrivium*:** The basic medieval university curriculum consisted of the *trivium* or disciplines related to language (grammar, rhetoric and dialectic) and the *quadrivium* or disciplines related to mathematics (arithmetic, geometry, astronomy, music etc.).

Appendix: Teaching Medieval British Literature into the Twenty-First Century

Susan Oldrieve with Joanna Wright Smith

Chapter Overview

This chapter is available online at:
www. continuumbooks.com/resources/9780826494092

Notes on Contributors

Gail Ashton is a freelance writer, poet and former academic (Universities of Manchester and Birmingham) based in the UK. She is the author of *Chaucer's The Canterbury Tales* (Continuum, 2007), *The Generation of Identity in Late Medieval Hagiography* (Routledge, 2001), *Chaucer: The Canterbury Tales* (Macmillan, 1998), co-editor of *Teaching Chaucer* (Palgrave, 2007), as well as co-editor of two poetry anthologies and author of a full-length poetry collection, *Ghost Songs* (all with Cinnamon Press).

Diane Cady (PhD, Cornell University) is an Associate Professor of English at Mills College. She has published articles on Chaucer, gender and commerce and is completing study entitled *Damaged Goods: Gender and Commerce in the Canterbury Tales.*

John L. Ganim (PhD, Indiana University) is a Professor of English at the University of California, Riverside. He is the author of *Style and Consciousness in Middle English Narrative* (Princeton, 1983), *Chaucerian Theatricality* (Princeton, 1990) and *Medievalism and Orientalism* (Palgrave, 2005). He has served as President of the New Chaucer Society, Chair of the Middle English Division of the Modern Language Association and has been a Guggenheim Fellow.

Brian Gastle (PhD, University of Delaware) currently is the Associate Dean of the Graduate School and an Associate Professor of English at Western Carolina University. He has published on late-medieval English authors such as Geoffrey Chaucer, John Gower and Margery Kempe, and he serves as the webmaster for the International John Gower Society (www.johngower.org).

Mathew Boyd Goldie (PhD, Graduate Center of the City University of New York) is an Associate Professor at Rider University and the editor of *Middle English Literature: A Historical Sourcebook* (Blackwell, 2003). He has published essays on Thomas Hoccleve and the play *Mankind* and is currently completing a book on the antipodes from the Greek and Roman era to the present day.

Julia Bolton Holloway (PhD, University of California-Berkeley), Hermit of the Holy Family, taught at Princeton and the University of Colorado-Boulder, took early retirement as Professor Emerita to enter her convent in Sussex, and then came to Florence where she directs the Mediatheca 'Fioretta Mazzei' and the 'English' Cemetery. She is the author of numerous studies, including *The Pilgrim and the Book: A Study of Dante, Langland and Chaucer* (Peter Lang, 1987 *Saint Bride and Her Book: Birgitta of Sweden's Revelations* (Boydell and Brewer, 1992), *Julian of Norwich, Showing of Love* (SISMEL, 2001). She has also edited several collections and is webmaster of www.umilta.com, a site devoted to medieval female mystics.

Daniel T. Kline (PhD, Indiana University) is an Associate Professor of English and the Coordinator of Graduate English at the University of Alaska-Anchorage. He edited *Medieval Children's Literature* (Routledge, 2003) and has published in *Chaucer Review, Comparative Drama, College Literature, Journal of English and Germanic Philology* and *Philological Quarterly*. He is currently completing a book the representation of children and childhood in Middle English literature and is the author/webmaster of The Electronic Canterbury Tales (www.kankedort.net).

Bonnie Millar (PhD, University of Nottingham) is on the faculty at Castle College (Nottingham, UK) and is the author of *The Siege of Jerusalem in its Physical, Literary, and Historical Contexts* (Four Courts, 2000).

Sol J. Neely (PhD, Purdue University) specializes in nineteenth- and twentieth-century Continental philosophy, medieval and modernist literature and Jewish studies. Sol is co-founder and president of the North American Levinas Society (www.levinas-society.org), and has published and presented internationally on philosophy, pedagogy and 'the ethical turn' in literary studies.

Susan Oldrieve (PhD, University of Virginia) is a Professor of English at Baldwin Wallace College and is an Associate Editor for Pedagogy for *Shakespeare and the Classroom*. She has published in the areas of Anglo-Saxon literature and Shakespeare and is currently working on a study of the relationship between sixteenth-century poetic theory and Spenser's *Faerie Queen*.

Nancy Bradley Warren (PhD, Indiana University) is a Professor of English and Courtesy Professor of Religion at Florida State University. She is the author of two books and numerous articles on medieval and early modern female spirituality. Her current book project is entitled *The Embodied Word: Female Spiritualities, Contested Orthodoxies, and English Religious Cultures, 1350–1700*.

References

Aarne, Antti, *The Types of the Folk-Tale: A Classification and Bibliography*, Stith Thompson (rev. ed.), New York: Burt Franklin, 1971. A revised and expanded index that classifies and describes tales from Northern, Southern and Eastern Europe and India, into animal, ordinary, joke and anecdote types.

Abrams, Meyer H. (gen. ed.), *Norton Anthology of English Literature, vol. 1* (3rd ed.), New York: W. W. Norton, 1975. Standard anthology for sophomore-level college survey classes in American universities, now in its 8th edition.

——, *Norton Anthology of English Literature, vol. 1* (4th ed.), New York: W. W. Norton, 1979.

——, *Norton Anthology of English Literature, vol. 1* (5th ed.), New York: W. W. Norton, 1986.

——, *Norton Anthology of English Literature, vol. 1* (6th ed.), New York: W. W. Norton, 1993.

——, *Norton Anthology of English Literature, vol. 1* (7th ed.), New York: W. W. Norton, 2000.

Aers, David, *Sanctifying Signs: Making Christian Tradition in Late Medieval England*, Notre Dame: Notre Dame University Press, 2004. Re-evaluates the nature of medieval spirituality and its literary and cultural expression.

——, *Faith, Ethics, and Church: Writing in England, 1360–1409*, Woodbridge, Suffolk New York: D. S. Brewer, 2000. Examines the relationship between the late-medieval Church and lay powers and the interplay of faith and ethics in a range of Middle English texts by Chaucer, Gower, Langland and the *Gawain*-poet.

——, 'Faith, ethics, and community: Reflections on reading late medieval English writing', *Journal of Medieval and Early Modern Studies* 28 (1998), 341–69. Offers a critically nuanced approach to questions of faith and reason as played out across conflicting literary accounts and exposes the sublimated assumptions of liberal humanism that uncritically inform many approaches to medieval literature.

—— (ed.), *Culture and History, 1350–1600: Essays on English Communities, Identities, and Writing*, Detroit: Wayne State University Press, 1992. Six essays centred upon the formation of subjectivity and the analysis of agency in late-medieval England.

——, 'A whisper in the ear of early modernity: Or reflections on literary critics writing the "history of the subject"', in Aers (ed.), 1992, 177–204. Reviews the contributions of New Historicism and other recent critical approaches and discourses, and their relationship to earlier conceptualizations of the Middle Ages.

——, *Community, Gender and Individual Identity, 1360–1430*, New York: Routledge, 1988. Examines the social, cultural and ideological values of medieval British literature in essays on Langland's Piers Plowman, *The Book of Margery Kempe*, Chaucer's *Troilus and Criseyde*, and *Sir Gawain and the Green Knight*.

——, *Piers Plowman and Christian Allegory*, London: Arnold, 1988. Analyses Piers Plowman in the light of late-medieval literary, religious and ideological currents.

——, *Chaucer, Langland and the Creative Imagination*, New York: Routledge, 1980. Deals with fourteenth-century literature and the intersections of history, language, literature and religion.

Alain de Lille, *The Plaint of Nature*, James J. Sheridan (trans.), Toronto: Pontifical Institute of Medieval Studies, 1980. Widely influential twelfth-century text, modeled upon Boethius' *Consolation*, in which Nature personified condemns homosexuality as a grammatical error.

Allen, Judson Boyce, *The Ethical Poetic of the Later Middle Ages: A Decorum of Convenient Distinction*, Toronto: University of Toronto Press, 1982. Analyses the relationship of literature to moral life through the use of medieval Latin terms drawn from the commentary tradition and applied to Dante, Chaucer, Langland, and Mallory.

Allen, Mark E., *The Online Chaucer Bibliography*, University of Texas San Antonio, available online at <http://uchaucer.utsa.edu/>.

Anderson, Benedict, *Imagined Communities: Reflections on the Origin and Spread of Nationalism*, London: Verso, 1983. Investigates the emergence of nationalism in relation to the media and vernacular languages and famously defines 'nation' as 'an imagined political community and imagined as both inherently limited and sovereign'.

Anderson, Perry, *Lineages of the Absolutist State*, London: NLB, 1974. A 'comparative study of the nature and development of the Absolutist State in Europe' (7) that views early modern absolutism against the background of medieval feudalism in Eastern and Western Europe.

——, *Passages from Antiquity to Feudalism*, London: NLB, 1974. The prologue to *Lineages* that traces the European political development from the Greeks to the absolutist monarchies.

Ariès, Philippe, *Centuries of Childhood: A Social History of Family Life*, New York: Knopf, 1962. Initiated the contemporary cultural study of childhood and introduced the idea, since refuted, that the Middle Ages considered children only 'miniature adults' and that medieval parents were not emotionally committed to their children.

Ashton, Gail, 'Introduction', in Ashton and Sylvester (eds.), *Teaching Chaucer*, New York: Palgrave Macmillan, 2007, 1–16. Sets the agenda for new approaches to teaching Chaucer.

——, and Louise Sylvester (eds.), *Teaching Chaucer*, New York: Palgrave Macmillan, 2007. Innovative series of essays.

Astell, Ann W., 'Nietzsche, Chaucer, and the sacrifice of art', *Chaucer Review* 39.3 (2005), 323–40. Examines the *Manciple's Tale* in terms of how it stages an anti-mythic, anti-sacrificial Girardian reading of culture that is opposed to a Nietzschean sacrificial approach.

Baker, Denise N. (ed.), *The Showings of Julian of Norwich*, New York: W. W. Norton, 2005. The Norton critical edition of Julian's *Showings*, including a critical text, background materials and academic essays.

Bakhtin, Mikhail, *The Dialogic Imagination: Four Essays*, Michael Holquist (ed.) and C. Emerson and M. Holquist (trans.), Austin: University of Texas Press, 1981. Puts forward the influential concepts of the heteroglossia, dialogic versus the monologic, and the chronotope.

——, *Rabelais and His World*, Boston: M.I.T. Press, 1968. Presents the concept of the carnivalesque as a means of subverting the officially prescribed social order.

Bambaras, Toni Cade, 'Foreword' to *This Bridge Called My Back: Writings by Radical Women of Color*, Cherrie Moraga and Gloria Anzaldua (eds.), New York: Women of Color Press, 1983. Famous anthology calling for political change in the US and utilizing a wide variety of discourses, like poetry, photography, free writing, graphics and academic essays.

Barber, Richard (ed.), *The Arthurian Legends: An Illustrated images Anthology*, Rochester, NY: The Boydell Press, 1992. Includes images from the ancient Welsh traditions to the present.

Barnhouse, Rebecca, 'Students editing manuscripts', *SMART: Studies in Medieval and Renaissance Teaching* 7.2 (Fall 1999), 17–21.

Barr, Helen, *Socioliterary Practice in Late Medieval England*, New York: Oxford University Press, 2001. Reconceptualizes Middle English literature as forms of social discourse operating within fractious and changing political, economic and religious circumstances.

Barratt, Alexandra (ed.), *Women's Writing in Middle English*, London: Longmans, 1992. An excellent and varied anthology of women's writing from the fourteenth through sixteenth centuries, including Trotula texts, Marie de France and Christine de Pizan, women mystics (Mechtild of Hackeborn, Bridget of Sweden, Catherine of Siena, Julian of Norwich, Margery Kempe), and collections of prayers, letters and poems.

Barthes, Roland, *Image, Music, Text*, London: Fontana, 1977. Collection of influential essays on a variety of cultural topics, including 'Introduction to the Structural Analysis of Images', 'The Grain of the Voice' and 'The Death of the Author'.

Bartlett, Robert, 'Medieval and modern concepts of race and ethnicity', *Journal of Medieval and Early Modern Studies* 31.1 (2001), 39–56. Argues controversially that 'race' and 'ethnicity' should be treated as synonyms in the Western Middle Ages.

Baswell, Christopher, 'Multilingualism on the page', in Strohm (ed.), 2007, 38–50. Analyses the important occurrences of macaronic texts and assesses their theoretical implications for understanding Middle English literature.

Baugh, Albert C. and Thomas Cable, *A History of the English Language* (5th ed.), Upper Saddle River, NJ: Prentice Hall, 2002. A standard text in many courses on the History of the English Language, this book discusses the historical and cultural environment that paralleled the changes in the English language.

Baumgarten, Elisheva, *Mothers and Children: Jewish Family Life in Medieval Europe*, Princeton: Princeton University Press, 2004. A synthetic history of family life, focusing upon mothers and children, from birth until age seven, among the medieval Ashkenazi Jews of Germany and northern France.

Beauvoir, Simone de, *The Second Sex*, New York: Bantam, 1952. Important mid-century feminist manifesto that declares no one is born a woman but is made one.

Beckwith, Sarah, *Signifying God: Social Relation and Symbolic Act in the York Corpus Christi Plays*, Chicago: The University of Chicago Press, 2001. Argues that the York Plays served a political function by organizing and regulating labour and that the drama performed important theological and sacramental work in the city.

——, 'Making the world in York and the York cycle', in Miri Rubin and Sarah Kay (eds.), *Framing Medieval Bodies*, Manchester: Manchester University Press, 1994, 254–76. Discusses the role of work in the York mystery plays and how it can be used as a form of control.

——, *Christ's Body: Identity, Religion and Society in Medieval English Writing*, New York: Routledge, 1993. Deals with the materiality of medieval spirituality, particularly how the body of Christ symbolically informs late-medieval devotional writing.

——, 'Ritual, church and theatre: medieval dramas of the sacramental body', in Aers (ed.), 992, 65–90. Reevaluates the social, religious and literary functions of ritual.

Beer, Francis (ed.), *Julian of Norwich's Revelations of Divine Love: The Shorter Version Edited from BL Add. MS 37790*, Heidelberg: Carl Winter, 1978. Critical edition of the 'shorter' of Julian's showings, probably set down very soon after her critical illness, while the 'long' version was probably written about 20 years later.

Bennett, Judith M, 'Medievalism and feminism', *Studying Medieval Women: Sex, Gender, Feminism*, Nancy F. Partner (ed.), Cambridge, MA: Medieval Academy of America, 1993, 7–29. Analyses the gulf between feminism and history and argues that women's history has not yet been fully incorporated into 'history' per se.

Benson, C. David, 'Chaucer's Pardoner: His sexuality and modern critics', *Medievalia* 8 (1982), 351–8. Argues that the Pardoner is an effeminate womanizer, like Absolon in the *Miller's Tale*.

Benson, Larry D., 'Why study the Middle Ages?' *Teaching the Middle Ages: Studies in Medieval and Renaissance Teaching, vol. 1*, Robert V. Graybill, Robert L. Kindrick, and Robert E. Lovell (eds.), Warrensburg, MO: Central Missouri State University, 1982, 1–16.

——, (gen. ed.), *The Riverside Chaucer*, Boston: Houghton-Mifflin, 1987. The standard critical edition of Chaucer for scholars, a revision of Robinson's 1957 edition.

——, *The Harvard Chaucer Page*, Harvard University, available online at <http://www.courses.fas.harvard.edu/~chaucer/>.

Bhabha, Homi K. (ed.), *Nation and Narration*, London: Routledge, 1990. Criticizes the tendency to see all colonized and postcolonial states under the same rubric.

Biddick, Kathleen, *The Shock of Medievalism*, Durham: Duke University Press, 1998. Analyses the nineteenth-century roots of academic medieval studies and the consequences of the unexamined and often sentimentalized conceptions still informing contemporary medieval studies.

'Bin Laden alleges "crusader war" against Islam' (11 November 2001), *PBSOnline News Hour*, available online at <http://www.pbs.org/newshour/updates/

november01/letter_11-1.html>. Contains Bin Laden's statement concerning the Crusades.

Birgitta of Sweden, *Saint Bride and Her Book*, Julia Bolton Holloway (trans.), Newburyport, MA: Focus, 1992. Contemporary English translation of the important female mystic and saint who influenced other mystics across Europe and attempted to mediate in the Hundred Years War.

Bloch, R. Howard, *Medieval Misogyny and the Invention of Western Romantic Love*, Chicago: University of Chicago Press, 1991. Progressing from biblical conceptions and patristic commentators on women and gender to the late Middle Ages, argues that the idealization of women in the twelfth and thirteenth centuries is itself a form antifeminism.

——, and Stephen G. Nichols (eds.), *Medievalism and the Modernist Temper*, Baltimore: Johns Hopkins University Press, 1996. Reassesses the development of medieval studies in the West and brings fresh attention to seemingly previously settled questions.

——, *The Anonymous Marie de France*, Chicago: University of Chicago Press, 2003. Reevaluates Marie de France based upon her writings and historical moment and finds a self-conscious artist of profound scope and skill, 'the Joyce of the twelfth century'.

Bloom, Harold, *The Western Canon: The Books and School of the Ages*, New York: Harcourt Brace, 1994. Argues against the theorization of literature and for the traditional canon of great Western, primarily male, writers, with Shakespeare at the centre of the canon.

Bloomfield, Martin, 'Teaching medieval romance', *Teaching the Middle Ages II: Studies in Medieval and Renaissance Teaching*, vol. 2, Robert V. Graybill, Robert L. Kindrick, and Robert E. Lovell (eds.), Warrensburg, MO: Central Missouri State University, 1985.

Bloomfield, Morton W., *Essays and Explorations: Studies in Ideas, Language and Literature*, Cambridge: Harvard University Press, 1970. Argues the need for a historicist approach establishing the original context of literature as a basis of literary criticism.

Blyth, Charles R., (ed.), *Thomas Hoccleve: The Regiment of Princes*, Kalamazoo, MI: Medieval Institute Publications, 1999. Critical text of Hoccleve's poem, in which he places Chaucer as the father of English letters and himself as descendent.

Blythe, James M. and Sarah L. E. Pratt, 'The Crusades game', *SMART: Studies in Medieval and Renaissance Teaching* 4.2. (Fall 1993), 13–25.

Boswell, John, *Christianity, Social Tolerance, and Homosexuality*, Chicago: University of Chicago Press, 1980. Groundbreaking, comprehensive study of attitudes towards homosexuality in the West and the mechanisms deployed to constrain social conformity.

Bourdieu, Pierre, *Outline of a Theory of Practice*, Cambridge: Cambridge University Press, 1977. Offers the concept of the *habitus* as a mediating principle between objective structures and subjective agents.

——, *The Logic of Practice*, Cambridge, UK; Oxford, UK: Polity Press, 1990. Critiques both objectivism and subjectivism through an interrogation of imaginary or symbolic relations that reproduce cultural norms.

——, and Randal Johnson, *The Field of Cultural Production: Essays on Art and Literature*, New York: Columbia University Press, 1993. Serves both as an introduction to Bourdieu's sociological practice and its application to the humanities: The field of cultural production entails not only the social system itself but the mechanisms by which it legitimates itself and disguises those mechanisms as 'natural' as in the example of artistic 'taste'.

Bowers, John M., *Chaucer and Langland: The Antagonistic Tradition*, Notre Dame: University of Notre Dame Press, 2007. Argues for the reinterpretation of English literary history with Langland rather than Chaucer as the putative father.

Braswell, Mary Flowers, 'Promoting the text: Teaching Chaucer through the Kress collection', *SMART: Studies in Medieval and Renaissance Teaching* 7.2 (Fall 1999), 23–31.

Brewer, Derek, 'Retellings', in T. Hahn and A. Lupack (eds.), *Retelling Tales: Essays in Honour of Russell Peck*, Cambridge: D. S. Brewer, 1997, 9–34. Surveys the key concepts and topics involved in the retelling of tales and critical appraisals of such redactions.

Bruce, Alexander, 'Strategies for introducing Old and Middle English language and literature to beginning students', *SMART: Studies in Medieval and Renaissance Teaching* 7.2 (Fall 1999), 33–41.

Bruns, Gerald, 'Midrash and allegory', *The Literary Guide to the Bible*, Robert Alter and Frank Kermode (eds.), Cambridge: Harvard University Press, 1987, 625–46. Recovers theoretically robust understanding of allegory to explicate the efficacy of midrash, a Rabbinic approach to interpretation aware of the complex relations between God, text, individual and community.

Bullough, Vern L, 'On being a male in the Middle Ages', in Lees (ed.), 1994, 31–45. Explores medieval definitions of masculinity and the significance of virility in religious and medical discourses.

——, with G. W. Brewer, 'Medieval masculinities and modern interpretations: The problem of the Pardoner', in J. Murray (ed.), *Conflicted Identities and Multiple Masculinities: Men in the Medieval West*, New York: Garland Publishing, 1993, 93–110. Proposes that sexual and gender ambiguity was present in medieval society.

Burger, Glenn, 'Erotic desire . . . or "tee hee, I like my boys to be girls": Inventing with the body in Chaucer's *Miller's Tale*', in Cohen and Wheeler, 1997, 245–60. Argues that through the thematic of the 'nether ey' the *Miller's Tale* queers the masculinist system and opens a space for alternative gender analysis.

——, *Chaucer's Queer Nation*, Minneapolis: University of Minnesota Press, 2003. Engages queer and postcolonial theory to rethink Chaucer's engagement with gendered and community identity to rethink the relationship between the body and nation.

Burkhardt, Jacob, *The Civilization of the Renaissance in Italy*, New York: Penguin, 1990. Classic nineteenth-century analysis of the rise of Renaissance Humanism and the artistic, cultural and political transformations begun in thirteenth-century Italy.

Butler, Judith, 'Performative acts and gender constitution: An essay in phenomenology and feminist theory', in Sue-Ellen Case (ed.), *Performing Feminisms: Feminist Critical Theory and Theatre*, Baltimore: Johns Hopkins University Press, 1990, 270–82. An early and succinct statement of gender as discontinuous, stylized performance ultimately constituting a form and object of belief.

——, *Gender Trouble: Feminism and the Subversion of Identity*, New York: Routledge, 1990. Central to feminist and gender theories, this monograph has not only changed the perception of gender, sexuality and femininity, but also challenged the putative naturalness of these categories.

——, *Bodies that Matter: On the Discursive Limits of 'Sex'*, New York: Routledge, 1993. Develops the theories presented in *Gender Trouble*, focusing on the materiality of gender representation.

——, *Undoing Gender*, New York: Routledge, 2004. A reconsideration of the claims of performativity in *Gender Trouble* that questions gender norms as it investigates new forms of personhood and community, particularly alternative forms of family.

Bynum, Carolyn Walker, *Jesus as Mother: Studies in the Spirituality of the High Middle Ages*, Berkeley: University of California Press, 1982. Foundational text in the feminist analysis of medieval culture, religion and spirituality.

——, *Holy Feast and Holy Fast: The Religious Significance of Food to Medieval Women*, Berkeley: University of California Press, 1987. Analyses the significance of food for medieval female spirituality throughout the medieval period, including fasting, feasting, the Eucharist and anorexia.

Cadden, Joan, *Meanings of Sex Difference in the Middle Ages: Medicine, Science, and Culture*, New York: Cambridge University Press, 1993. Investigates how scientific, philosophical and medical conceptions of sexual difference in the later Middle Ages informed the cultural construction of gender and gender roles, including biological distinction, sexual desire, gender roles, marriage and reproduction.

Calabrese, Michael A., '"Make a mark that shows': Orphean song, Orphean sexuality, and the exile of Chaucer's Pardoner', *Viator: Medieval and Renaissance Studies*, 24 (1993), 269–86. Uses Genius's discussion of Orpheus in the *Romance of the Rose* to analyse Chaucer's Pardoner.

Cannon, Christopher, 'Form', in Strohm (ed.), *Middle English*, Oxford: Oxford University Press 2007, 177–90. Reassess the place and importance of the formal and aesthetic elements of Middle English texts.

——, *The Grounds of English Literature*, Oxford: Oxford University Press, 2004. Looks to texts from the twelfth and thirteenth centuries – like Layamon's *Brut*, the *Ormulum*, *The Owl and the Nightingale*, the *Ancrene Wisse* and *Katherine*-group, and the *Horn* child romances – as a source of literary variety and richness that laid the foundation for English literature.

Carlson, Cindy L. and Angela Jane Weisl (eds.), *Constructions of Widowhood and Virginity in the Middle Ages*, New York: St. Martin's Press, 1999. Twelve essays detailing the unstable and contested status of two seemingly stable gendered categories.

Carlson, David R. (ed.), *Richard Maidstone: Concordia (The Reconciliation of Richard II with London)*, Kalamazoo: Medieval Institute Publications, 2003. Extraordinary poem – written after the civic administrators of the city of London, who attempted to withhold payment from the crown, were forced to capitulate – that documents Richard II's royal entry into and reconciliation with London in 1392.

Carruthers, Mary, *The Book of Memory: A Study of Memory in Medieval Culture*, Cambridge: Cambridge University Press, 1996. A comprehensive study of the function and practice of memory in medieval culture and society drawing upon on literary theory, anthropology and psychology.

Chambers, E. K., *The Mediaeval Stage*, London: Oxford University Press, 1903. Argues for an evolutionary development of medieval drama which led from relatively simple liturgical and folk plays to increasingly complex and secularized urban cycle plays, or as it is still too often asserted, drama moved from the church, to the courtyard, and finally into the hall and city. This view was definitively disproved by O. B. Hardison in 1965.

Chance, Jane (ed.), *Women Medievalists and the Academy*, Madison: University of Wisconsin Press, 2005. Addresses the gaps in most accounts of the development of contemporary medieval studies by assessing the work of more than 70 female scholars and their contributions to the range of disciplines.

Christine de Pizan, *The Book of the City of Ladies*, Earl Jeffrey Richards (trans.), New York: Persea Books, 1989. Christine's learned apologetic against misogyny, slyly referencing Augustine's *City of God*, in which Christine converses with three allegorical interlocutors (Reason, Rectitude and Justice) who instruct her about the women without whose contributions civilization would not exist.

——, 'L'epistle au Dieu d'Amours', Madeline Jeay and Kathleen Garay (trans.), McMaster University Scriptorium, 2000, available online at <http://mw. mcmaster.ca/scriptorium/cdpizan8.html>. In which Christine, through reading a letter from the God of Love in the presence of Cupid and his court, criticizes Ovid (*The Arts of Love*) and Jean de Meun (*The Romance of the Rose*) for their misogyny.

Cixous, Hèléne, 'Laugh of the medusa', (Keith Cohen and Paula Cohen, trans.), *Signs* 1 (1976), 875–93. The famous articulation of transformative écriture féminine and 'writing the body', as informed by Lacanian psychoanalysis and Derridean deconstruction.

Clifford, James, *The Predicament of Culture: Twentieth-Century Ethnography, Literature, and Art*, Cambridge: Harvard University Press, 1988. A critical ethnography of Western thought that attempts to domesticate other cultures through anthropology, travel writing, artifact collecting and museum displays, and other disciplinary practices.

——, and George E. Marcus (eds.), *Writing Culture: The Poetics and Politics of Ethnography*, Berkeley: University of California Press, 1986. Nine essays critiquing different forms of writing about culture as imbued with persistent allegorical structures, teleological strategies and rhetorical tropes consistent with Western preconceptions.

Clopper, Lawrence M., 'The history and development of the Chester cycle', *Modern Philology* 75 (1978), 219–46. Traces the revision and performance history of the Chester cycle from its founding to its dissolution.

——, *Drama, Play and Game: English Festive Culture in the Medieval and Early Modern Period*, Chicago: University of Chicago Press, 2001. Revises traditional linear histories of early English drama, providing a philological inquiry into the terminology, examining the nature of the texts, performance history, official pronouncements and dramatic content of disparate works into the sixteenth century.

Cohen, Jeffrey Jerome, 'Postcolonial theory', available online at <http:// jjcohen.blogspot.com/2006/01/postcolonialtheory.html>. A brief excerpt from

Cohen's article on 'Postcolonial Theory' in *Women and Gender in Medieval Europe: An Encyclopedia*, Margaret Schaus (ed.), New York: Routledge, 2005.

——, *Medieval Identity Machines*, Minneapolis: University of Minnesota Press, 2003. Reads medieval literature and culture in the light of Deleuzian conceptions race, gender, sexuality and nationality in order to understand the fluidity of potentially 'posthuman' medieval subjectivities and identities.

—— (ed.), *The Postcolonial Middle Ages*, New York: St. Martin's Press, 2000. The first collection of essays about the intersections between medieval and postcolonial studies, concentrating on medieval British literature to reveal the practices by which non-English cultures are obscured or subsumed.

—— and Bonnie Wheeler (eds.), *Becoming Male in the Middle Ages*, New York: Garland Publishing, 1999. Seventeen essays that explore the construction of masculinity in relation to Christianity, sexuality, childhood, penance, discipline, drag, castration and other aspects of medieval masculinity and male subjectivity.

——, *Of Giants: Sex, Monsters and the Middle Ages*, Minneapolis: University of Minnesota Press, 1999. Offers a critical psychoanalytic assessment of identity formation that takes into account the philological and narrative representation of the monster, the intimate stranger who straddles the limits of selfhood and subjectivity.

——, 'Gowther among the dogs: Becoming inhuman c.1400', in Cohen and Wheeler (eds.), 1997, 219–44. Argues that the hybridity of Gowther's monstrous heritage and the fluid multiplicity of his subjectivity are foreclosed by his identification as God's child while simultaneously banishing the feminine from the narrative completely.

—— (ed.), *Monster Theory: Reading Culture*, Minneapolis: University of Minnesota Press, 1996. Analyses the liminal, monstrous forces and figures that threaten medieval society and need to be controlled. Includes Cohen's influential introductory essay, 'Monster Culture (Seven Theses)'.

Coletti, Theresa, *Mary Magdalene and the Drama of Saints: Theatre, Gender, and Religion in Late Medieval England*, Philadelphia: University of Pennsylvania Press, 2004. A cultural reading of the Digby play in relation to late medieval and specific local ideologies, literature, religious and gender negotiations.

——, 'Reading REED: History and the records of early English drama', in Lee Patterson (ed.), *Literary Practice and Social Change in Britain, 1380–1530*, Berkeley: University of California Press, 1990, 248–84. Critiques the limitations of a historicist approach that relies on documentary evidence of the origins of drama and performance history as the basis of literary analysis.

Colledge, Edmund and James Walsh (ed.), *A Book of Showings to the Anchoress Julian of Norwich*, Toronto: Pontifical Institute of Mediaeval Studies, 1978. Academic edition of Julian's *Showings* with critical apparatus.

Cooney, Helen (ed.), *Nation, Court and Culture: New Essays on Fifteenth-Century English Poetry*, Dublin: Four Courts Press, 2001. Suggest that fifteenth-century literature, far from being dull, constitutes a body of work that self-consciously engages with political, cultural and aesthetic changes.

Coote, Lesley, 'Chaucer and the visual image: Learning, teaching, assessing', in Ashton and Sylvester (eds.), *Teaching Chaucer*, New York: Palgrave Macmillan, 2007, 139–152.

Copeland, Rita, *Rhetoric, Hermeneutics, and Translation in the Middle Ages: Academic Traditions and Vernacular Texts*, Cambridge: Cambridge University Press, 1991. Surveys the role of language, translation and education in the late Middle Ages, and the contribution of the Lollard movement.

——, 'Why women can't read: Medieval hermeneutics, statutory law, and the Lollard heresy', in S. S. Heinzelman and Z. B. Wiseman (eds.), *Representing Women: Law, Literature, and Feminism*, Durham: Duke University Press, 1994, 253–86. Considers medieval interpretation in light of legal restrictions on Lollardy.

——, *Pedagogy, Intellectuals, and Dissent in the Later Middle Ages: Lollardy and Ideas of Learning*, Cambridge: Cambridge University Press, 2001. Analyses the place of pedagogy, especially lay education, and the function of intellectual work in the formation and transmission of medieval Lollard dissent and heterodoxy.

Coss, Peter R., 'Aspects of cultural diffusion in medieval England: Robin Hood', in Stephen Knight (ed.), *Robin Hood: An Anthology of Scholarship and Criticism*, Cambridge: D.S. Brewer, 1999, 329–43. Investigates the cultural forces which result in the formation and distribution of the legend.

Crampton, Georgia Ronan (ed.), *The Shewings of Julian of Norwich*, Kalamazoo, MI: Medieval Institute Publications, 1994. An edition of Julian's 'long text' based primarily upon British Library MS Sloane 2499 (c. 1650).

Crane, Susan, *The Performance of Self: Ritual, Clothing and Identity During the Hundred Years' War*, Philadelphia: University of Pennsylvania Press, 2002. Examines the literary and cultural formation and performance of identity, focusing on England and France in the fourteenth and fifteenth centuries.

——, 'Knights in disguise: Identity and incognito in fourteenth-century chivalry', in F. R. P. Akehurst and S. C. Van D'Elden (eds.), *The Stranger in Medieval Society*, Minnesota: University of Minneapolis Press, 1997, 63–79. Explores the tension between the private and the public that is enacted through self-presentation and dramatization.

——, *Gender and Romance in Chaucer's Canterbury Tales*, Princeton: Princeton University Press, 1994. Examines Chaucer's relationship to English and French romance and finds that gender, especially late-medieval complications and elaborations of heterosexual relationships, is romance's key concern.

Culler, Jonathan D., *Structuralist Poetics: Structuralism, Linguistics and the Study of Literature*, London: Routledge & Kegan Paul, 1975. Introduced French structuralist thought and literary analysis to an Anglo-American audience.

Curry, Walter Clyde, *Chaucer and the Mediaeval Sciences*, (2nd ed.), New York: Barnes & Noble, 1960. Still definitive, presents eleven essays on different aspects of Chaucer's use of medieval medicine, physiognomy, juridical astrology and dream psychology.

Damian, Peter, *The Book of Gomorrah: An Eleventh-Century Treatise Against Clerical Homosexual Practices*, Pierre J. Payer (trans.), Waterloo, Ontario, Canada: Wilfrid Laurier University Press, 1982. The only medieval tract devoted exclusively to homosexuality defines sex between men, as well as masturbation, as sins 'against nature' and the cause moral disorder and madness brought about by immoderate lust.

Daumer, Elisabeth D., 'Queer ethics: Or, the challenge of bisexuality lesbian ethics', *Hypatia* 7.4 (1992), 91–105. Argues that bisexuality, because it violates bipartite ideas of fixed gender, offers an ethical alternative because 'bisexual and transgender movements expose and politicize the middle ground' (99).

Davis, Kathleen, 'Time behind the veil: The media, the Middle Ages, and Orientalism now', in Jeffrey Jerome Cohen (ed.), *The Postcolonial Middle Ages*, New York: Palgrave, 2000, 105–22. Davis revisions postcolonial medieval studies in a three-fold discussion of contemporary culture, critical theory (specifically Said's *Orientalism*) and Chaucer's *Man of Law's Tale*.

Dean, James M. (ed.), *Six Ecclesiastical Satires*, Kalamazoo: Medieval Institute Publications, 1991. Editions of the Middle English *Piers the Plowman's Crede, The Plowman's Tale, Jack Upland, Friar Daw's Reply, Upland's Rejoinder*, and *Why I Can't Be a Nun*.

——, *Medieval English Political Writings*, Kalamazoo: Medieval Institute Publications, 1996. Includes political prophecies (like *The Prophecy of Merlin* and *Ercyldoun's Prophecy*) as well as anticlerical poems and documents (like 'Thou That Sellest the Worde of God'), literature concerning Richard II and the Peasant's Revolt ('The Letter of John Ball' and Knighton's 'Address of the Commons'), poems against simony and monetary abuse ('The Simonie' and 'London Lickpenny'), and a variety of plowman texts ('Song of the Husbandman' and 'God Spede the Plough').

Delany, Sheila, '"Mothers to think back through": Who are they? The ambiguous example of Christine de Pizan', in Finke and Shichtman (eds.), 1987, 177–97. Argues that although Christine mounted a spirited textual defense against misogynistic writers and called for a recognition of this injustice, she ultimately reaffirmed conventional social roles.

——, *Medieval Literary Politics: Shapes of Ideology*, Manchester: Manchester University Press, 1990. Collection of previously published essays, including 'Mothers to think back through'.

——, *A Legend of Holy Women: A Translation of Osbern Bokenham's Legends of Holy Women*, Notre Dame: University of Notre Dame Press, 1992a. Based upon the 1938 Early English Text Society edition, offers a translation of the first all-female collection of saints' lives in English (c. 1443).

——, 'History, Politics, and Christine Studies: A Polemical Reply', in Margaret Brabant (ed.), *Politics, Gender and Genre: The Political Thought of Christine de Pizan*, Boulder, CO: Westview, 1992b, 193–206. Responds to those criticizing her understanding of Christine's political conservatism.

——, *Impolitic Bodies: Poetry, Saints, and Society in Fifteenth-Century England: The Work of Osbern Bokenham*, Oxford: Oxford University Press, 1997. Analysis of the fifteenth-century Augustinian Friar's *Legends of Holy Women* in terms of his sources and influences, treatment of the body, and construction of the body politic during the fifteenth century's crises of succession and war.

Deleuze, Gilles and Félix Guattari, *Anti-Oedipus: Capitalism and Schizophrenia*, New York: Viking Press, 1977. Influential critique of psychoanalysis and capitalism ('schizoanalysis') that conceives of desire as a 'desiring machine', of the social 'body without organs', and a 'deterritorialized' 'rhizomatic' sense of fluid identity.

——, *A Thousand Plateaus: Capitalism and Schizophrenia*, Minneapolis: University of Minnesota Press, 1987. The second part of the critique organized around an accumulation of 'plateaus' or 'fields of intensity' rather than chapters, a 'rhizomatic' organization rather than an 'arborescent' hierarchy in which the 'nomad' is favoured over the 'apparatus'.

Derrida, Jacques, *Of Grammatology*, Gayatri Chakravorty Spivak (trans.), Baltimore: Johns Hopkins University Press, 1976. Probably Derrida's most influential work, in which he initiated 'grammatology', or the deconstructive analysis of writing systems, their associated metaphysical preconceptions and controlling tropes, and a developed series of concepts crucial to deconstruction, including *différance*, logocentrism, trace and the supplement.

——, 'Structure, sign, and play in the discourse of the human sciences', in *Writing and Difference*, Chicago: University of Chicago Press, 1978, 278–93. Offers a remarkable critique of the limitations of structuralism and helped initiate what has become deconstruction and post-structuralism.

Dinshaw, Carolyn, 'Pale faces: Race, religion, and affect in Chaucer's texts and their readers', *Studies in the Age of Chaucer*, 23 (2001), 19–41. Deals with the production and reception of alterity, race and religion in Chaucer's works through an autobiographical lens.

——, *Getting Medieval: Sexualities and Communities, Pre- and Postmodern*, Durham: Duke University Press, 1999. Applies the queer 'touch' to a range of disparate texts (for example the *Cook's Tale*, the Lollard's *Twelve Conclusions*, Robert Gluck's *Margery Kempe*, and Tarantino's *Pulp Fiction*) that transect time, place, genre and circumstance, and engage with sexualities.

——, 'Getting medieval: *Pulp Fiction*, Gawain, Foucault', in Dolores W. Frese and Katherine O' Keefe (eds.), *The Book and the Body*, Notre Dame: University of Notre Dame Press, 1997, 116–63. Early version of what became the final chapter in *Getting Medieval* ('Getting Medieval: Pulp Fiction, Foucault, and the Uses of the Past').

——, 'Chaucer's queer touches/A queer touches Chaucer', *Exemplaria* 7 (1995), 76–92. Considers Chaucer's Pardoner and sets out the notion of a queer theory which 'touches' or 'vibrates' across specific moments in time, culture and texts.

——, *Chaucer's Sexual Poetics*, Madison: University of Wisconsin Press, 1989. A revolutionary study of medieval sexuality that offers new ways of engaging with the representation of gender and sexuality.

Doane, A. N. and C. B. Pasternack (eds.), *Vox Intextua: Orality and Textuality in the Middle Ages*, Madison: University of Wisconsin Press, 1991. Contributors discuss the semiotic, physical and social aspects of medieval oral production and reception.

Dobson, Richard Barrie, *The Peasants' Revolt of 1381* (2nd ed.), Basingstroke, Hampshire: Macmillan Press, 1983. Still the standard history of the 1381 Rebellion.

Donaldson, E. Talbot, *Speaking of Chaucer*, London: Athlone Press, 1970. A sustained exercise in the methodology of close literary reading, including the influential essays 'Chaucer the Pilgrim', 'Idiom of Popular Poetry in the Miller's Tale' and 'The Myth of Courtly Love'.

——, (ed. and trans.), *Will's Vision of Piers Plowman: An Alliterative Verse Translation*, New York: Norton, 1990. Donaldson's edition and translation of *Piers Plowman*.

Dronke, Peter, *Women Writers of the Middle Ages: A Critical Study of Texts from Perpetua († 203) to Marguerite Porete († 1310)*, Cambridge: Cambridge University

Press, 1984. An early and still important study of medieval women's writing from across Europe.

Duggan, Joseph J., 'Medieval epic as popular historiography: Appropriation of historical knowledge in the vernacular epic', *Gundriss der Roamanischen Literaturen des Mittelalters*, 11 (1981), 285–311. An exploration of the relationship between facts and narrative, genre and language, and the nature of authority and truth in the *chanson de geste*.

Eagleton, Terry, *Criticism and Ideology: A Study in Marxist Literary Theory*, London: NLB, 1976. Reestablish a dynamic materialist criticism that brings Marxism together with literary criticism to offer a compelling account of ideology and the social pressures ideological forces bring to bear on literary production.

——, *Literary Theory: An Introduction*, Minneapolis: University of Minnesota Press, 1996. An essential though sometimes polemical introduction to the broader movements of literary theory, including the rise of English, phenomenology, structuralism, semiotics, post-structuralism and psychoanalysis – all of which are understood in terms of their political work and consequences.

Eco, Umberto, *Travels in Hyperreality*, New York: Harcourt Brace, 1986. Includes the two important essays, 'Dreaming the Middle Ages' (61–72) and 'Living in the Middle Ages' (73–84).

Edwards, Robert (ed.), *John Lydgate: Troy Book: Selections*, Kalamazoo: Medieval Institute Publications, 1998. Selections from one of the longest poems in Middle English.

——, *John Lydgate: Siege of Thebes*, Kalamazoo: Medieval Institute Publications, 2001. Only Middle English version of the story of Thebes, here updating Eerdman and Ekwall's two volume edition (Early English Text Society, Extra Series 108, 125) from London, British Library Arundel 119.

Eisenstein, Elizabeth L., *The Printing Press as an Agent of Change: Communications and Cultural Transformations in Early-Modern Europe*, Cambridge: Cambridge University Press, 1980. Seminal study concerning the cultural impact of the introduction and dissemination of the printing press and moveable type.

Ellis, Steve, *Chaucer at Large: The Poet in the Modern Imagination*, Minneapolis: University of Minnesota Press, 2000. Answers the question posed in the first sentence, 'Where in the last 150 years do we find Chaucer at large (i.e. outside universities)?' and analyses the modern reception of Chaucer in popular culture.

Emmerson, Richard K. (ed.), *Approaches to Teaching Medieval English Drama*, New York: The Modern Language Association of America, 1990.

Enders, Jody, *Rhetoric and the Origins of Medieval Drama*, Ithaca: Cornell University Press, 1992. Examines the relationship between legal or forensic and dramatic or disputational discourse to argue that legal as well as liturgical ritual was a source for what became medieval drama.

Evans, Ruth, Sarah Salih and Anke Bernau (eds.), *Medieval Virginities*, Toronto: University of Toronto Press, 2003. Twelve essays engaging the contested and paradoxical status of the both female and male virgins in medieval Europe.

Fanon, Frantz, *The Wretched of the Earth*, Constance Farrington (trans.), New York: Grove Press, 1963. A trenchant exploration of the psychological effects of colonization and linguistic domination on both individuals and nations, and a précis for the effects of violence on the colonized and the potential for cathartic violence as a means of liberation.

——, *Black Skin, White Masks*, New York: Grove Press, 1967. Analyses psycho-analytically the feelings of dependency and inadequacy that those in a minority culture (in this case, Blacks) experience within the dominant culture (Whites) and the mechanisms that propel the subjugated to embrace the culture of the colonial oppressor.

Fee, Christopher, 'ENG 317: Studies in Middle English literature & the language of the age of Chaucer course syllabus', *Gettysburg College*, available online at <http://public.gettysburg.edu/~cfee/courses/English317.html#info>.

——, 'Medieval drama at Gettysburg College', *Gettysburg College*, available online at <http://public.gettysburg.edu/~cfee/courses/English312/Medieval%20 Drama%20Homepage.html#Webpages>.

——, Feinstein, Sandy, 'Teaching Chaucer cross-culturally', *SMART: Studies in Medieval and Renaissance Teaching* 7.1 (Spring 1999), 30–42.

Ferrante, Joan, *Woman as Image in Medieval Literature from the Twelfth Century to Dante*, New York: Columbia University Press, 1975. Early feminist analysis of the representation of women in medieval literature.

Fiedler, Leslie A., *Love and Death in the American Novel*, New York: Criterion, 1960. Influential psychoanalytic analysis which found an obsession with death and sexuality in the American novel.

Finke, Laurie M., *Feminist Theory, Women's Writing*, Ithaca: Cornell University Press, 1992. Important analysis of feminist theory.

—— and Martin B. Schichtman (eds.), *Medieval Texts and Contemporary Readers*, Ithaca: Cornell University Press, 1987. Varied collection applying contemporary theory to literary texts.

Finucane, Ronald C., *Rescue of the Innocents: Endangered Children in Medieval Miracles*, New York: Macmillan, 1997. Using accounts recorded at shrines, demonstrates that parents sought saintly intervention for their ill, injured or dead children, thus demonstrating medieval parents' care and commitment for their children.

Fitzgibbons, Moira, ' "Cross-voiced" assignments and the critical "I" ', in Ashton and Sylvester (eds.), *Teaching Chaucer*, New York: Palgrave Macmillan, 2007, 65–80.

Forest-Hill, Lynn, *Transgressive Language in Medieval English Drama: Signs of Challenge and Change*, Aldershot: Ashgate, 2000. An historicist analysis of medieval drama that reveals a space between dramatic representations of society and the actuality where social critique and religious instruction can operate.

Foucault, Michel, *Language, Counter-Memory, Practice: Selected Essays and Inter-views*, Ithaca: Cornell University Press, 1977. Essential set of essays, including 'What is an Author?'

——, *The History of Sexuality, Vol. 1*, New York: Pantheon, 1978. Foundational text in gender and cultural analysis that sets forth the 'Repressive Hypothesis'.

——, *The Archaeology of Knowledge*, New York: Pantheon Books, 1972. Program-matic text that offers an early attempt to outline Foucault's 'archeological' (as opposed to the later 'genealogical') approach to the theoretical problems and hidden assumptions that organize our approach to knowledge, history, language, and practice.

——, *Discipline and Punish: The Birth of the Prison*, New York: Pantheon Books, 1977. Revolutionary and influential genealogical study of the prison, of technologies of discipline and cultures of surveillance, including 'the panopticon' and 'carceral archipelago', and of the production of subjectivity as constituted in the dialectic of discursive and non-discursive practices.

——, 'Nietzsche, genealogy, history', in Paul Rabinow and Nikolas Rose (eds.), *The Essential Foucault*, New York: New Press, 1994, 351–69. Shifts historical analysis from metaphysical history, as the pursuit of transcendent origins, to a concern for excavating the histories of injustice upon which knowledge is built.

Fradenburg, Louise O. Aranye, *City, Marriage, Tournament: Arts of Rule in Late Medieval Scotland*, Madison: University of Wisconsin Press, 1991. An influential study that argues that the city is the locale in which change and artifice become more visible and where the public and the private interact.

——, 'The love of thy neighbor', in K. Lochrie, P. McCracken and J. A. Schultz (eds.), *Constructing Medieval Sexuality*, Minneapolis: University of Minnesota Press, 1997, 135–57. Takes a Lacanian approach to courtly love.

——, and Carka Freccero (eds.), *Premodern Sexualities*, New York: Routledge, 1995. A collection of rigorous approaches to the history of sexuality from a variety of perspectives and disciplines that call for a rethinking of the categories of history and sexuality.

——, *Sacrifice Your Love: Psychoanalysis, Historicism, Chaucer*, Minneapolis: University of Minnesota Press, 2002. Redraws psychoanalytical theory (by tracing a 'history of the signifier'), historicism and Chaucer's texts through a consideration of the desire for sacrifice.

Fries, Maureen and Jeanie Watson (eds.), *Approaches to Teaching the Arthurian Tradition*, New York: The Modern Language Association of America, 1992

Frye, Northrup, *Anatomy of Criticism: Four Essays*, Princeton: Princeton University Press, 1957. Provides a psychoanalytic treatment of medieval romance and literature, and reads it in the light of dreams and archetypal quests.

Fugelso, Karl (ed.), *Memory and Medievalism*, Cambridge: D. S. Brewer, 2007. Nine essays covering material from the Anglo-Saxons to *A Confederacy of Dunces* and detailing how the medieval period is remembered, reconditioned and recycled in the present.

Ganim, John M., *Chaucerian Theatricality*, Princeton: Princeton University Press, 1990. Provides a reading of Chaucer's troubled relations and negotiations with popular literary forms, drawing on Bahktian notions of the 'carnivalesque'.

——, 'The literary uses of the new history', in James M. Dean (ed.), *The Idea of Medieval Literature: New Essays on Chaucer and Medieval Culture in Honor of Donald R. Howard*, Newark: University of Delaware Press, 1992, 209–26. An incisive account of the history of the Annales school and its progeny.

Gans, Eric, 'Sacrificing Culture', *Chronicles of Love and Resentment*, No. 184 (9 October 1999), available online at <http://www.anthropoetics.ucla.edu/views/vw184.htm>. On the possibilities of deconstructing sacrificial culture.

Gates, Henry Louis, Jr., *Race, Writing and Difference*, Chicago: University of Chicago Press, 1986. Classic analysis of race as an analytical concept with which to interrogate writing and the construction of racial otherness.

Geertz, Clifford C., *The Interpretation of Cultures: Selected Essays*, New York: Basic, 1973. Influential collection of essays demonstrating Geertz's anthropological practice of 'thick description'.

Gellrich, Jesse M., *The Idea of the Book in the Middle Ages: Language Theory, Mythology, and Fiction*, Ithaca: Cornell University Press, 1985. Early argument against conventional notions of periodization, using a Derridean 'idea of the book' to interrogate medieval efforts to maintain homogeneity and logocentrism, the idea of presence or being in a text, particularly through the work of vernacular poets like Dante and Chaucer.

Georgianna, Linda, 'The Protestant Chaucer', in C. David Benson and Elizabeth Ann Robertson (eds.), *Chaucer's Religious Tales*, Cambridge: D. S. Brewer, 1990, 55–69. Contrasts the 'protestant' Chaucer, a product of Reformation apologists like John Foxe (and his book of martyrs) and subsequent editors, with the historically 'Catholic' Chaucer and traces the affect of the protestant Chaucer on subsequent scholarship.

Gezari, Janet, 'Gilbert and Susan Gubar's *The Madwoman in the Attic*', *Essays in Criticism* 56.3 (2006), 264–79. Reassesses Gilbert and Gubar's landmark study.

Gibaldi, Joseph (ed.), *Approaches to Teaching Chaucer's Canterbury Tales*, New York: The Modern Language Association of America, 1980.

Gibson, Gail McMurray, *The Theater of Devotion: East Anglian Drama and Society in the Late Middle Ages*, Chicago: University of Chicago Press, 1989. Seminal interdisciplinary study that reassesses fifteenth-century drama and dramatic episodes through detailed investigation into the public and private manifestations of spirituality in medieval East Anglia (Norfolk and Suffolk).

Giladi, Avner, *Children of Islam: Concepts of Childhood in Medieval Muslim Society*, New York: St. Martin's, 1992. Treats infancy, education and child mortality by examining medical, juricidal and theological treatises, as well as belles-lettres, biography, and the Quran.

Gilbert, Sandra M. and Susan Gubar, *The Madwoman in the Attic: The Woman Writer and the Nineteenth-Century Literary Imagination*, New Haven: Yale University Press, 1975. Groundbreaking feminist literary analysis of women figures in, particularly, the nineteenth-century novel.

Girard, René, *Things Hidden Since the Foundation of the World*, Stanford: Stanford University Press, 1978. Analysis of the foundational role of the mimeticism, scapegoating and violence that organize culture and examination of the relationship between violence and the sacred.

Glück, Robert, *Margery Kempe*, New York: Serpent's Tail, 1994. Novel graphically parallels the desire of 'G' (the narrator) for his younger lover 'G' with a re-imagining of Margery Kempe's lust for Jesus, thereby queering the *Book of Margery Kempe*.

Glasscoe, Marion (ed.), *Julian of Norwich, A Revelation of Love*, Exeter: University of Exeter Press, 1976. An edition of the Sloane version of the Long Text.

Glover, David and Cora Kaplan, *Genders*, New York: Routledge, 2000. Traces the debate concerning the idea of gender from 18th to its current use in gender theory, including feminist, masculinist and queer theory approaches.

Goldberg, P. J. P., *Medieval England: A Social History 1250–1550*, New York: Oxford University Press, 2004. Provides a broad and current survey of late medieval English social history, focusing on issues like social structures, classes and the economy by focusing on common people as well as the political and religious elites.

Goldie, Mathew Boyd (ed.), *Middle English Literature: A Historical Sourcebook*, Oxford: Blackwell, 2003. Collection of primary historical texts organized by topic and linking those historical texts to specific literary works of the time.

Goodhart, Sandor, *Sacrificing Commentary: Reading the End of Literature*, Baltimore: Johns Hopkins University Press, 1996. Following Girard, develops important insights into the foundational role of mimeticism and sacrifice and extends these concerns to show how great literature – of which he includes Sophocles, Shakespeare, and the Hebrew Bible – already performs the function of critical theory that commentary ordinarily reserves for itself.

Goodich, Michael, *The Unmentionable Vice: Homosexuality in the Later Medieval Period*, Santa Barbara: Rose-Erickson Press, 1979. Early monograph, linking sodomy and heresy, includes a 30-page translation from thirteenth-century inquisition records of Jacques Fournier.

Goodman, Jennifer R., *Chivalry and Exploration 1298–1630*, Woodbridge, Suffolk: Boydell Press, 1998. Undertakes a comparative analysis of chivalric romances and histories of explorers and highlights the connections between the two.

Gottlieb, Beatrice, 'The Problem of Feminism in the fifteenth century', in Julius Kirshner and Suzanne F. Wemple (eds.), *Women of the Medieval World*, Oxford: Basil Blackwell, 1985, 337–62. Addresses medieval misogyny primarily through the works of Christine de Pizan.

Gower, John, *Vox clamantis, The Major Latin Works of John Gower*, Eric W. Stockton (trans.), Seattle: University of Washington Press, 1962. Translation of Gower's 10,000 line Latin poem decrying the 1381 Revolt.

Grady, Frank, 'The generation of 1399', in Emily Steiner and Candace Barrington (eds.), *The Letter of the Law: Legal Practice and Literary Production in Medieval England*, Ithaca: Cornell University Press, 2002, 202–29. Attempts to define a 'Lancastrian poetic' by examining *Mum and Sothsegger, Richard the Redeless* and John Gower's *Cronica Tripertita*.

Gramsci, Antonio, *A Gramsci Reader: Selected Writings, 1916–1935*, David Forgacs (ed.), London: Lawrence and Wishart, 1988. Key essays by the Italian Marxist.

Gravdal, Kathryn, *Ravishing Maidens: Writing Rape in Medieval French Literature and Law*, Philadelphia: University of Pennsylvania Press, 1991. Examines 'the naturalization of the subordination of women in medieval French culture by examining representations of rape in different discursive genres, both literary and legal' (1).

Green, Richard Firth, 'The sexual normality of Chaucer's Pardoner', *Medievalia* 8 (1982), 351–8. Argues that the Pardoner is effeminate, and thus linked to carnality, and not homosexuality.

Greenblatt, Stephen, *Renaissance Self-Fashioning from More to Shakespeare*, Chicago: University of Chicago Press, 1980. A foundational text of New Historicism that examines the process of subjectivation – 'self fashioning' – in sixteenth-century figures like More, Tyndale, Wyatt, Spencer and Shakespeare.

——, 'Towards a poetics of culture', in H. Aram Veeser (ed.), *New Historicism*, New York: Routledge, 1989, 1–14. One of the more important articulations of the tenets of New Historicism.

——, *Learning to Curse: Essays in Early Modern Culture*, New York: Routledge, 1990. Collection of essays further developing Greenblatt's sense of New Historicism, or what he terms 'cultural poetics'.

——, *Marvelous Possessions: The Wonder of the New World*, Oxford: Clarendon Press, 1991. Examines European responses to the New World as reflected in travel accounts from Mandeville, Columbus and Frobisher, compelling 'at the level of the anecdote' (2).

——, *The Norton Anthology of English Literature, Vol. 1*, 8th ed., New York: Norton, 2006. Most recent edition of the venerable anthology, now updated to reflect a broader range of texts and languages.

Grim, Edward, 'The murder of Thomas Becket', from *Vita S. Thomae, Cantuariensis Archepiscopi et Martyris*, James Robertson (ed.), *Materials for the Life of Thomas Becket* (7 vols). London: Rolls Series, 1875–1885, available online at <http://www.fordham.edu/halsall/source/grim-becket.html>. Eyewitness account of Becket's martyrdom.

Guillaume de Lorris and Jean de Meun, *The Romance of the Rose*, Oxford: Oxford University Press, 1999. Translation of this key late-medieval text which influenced writers throughout Europe.

Hahn, Thomas, 'The difference the Middle Ages makes: Color and race before the modern world', *Journal of Medieval and Early Modern Studies* 31.1 (2001), 1–37. Argues that medievalists should 'recognize race studies as something other than a fashionable, politically driven niche subject whose single-minded, universalizing models import inappropriate or irrelevant interests to the study of the past' (4).

Halsall, Paul, 'Medieval history in the movies', *Internet Medieval Sourcebook*, available online at <http://www.fordham.edu/halsall/medfilms.html>.

——, *Internet Medieval Sourcebook*, Fordham University, available online at <http://www.fordham.edu/halsall/Sbook.html>.

Hanawalt, Barbara A., *Growing Up in Medieval London: The Experience of Childhood in History*, London: Oxford University Press, 1993. Details the experience of childhood in fourteenth- and fifteenth-century London based upon courtesy and conduct books, court records, literary texts and historical archives.

——, 'Medievalists and the study of childhood', *Speculum* 77.2 (2002), 440–60. Assesses the promise of medieval children's studies.

——, 'Ballads and bandits: Fourteenth-century outlaws and the Robin Hood poems', in Stephen Knight (ed.), *Robin Hood: An Anthology of Scholarship and Criticism*, Cambridge: D. S. Brewer, 1999, 263–84. Explores fictional and historical accounts of medieval outlaws, those on the margins of society.

——, *Ties That Bound: Peasant Families in Medieval England*, London: Oxford University Press, 1986. A compelling and detailed view of everyday life among the lower classes in medieval England based upon a wealth of archival sources that argues the basic structure of the family has not changed substantially since the Middle Ages.

Hanna, Ralph, *London Literature, 1300–1380*, Cambridge: Cambridge University Press, 2005. Turns to London's textual production in the Edwardian era, prior to Richard II and Henry IV, defining generally neglected London texts on the basis of manuscript, handwriting, and dialect and calling Langland London's most important Edwardian writer.

Hansen, Elaine Tuttle, *Chaucer and the Fictions of Gender*, Berkeley: University of California Press, 1992. Addresses how masculinist assumptions are smuggled into critical approaches that call themselves 'humanist', thus reinforcing fictions of gender.

Hardison, O. B., *Christian Rite and Christian Drama in the Middle Ages: Essays in the Origin and Early History of Modern Drama*, Baltimore: Johns Hopkins Press, 1965. Put to rest the linear, evolutionary paradigm of medieval drama.

Harty, Kevin J., 'Arthurian film: An *Arthuriana*/Camelot project bibliography', *The Camelot Project at the University of Rochester*, available online at <http://www.library.rochester.edu/camelot/ACPBIBS/HARTY.HTM>.

——, *The Reel Middle Ages: American, Western and Eastern European, Middle Eastern, and Asian Films about Medieval Europe*, Jefferson, NC: McFarland, 2006.

Heng, Geraldine, 'The romance of England: *Richard Coer de Lyon*, Saracens, Jews, and the politics of race and nation', in Jeffrey Jerome Cohen (ed.), *The Postcolonial Middle Ages*, New York: St. Martin's Press, 2000, 135–71. Argues that *Richard Coer de Lyon* transforms the cannibalistic memory of the First Crusade into romance through the heroism of King Arthur.

——, *Empire of Magic: Medieval Romance and the Politics of Cultural Fantasy*, New York: Columbia University Press, 2003. Argues that romance emerged in the twelfth century as a response to the horrors of the Crusades ('cannibalism performed by Latin Christian crusaders on Turkish Muslim cadavers at Ma'arra an-Numan in Syria, in 1098, during the First Crusade' [334]) and shows the role of romance in the development of English national identity, particularly in the figure of Arthur.

Henryson, Robert. *Testament of Cresseid*, Bruce Dickens (ed.), London: Faber and Faber, 1925. Henryson's rewriting of Chaucer's *Troilus and Criseyde*.

Hilton, Walter, *The Scale of Perfection*, Thomas H. Bestul (ed.), Kalamazoo: Medieval Institute Publications, 2000. A devotional treatise concerning the spiritual pursuit of the New Jerusalem by the head of the Augustine Canons at Thurgarton Priory, Nottinghamshire.

Hobsbawm, E. J., *Bandits*, New York: Delacorte Press, 1971. Seminal historical study of outlaws and their paradoxical position in society.

——, *Primitive Rebels: Studies in Archaic Forms of Social Movement in the 19th and 20th Centuries*, New York: Praeger, 1963. Describes 'archaic forms of social agitation: Robin Hood type, rural secret societies, various peasant revolutionary movements of the millenarian sort, pre-industrial urban "mobs" and their riots, some labour sects and the use of ritual in early labour and revolutionary organizations' (1).

Holland, Norman, *The Dynamics of Literary Response*, New York: Oxford University Press, 1968. Early reader-response investigation using psychodynamic theory.

Holloway, Julia Bolton (ed.), *Birgitta of Sweden's Revelations: Saint Bride and Her Book Translated from Latin and Middle English with Introduction, Notes and Interpretative Essay*, Newburyport: Focus Books, 1992. Translates Birgitta's life from two medieval manuscripts, one in Latin and the other in Middle English.

——, *The Mystics' Internet*, available online at <http://www.umilta.net/mystics.html>. Excellent source of online sources related to medieval mystics and mysticism, including texts, translations, sources and images.

Holsinger, Bruce W., *Neomedievalism, Neoconservatism, and the War on Terror*, Chicago: Prickly Paradigm Press, 2007. Argues that the neoconservatives of the Bush Administration have manipulated a politically polemical notion of the Middle Ages, termed neomedievalism, for partisan political and foreign policy objectives.

——, *The Premodern Condition: Medievalism and the Making of Theory*, Chicago: University of Chicago Press, 2005. An important contribution to critical theory, medievalism and medieval studies, this book highlights the centrality of the medieval era in philosophical, literary-critical and sociological theories developed especially in 1960s France.

——, *Music, Body and Desire in Medieval Culture: Hildegard of Bingen to Chaucer, Stanford*: Stanford University Press, 2001. A wide-ranging study of twelfth- through fifteenth-century vernacular and Latin texts that reads medieval musical practice and ideology as a means of expressing physicality and bodily desires.

Horobin, Simon, 'Teaching the language of Chaucer manuscripts', in Ashton and Sylvester (eds.), *Teaching Chaucer*, New York: Palgrave Macmillan, 2007, 96–104.

Howard, Donald R., *The Idea of the Canterbury Tales*, Berkeley: University of California Press, 1976. Influential reading of the *Tales* that finds it 'unfinished but complete'.

Hudson, Anne, *The Premature Reformation: Wycliffite Texts and Lollard History*, Oxford: Clarendon Press, 1988. Groundbreaking history of Wycliff's writings and their use by the Lollards that launched the contemporary study of Lollardy in medieval studies.

Hudson, Harriet, 'Teaching medieval literature with medieval books', *Teaching the Middle Ages III: Studies in Medieval and Renaissance Teaching III*, Robert V. Graybill, Judy G. Hample, Robert L. Kindrick and Robert E. Lovell. (eds.), Warrensburg, MO: Central Missouri State University, 1989.

Ingham, Patricia Clare, *Sovereign Fantasies: Arthurian Romance and the Making of Britain*, Philadelphia: University of Pennsylvania Press, 2001. Describes the symbolic work the Arthurian legends do to create the 'sovereign fantasy' of a united English nation, through appropriation of Celtic legend.

——, and Michelle R. Warren (eds.), *Postcolonial Moves: Medieval through Modern*, New York: Palgrave Macmillan, 2003. Series of essays interrogating contemporary formulations of the postcolonial that image a unified premodern Europe as the basis of their theorizing.

Internet Medieval Sourcebook, Paul Halsall (ed.), online at <http://www.fordham.edu/halsall/sbook.html>. Provides a wide range of excerpted and complete primary medieval texts organized by subject area and include legal, literary, religious and nationally specific materials. The single best medieval website on the Internet.

Irigaray, Luce, 'La Mystérique', *Speculum of the Other Woman*, Ithaca, NY: Cornell University Press, 1985, 191–202. A nearly untranslatable term, 'La Mystérique' indicates mystic and mysticism, the mysterious hysteric, and femaleness, all of which point to the mystery of God and a space of liberation outside the masculine symbolic.

Irvine, Martin and Deborah Everhart, *The Labyrinth*, Georgetown University, available online at <http://labyrinth.georgetown.edu/>.

Jameson, Fredric, *Marxism and Form: Twentieth-Century Dialectical Theories of*

Literature, Princeton: Princeton University Press, 1971. Attempts a structural Marxist reading of literature that takes seriously the material forms of production and consumption.

——, *The Political Unconscious: Narrative as a Socially Symbolic Act*, Ithaca: Cornell University Press, 1981. An important Marxist study of romance dealing with personal expression, political mediations and social control.

Jamison, Carol. 'King Arthur online: A brief navigational tour of a web-enhanced Arthurian survey course', *SMART: Studies in Medieval and Renaissance Teaching* 12.1 (Spring 2005), 65–79.

Jauss, Hans Robert, *Toward an Aesthetic of Reception*, Minneapolis: University of Minnesota Press, 1982. The preeminent statement of what has developed into reception theory.

Jokinen, Anniina, *The Luminarium*, available online at <http://www.luminarium.org/lumina.htm>.

Jones, Terry, *Chaucer's Knight: The Portrait of a Medieval Mercenary*, London: Methuen, 1994. Important and controversial rereading of Chaucer's Knight as a mercenary rather than an idealized figure.

Jordan, Mark D., *The Invention of Sodomy in Christian Theology*, Chicago: University Chicago Press, 1997. Historically traces the roots of the conception of sodomy in medieval Christianity and assesses its effect on medieval and contemporary ethics.

Jost, Jean E., 'Teaching *The Canterbury Tales:* The process and the product', *SMART: Studies in Medieval and Renaissance Teaching* 8.1 (Spring 2000), 61–70.

Julian, Anna Maria Reynolds and Julia Bolton Holloway (ed.), *Showing of Love: Extant Texts and Translation*. Biblioteche e archivi, 8 Florence: SISMEL Edizioni del Galluzzo, 2001. Exactly renders Julian's surviving manuscript texts (letter for letter, line by line, folio by folio), with a facing translation in Modern English and including manuscript variants, explanatory notes, and history of the manuscripts (Westminster, Paris, Sloane and Amherst).

Justice, Steven, *Writing and Rebellion: England in 1381*, Berkeley: University of California Press, 1994. Important study rearticulating the aims and activities of the 1381 Revolt from that of a rebellious mob to an ideologically driven attempt at rule through their destruction of official archives and other symbols of power.

Kabir, Ananya Jahanara and Deanne Williams (eds.), *Postcolonial Approaches to the European Middle Ages: Translating Cultures*, Cambridge: Cambridge University Press, 2005. Builds upon the interplay of medieval and postcolonial studies by drawing attention to material and linguistic features of texts and artifacts.

Kendrick, Laura, *Chaucerian Play: Comedy and Control in the Canterbury Tales*, Berkeley: University of California Press, 1988. Locates Chaucer's work in terms of popular lower-class plays and spectacles and argues that it deals with social control and resistance.

Ker, W. P., *Epic and Romance: Essays on Medieval Literature* (repr. ed.), New York: Dover, 1957. An early account of medieval literature heavily influenced by eighteenth-, nineteenth-, twentieth-century ideals and aesthetic tastes.

Kerby-Fulton, K., *Books Under Suspicion: Censorship and Tolerance of Revelatory Writing in Late Medieval England*, Notre Dame: University of Notre Dame Press, 2006. Argues that official censorship drove medieval authors like Langland, Chaucer and Julian of Norwich towards creating visionary literature.

King of Tars, in *The Auchineleck Manuscript* (Version 1.2, 5 July 2003), David Burnely and Alison Wiggins (eds.), available online at <http://www.nls.uk/auchinleck/mss/tars.html>.

Kinney, Clare R, 'The (dis)embodied hero and the signs of manhood in *Sir Gawain and the Green Knight*', in Lees (ed.), 1994, 47–57. Illustrates the fluid nature of the material presence of masculinity through the construction and deconstruction of Gawain's body in *Sir Gawain and the Green Knight*.

Kinoshita, Sharon, ' "Pagans are wrong and Christians are right": Alterity, gender, nation in the *Chanson de Roland*', *Journal of Medieval and Early Modern Studies* 31.1 (2001), 79–111. Argues that the instability of religious identity in Roland is stabilized through the stock figure of Saracen queen, Bramimonde, and her conversion to Christianity.

——, *Medieval Boundaries: Rethinking Difference in Old French Literature*, Philadelphia: University of Pennsylvania Press, 2006. Investigates cross-cultural contact in French texts from 1150–1225 to ascertain how constructions of racial and ethic otherness destabilize notions of identity.

Kirken, J., and R. Chilson, *All Will be Well: Based on the Classic Spirituality of Julian of Norwich: 30 Days with a Great Spiritual Teacher*, Notre Dame: Ave Maria Press, 1995. Devotional text derived from Julian's work.

Kline, Daniel T. (ed.), *Medieval Literature for Children*, New York: Routledge, 2003. An academic anthology of 16 primary texts (with introductory critical essays and bibliography) whose audience was primarily children and youth from late antiquity to the early modern period, including courtesy texts, school texts, drama, romance and didactic literature.

——, 'Taming the labyrinth: An introduction to medieval resources on the World Wide Web', *SMART: Studies in Medieval and Renaissance Teaching* 8.2(2000), 37–55.

——, *The Electronic Canterbury Tales*, University of Alaska Anchorage, available online at <http://www.kankedort.net>.

Knapp, Peggy A., 'Chaucer for fun and profit', in Ashton and Sylvester (eds.), *Teaching Chaucer*, New York: Palgrave Macmillan, 2007, 17–29.

Knight, Stephen, *Robin Hood: A Mythic Biography*, Ithaca: Cornell University Press, 2003. An award-winning survey of the mythological development and representation of Robin Hood.

—— (ed.), *Robin Hood: An Anthology of Scholarship and Criticism*, Cambridge: D. S. Brewer, 1999. Thirty-one essays surveying all aspects of the Robin Hood legend from early manuscripts to contemporary films.

——, *Robin Hood: A Complete Study of the English Outlaw*, Oxford: Cambridge University Press, 1994. A cultural study of the historical, literary, and textual production and circulation of Robin Hood mythology.

——, *Arthurian Literature and Society*, London: Macmillan, 1983. Reorients historical and Marxist studies of Arthurian literature to take into account literary and cultural representations of the legend.

Kolve, V. A., *The Play Called Corpus Christi*, London: Edward Arnold, 1966. Initiated the contemporary study of the late-medieval cycle plays.

Krause, F. (ed.), 'Kleine publicationen aus der Auchinleck-hs. IX. The King of Tars', *Englische Studien* 11 (1888), 1–62. An edition of the Auchinleck manuscript of the *King of Tars*, in parallel with the Vernon manuscript.

Kristeva, Julia, *Desire in Language: A Semiotic Approach to Literature and Art*, New

York: Columbia University Press, 1980. Influential engagement with Lacanian concepts through linguistic feminism that introduced the 'semiotic', related to the infantile pre-Oedipal moment, which opposes the symbolic order of language.

Kruger, Steven F., 'A series of linked assignments for the undergraduate course on Chaucer's *Canterbury Tales*', in Ashton and Sylvester (eds.), *Teaching Chaucer*, New York: Palgrave Macmillan, 2007, 30–45.

Kruger, Steven, 'Claiming the Pardoner: Toward a gay reading of Chaucer's *Pardoner's Tale*', *Exemplaria* 6 (1994), 115–39. Influential queer reading of one of Chaucer's most controversial characters and tales.

——, *The Spectral Jew: Conversion and Embodiment in Medieval Europe*, Minneapolis: University of Minnesota Press, 2006. A historically grounded study in which queer theory and deconstructive mechanisms are used to generate an understanding of the reciprocal influence of Jews and Judaism on Christianity and its practitioners.

López, Ian F. Haney, 'The social construction of race', in Rivkin and Ryan (eds.), 2004, 964–74. Essential article on the social construction of race from a legal perspective.

Labbie, Erin Felicia, *Lacan's Medievalism*, Minneapolis: University of Minnesota Press, 2006. Traces how Lacan's thinking was influenced by medieval texts and concepts.

Lacan, Jacques, 'The mirror stage as formative of the function of the I', *Ecrits: A Selection*, New York: W. W. Norton, 1982, 1–7. Perhaps Lacan's most famous essay, first published in 1937, concerning the formation of the subject.

——, *The Ethics of Psychoanalysis, 1959–1960*, New York: Norton, 1992. Important psychoanalytic statement concerning courtly love as anamorphosis.

——, 'The mirror stage as formative of the I function as revealed in psychoanalytic experience', in Bruce Fink (trans.), *Ecrits: The First Complete Edition in English*, New York: W. W. Norton, 2005, 75–81. New translations of the complete French edition of Lacan's writings.

Lampert, Lisa, *Gender and Jewish Difference from Paul to Shakespeare*, Philadelphia: University of Pennsylvania Press, 2004. Asserts that medieval Christian identity is constructed through reference to Others, like women and Jews, who also are inextricably tied to Christian origins.

Laqueur, Thomas, *Making Sex: Body and Gender from the Greeks to Freud*, Cambridge: Harvard University Press, 1990. A historical investigation into scientific conceptions of sexual difference arguing that medical theory shifted at the Enlightenment from a 'one sex' view (females as lesser versions of males) to a 'two sex' model (males and females as incommensurable opposites).

Lavezzo, Kathy, review of Jeffrey Jerome Cohen's *The Postcolonial Middle Ages, Journal of Colonialism and Colonial History*, 3.3 (2002), available online at <http://muse.jhu.edu.proxy.lib.fsu.edu/journals/journal_of_colonialism_and_colonial_history/v003/3.1lavezzo.html>.

—— (ed.), *Imagining a Medieval English Nation*, Minneapolis: University of Minnesota Press, 2004. Essays address the development of English national identity in the late Middle Ages, particularly in the development of the institutions and discourses of state.

Lawton, David, 'Dullness and the fifteenth century', *English Literary History*, 54 (1987), 761–99. Landmark essay opposing the previously conventional academic view that fifteenth-century literature is overly dull and stylized and launched renewed interest in the work of fifteenth-century writers.

Lees, Claire A. (ed.), *Medieval Masculinities: Regarding Men in the Middle Ages*, Minneapolis: University of Minnesota Press, 1994. One of the earliest anthologies to approach medieval masculinity, male gender roles, and the institutions and discourses of power that maintained masculine privilege.

Leicester Jr., H. Marshall, 'Our tonges différance: Textuality and deconstruction in Chaucer', in Finke and Schichtman (eds.), 1987, 15–26. An early attempt to bring contemporary literary theory – especially deconstruction, psychoanalysis and social concerns of poststructuralism – to an understanding of how Chaucer's work constructs and calls into question notions of the self, the subject, agency, representation and imagination.

——, *The Disenchanted Self: Representing the Subject in the Canterbury Tales*, Berkeley: University of California Press, 1990. Questions the 'dramatic theory' of interpreting the *Tales* through reference to deconstructive ideas of agency, subjectivity, gender and representation.

Lerer, Seth, *Chaucer and His Readers: Imagining the Author in Late-Medieval England*, Princeton: Princeton University Press, 1993. Important study of Chaucer's reception in the fifteenth and sixteenth century and the discursive mechanisms and Chaucerian imitators that elevated Chaucer to the 'father' of English poetry.

——, 'The endurance of formalism in Middle English studies', *Literature Compass* 1.1 (2003), n.p., available online at <http://www.literaturecompass.com>. Argues that any return to formalism must be equally aware of ideological concerns.

——, '"Representyd now in yower syght": The culture of spectatorship in late fifteenth-century England', in David Wallace and Barbara Hanawalt (eds.), *Intersections: History and Literature in the Fifteenth Century*, Minneapolis: University of Minneapolis Press, 1995. Reexamines the reception of literature and drama in the fifteenth century and reconceptualizes the notion of authority.

Levinas, Emmanuel, *Totality and Infinity: An Essay on Exteriority*, Alphonso Lingis (trans.), Pittsburgh: Duquesne University Press, 1969. The first major volume in Levinas' rethinking of 'ethics as first philosophy' through the image of the face, the second being *Otherwise Than Being: Or Beyond Essence* (1998).

——, 'Revelation in the Jewish tradition', in Sean Hand (ed.), *The Levinas Reader*, Oxford: Blackwell, 1989, 190–210. Makes the claim that the Bible is the hermeneutical model for ethical philosophy and describes midrashic interpretative procedures.

——, 'Useless suffering', in Michael B. Smith and Barbara Harshav (eds.), *Entre Nous: Thinking-of-the-Other*, New York: Columbia University Press, 1998, 91–102. Argues that the suffering of the Other must remain 'useless' or non-instrumentalized lest that suffering be compounded through the violence of appropriation.

Levinson, Marjorie, 'What is new formalism?' *PMLA: Publications of the Modern Language Association of America*, 122 (2007), 558–69. Differentiates distinct approaches to the newly revived concern for form and aesthetics in contemporary literary study.

Lewis, C. S., *English Literature in the Sixteenth Century Excluding Drama*, Oxford: Oxford University Press, 1954. Formalist and aesthetic analysis of late-medieval literature canonizes certain literary works while, at the same time, denigrating fifteenth-century literature as 'dull' and the period as a 'time of decay'.

Leyser, Conrad, 'Cities of the plain: The rhetoric of sodomy in Peter Damian's *Book of Gomorrah'*, *Romanic Review* 86.2 (1995), 191–211. Relates the medieval discourse concerning sodomy to the rise and development of cities in the eleventh and twelfth century.

Lindahl, Carl, *Earnest Games: Folkloric Patterns in the Canterbury Tales*, Bloomington: University of Indiana Press, 1987. A comparative study of traditional tales and Chaucer's literary endeavor that examines their common ground, shared formulae, and literary elements.

Lindenbaum, Sheila, 'London texts and literate practice', in Wallace (ed.), 1999, 284–309. Perceives London as a permeable space without a fixed social, economic or political centre, even the traditional mercantile elites, whose overlapping and competing institutions produced texts and discourse whose conditions of production Chaucer tended to suppress.

Liu, Alan, *Voice of the Shuttle*, University of California, available online at <http://vos.ucsb.edu/index.asp>.

Lochrie, Karma, *Covert Operations: The Medieval Uses of Secrecy*, Philadelphia: University of Pennsylvania Press, 1999. Examines forms of secrecy in five areas (confession, gossip, medicine, marriage, and sodomitic discourse) and analyses a variety of texts to ascertain the suppressive and revelatory aspects of keeping secrets.

——, *Heterosyncrasies: Female Sexuality When Normal Wasn't*, Minneapolis: University of Minnesota Press, 2005. Investigates the history of a discourse of sexual normalization that begins in the nineteenth century and argues that the medieval discourse of natural and unnatural is different from modern notions of normal and abnormal.

Lomperis, Linda and Sarah Stanbury (eds.), *Feminist Approaches to the Body in Medieval Literature*, Philadelphia: University of Pennsylvania Press, 1993. Important collection of theoretically sophisticated feminist analyses of materiality in medieval literature.

Loomis, Laura H., *Medieval Romance in England: A Study of the Sources and Analogues of the Non-Cyclic Metrical Romances*, New York: Oxford University Press, 1924. Surveys a wide selection of Middle English romances and classifies them into thematic groupings.

Lynch, Jack, *Literary Resources on the Net*, Rutgers University, available online at <http://andromeda.rutgers.edu/~jlynch/Lit/>.

Mankind, in *The Macro Plays*, Mark Eccles (ed.), Early English Text Society, Original Series 262, London: Oxford University Press, 1969, 153–84. The current critical text of this important medieval morality play.

Mann, Jill, *Chaucer and Medieval Estates Satire*, Cambridge: Cambridge University Press, 1973. Argues that Chaucer drew his characters from the estates of contemporary social life rather than from any archetype and asserts that Chaucer's unconventional use of the estates satire makes moral judgment upon the characters difficult.

Mapping Margery Kempe, Sarah Stanbury and Virginia Raguin (eds.), Holy Cross University, available online at <http://www.holycross.edu/departments/visarts/projects/kempe/>. A valuable resource for 'studying Kempe in her cultural and social context, particularly the material culture of the fifteenth-century East Anglian parish'.

Marcus, Ivan G., *Rituals of Childhood: Jewish Acculturation in Medieval Europe*, New Haven: Yale University Press, 1989. Examines anthropologically the Ashkenazi ritual enabling boys to study Torah at age 5 and demonstrates how medieval Judaism transformed Christian symbols for their own uses in a predominantly Christian culture.

Margherita, Gayle, *The Romance of Origins: Language and Sexual Difference in Middle English Literature*, Philadelphia: University of Pennsylvania Press, 1994. Attempts 'to foreground the epistemological question of origins in rethinking the ethical and political basis of aesthetic judgments, and to interrogate some of the ideologies of "medievalism" from a feminist and psychoanalytic perspective' (1).

——, 'Originary fantasies and Chaucer's *Book of Duchess*', in Linda Lomperis and Sarah Stanbury (eds.), *Feminist Approaches to the Body in Medieval Literature*, Philadelphia: University of Pennsylvania Press, 1993, 116–41. Combines a feminist critique with Lacanian psychoanalysis to trace out the dramatic implications of the critical blindness endemic to Robertsonianism and still prevalent in contemporary poststructuralist criticism.

Marie de France, *Lanval*, in *The Lais of Marie de France*, Robert Hanning and Joan Ferrante (trans.), New York: E. P. Dutton, 1978, 105–25. An excellent and readable translation of Marie's *Lais* with introductory essays.

Marks, Elaine and Isabelle de Courtivron (eds.), *New French Feminisms: An Anthology*, Amherst: University of Massachusetts Press, 1980. Important early anthology that put brought French feminism to a broader Anglo-American audience.

Marotta, Joseph., 'The part in the whole: The use of the episode in teaching medieval narrative'. *Teaching the Middle Ages III: Studies in Medieval and Renaissance Teaching*. Warrensburg, Missouri: Central Missouri State University, 1989, 1–21.

Marshall, David W. (ed.), *Mass Market Medieval: Essays on the Middle Ages in Popular Culture*, Jefferson, NC: McFarland, 2007. Addresses the appearance of medieval tropes in a variety of media.

Marx, Karl, 'Manifesto of the Communist Party', in *The Marx-Engels Reader* (2nd ed.), Robert C. Tucker (ed.), New York: W. W. Norton, 1978, 469–500. Both a course of action for social revolution and an important introduction to Marx's notion of historical materialism, which understands history in terms of the dialectic of class struggle.

Massey, Jeff, '"What's wrong with this picture?": Teaching Arthuriana via the *via negativa*', *SMART: Studies in Medieval and Renaissance Teaching* 12.1 (Spring 2005), 53–64.

Mathews, David, *The Making of Middle English, 1765–1910*, Minneapolis: University of Minneapolis Press, 1999. Explores the formation of Middle English studies and the need for current scholars to engage in a dialogue with its legacy.

McAlpine, Monica E., 'The Pardoner's homosexuality and how it matters', *PMLA: Publications of the Modern Language Association of America*, 95 (1980), 8–22. Argues that the Pardoner fits three medieval characteristics that were associated with homosexuality: being effeminate, a eunuch, and a hermaphrodite.

McClain, Lee Tobin, 'Introducing medieval romance via popular films: Bringing the other closer', *SMART: Studies in Medieval and Renaissance Teaching* 5.2 (Fall 1997), 59–63.

McClintock, Anne, 'The angel of progress: Pitfalls of the term "post-colonialism"', in Rivkin and Ryan (eds.), 2004, 1183–96. Argues that the 'post' in postcolonial collapses a multitude of distinct histories, locales, and experiences under a single rubric, the teleological triumph of colonialism to which everything else is still 'pre'.

McPhillips, Robert (ed.), *The New Formalism: A Critical Introduction*, Cincinnati, OH: Textos Books, 2005. Overview of New Formalist poetry and poets.

Meñocal, Maria Rosa (ed.), *The Literature of Al-Andalus*, New York: Cambridge University Press, 2000. A volume in *The Cambridge History of Arabic Literature* that attends to the interplay of Islamic, Judaic and Christian culture in medieval Spain.

Meech, Stanford B. with H. E. Allen (eds.), *The Book of Margery Kempe*, Early English Text Society, Original Series 212, Oxford: Oxford University Press, 1940. Critical edition of the unique manuscript of *The Book of Margery Kempe*, with full critical apparatus.

Memmi, Albert, *The Colonizer and the Colonized*, New York: Orion Press, 1965. Incisive analysis of the dynamics of colonialism and its effect on individuals and offers a critique of leftist and rightist colonialists.

Middle English Dictionary, Hans Kurath (gen. ed.), online at <http://ets.umdl.umich.edu/m/med/>. The most comprehensive and scholarly dictionary of the English language during the later Middle Ages, with 15,000 searchable pages of entries spanning 1000–1500 CE.

Middleton, Anne, 'The idea of public poetry in the reign of Richard II', *Speculum* 53.1 (1978), 94–114. Trailblazing article identifying a form of public poetry, a poetry of direct address, that first emerges during the reign of Richard II, which is only indirectly evident in Chaucer.

Miller, Miriam Youngerman and Jane Chance (eds.), *Approaches to Teaching Sir Gawain and the Green Knight*, New York: The Modern Language Association of America, 1986.

Millet, Bella and Joyce Wogan-Browne (eds.), *Medieval English Prose for Women: Selections from the Katherine Group and Ancrene Wisse*, Oxford: Oxford University Press, 1990. Introduction, commentary, notes and parallel contemporary English translations of Middle English texts.

Millett, Kate, *Sexual Politics*, London: Virago, 1970. Presents an influential account of sexual politics and essays on 'the sexual revolution' from 1830 to 1960 with examples from D. H. Lawrence, Henry Miller, Norman Mailer and Jean Genet.

Mills, Sara, 'Post-colonial feminist theory', in Stevi Jackson and Jackie Jones (eds.), *Contemporary Feminist Theories*, New York: New York University Press, 1998, 98–112. Maps the confluence of feminist thought and postcolonial theory and suggests new areas of investigation.

Minnis, A. J., *Medieval Theory of Authorship: Scholastic Literary Attitudes in the Later Middle Ages*, London: Scolar Press, 1984. Milestone work that examines the writings of Latin authorities studies in universities from 1100–1400 to reconceive the medieval notion of *auctor* and *auctoritas*.

Moller, Herbert, 'The social causation of the courtly love complex', *Comparative Studies in Society and History* 1.2 (1959), 137–63. In periods of demographic imbalance, considers hypergamy, wherein an upper class male may marry a woman below his station, though a woman cannot do the same thing.

Morris, Richard and Pamela Gradon (eds.), *Dan Michel's Ayenbite of Inwyt, or, Remorse of Conscience* (rev. ed.), Oxford: Oxford University Press, 1965. Often called 'The Prick of Conscience', translates a French confessional manual on the virtues and vices.

Morrison, Toni, *Playing in the Darkness: Whiteness and Literary Imagination*, New York: Vintage Books, 1993. Criticizes the accepted notion that whiteness signifies the normal or universal human condition, while ignoring the race or the 'Africanist Presence'.

Morte Arthure, or The Death of Arthur, Edmund Brock (ed.), Early English Text Society, Original Series 8, London: Oxford University Press, 1871. An expanded adaptation of Geoffrey of Monmouth's *History of the Kings of England* (books 9 and 10), with a realistic depiction of Arthur's military and chivalric exploits leading to his death at Mordred's hands.

Muhlberger, Stephen, 'Medieval England', *ORB: On-line Reference Book for Medieval Studies*, online at <http://www.the-orb.net/textbooks/muhlberger/muhlindex.html>. Excellent, easily accessible introductory essay.

Mullally, Evelyn, and John Thompson (eds.), *The Court and Cultural Diversity: Selected Papers from the Eight Triennial Congress of the International Courtly Literature Society, The Queen's University of Belfast 26 July – 1 August 1995*, Cambridge: D. S. Brewer, 1997. Essays consider the liminality of the court and outsiders, as well as the interplay and distribution of courtly cultures and ideologies in a range of registers and discourses.

Mulvey, Laura, 'Visual pleasure and narrative cinema', *Screen* 16.3 (1975), 6–18. Essential essay that initiated the discussion concerning 'scopophilia' and Lacanian approaches to film.

Muscatine, Charles, *Chaucer and the French Tradition: A Study in Style and Meaning*, Berkeley: University of California Press, 1957. Focuses on style and convention in order to explore Chaucer's 'stylistic heritage'.

Nissé, Ruth, 'Reversing discipline: *The Tretise of Miraclis Pleyinge*, Lollard exegesis, and the failure of representation', *The Yearbook of Langland Studies*, 11 (1997), 163–96. Sets *The Tretise* in the context of various Wycliffite texts to ascertain the links between exegetical and political practices.

——, *Defining Acts: Drama and the Politics of Interpretation in Late Medieval England*, Notre Dame: University of Notre Dame Press, 2005. Analyses drama's mediation of political and theological concerns based on performance and literary contexts.

'Of Feigned Contemplative Life', *The English Works of Wyclif Hitherto Unprinted*, F. D. Matthew (ed.), London: Trubner, 1880, 187–96. Likely an early treatise by Wycliffe that argues against the contemplative life and for preaching in the community.

Ong, Walter J., *Orality and Literacy: The Technologizing of the Word*, London: Methuen, 1982. Analyses the relationship between orality and literacy and assesses the production of literature for oral delivery in a culture that possesses the technology of writing.

ORB: On-line Reference Book for Medieval Studies, online at <http://www.the-orb.net>. Provides a peer reviewed online encyclopedia, a collection of full-length textbooks, complete and excerpted e-texts, and an extensive bibliography of online and print sources.

Orme, Nicholas, *Medieval Children*, New Haven: Yale University Press, 2001. Beautifully illustrated, comprehensively researched encyclopedic synthesis of the lives of children in all classes from birth, including chapters on children's culture (family life, education, learning to read, toys and games).

——, *Medieval Schools*, New Haven: Yale University Press, 2006. Companion volume to *Medieval Children* that synthesizes Orme's 40 years of research into medieval education.

Osborne, Monica, 'Midrash and postmodernity: Art after the Holocaust', *Tikkun* (26 Dec. 2006), available online at <http://www.tikkun.org/magazine/ specials/article.2006-12-26.0924>. Accessible and comprehensive history of the attention given to midrashic approaches in literature that argues we are at the beginning of a 'third wave' that is capable of responding to the dilemmas of postmodern aesthetic theory.

Parry, Milman and Alfred Lord, *The Singer of Tales*, Cambridge: Harvard University Press, 1968. Investigates oral composition and improvisation based on surviving oral traditions, like the guslari in Serbia-Herzegovina.

Patterson, Lee, 'Chaucer's Pardoner on the couch: Psyche and Clio in medieval literary studies', *Speculum* 76 (2001), 638–80. Argues stridently against the usefulness of psychoanalytic approaches to medieval literature because (1) the truth-claims of psychoanalysis are suspect, (2) fictional characters are mute objects in what is supposed to be a therapeutic dialogue and (3) psychoanalytic approaches often claim superiority to caricatured historicist methods – and historicists themselves.

——, 'On the margin: Postmodernism, ironic history, and medieval studies', *Speculum* 65 (1996), 87–108. Argues for the need to break down the periodization and compartmentalization of medieval literary studies.

——, *Chaucer and the Subject of History*, Madison: University of Wisconsin Press, 1991. Analyses modes of temporality and their relation to subjectivity and social formations in the *Canterbury Tales*.

——, *Negotiating the Past: The Understanding of Medieval Literature*, Madison: University of Wisconsin Press, 1987. An influential critique of the legacy of medieval studies, proposing a thoroughgoing historicist approach.

Paxson, James. J., Lawrence M. Clopper and Sylvia Tomasch (eds.), *The Performance of Middle English Culture: Essays on Chaucer and the Drama*, Cambridge: D. S. Brewer, 1998. Approaches the works of Chaucer and medieval drama from an interdisciplinary standpoint grounded in close textual analyses that is historically situated and incorporates iconographical, anthropological and sociological mechanisms.

Pearsall, Derek, 'The idea of Englishness in the fifteenth century', in Helen Cooney (ed.), *Nation, Court and Culture: New Essays on Fifteenth Century English Poetry*, Dublin: Four Courts Press, 2001, 15–27. A wide-ranging study of the concept of English national identity.

——, 'Strangers in late fourteenth-century London', in F. R. P. Akehurst and S. C. Van D'Elden (eds.), *The Stranger in Medieval Society*, Minnesota: University of Minneapolis Press, 1997, 46–62. A philological and historical exploration of strangeness and strangers in England.

Percy, Thomas, *Reliques of Ancient English Poetry*, London, 1765. Early collection of medieval and early modern texts, especially ballads, with an introductory essay.

Petrarch, Francesco, 'Letter to a friend, 1340–1353', *Internet Medieval Sourcebook*, available online at <http://www.fordham.edu/halsall/source/14cpetrarch-pope.html>. Famous letter criticizing the Avignon papacy.

Petroff, Elizabeth A. (ed.), *Medieval Women's Visionary Literature*, Oxford: Oxford University Press, 1986. Important anthology focusing on epiphanic and visionary literature from Sts. Perpetua and Macrina but concentrating on twelfth through fourteenth-century mystical writings.

Poirion, Daniel, 'Literary meaning in the Middle Ages: From a sociology of genres to an anthropology of works', *New Literary History*, 10 (1978–79), 401–8. A detailed study of the two-way relationship between history and literature.

Pulp Fiction, Quentin Tarantino (dir.), Miramax Films (prod.), 1994. From whence the term 'getting medieval' springs.

Quinn, William A. and Audley S. Hall, *Jongleur: A Modified Theory of Oral Performance and Transmission of Middle English Romance*, Washington: University Press of America, 1982. Proposes that romances can be simultaneously composed from a store of memorized formulae recited from memory, or result from a combination of memory recall, improvisation, and public/private reading.

Rabaté, Jean-Michel (ed.), *The Cambridge Companion to Lacan*, Cambridge: Cambridge University Press, 2003. Fifteen specially commissioned essays forming an advanced introduction to Lacanian thought.

'Remarks by the President upon arrival' (16 September 2001), available online at <http://www.whitehouse.gov/news/releases/2001/09/20010916-2.html> contains President Bush's remarks concerning a 'crusade' against terrorism.

Rich, Adrienne, 'Compulsory heterosexuality and lesbian existence', in Henry Abelove, Michèle Aina Barale, David M. Halperin (eds.), *The Lesbian and Gay Studies Reader*, New York: Routledge, 1993, 227–54. Proceeds from the suggestion that if a child's first erotic attachment is to the mother, then why could not the sexual orientation of both men and women naturally extend towards women?

Riddy, Felicity (ed.), *Prestige, Authority and Power in Late Medieval Manuscripts and Texts*, Woodbridge, Suffolk: York Medieval Press, 2000. Investigates the textual authority, prestige, patronage, production and circulation of manuscripts.

Risden, E.I., 'Walking Hadrian's Wall', *SMART: Studies in Medieval and Renaissance Teaching* 11.2 (Fall 2004), 37–61.

Rivkin, Julie and Michael Ryan (eds.), *Literary Theory: An Anthology* (2nd ed.), Oxford: Blackwell Publishing, 2004. Major anthology of literary theory organized by school or approach.

Robertson, Durant W., *A Preface to Chaucer: Studies in Medieval Perspectives*, Princeton: Princeton University Press, 1962. Influential study that initiated patristic analysis of medieval literature.

Robeson, Lisa, 'Leaves that are part of the tree: Teaching the past through the present in a Humanities I course', *SMART: Studies in Medieval and Renaissance Teaching* 10.1 Spring 2003. 19–41.

Rolle, Richard, *The Fire of Love and The Mending of Life or The Rule of Living*, Ralph Harvey (ed.), Early English Text Society, Original Series 106, Woodbridge, Suffolk: Boydell and Brewer, 1996. Richard Rolle's famous spiritual meditation.

Romaine, Suzanne, *Bilingualism* (2nd ed.), Oxford: Oxford University Press, 1995.

Distinguishes code-switching from borrowing, and deals with the practice, function, conditions and constraints of language-switching.

Roper, Gregory, 'Making students do the teaching: Problems of "Brit Lit Survey I"', *SMART: Studies in Medieval and Renaissance Teaching* 9.1 (Spring 2002), 39–57.

Rougemont, Denis de, *Love in the Western World*, New York: Harcourt, 1940. Traces the psychology of love from Tristan and Isolde to Golden Age Hollywood and argues that contemporary notions of love originated in medieval courtly love traditions.

Rowland, Beryl, 'Animal imagery and the Pardoner's abnormality', *Neophilologus* 48 (1964), 56–60. Claims that because he is compared to a hare and a goat, both considered hermaphroditic or bisexual in the medieval period, the Pardoner should be considered a 'testicular pseudo-hermaphrodite of the feminine type' (58).

Rubin, Gayle, 'The traffic in women: Notes on the political economy of sex', in Rayna R. Reiter (ed.), *Toward an Anthropology of Women*, New York: Monthly Review Press, 1975, 157–210. Landmark feminist analysis arguing that masculine culture finds coherence in the exchange of women.

Rubin, Miri, 'The body whole and vulnerable in fifteenth-century England', *Bodies and Disciplines: Intersections of Literature and History in Fifteenth-Century England*, David Wallace and Barbara Hanawalt (eds.), Minneapolis: University of Minnesota Press, 1996, 19–28. Considers medieval bodies according to their social functions, as anomalies, markers of holiness and sanctity, vehicles of humanity and vulnerability, and the universal body of Christ.

——, 'The Eucharist and the construction of medieval identities', in Aers (ed.), 1992, 43–64. Develops her work on the relationship between medieval spirituality, ritual and the sacraments to analyse their implications for individual identity.

——, *Corpus Christi: The Eucharist in Late Medieval Culture*, Cambridge: Cambridge University Press, 1991. Influential study of the sacramental nature of medieval Christianity that deals with the significance of the Eucharist and embodiment, and especially the powerful symbolism of Christ's body.

Rudd, Gillian, *Greenery: Ecocritical Readings of Late Medieval English Literature*, Manchester: Manchester University Press, 2007. Brings ecocriticism by image pattern (earth, trees, wilds, sea, gardens, fields) to Malory's *Morte d'Arthur*, the *Knight's* and *Franklin's Tales*, *Piers Plowman*, and *Sir Gawain and the Green Knight*.

Sadler, Joseph, et al., *Freud's Models of the Mind: An Introduction*, Madison, CT: International Universities Press, 1998. Historical over view of the development of Freud's models of the psyche.

Said, Edward, *Orientalism*, New York: Pantheon Books, 1978. Influential study providing a framework for theorizing the conceptualization and domination of other races and ethnicities by colonial powers, particularly the English.

Salter, Elizabeth, Derek Pearsall, and Nicolette Zeaman (eds.), *English and International: Studies in the Literature, Art, and Patronage of Medieval England*, Cambridge: Cambridge University Press, 1988. Collection of Salter's essays and two projects left unfinished at her death.

Saunders, Corinne J., *The Forest of Medieval Romance: Avernus, Broceliande, Arden,*

Cambridge: D. S. Brewer, 1993. Explores the locale of the forest and its cultural implications in a range of texts from the twelfth to the sixteenth centuries.

Saussure, Ferdinand de, *Course in General Linguistics*, LaSalle: Open Court, 1986. Influential study instrumental in establishing modern linguistic theory in its structuralist insistence on studying language synchronically, seeking out is general structures, rather than diachronically, focusing on historical and comparative approaches.

Sawyer, Michael E., *A Bibliographical Index of Five English Mystics*, Pittsburgh: Clifford E. Barbour Library Pittsburgh Theological Seminary, 1978. Covers Richard Rolle, Julian of Norwich, the *Cloud of Unknowing*, Walter Hilton and Margery Kempe.

Scarry, Elaine, *The Body in Pain: The Making and Unmaking of the World*, New York: Oxford University Press, 1985. Important meditation on the suffering body and its relation to a variety of cultural discourses in the process of 'unmaking' and making' individuals and communities.

Schor, Nancy, 'Feminist and gender studies', *Introduction to Scholarship in Modern Languages and Literatures* (2nd ed.), Joseph Gibaldi (ed.), New York: Modern Language Association, 1992. Overview of the field as of its publication in 1992.

Sebastian, John, 'Chaucer and the theory wars: Attack of the historicists? The psychoanalysts strike back? Or a new hope?', *Literature Compass* 3.4 (2006), 767–77, available online at <http://www.literaturecompass.com>. Analyses the sometimes irreconcilable differences between historicist and psychoanalytic critics and offers several points of contact between the rival camps.

Sedgwick, Eve Kosofsky, *Between Men: English Literature and Male Homosocial Desire*, New York: Columbia University Press, 1985. The harbinger of queer theory, argued that male to male desire is triangulated through women.

——, *Touching Feeling: Affect, Pedagogy, Performativity*, Durham: Duke University Press, 2003. Investigates the relationships between feeling, teaching and acting.

Semper, Phillippa, ' "The wondres that they myghte seen or heere": Designing and using Web-based resources to teach medieval literature', in Ashton and Sylvester (eds.), *Teaching Chaucer*, New York: Palgrave Macmillan, 2007, 120–38.

Serjeantson, M. S. (ed.), *Osbern Bokenham: Legendys of Hooly Wummen*, Early English Text Society, Original Series 206, London: Oxford University Press, 1938. Critical text of Bokenham's collection.

Shahar, Shulamith, *Childhood in the Middle Ages*, New York: Routledge, 1990. Draws upon a wide variety of material from across western Europe to demonstrate, contra Ariès, that medieval children were understood to be different from adults and, as such, required parental care and emotional investment.

Shoaf, R. A., Dante, *Chaucer, and the Currency of the Word: Money, Images, and Reference in Late Medieval Poetry*, Norman, OK: Pilgrim, 1983. Reads *The Divine Comedy*, *Troilus and Criseyde*, and *The Canterbury Tales* through relationship of money and language (and hence poetry), both of which concern the problem of reference and the question of ethics.

Showalter, Elaine, 'Feminist criticism in the wilderness', *Critical Inquiry* 8 (1981), 179–205. Early and influential feminist essay.

Silence: A Thirteenth-Century French Romance, Sarah Roche-Mahdi (ed. and trans.), East Lansing, Michigan: Michigan State University Press, 1992. Fascinating French romance of the knight, Silence, who was born a female but raised a male.

Silverman, Kaja, *The Subject of Semiotics*, New York: Oxford University Press, 1983. Brings semiotics and structuralist theory together in important ways to emphasize the theoretical intimacy of the Lacanian 'subject', 'signification' and the 'symbolic order'.

Simpson, James, *Reform and Cultural Revolution: 1350–1547*, Oxford: Oxford University Press, 2002. Major reassessment of the intersection of textuality and ideology in late-medieval England.

Speed, Diane, 'The Saracens of *King Horn*', *Speculum* 65 (1990), 564–95. Argues that the significance of Horn's enemies, the Saracens, is their difference, the fact that they are non-Christian and hence can and should be controlled by the Christian king.

Spivak, Gayatri Chakravorty, 'Three women's texts and a critique of imperialism', *Critical Inquiry*, 12 (1985), 243–61. Critiques feminist approaches that 'reproduce the axioms of imperialism' (243).

Sponsler, Claire, *Drama and Resistance: Bodies, Goods, and Theatricality in Late Medieval Britain*, Minnesota: University of Minnesota Press, 1997a. Examines the politics of control and resistance in medieval drama, especially its expression through embodiment and commodification and its implications for identity formation.

——, 'Outlaw masculinities: Drag, blackface, and late medieval laboring-class festivities', in Cohen and Wheeler (eds.), 1997, 321–47. Looks at the paradoxical nature of men's seasonal celebrations and spectacles which through their incorporation of drag and blackface permit dissidence while suppressing difference.

Staley, Lynn (ed.), *The Book of Margery Kempe*, New York: W. W. Norton, 2001. The Norton critical edition of Margery's famous book, including critical text, backgrounds and academic essays.

Stallybrass, Peter, ' "Drunk with the cup of liberty": Robin Hood, the carnivalesque, and the rhetoric of violence in early modern England', in Knight (ed.), 1999, 297–327. Examines the 'carnivalesque' potential of the Robin Hood material, with its intrinsic transgressive, disruptive power and rhetoric of violence, which serves as social critique.

Stanbury, Sarah, *Seeing the Gawain-Poet: Description and the Act of Perception*, Philadelphia: University of Pennsylvania Press, 1991. Examines recurrent patterns of spatial imagery in Cotton Nero A.x.

——, 'The virgin's gaze: Spectacle and transgression in Middle English lyrics of the Passion', *PMLA: Publications of the Modern Language Association of America* 106.5 (1991), 1083–93. Argues that Passion lyrics invoke a complicated visual regime by requiring the reader to gaze not only upon the suffering Christ but the Blessed Virgin who suffers while she gazes upon her son, making the Virgin both an object of spectacle and the subject of the gaze.

Stein, Robert M., 'Multilingualism', in Strohm (ed.), 2007, 23–37. Surveys the occurrences and implications of multilingual medieval British literature.

Stevens, Martin, 'The performing self in twelfth-century culture', *Viator* 9 (1978), 193–218. Conceptualizes the cultural production of texts as performance that includes all segments of society.

——, *Four Middle English Mystery Cycles: Textual, Contextual, and Critical Interpretations*, Princeton: Princeton University Press, 1987. Brings textual, documentary and codicological evidence to bear on the four cycles and examines the cultural, ideological and political discourses contained therein.

Strohm, Paul, *Oxford Twenty-First Century Approaches to Literature: Middle English*, Oxford: Oxford University Press, 2007. State of the art collection of essays on the newest approaches to medieval literature that simultaneously takes into account abiding questions.

——, *Theory and the Premodern Text*, Minneapolis: University of Minnesota Press, 2006. Subtle and influential readings of medieval English literature through contemporary literary-critical theory.

——, *Politique: Languages of Statecraft between Chaucer and Shakespeare*, Notre Dame: University of Notre Dame Press, 2005. A comparative analysis of fifteenth-century English and continental political texts to reevaluate English writing as a mode of linguistically symbolic political and ideological expression.

——, 'Chaucer's Lollard joke: History and the textual unconscious', *Studies in the Age of Chaucer* 17 (1995), 23–42. A psychoanalytic reading of the Pardoner's reference to dung as the desacralization of the Eucharist.

——, *Hochon's Arrow: The Social Imagination of Fourteenth-Century Texts*. Princeton: Princeton University Press, 1992. Uses a sophisticated historicist approach that incorporates philological, anthropological and sociological elements to read well-known Ricardian literary works alongside lesser-known Latin and vernacular literary, historical and political texts.

——, *Social Chaucer*, Cambridge: Harvard University Press, 1989. Deploys Bakhtinian theories to discuss the polyphonic (multi-voiced) and hetero-geneous 'society' of Chaucer's *Canterbury Tales* as a model of social possibility.

Studies in Medievalism, Holland, MI: Studies in Medievalism, 1979–present. The first journal devoted to medievalism, the study of post-medieval representa-tions of medieval concerns.

Sweeney, Michelle, *Magic in Medieval Romances from Chrétien de Troyes to Geoffrey Chaucer*, Dublin: Four Courts Press, 2000. Argues that through the depiction of magic, romances could become vehicles of social and moral critique dealing with a broad range of morally ambiguous issues.

Sylvester, Louise, 'Teaching the language of Chaucer', in Ashton and Sylvester (eds.), *Teaching Chaucer*, New York: Palgrave Macmillan, 2007, 81–95.

Symes, Carol, 'Manuscript matrix, modern canon', in Strohm (ed.), 2007, 7–22. Using *Beowulf* and *Judith* as exemplars, argues that the reception history of a medieval text out of its manuscript matrix – its preservation, discovery, recovery, transcription, editing, translation and study – is less a medieval phenomenon than an historical process often governed by factors other than its literary qualities.

Talarico, Kathryn (gen. ed.), *ORB: The Online Reference Book for Medieval Studies*, College of Staten Island, City University of New York, available online at <http://the-orb.net/>.

Tardiff, Richard, 'The "mistery" of Robin Hood: A new social context for the texts', in Stephen Knight (ed.), *Robin Hood: An Anthology of Scholarship and Criticism*, Cambridge: D.S. Brewer, 1999, 345–61. Reads Robin Hood and the forest myth as a means of expressing and relieving the isolation felt by medieval urban tradesmen.

TEAMS Middle English Texts, University of Rochester, available online at <http://www.lib.rochester.edu/camelot/teams/tmsmenu.htm>.

The Anonimalle Chronicle, Middle English Literature: An Historical Sourcebook, Matthew Boyd Goldie (ed. and trans.), Oxford: Blackwell, 2003, 175–89. Anonymous late-medieval chronicle in Anglo-Norman recounting history from the time of Brutus to 1381.

'The Babees Book', in *Early English Meals and Manners*, Frederick J. Furnivall (ed.), Early English Text Society, Original Series 32, London: N. Trubner, 1868, 1–9. Fascinating compendium of texts related to childhood education in service, table manners and courteous conduct.

The Cloud of Unknowing, Phyllis Hodgson (ed.), Early English Text Society, Extra Series 218, London: Oxford University Press, 1944. Contemplative treatise designed to lead to a reader an apophatic, or imageless, contemplation of God who transcends all conception – the 'unknowing' of the title.

The Corpus of Middle English Prose and Verse, University of Michigan, available online at <http://quod.lib.umich.edu/c/cme/browse.html>.

The Labyrinth: Resources for Medieval Studies, online at <http://www8.george town.edu/departments/medieval/labyrinth/>. A searchable web site that links to databases, texts, images, and other online resources devoted to medieval studies.

The Middle English Dictionary, University of Michigan, available online at <http://quod.lib.umich.edu/m/med/>.

The Medieval Translator: Theory and Practice of Translation in the Middle Ages, Roger Ellis (ed.), 1981–present. Important series that reappraises the practices of medieval translation and translators.

Thiébaux, Marcelie (ed.), *The Writings of Medieval Women: An Anthology* (2nd ed.), New York: Garland Publications, 1994. Broad-based collection of writings including political, familial, poetic and mystical writings.

Thompson, Stith, *Motif-Index of Folk Literature: A Collection of Narrative Elements in Folktales, Ballads, Myths, Fables, Medieval Romances, Exempla, Fabliaux, Jest-Books, and Local Legends* (2nd ed., 6 vols), Bloomington: Indiana University Press, 1955–58. A magisterial guide of folkloric motifs for use in ascertaining the origin and dissemination of tales and asserts that these elements, although potentially widespread, can appear independently in different regions.

Tolhurst, Fiona, 'Why we should teach – and our students perform – *The Legend of Good Women*', in Ashton and Sylvester (eds.), *Teaching Chaucer*, New York: Palgrave Macmillan, 2007, 46–64.

Tolkien, J. R. R. and E. V. Gordon (eds.), *Sir Gawain and the Green Knight*, 2nd ed. revised by Norman Davis, Oxford: Oxford University Press, 1967. Famous edition of the important Arthurian romance.

Tomasch, Sylvia and S. Gilles (eds.), *Text and Territory: Geographical Imagination in the European Middle Ages*, Philadelphia: University of Pennsylvania Press, 1999. Collection employing feminist, queer, cultural and postcolonial theory to examine the interconnections between geographical categories and the transmission of ideology, religion, power relations and political control.

Treharne, Elizabeth (ed.), *Old and Middle English c. 890–1400*, Oxford: Blackwell, 2004. Recent anthology of Anglo-Saxon and Middle English texts.

A Tretise of Miraclis Pleyinge, in Goldie (ed.), 2003, 262–72. Lollard treatise against secular entertainments.

Trigg, Stephanie, *Congenial Souls: Reading Chaucer from Medieval to Postmodern,* Minneapolis: University of Minnesota Press, 2002. Surveys post-Chaucerian responses to Chaucer's work in the creation of literary critical, even Chaucerian, communities.

Trotter, D. A. (ed.), *Multilingualism in Later Medieval Britain,* Cambridge: D. S. Brewer, 2000. Discusses the historical evidence for language contact, language-mixing and tri-lingualism in Medieval England and notes the lexicographical consequences of this language interplay.

Trounce, A. M. (1932–34), 'The English tail-rhyme romance', *Medium Ævum* 1 (1932), 86–108, 168–82; 2 (1933), 34–57, 189–98; 3 (1934), 30–50. Provides a classic example of categorization according to metrical type, discussing in a series of articles the English tail-rhyme romances.

Turville-Petre, Thorlac, *England the Nation: Language, Literature and National Identity 1290–1340,* Oxford: Clarendon Press, 1996. Examines early fourteenth-century literature to interrogate ideas of Englishness and nationhood.

Utz, Richard J., *Chaucer and the Discourse of German Philology: A History of Reception and an Annotated Bibliography of Studies, 1793–1948,* Turnhout: Brepols, 2002. Traces the reception of Chaucer's works in Germany beginning in the late eighteenth century.

Vance, Eugene, *Mervelous Signals: Poetics and Sign Theory in the Middle Ages,* Lincoln; London: University of Nebraska Press, 1986. Joins medieval semiotics and poetics both to analyse medieval works and to assess contemporary critical vocabularies.

——, *From Topic to Tale: Logic and Narrativity in the Middle Ages,* Minneapolis: University of Minnesota Press, 1987. Uses rhetorical, structural and ideological strategies to investigate the logic of medieval narratives.

Veeser, H. Aram, 'Introduction', in Veeser (ed.), *New Historicism,* New York: Routledge, 1989, xi–xvi. An important contribution to the general development of New Historicism that includes essays by Stephen J. Greenblatt, Louis A. Montrose, Catherine Gallagher, Elizabeth Fox-Genovese, Gerald Graff, Jean Franco, Gayatri Chakravorty Spivak, Frank Lentricchia, Vincent Pecora, Jane Marcus, Jon Klancher, Jonathan Arac, Hayden White, Stanley Fish, Judith Newton, Joel Fineman, John Schaffer, Richard Terdiman, Donald Pease, Brooks Thomas.

Verkerk, Dorthy Hoogland, 'Black servant, black demon: Color ideology in the Ashburnham Pentateuch', *Journal of Medieval and Early Modern Studies* 31 (2001), 57–78. Demonstrates that 'the depiction of blacks [is] necessary to construct a white and Christian identity'.

Vitto, Cindy, 'The periis of translation, or when is a kni3t a gnome?' *SMART: Studies in Medieval and Renaissance Teaching* 7.2. (Fall 1999), 75–87.

Wallace, David (ed.), *The Cambridge History of Medieval English Literature,* Cambridge: Cambridge University Press, 1999. Collection of over thirty essays from preeminent medieval scholars introducing the major genres, authors, motifs, geographical locales, institutions and historical events that characterize Middle English literature.

——, *Chaucerian Polity: Absolutist Lineages and Associational Forms in England and*

Italy, Stanford: Stanford University Press, 1997. Deconstructs the distinction between medieval and early modern by examining Chaucer's interaction with Trecento Italian (Renaissance) authors associated with Florence (oligarchic rule) and Milan (despotic rule).

——, *Premodern Places: Calais to Surinam, Chaucer to Aphra Behn*, Malden, MA: Blackwell Publishing, 2004. Important study challenging the conventional demarcations between medieval and early modern, old and new world, and male and female.

——, 'Periodizing women: Mary Ward (1585–1645) and the premodern canon', *Journal of Medieval and Early Modern Studies*, 36 (2006), 398–453. Uses the case of Mary Ward to show the failure of traditional periodizing.

Warren, Michelle R., *History on the Edge: Excalibur and the Borders of Britain, 1100–1300*, Minneapolis: University of Minnesota Press, 2000. Demonstrates how Arthurian legends form at the borders of Britain where it is used by different communities to articulate their resistance to colonization and domination.

Warren, Nancy Bradley, 'Feminist approaches to Middle English religious writing: The cases of Margery Kempe and Julian of Norwich', *Literature Compass* 4.5 (2007), 1378–96, available online at <http://www.literaturecompass.com>. Excellent overview of feminist analyses of medieval female mystical writings, particularly those of Margery Kempe and Julian of Norwich.

Watson, Nicholas, 'Censorship and cultural change in late-medieval England: Vernacular theology, the Oxford translation debate, and Arundel's Constitution of 1409', *Speculum* 70 (1995), 822–64. Examines 'the shift from fourteenth-century "Ricardian" to fifteenth-century "Lancastrian" cultures' via an examination of the 'vernacular theology' in late-medieval mystical and theological texts (823) composed in response to Arundel's Constitutions.

——, and J. Jenkins (eds.), *The Writings of Julian of Norwich: A Vision Showed to a Devout Woman and a Revelation of Love*, University Park: Pennsylvania State University Press, 2006. A stellar example of contemporary textual and codicological studies that has quickly become the standard source for Julian of Norwich's writings.

White, Hayden, *Tropics of Discourse: Essays in Cultural Criticism*, Baltimore: John Hopkins Press, 1978. Classic study of the construction and elements of historical narratives.

Wilbur, Richard, *The Beautiful Changes and Other Poems*, New York: Harcourt, Brace, and Co., 1947. Wilbur's first collection of poems.

Williams, Raymond, 'Base and superstructure in Marxist cultural theory', *Contemporary Literary Criticism*, Robert Con Davis and Ronald Schleifer (eds.), New York: Longman, 1998, 489–501. A reevaluation of the Marxist base/super-structure distinction into a more dynamic and affective social activity than previously imagined by the rigidly determining base of economic activity emphasized by Marx.

Wilson, Katharina, M, (ed.), *Medieval Women Writers*, Athens, GA.: University of Georgia Press, 1984. Fine collection of medieval women writers, both secular and religious, with excellent introductory essays.

Wilson-Okamura, David, *Geoffrey Chaucer Online*, East Carolina University, available online at <http://geoffreychaucer.org>.

Wittig, Susan, *Stylistic and Narrative Structures in Middle English Romances*, Austin:

University of Texas Press, 1978. Provides a detailed structural analysis of the elements of medieval romances.

Wogan-Brown, Joyce, 'The virgin's tale', in Ruth Evans and Lesley Johnson (eds.), *Feminist Readings in Middle English Literature: The Wife of Bath and All Her Sect*, London: Routledge, 1994, 165–94. Argues that texts representing virginity counter the conventions of romance that tend to disempower women by making women readers the heroines of 'divine romance' (171).

Wood, Charles T., 'In medieval studies, is "to teach" a transitive verb?' *SMART: Studies in Medieval and Renaissance Teaching* 3.2 (Fall 1992), 3–13.

Yandell, Stephen, 'Undergraduate readers as narrative cartographers' *SMART: Studies in Medieval and Renaissance Teaching* 11.2 (Fall 2004), 19–35.

Žižek, Slavoj, *Enjoy Your Symptom! Jacques Lacan in Hollywood and Out*, New York: Routledge, 1992. Explicates Lacanian psychoanalytic concepts through reference to classic Hollywood films, particularly Hitchcock.

Zumthor, Paul, *Toward a Medieval Poetics*, Minneapolis: University of Minnesota Press, 1999. Examines 'the ensemble of poetic texts' as well as 'the activity by which they are produced' (xx).

Index

Please note that titles of works beginning with 'A' and 'The' are filed under the first significant word

Index

Écriture Féminine (feminine
    writing) 206–7, 209–10
Edward II 74
Edward III 32, 33
Edward the Confessor 24–5
Ellesmere Manuscript (*El*) 64
Ellis, Steve 180
embodiment 125
Empire of Magic (Heng) 171,
    172
Empson, William 228–9
Enders, Jody 180
Engels, Friedrich 231
Enjoy Your Symptom (Zizek)
    174
essentialism 209, 210–11, 247
*The Ethical Poetic of the Later
    Middle Ages* (Allen) 178
ethical turn 16, 228, 236–8;
    and deconstruction 234;
    Osborn on 244; and
    terminology 6, 135, 146,
    191, 229
eunuch hermeneutics 116
exegetical criticism 228
experiential learning 259–60
extimité 125, 128

fabliau, genre of 121
famine 8, 31–2
Fanon, Franz 170
Fee, Christopher 266
feminism: Anglo-American
    203; development of
    feminist criticism 187–8;
    and expansion of canon
    186; and feminisms
    202–3; French 161, 206;
    and gender studies
    160–1, 247; and medieval
    texts 161–2; queer and
    gender theory 116; Third
    World, and Third Wave
    209–10
Festial (Mirk) 70
Fiedler, Leslie 162
fifteenth-century literature
    192–3
film, and popular culture 260
film theory 160
Filostrato (Boccaccio) 57
Fineman, Joel 233
folios 53
Forest-Hill, Lynn 146
Foucault, Michel 138, 158;
    archaeological work 230;
    genealogical work 230;
    History of Sexuality 153,

215; and New
    Historicism 157; and
    Nietzsche 233; power
    matrix 146; 'Repressive
    Hypothesis' 215–16, 249;
    on subject 230
Fradenburg, Louise O.
    Aranye 110, 148, 174
Franciscans 7
Frankfurt School 167
Fraternal orders 28
French feminism 206
Freud, Sigmund 14, 173
Froissart, Jean 87–8
Frye, Northrop 135, 173
Furnivall, Frederick 134

Galen 212–13
Ganim, John 145, 152
Gates, Henry Louis 219
Gawain-Poet 34, 72, 162, 185
Gaylord, Alan T. 243, 244
gaze 124, 125, 162
Geertz, Clifford 153, 233
Gellrich, Jesse 159
gender: concept of 139–40;
    feminism and gender
    studies 160–1;
    hermeneutics, gendered
    114–15; identity and
    queer studies 163–4, 248;
    and Latinity 95–6; and
    politics 235–6; race and
    sexuality 223–4; and
    religious difference
    165–6; and secrecy 120–1;
    sex/gender system 212
Gender and Jewish Difference
    (Lampert) 165
*Gender and Romance in
    Chaucer's Canterbury Tales*
    (Crane) 162
gender studies 211–12; and
    feminism 160–1, 247
General Prologue (Chaucer)
    157, 164, 217
Geoffrey of Monmouth 54,
    143, 171–2; *History of the
    Kings of Britain* 34, 65,
    128, 172
Georgianna, Linda 176
Gesta Regum Anglorum (*The
    Deeds of the Kings of
    England*) (William of
    Malmesbury) 34
Getting Medieval (Dinshaw)
    114, 117, 118, 126, 163
giant, image of 124–5

Gibson, Gail 13
gigantomachia 124, 126
Gilbert, Sandra M. 203–4,
    210
Glasscoe, Marion, and
    feminist criticism 187
Gluck, Robert 189
Goidelic language 52
Goldberg, Jonathan 233
Golden Age, fourteenth
    century as 155, 170
Gollancz, Israel 134
Goodhart, Sandor 227, 239,
    241, 244
Goodman, Jennifer R. 141
*Gothic Architecture and
    Scholasticism* (Panofsky)
    16
Gower, John 10, 30;
    allegorical beasts, 90; and
    Chaucer 65; on Clement
    29; *Confessio Amantis* 27,
    29, 36, 63; on Crusades
    27; *Vox clamantis* 29, 33,
    88–9, 93
Grady, Frank 170
Gramsci, Antonio 168, 232
Great Rising of AD 1381
    (Peasants' Revolt) 32–3,
    87; comparing accounts
    of 92–3; New Historicist
    studies of 168; and
    Richard II 74
Great Schism (1378–1417) 8,
    28–9
Greek Orthodox Church 7
Greenblatt, Stephen 168, 169,
    173, 187, 188, 233
Gregory XI (Pope) 29
Grey Friars 71
Gubar, Susan 203–4
Guinevere 84, 85, 86
guslars (bards) 144
gynocriticism 203–4

Habermas, Jürgen 167
habitus 16, 138
Hagiography (Saints'
    Legends) 75
Hali Meidhad ('Holy
    Maidenhood') 77
Hall, A. S. 144
Hanawalt, Barbara A. 142
Hanna, Ralph 12, 170
Hansen, Elaine Tuttle 162,
    205
Hardison, O. B. 144, 179
Harold Hardraada 25